Readings in the History and Systems of Psychology

James F. Brennan

University of Massachusetts at Boston

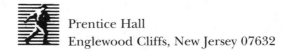

Prentice Hall
Englewood Cliffs, New Jersey 07632

Library of Congress Cataloging-in-Publication Data

BRENNAN, JAMES F.
    Readings in the history and systems of psychology / James F.
Brennan.
        p.   cm.
    Includes bibliographical references and index.
    ISBN 0-13-103763-3
    1. Psychology—History.   2. Psychology—History—20th century.
3. Psychology—Philosophy.   I. Title.
    BF81.B674   1995
    150—dc20   93-50565
                                                              CIP

Acquisitions editors: *Heidi Freund/Pete Janzow*
Production editor: *Jean Lapidus*
Cover design: *Patricia McGowan*
Production coordinator: *Tricia Kenny*

 © 1995 by Prentice-Hall, Inc.
A Paramount Communications Company
Englewood Cliffs, New Jersey 07632

Printed in the United States of America

10   9   8   7   6   5   4   3   2   1

ISBN 0-13-103763-3

PRENTICE-HALL INTERNATIONAL (UK) LIMITED, *London*
PRENTICE-HALL OF AUSTRALIA PTY. LIMITED, *Sydney*
PRENTICE-HALL CANADA INC., *Toronto*
PRENTICE-HALL HISPANOAMERICANA, S.A., *Mexico*
PRENTICE-HALL OF INDIA PRIVATE LIMITED, *New Delhi*
PRENTICE-HALL OF JAPAN, INC., *Tokyo*
SIMON & SCHUSTER ASIA PTE. LTD., *Singapore*
EDITORA PRENTICE-HALL DO BRASIL, LTDA., *Rio de Janeiro*

Alla mia moglie Maria Candida che è sempre là.

⤜ Contents ⤛

⁓ Preface ⁓

The purpose of this book is to provide a selection of primary source readings to accompany the study of psychology's long past. From the time of ancient societies, intellectual writers have recorded their observations and interpretations of human activities, motives, and emotions. The progression of ideas that led to the post-Renaissance development of empirical science in Europe allowed psychology to assume its present, diverse form. Accordingly, the scope of twentieth-century systems of psychology may be best understood in terms of the evolution of Western thought from the time of antiquity.

While a textbook can provide the outline of this historical development, the writers themselves perhaps best document their thoughts on psychology. This collection of readings can supplement any textual exposition of the history and systems of psychology, and it offers a coherent perspective by itself as well.

After presenting approaches to the scholarly study of psychology's past, the readings follow a general chronology. Following the outlines of most textbooks, the selections introduce the major themes of psychological inquiry, initially considered by Greek scholars and subsequently modified by early Christian writers. As modern science grew out of the Renaissance, the place of psychological inquiry became a source of controversy that resulted in competing philosophical models of the nature of psychology, represented in the writings of René Descartes (1596-1650) and Baruch Spinoza (1632-1677). These models followed trends of psychological views proposed by scholars selected from the intellectual climates of France (Étienne Bonnot de Condillac, 1715-1780), Britain (John Locke, 1632-1704; George Berkeley, 1885-1753; John Stuart Mill, 1806-1873) and Germany (Immanuel Kant, 1724-1804). The tremendous advances of the empirical disciplines, which culminated in the nineteenth century, led to the articulation of the formal study of psychology in the 1870s. This period is represented by the writings of Wilhelm Wundt (1832-1920), Franz Brentano (1838-1917), and Edward Bradford Titchener (1867-1927).

The remainder of the readings deals with the major twentieth-century systems of psychology: the American functional movement (William James, 1842-1910; John Dewey, 1859-1952; James Angell, 1869-1949), Gestalt psychology (Kurt Koffka, 1886-1941; Wolfgang Köhler (1887-1967), psychoanalysis (Sigmund Freud, 1856-1939), reflexology and behaviorism (Ivan Pavlov, 1849-1936; John Broadus Watson, 1878-1958; Edward C. Tolman, 1886-1959; B.F. Skinner, 1904-1990), and the third force movement (Amedeo Giorgi, b. 1931; Maurice Merleau-Ponty, 1908-1961; Carl Rogers (1902-1987).

A project such as this develops in competition with a wide range of faculty demands, and I want to thank those colleagues and research assistants who have helped throughout this project. I especially want to acknowledge the help of Phyllis Doucette and Majid Zandipour, staff members of the Department of Psychology at the University of Massachusetts/Boston. They often worked wonders in dealing with the logistics of meeting publication deadlines while I was on sabbatical leave in Italy.

For their continuing help and support, I am grateful to my wife Maria and daughters Tara and Mikala, who have always been a source of support for these projects.

James F. Brennan
Boston, Massachusetts

I. Introduction to the Study of the History of Psychology

Historical progress does not seem to be the product of random events. Historians devote considerable energy to discerning the various relationships among events—from sequential series to conceptual linkages to cause-effect determinism—in order to discover trends that might help us understand why events occurred the way they did. Any history may be made more attractive and personal when we learn about past events through the biographical stories of important, and even not so important, men and women who are the major actors in historical dramas. However, most historians recognize that it is the "spirit of the times" that sets the contextual stage for historical events and therefore provides the focus for understanding historical relationships.

In this first section of readings, we are introduced to the formal study of history by two related writings. In Boring's (1955) article, the *zeitgeist* or "spirit of the times" is broadly defined as "the total body of knowledge and opinion available at any time to a person living within a given culture" (p. 10). With the scientist firmly embedded in her or his cultural frame of reference, Boring argued that the *zeitgeist* may either facilitate or impede progress relative to some particular stage of scientific development. As perhaps the major figure in the modern study of the history of psychology, Edwin G. Boring (1886-1968) recorded the emergence of Psychology, distinct from the disciplinary provinces of Philosophy, Physics, and Physiology in his famous work, *A history of experimental psychology* (1950). Others (e.g., Watson, 1971) followed in his footsteps by setting a solid foundation for the scholarly study of psychology's past.

The second paper in this section is excerpted from the writings of Thomas Kuhn (b. 1922) who has greatly influenced scholars of the history of science through his particular interpretation of the *zeitgeist* as it acts on scientific progress. In this reading taken from his *The Structure of Scientific Revolutions,* Kuhn (1970) posited paradigm changes that account for the extension of science to accommodate new observations. By paradigm, Kuhn referred to a model that is able to deal with specific observations in a coherent way. When observations arise that do not fit well within the paradigm, they are termed anomalies, and the coherence of the model begins to crumble. Kuhn proposed that scientific progress is supported by the shortcomings of existing ways of thinking about science, which results in a search for new, promising alternatives that can, in turn, better deal with the new observations. In this excerpt on "The Route of Normal Science", Kuhn cited classical examples from the history of science to support his view of how a given paradigm failed to accommodate new findings, and a search eventually found a new, better and more encompassing paradigm. These processes of transformation are scientific revolutions for Kuhn. The new paradigm then defines a new vision, and the cycle continues.

REFERENCES

BORING, E.G. (1950). *A history of experimental psychology* (2nd.ed). Englewood Cliffs, N.J.: Prentice Hall.

BORING, E.G. (1955). Dual role of the *Zeitgeist* in scientific creativity. *Scientific Monthly, 80,* 101–106.

KUHN, T. (1970). *The structure of scientific revolutions,* 2nd ed. Chicago: University of Chicago Press.

WATSON, R.I. (1971). Prescriptions as operative in the history of psychology. *Journal of the History of the Behavioral Sciences, 7,* 311–322.

∽ 1 ∽

Edwin G. Boring,
"Dual role of the *Zeitgeist*
in scientific creativity" (1955).*

This "magic" term *Zeitgeist* means at any one time the climate of opinion as it affects thinking, yet it is also more than that, for the *Zeitgeist* is forever being altered, as if the thinker whom it affects were shifting latitude and longitude over sea and land so that his climate keeps changing in unpredictable ways. Goethe, who in 1827 may have been the first to use this word with explicit connotation, limited it to the unconscious, covert, and implicit effects of the climate of opinion, at the same time ruling out thought control by such explicit processes as persuasion and education (*1*).

Such a concept proves useful in those cases where plagiarism is clearly unconscious, as so often it is. No man clearly understands the sources of his own creativity, and it is only since Freud that we have begun to have an inkling of how general is this lack of understanding of one's own motives and of the sources of one's own ideas. On the other hand, this conception long antedates Freud, for it was the essence of Tolstoy's argument in 1869 that "a king is history's slave" whose conscious reasons for action are trivial and unimportant. Charles Darwin, Herbert Spencer, and Francis Galton all supported Tolstoy's view of the unconscious determination of the actions of great men, against the more voluntaristic views of Thomas Carlyle, William James, and some lesser writers.

Later the historians of science and of thought in general found themselves faced with the essential continuity of originality and discovery. Not only is a new discovery seldom made until the times are ready for it, but again and again it turns out to have been anticipated, inadequately perhaps but nevertheless explicitly, as the times were beginning to get ready for it. Thus the concept of a gradually changing *Zeitgeist* has been used to explain the historical

* Boring, E.G. (1955). Dual role of the *Zeitgeist* in scientific creativity. *Scientific Monthly*, *80*, 101-106. Reprinted by permission of the American Association for the Advancement of Science.

continuity of thought and the observation that the novelty of a discovery, after the history of its anticipations has been worked out, appears often to be only a historian's artifact.

In addition to these anticipations there are, however, also the near-simultaneities and near-synchronisms that are clearly not plagiarisms. Napier and Briggs on logarithms. Leibnitz and Newton on the calculus. Boyle and Mariotte on the gas law. D'Alibard and Franklin on electricity. The sociologists Ogburn and Thomas have published a list of 148 contemporaneous but independent discoveries or inventions. Since you cannot in these pairs assume that one man got the crucial idea from the other, you are forced to assume that each had his novel insight independently by his ordinary processes of thought, except that each was doing his thinking in the same climate of opinion. Some such appeal to a maturing *Zeitgeist* is necessary to explain the coincidence (*2*).

Now how, we may ask, does the *Zeitgeist* of the present time interpret the generic concept of the *Zeitgeist?* Today the *Zeitgeist* is certainly *not* a superorganic soul, an immortal consciousness undergoing maturation with the centuries, an unextended substance interpenetrating the social structure. The *Zeitgeist* must be regarded simply as the sum total of social interaction as it is common to a particular period and a particular locale. One can say it is thought being affected by culture, and one would mean then that the thinking of every man is affected by the thinking of other men in so far as their thinking is communicated to him. Hence the importance of communication in science, which both helps and hinders progress. That is the thesis of this paper.

It is always hard to be original, to make progress in a minority thinking that goes against the majority. In science, moreover, even the dead help to make up the majority, for they communicate by the printed word and by the transmitted conventions of thought. Thus the majority, living and dead, may slow up originality. On the other hand, the chief effect of scientific communication and of the availability of past thought is facilitative. We all know how the invention of printing advanced science.

We shall not be far wrong—being prejudiced, of course, by the *Zeitgeist* of the present—if we regard the scientist as a nervous system, influenced by what it reads and hears as well as by what it observes in nature and in the conduct of other men—the smile of approbation, the sneer of contempt—and affected also by its own past experience, for the scientist is forever instructing himself as he proceeds toward discovery and is also forever being instructed by other men, both living and dead.

The single investigator works pretty much like a rat in a maze—by insight, hypothesis, trial, and then error or success. I am not trying to say that rats are known to prefer deduction to induction because they use hypotheses in learning a maze. The maze is set up to require learning by trial and error, which is to say, by hypothesis and test. The rat's insight, as it learns, may indeed be false: the rat looks down the alley, sees it is not immediately blind but later finds it is blind after all. An error for the rat. And its trial may be vicarious. The rat looks tentatively down an alley, entertains it as a hypothesis, rejects it, chooses to go the other way. Anybody's hypothesis can come as the brilliant perception of an unexpected relationship and yet be wrong. It may be a hunch. Rodent hypotheses begin as hunches—and by this I mean merely that the rat does not understand the ground of its motives.

The human investigator, on the other hand, may consciously base his new hypothesis on his own earlier experiment, or on something other persons did. For this reason erudition is important, and communication is vital in modern science. Nevertheless it remains possible to regard the single scientist as an organic system, as a discovery machine, with a certain input from the literature and from other forms of social communication and also—let the essential empiricism of science not be forgotten—from nature, which comes through to insights and a conclusion by that method of concomitant variation which is experiment. There we have the individual investigator, who, as he grows older, gains in erudition and wisdom and becomes more mature, with his past discoveries now available as part of his knowledge.

A broader and more interesting question, however, concerns, not the individual, but the maturation of scientific thought itself. The mechanics of one person applies to too small a system to throw much light on the history of science. The larger view substitutes social interaction and communication for an individual's input, thus exposing the whole dynamic process as it undergoes maturation down the years, the centuries, and the ages. This interaction *is* the *Zeitgeist*, which is not unlike a stream. It is bounded on its sides by the limits of communication, but it goes on forever unless, of course, some great cataclysm, one that would make Hitler's effect on German science seem tiny and trivial, should some day stall it.

Here we have a physicalistic conception of the *Zeitgeist*. The *Zeitgeist*, of course, inevitably influences the conception of the *Zeitgeist*. And the *Zeitgeist* ought to be the property of psychologists, for the psychologists have a proprietary right in all the *Geister*. Now the psychology of the 19th century was dualistic, mentalistic, spiritualistic. In those days the *Zeitgeist* would certainly have had to be the maturing superconsciousness of science, something comparable to the immediate private experience that everyone then believed he had. The 20th century, on the other hand, at least since 1925, is physicalistic and behavioristic. Nowadays the term *behavioral sciences* is on everyone's lips and there is no English equivalent for *Geisteswissenschaften*.

Between 1910 and 1930 the *Zeitgeist* changed. Mind gave way to behavior. This transition was eased by the positivists who supplied the transformation equations from the old to the new, transformations by way of the operational definitions of experience: but only a few bother to use these equations. It is enough for most persons that they are using the convenient language of the great majority. And truth in science, as S. S. Stevens has pointed out, is simply what competent opinion at the time in question does not dissent from (*3*). In a physicalistic era, we, physicalistically minded scientists, choose a physicalistic definition of the *Zeitgeist*. Our predecessors in 1900 would not so easily have accepted such nonchalance toward Cartesian dualism.

We are wise thus to accept the wisdom of the age. Nor is my personal history without interest in this respect, for I was brought up in the introspective school of E.B. Titchener and for 20 years believed firmly in the existence of my own private immediate consciousness. Then, about 1930, en route to Damascus, as it were, I had a great insight. I knew that I was unconscious and never had been conscious in the sense that to have experience is to know instantaneously that you have it. Introspection always takes time, and the most immediate conscious datum is, therefore, obtained retrospectively. Once this basic truth is assimilated, once one realizes that no system can include the report of itself and that to one's own introspection one's own consciousness is as much the consciousness of some "Other One" as is the consciousness of a different person, then it becomes clear that consciousness is not in any sense immediate, and then—just exactly then—the introspectionist gladly and sincerely joins the behavioristic school (*4*).

THE ZEITGEIST'S DUAL ROLE

The *Zeitgeist* has a dual role in scientific progress, sometimes helping and sometimes hindering. There can be nothing surprising in such a statement. Forces in themselves are not good or bad. Their effects can be, depending on what it is you want. Inevitably by definition the *Zeitgeist* favors conventionality, but conventionality itself keeps developing under the constant pressures of discoveries and novel insights. So the *Zeitgeist* works against originality; but is not originality, one asks quite properly, a good thing, something that promotes scientific progress? In the cases of Copernicus, Galileo, Newton, and other comparably great men of science, originality was good—good for what posterity has called progress. These are the men to emulate. The indubitably original people are, however, the cranks, and close to them are the paranoid enthusiasts. Velikovsky's conception of the collision of two worlds is original. Does science advance under his stimulus? Hubbard's dianetics is original. Is it good? Most of us right now think not, yet these men point in self-defense to Galileo who also resisted the *Zeitgeist* (*5*). This dilemma arises because it is well to know and respect the wisdom of the ages and also to correct it when the evidence for change is adequate. If men were logical machines and evidence could be weighed in balances, we should not be mentioning the *Zeitgeist* at all. The *Zeitgeist* comes into consideration because it can on occasion work irrationally to distort the weight of the evidence.

When does the *Zeitgeist* help and when does it hinder the progress of science?

1) It is plain that knowledge helps research, and knowledge, whether it be explicit on the printed page of a handbook or implicit in the unrecognized premises of a theory, is in the *Zeitgeist*. There is no use trying to limit the *Zeitgeist* to that knowledge which you have without knowing it, for the line simply cannot be kept. One discovery leads to another, or one experiment leads to a theory that leads to another experiment, and the history of science tells the story. The law of multiple proportions, for instance, validates the atomic theory, and then the atomic theory leads off to all sorts of chemical research and discovery.

On the other hand, the *Zeistgeist* does not always help, for there is bad knowledge as well as good, and it takes good knowledge to get science ahead. It is useful to be ignorant of bad knowledge.

The idea that white is a simple color was a bit of bad knowledge that was in the *Zeistgeist* in the middle of the 17th century. It was not a silly idea. It was empirically based. You can see colors, can you not? And white is a color. And you can see that it is simple and not a mixture, can you not? It is not clear whether Newton was lucky enough not to have absorbed this bit of false knowledge from the *Zeistgeist* or whether he was just stubborn, when, having bought his prism at the Stourbridge Fair, he concluded that white is a mixture of other colors. He was probably consciously flouting the *Zeistgeist*, for he sent his paper up to the Royal Society with the remark that it was in his "judgment the oddest if not the most considerable detection which hath hitherto been made into the operations of nature." But Robert Hooke and the others at the Royal Society would have none of it. They were restrained from belief by the *Zeistgeist*. White is obviously not colored, not a mixture. There was bitter controversy before the conventional scientists gave in, before the truth shifted over to Newton's side (*6*).

Helmholtz ran into a similar difficulty when in 1850 he measured the velocity of the nervous impulse. The *Zeitgeist* said: The soul is unitary; an act of will is not spread out over a period of time; you move your finger; you do not will first that the finger move with the finger not moving until the message gets to it. Thus Helmholtz' father had religious scruples against accepting his son's discovery. And Johannes Müller, then the dean of experimental physiology, doubted that the conduction times could be so slow. At the very least, he thought, the rate of the impulse must approximate the speed of light (*7*).

The persistence of the belief in phlogiston is still another example of the inertia that the *Zeitgeist* imposes on progress in thought. Here both Lavoisier and Priestley broke away from convention enough to discover oxygen, but Lavoisier, with the more negativistic temperament, made the greater break and came farther along toward the truth, whereas Priestley could not quite transcend his old habits of thought. His theory was a compromise, whereas we know now—insofar as we ever know truth in science—that that compromise was not the way to push science ahead then (*8*).

So it is. Good knowledge promotes progress, bad knowledge hinders, and both kinds make up the *Zeitgeist*. Ignorance of good knowledge and awareness of bad hinder; awareness of good and ignorance of bad help. The history of science is full of instances of all four.

2) Not only do the discovery of fact and the invention of theory help progress when fact and theory are valid, but comparable principles apply to the discovery and invention of new scientific techniques. The telescope seems to have come out of the *Zeitgeist*, for it was invented independently by half a dozen different persons in 1608, although lenses had been made and used for magnification for at least 300 years. But then Galileo's discovery of Jupiter's moons the next year created, as it were, a new phase in the *Zeitgeist*, one that promoted astronomical discovery. So it was with the invention of the simple microscope, the compound microscope, the Voltaic pile, the galvanic battery, the galvanometer, the electromagnet, and recently the electron tube—the possibilities opened up by the availability of a new important instrument change the atmosphere within a field of science and lead quickly to a mass of valid research. Within psychology the experimental training of a rat in a maze in 1903, in order to measure its learning capacity, led at once to a long series of studies in the evolution of animal intelligence with the maze as the observational instrument.

It is true that the negative instances of this aspect of the *Zeitgeist* are not so frequent or obvious: yet they occur. For years the Galton whistle, used for the determination of the upper limit of hearing, was miscalibrated, because its second harmonic had been mistaken for its first. The highest audible pitch was thought to occur at about 40,000 cycles per second, whereas the correct figure is about 20,000. Did this error of an octave hold back science? Not much, but a little. For a couple of decades investigators reported facts about the octave above 20,000 cycles per second, an octave that is really inaudible. One experimenter even found a special vowel quality for it to resemble. Thus bad knowledge about the whistle led to confusion and hindered the advance of science.

3) The *Zeitgeist* acts as inertia in human thinking. It makes thought slow but also surer. As a rule scientific thinking does not suddenly depart widely from contemporary opinion. In civilization, as in the individual, the progress of thought is sensibly continuous. Consider, for example, the history of the theory of sensory quality.

Empedocles believed that eidola of objects are transmitted by the nerves to the mind so that it may perceive the objects by their images. Later there arose the notion that there are animal spirits in the nerves to conduct the eidola. Then, under the influence of materialism, the animal spirits came to be regarded as a *vis viva* and presently a *vis nervosa*. Next Johannes Müller, seeing that every sensory nerve always produces its own quality, substituted for the *vis nervosa* five specific nerve energies, using the word *energy*, in the days before the theory of conservation of energy, as equivalent to *force* or *vis*. He said that the mind, being locked away in the skull, cannot perceive the objects themselves, or their images, but only the states of the nerves that the objects affect, and he fought a battle against the Empedoclean theory—as indeed had John Locke and Thomas Young and Charles Bell before him, and as still others were to do after him. After a while it was seen, however, that the specificity of the five kinds of nerves lies not in the peculiar energies that they conduct to the brain but in where they terminate in the brain. Thus there arose the concept of sensory centers in the cerebrum. Nowadays we see that a cerebral center is nothing more than a place where connections are made and that sensory quality must be understood in terms of the discriminatory response in which stimulation eventuates—or at least many of us see this fact while we fight a *Zeitgeist* that still supports the theory of centers (*9*).

Is there any reason why Galen in A.D. 180 or Albrecht von Haller in 1766 should not have invented the modern theory of sensory quality? None, except that most of the supporting evidence was lacking and, being contrary to the accepted notions of the time, it would have sounded silly. Yet each contribution to this strand of scientific maturation was original, and several contributors had to fight against the battle against the notion that the mind perceives an object by embracing it, or, if it cannot get at the object itself, by getting itself impressed by the object's eidolon or simulacrum. Nor has the *Zeitgeist* even yet been thoroughly disciplined in this affair, as you can tell whenever you hear the remark: "If the lens of the eye inverts the image of the external world on the retina, why do we not see upside down?"

The *Zeitgeist* was hindering progress in this piece of history. It made originality difficult and it made it necessary to repeat the same arguments in 1690 (John Locke) and in 1826 (Johannes Müller) and, if one may believe current advertisements of a scientific film, nowadays too. Yet let us remember that this *Zeitgeist* also helped progress. The continuity of development lay always within the *Zeitgeist*. It was a conservative force that demanded that originality remain responsible, that it be grounded on evidence and available knowledge. Had Galen espoused a connectionist's view of sensory quality in the second century, he would have been irresponsibly original, a second-century crank, disloyal to the truth as it existed then. Loyalty may be prejudice and sometimes it may be wrong, but it is nevertheless the stuff of which responsible continuous effort is made. Science needs responsibility as well as freedom, and the *Zeitgeist* supports the one virtue even though it may impede the other.

4) What may be said of the big *Zeitgeist* may also be said of the little *Zeitgeister* of schools and of the leaders of schools and of the egoist who has no following. They have their inflexible attitudes and beliefs, their loyalties that are prejudices, and their prejudices that are loyalties. Every scientific in-group with strong faith in a theory or a method is a microcosm, mirroring the macrocosm which is the larger world of science.

Take egoism. Is it bad? It accounts for a large part of the drive that produces research, for the dogged persistence that is so often the necessary condition of scientific success. So egoism yields truth. It accounts also for the hyperbole and exaggeration of the investigating enthusiast, and then it may yield untruth. When two incompatible egoisms come together, they account for the wasted time of scientific warfare, for the dethronement of reason by rationalization. Egoism is both good and bad.

Take loyalty. Think how it cements a group together and promotes hard work. Yet such in-groups tend to shut themselves off from other out-groups, to build up their special vocabularies, and so, while strengthening their own drives, to lessen communication with the outside, the communication that advances science. Loyalty is both good and bad, and with loyalty a person sometimes has to choose whether he will eat his cake or will keep it.

This dilemma posed by the little *Zeitgeister* of the in-groups and the scientific evangelists has its root in basic psychological law. Attention to this is inevitably inattention to that. Enthusiasm is the friend of action but the enemy of wisdom. Science needs to be both concentrated and diffuse, both narrow and broad, both thorough and inclusive. The individual investigator solves this problem as best he can, each according to his own values, as to when to sell breadth in order to purchase depth and when to reverse the transaction. He, the individual, has limited funds and he has to sell in order to buy, and he may never know whether he made the best investment. But posterity will know, at least better than he, provided that it troubles to assess the matter at all, for posterity, having only to understand without hard labor, can assess the effect of prejudice and loyalty and enthusiasm, of tolerance and intolerance, as no man ever can in himself.

Coda

This is a broad meaning for the word *Zeitgeist*—the total body of knowledge and opinion available at any time to a person living within a given culture. There is, certainly, no rigorous way of distinguishing between what is explicit to a scientist and what is implicit in the forms and patterns of communication, between what is clear conclusion and what is uncritically accepted premise. Available knowledge is communicated whenever it becomes effective, and this is the *Zeitgeist* working.

The *Zeitgeist* is a term from the language of dualism, while its definition is formally physicalistic. That paradox is for the sake of convenience in the present communication and is allowable because every statement can be transformed into physicalistic language when necessary. Dualism has the disadvantage of implying a mystery, the existence of a *Zeitgeist* as a vague supersoul pervading and controlling the immortal body of society. We need no such nonsense, even though this abstinence from mystery reduce us to so ordinary a concept as a *Zeitgeist* inclusive of all available knowledge that affects a thinker's thinking.

That such a *Zeitgeist* sometimes helps progress and sometimes hinders it should be clear by now. As a matter of fact, the distinction between help and hindrance can never be absolute but remains relative to some specific goal. The *Zeitgeist* hindered Copernicus, who, resisting it, helped scientific thought onward and presently changed the *Zeitgeist* on this matter to what it was in Newton's day. Did the *Zeitgeist* that Newton knew help relativity theory? No; relativity had to make its way against that *Zeitgeist*. The newest *Zeigeist*, which will include the principles of relativity and uncertainty and complementarity, presumably exists today within the in-group of theoretical physicists. It will become general eventually, and then it will reinforce progress, and after that, much later, perhaps our posterity will find today's truth tomorrow's error. The one sure thing is that science needs all the communication it can get. The harm communication does to progress never nearly equals the good.

REFERENCES AND NOTES

1. The term *Zeitgeist* seems to have originated in this sense in 1827 with Goethe who, in discussing the way in which Homer had influenced thought, remarked in the last sentence of his essay, *Homer noch einmel*, "Und dies geschieht denn auch im Zeitgeiste, nicht verabredet noch überliefert, sondern *proprio motu*, der sich mehrfältig unter verschiedenen Himmelsstrichen hervortut." *Himmelsstrichen* can be translated "climates," thus justifying the figure of the text, but it must also be noted that Goethe meant to use the term *Zeitgeist* when the effect is "self-determined," brought about "neither by agreement nor fiat." See, for instance, *Goethes sämtliche Werke*, (I.J. Cotta, Berlin, 1902–07), vol. 38, p. 78.

2. The discussion of this paragraph and all the references will be found *in extenso* in E.G. Boring, "Great men and scientific progress," *Proc. Am. Phil. Soc.* 94, 339 (1950). The reference to Tolstoy is, of course, to his *War and Peace*. For the longest list of nearly simultaneous inventions and discoveries, see W.F. Ogburn and D. Thomas, "Are inventions inevitable?'" *Polit. Sci. Quart.* 37, 83 (1922).

3. On the social criterion of truth, on scientific truth's being what scientists agree about, see S.S. Stevens, "The operational basis of psychology," *Am. J. Psychol.* 47, 323 (1935), especially p. 327; "The operational definition of psychological concepts," *Psychol. Rev.* 42, 517 (1935), especially p. 517: E.G. Boring, "The validation of scientific belief," *Proc. Am. Phil. Soc.* 96, 535 (1952), especially pp. 537 f.

4. On the point that a self cannot observe itself, that in self-observation a person must regard himself as if he were another person, see M. Meyer, *Psychology of the Other One* (Missouri Book Co., Columbia, Mo., 1921); Stevens, *op. cit.*, especially pp. 328 f.; E.G. Boring, "A history of introspection," *Psychol. Bull.* 50, 169 (1953), specially p. 183.

5. On the sincerity of cranks in science, see I.B. Cohen, J.L. Kennedy, C. Payne-Gaposchkin. T.M. Riddick, and E.G. Boring, "Some unorthodoxies of modern science," *Proc. Am. Phil. Soc.* 96, 505 (1952).

6. On Newton's difficulty in changing the *Zeitgeist* with respect to the complexity of white, see E.G. Boring, *Sensation and Perception in the History of Experimental Psychology* (Appleton-Century, New York, 1942), pp. 101 f. This discovery of Newton's was exceptional in that it had no anticipations (unless my wisdom is at fault). In other words, the *Zeitgeist* was strongly fixed, and to break it Newton must have been very stubborn—as indeed other evidence indicates that he was.

7. On Helmholtz' trouble with the *Zeitgeist* with respect to the velocity of the nervous impulse, see E.G. Boring, *A History of Experimental Psychology* 2 ed. (Appleton-Century-Crofts, New York, 1950), pp. 41 f., 47 f.

8. On Priestley and Lavosier and the *Zeitgeist's* support of the phlogiston theory, see J.B. Conant. *The Overthrow of the Phlogiston Theory*, Harvard Case Histories in Experimental Science, Case 2 (Harvard Univ. Press, Cambridge, Mass., 1950).

9. On the history of the physiological theories of sensory quality and the retardation of progress in thinking by successive phases of this *Zeitgeist*, see E.G. Boring, *Sensation and Perception* (*op. cit.*), pp. 68–83, 93–95.

2

Thomas Kuhn, Excerpt from *The structure of scientific revolutions* (1970).*

II. THE ROUTE TO NORMAL SCIENCE

In this essay, 'normal science' means research firmly based upon one or more past scientific achievements, achievements that some particular scientific community knowledges for a time as supplying the foundation for its further practice. Today such achievements are recounted, though seldom in their original form, by science textbooks, elementary and advanced. These textbooks expound the body of accepted theory, illustrate many or all of its successful applications, and compare these applications with exemplary observations and experiments. Before such books became popular early in the nineteenth century (and until even more recently in the newly matured sciences), many of the famous classics of science fulfilled a similar function. Aristotle's *Physica*, Ptolemy's *Almagest*, Newton's *Principia* and *Opticks*, Franklin's *Electricity*, Lavoisier's *Chemistry*, and Lyell's *Geology*—these and many other works served for a time implicitly to define the legitimate problems and methods of a research field for succeeding generations of practitioners. They were able to do so because they shared two essential characteristics. Their achievement was sufficiently unprecedented to attract an enduring group of adherents away from competing modes of scientific activity. Simultaneously, it was sufficiently open-ended to leave all sorts of problems for the redefined group of practitioners to resolve.

Achievements that share these two characteristics I shall henceforth refer to as 'paradigms,' a term that relates closely to 'normal science.' By choosing it, I mean to suggest that some accepted examples of actual scientific practice—examples which include law, theory, application, and instru-

---

* Kuhn, T. (1970). Excerpt from *The structure of scientific revolutions*, 2nd ed. Chicago: University of Chicago Press, Ch. 2, 10–22. Reprinted by permission of the University of Chicago Press.

mentation together—provide models from which spring particular coherent traditions of scientific research. These are the traditions which the historian describes under such rubrics as Ptolemaic astronomy' (or 'Copernican'), 'Aristotelian dynamics' (or 'Newtonian'), 'corpuscular optics' (or 'wave optics'), and so on. The study of paradigms, including many that are far more specialized than those named illustratively above, is what mainly prepares the student for membership in the particular scientific community with which he will later practice. Because he there joins men who learned the bases of their field from the same concrete models, his subsequent practice will seldom evoke overt disagreement over fundamentals. Men whose research is based on shared paradigms are committed to the same rules and standards for scientific practice. That commitment and the apparent consensus it produces are prerequisites for normal science, i.e., for the genesis and continuation of a particular research tradition.

Because in this essay the concept of a paradigm will often substitute for a variety of familiar notions, more will need to be said about the reasons for its introduction. Why is the concrete scientific achievement, as a locus of professional commitment, prior to the various concepts, laws, theories, and points of view that may be abstracted from it? In what sense is the shared paradigm a fundamental unit for the student of scientific development, a unit that cannot be fully reduced to logically atomic components which might function in its stead? When we encounter them in Section V, answers to these questions and to others like them will prove basic to an understanding both of normal science and of the associated concept of paradigms. That more abstract discussion will depend, however, upon a previous exposure to examples of normal science or of paradigms in operation. In particular, both these related concepts will be clarified by noting that there can be a sort of scientific research without paradigms, or at least without any so unequivocal and so binding as the ones named above. Acquisition of a paradigm and of the more esoteric type of research it permits is a sign of maturity in the development of any given scientific field.

If the historian traces the scientific knowledge of any selected group of related phenomena backward in time, he is likely to encounter some minor variant of a pattern here illustrated from the history of physical optics. Today's physics textbooks tell the student that light is photons, i.e., quantum-mechanical entities that exhibit some characteristics of waves and some of particles. Research proceeds accordingly, or rather according to the more elaborate and mathematical characterization from which this usual verbalization is derived. That characterization of light is, however, scarcely half a century old. Before it was developed by Planck, Einstein, and others early in this century, physics texts taught that light was transverse wave motion, a conception rooted in a paradigm that derived ultimately from the optical writings of Young and Fresnel in the early nineteenth century. Nor was the wave theory the first to be embraced by almost all practitioners of optical science. During the eighteenth century the paradigm for this field was provided by Newton's *Opticks*, which taught that light was material corpuscles. At that time physicists sought evidence, as the early wave theorists had not, of the pressure exerted by light particles impinging on solid bodies.[1]

These transformations of the paradigms of physical optics are scientific revolutions, and the successive transition from one paradigm to another via revolution is the usual developmental pattern of mature science. It is not, however, the pattern characteristic of the period before Newton's work, and that is the contrast that concerns us here. No period between remote antiquity and the end of the seventeenth century exhibited a single generally accepted view about the nature of light. Instead there were a number of competing schools and subschools, most of them espousing one variant or another of Epicurean, Aristotelian, or Platonic theory. One group took light to be particles emanating from material bodies; for another it was a modification of the medium that intervened between the body and the eye; still another explained light in terms of an interaction of the medium with an emanation from the eye; and there were other combinations and modifications besides. Each of the corresponding schools derived strength from its relation to some particular metaphysic, and each emphasized, as paradigmatic observations, the particular cluster of optical phenomena that its own theory could do most to explain. Other observations were dealt with by *ad hoc* elaborations, or they remained as outstanding problems for further research.[2]

At various times all these schools made significant contributions to the body of concepts, phenomena, and techniques from which Newton drew the first nearly uniformly accepted paradigm for physical optics. Any definition of the scientist that excludes at least the more creative members of these various schools will exclude their modern successors as well. Those men were scientists. Yet anyone examining a survey of physical optics before Newton may well conclude that, though the field's practitioners were scientists, the net result of their activity was something less than science. Being able to take no common body of belief for granted, each writer on physical optics felt forced to build his field anew from its foundations. In doing so, his choice of supporting observation and experiment was relatively free, for there was no standard set of methods or of phenomena that every optical writer felt forced to employ and explain. Under these circumstances, the dialogue of the resulting books was often directed as much to the members of other schools as it was to nature. That pattern is not unfamiliar in a number of creative fields today, nor is it incompatible with significant discovery and invention. It is not, however, the pattern of development that physical optics acquired after Newton and that other natural sciences make familiar today.

The history of electrical research in the first half of the eighteenth century provides a more concrete and better known example of the way a science

---

[1] Joseph Priestley, *The History and Present State of Discoveries Relating to Vision, Light, and Colours* (London, 1772), pp. 385–90.

[2] Vasco Ronchi, *Histoire de la lumière*, trans. Jean Taton (Paris, 1956), chaps. i–iv.

develops before it acquires its first universally received paradigm. During that period there were almost as many views about the nature of electricity as there were important electrical experimenters, men like Hauksbee, Gray, Desaguliers, Du Fay, Nollett, Watson, Franklin, and others. All their numerous concepts of electricity had something in common—they were partially derived from one or another version of the mechanico-corpuscular philosophy that guided all scientific research of the day. In addition, all were components of real scientific theories, of theories that had been drawn in part from experiment and observation and that partially determined the choice and interpretation of additional problems undertaken in research. Yet though all the experiments were electrical and though most of the experimenters read each other's works, their theories had no more than a family resemblance.[3]

One early group of theories, following seventeenth-century practice, regarded attraction and frictional generation as the fundamental electrical phenomena. This group tended to treat repulsion as a secondary effect due to some sort of mechanical rebounding and also to postpone for as long as possible both discussion and systematic research on Gray's newly discovered effect, electrical conduction. Other "electricians" (the term is their own) took attraction and repulsion to be equally elementary manifestations of electricity and modified their theories and research accordingly. (Actually, this group is remarkably small—even Franklin's theory never quite accounted for the mutual repulsion of two negatively charged bodies.) But they had as much difficulty as the first group in accounting simultaneously for any but the simplest conduction effects. Those effects, however, provided the starting point for still a third group, one which tended to speak of electricity as a "fluid" that could run through conductors rather than as an "effluvium" that emanated from non-conductors. This group, in its turn, had difficulty reconciling its theory with a number of attractive and repulsive effects. Only through the work of Franklin and his immediate successors did a theory arise that could account with something like equal facility for very nearly all these effects and that therefore could and did provide a subsequent generation of "electricians" with a common paradigm for its research.

Excluding those fields, like mathematics and astronomy, in which the first firm paradigms date from prehistory and also those, like biochemistry, that arose by division and recombination of specialties already matured, the situations out-

---

[3] Duane Roller and Duane H.D. Roller, *The Development of the Concept of Electric Charge: Electricity from the Greeks to Coulomb* ("Harvard Case Histories in Experimental Science," Case 8; Cambridge, Mass., 1954); and I.B. Cohen, *Franklin and Newton: An Inquiry into Speculative Newtonian Experimental Science and Franklin's Work in Electricity as an Example Thereof* (Philadelphia, 1956), chaps. vii–xii. For some of the analytic detail in the paragraph that follows in the text, I am indebted to a still unpublished paper by my student John L. Heilbron. Pending its publication, a somewhat more extended and more precise account of the emergence of Franklin's paradigm is included in T.S. Kuhn, "The Function of Dogma in Scientific Research," in A.C. Crombie (ed.), "Symposium on the History of Science, University of Oxford, July 9–15, 1961," to be published by Heinemann Educational Books, Ltd.

lined above are historically typical. Though it involves my continuing to employ the unfortunate simplification that tags an extended historical episode with a single and somewhat arbitrarily chosen name (e.g., Newton or Franklin), I suggest that similar fundamental disagreements characterized, for example, the study of motion before Aristotle and of statics before Archimedes, the study of heat before Black, of chemistry before Boyle and Boerhaave, and of historical geology before Hutton. In parts of biology—the study of heredity, for example—the first universally received paradigms are still more recent; and it remains an open question what parts of social science have yet acquired such paradigms at all. History suggests that the road to a firm research consensus is extraordinarily arduous.

History also suggests, however, some reasons for the difficulties encountered on that road. In the absence of a paradigm or some candidate for paradigm, all of the facts that could possibly pertain to the development of a given science are likely to seem equally relevant. As a result, early fact-gathering is a far more nearly random activity than the one that subsequent scientific development makes familiar. Furthermore, in the absence of a reason for seeking some particular form of more recondite information, early fact-gathering is usually restricted to the wealth of data that lie already to hand. The resulting pool of facts contains those accessible to casual observation and experiment together with some of the more esoteric data retrievable from established crafts like medicine, calendar making, and metallurgy. Because the crafts are one readily accessible source of facts that could not have been casually discovered, technology has often played a vital role in the emergence of new sciences.

But though this sort of fact-collecting has been essential to the origin of many significant sciences, anyone who examines, for example, Pliny's encyclopedic writings or the Baconian natural histories of the seventeenth century will discover that it produces a morass. One somehow hesitates to call the literature that results scientific. The Baconian "histories" of heat, color, wind, mining, and so on, are filled with information, some of it recondite. But they juxtapose facts that will later prove revealing (e.g., heating by mixture) with others (e.g., the warmth of dung heaps) that will for some time remain too complex to be integrated with theory at all.[4] In addition, since any description must be partial, the typical natural history often omits from its immensely circumstantial accounts just those details that later scientists will find sources of important illumination. Almost none of the early "histories" of electricity, for example, mention that chaff, attracted to a rubbed glass rod, bounces off again. That effect seemed mechanical, not electrical.[5] Moreover, since the casual fact-gatherer seldom possesses the time or the tools to be critical, the natural histories

[4] Compare the sketch for a natural history of heat in Bacon's *Novum Organum.* Vol. VIII of *The Works of Francis Bacon*, ed. J. Spedding, R.L. Ellis, and D.D. Heath (New York, 1869), pp. 179–203.

[5] Roller and Roller, *op cit.*, pp. 14, 22, 28, 43. Only after the work recorded in the last of these citations do repulsive effects gain general recognition as unequivocally electrical.

often juxtapose descriptions like the above with others, say, heating by antiperistasis (or by cooling), that we are now quite unable to confirm.[6] Only very occasionally, as in the cases of ancient statics, dynamics, and geometrical optics, do facts collected with so little guidance from pre-established theory speak with sufficient clarity to permit the emergence of a first paradigm.

This is the situation that creates the schools characteristic of the early stages of a science's development. No natural history can be interpreted in the absence of at least some implicit body of intertwined theoretical and methodological belief that permits selection, evaluation, and criticism. If that body of belief is not already implicit in the collection of facts—in which case more than "mere facts" are at hand—it must be externally supplied, perhaps by a current metaphysic, by another science, or by personal and historical accident. No wonder, then, that in the early stages of the development of any science different men confronting the same range of phenomena, but not usually all the same particular phenomena, describe and interpret them in different ways. What is surprising, and perhaps also unique in its degree to the fields we call science, is that such initial divergences should ever largely disappear.

For they do disappear to a very considerable extent and then apparently once and for all. Furthermore, their disappearance is usually caused by the triumph of one of the pre-paradigm schools, which, because of its own characteristic beliefs and pre-conceptions, emphasized only some special part of the too sizable and inchoate pool of information. Those electricians who thought electricity a fluid and therefore gave particular emphasis to conduction provide an excellent case in point. Led by this belief, which could scarcely cope with the known multiplicity of attractive and repulsive effects, several of them conceived the idea of bottling the electrical fluid. The immediate fruit of their efforts was the Leyden jar, a device which might never have been discovered by a man exploring nature casually or at random, but which was in fact independently developed by at least two investigators in the early 1740's.[7] Almost from the start of his electrical researches, Franklin was particularly concerned to explain that strange and, in the event, particularly revealing piece of special apparatus. His success in doing so provided the most effective of the arguments that made his theory a paradigm, though one that was still unable to account for quite all the known cases of electrical repulsion.[8] To be accepted as a paradigm, a theory must seem better than its competitors, but it need not, and in fact never does, explain all the facts with which it can be confronted.

What the fluid theory of electricity did for the subgroup that held it, the Franklinian paradigm later did for the entire group of electricians. It suggest-

[6] Bacon, *op. cit.*, pp. 235, 337, says, "Water slightly warm is more easily frozen than quite cold." For a partial account of the earlier history of this strange observation, see Marshall Clagett, *Giovanni Merliani and Late Medieval Physics* (New York, 1941), chap. iv.

[7] Roller and Roller, *op. cit.*, pp. 51–54.

[8] The troublesome case was the mutual repulsion of negatively charged bodies, for which see Cohen, *op. cit.*, pp. 491–94, 531–43.

ed which experiments would be worth performing and which, because directed to secondary or to overly complex manifestations of electricity, would not.
Only the paradigm did the job far more effectively, partly because the end of
interschool debate ended the constant reiteration of fundamentals and partly
because the confidence that they were on the right track encouraged scientists
to undertake more precise, esoteric, and consuming sorts of work.[9] Freed from
the concern with any and all electrical phenomena, the united group of electricians could pursue selected phenomena in far more detail, designing much
special equipment for the task and employing it more stubbornly and systematically than electricians had ever done before. Both fact collection and theory articulation became highly directed activities. The effectiveness and efficiency of electrical research increased accordingly, providing evidence for a
societal version of Francis Bacon's acute methodological dictum: "Truth
emerges more readily from error than from confusion."[10]

We shall be examining the nature of this highly directed or paradigm-
based research in the next section, but must first note briefly how the emergence of a paradigm affects the structure of the group that practices the field.
When, in the development of a natural science, an individual or group first
produces a synthesis able to attract most of the next generation's practitioners, the older schools gradually disappear. In part their disappearance is
caused by their members' conversion to the new paradigm. But there are
always some men who cling to one or another of the older views, and they are
simply read out of the profession, which thereafter ignores their work. The
new paradigm implies a new and more rigid definition of the field. Those
unwilling or unable to accommodate their work to it must proceed in isolation or attach themselves to some other group.[11] Historically, they have often

---

[9] It should be noted that the acceptance of Franklin's theory did not end quite all debate.
In 1759 Robert Symmer proposed a two-fluid version of that theory, and for many years thereafter
electricians were divided about whether electricity was a single fluid or two. But the debates on
this subject only confirm what has been said above about the manner in which a universally recognized achievement unites the profession. Electricians, though they continued divided on this
point, rapidly concluded that no experimental tests could distinguish the two versions of the theory and that they were therefore equivalent. After that, both schools could and did exploit all the
benefits that the Franklinian theory provided (*ibid.*, pp. 543–46, 548–54).

[10] Bacon, *op. cit.*, p. 210.

[11] The history of electricity provides an excellent example which could be duplicated from
the careers of Priestley, Kelvin, and others. Franklin reports that Nollet, who at mid-century was
the most influential of the Continental electricians, "lived to see himself the last of his Sect, except
Mr. B.—his Eleve and immediate Disciple" (Max Farrand [ed.], *Benjamin Franklin's Memoirs*
[Berkeley, Calif., 1949], pp. 384–86). More interesting, however, is the endurance of whole schools
in increasing isolation from professional science. Consider, for example, the case of astrology,
which was once an integral part of astronomy. Or consider the continuation in the late eighteenth
and early nineteenth centuries of a previously respected tradition of "romantic" chemistry. This is
the tradition discussed by Charles C. Gillispie in "The *Encyclopédie* and the Jacobin Philosophy of
Science: A Study in Ideas and Consequences," *Critical Problems in the History of Science*, ed. Marshall
Clagett (Madison, Wis., 1959), pp. 255–89; and "The Formation of Lamarck's Evolutionary
Theory," *Archives internationales a'histoire des sciences*, XXXVII (1956), 323–38.

simply stayed in the departments of philosophy from which so many of the special sciences have been spawned. As these indications hint, it is sometimes just its reception of a paradigm that transforms a group previously interested merely in the study of nature into a profession or, at least, a discipline. In the sciences (though not in fields like medicine, technology, and law, of which the principal *raison d'être* is an external social need), the formation of specialized journals, the foundation of specialists' societies, and the claim for a special place in the curriculum have usually been associated with a group's first reception of a single paradigm. At least this was the case between the time, a century and a half ago, when the institutional pattern of scientific specialization first developed and the very recent time when the paraphernalia of specialization acquired a prestige of their own.

The more rigid definition of the scientific group has other consequences. When the individual scientist can take a paradigm for granted, he need no longer, in his major works, attempt to build his field anew, starting from first principles and justifying the use of each concept introduced. That can be left to the writer of textbooks. Given a textbook, however, the creative scientist can begin his research where it leaves off and thus concentrate exclusively upon the subtlest and most esoteric aspects of the natural phenomena that concern his group. And as he does this, his research communiqués will begin to change in ways whose evolution has been too little studied but whose modern end products are obvious to all and oppressive to many. No longer will his researches usually be embodied in books addressed, like Franklin's *Experiments ... on Electricity* or Darwin's *Origin of Species*, to anyone who might be interested in the subject matter of the field. Instead they will usually appear as brief articles addressed only to professional colleagues, the men whose knowledge of a shared paradigm can be assumed and who prove to be the only ones able to read the papers addressed to them.

Today in the sciences, books are usually either texts or retrospective reflections upon one aspect or another of the scientific life. The scientist who writes one is more likely to find his professional reputation impaired than enhanced. Only in the earlier, pre-paradigm, stages of the development of the various sciences did the book ordinarily possess the same relation to professional achievement that it still retains in other creative fields. And only in those fields that still retain the book, with or without the article, as a vehicle for research communication are the lines of professionalization still so loosely drawn that the layman may hope to follow progress by reading the practitioners' original reports. Both in mathematics and astronomy, research reports had ceased already in antiquity to be intelligible to a generally educated audience. In dynamics, research became similarly esoteric in the later Middle Ages, and it recaptured general intelligibility only briefly during the early seventeenth century when a new paradigm replaced the one that had guided medieval research. Electrical research began to require translation for the layman before the end of the eighteenth century, and most other fields of physical science ceased to be generally accessible in the nineteenth.

During the same two centuries similar transitions can be isolated in the various parts of the biological sciences. In parts of the social sciences they may well be occurring today. Although it has become customary, and is surely proper, to deplore the widening gulf that separates the professional scientist from his colleagues in other fields, too little attention is paid to the essential relationship between that gulf and the mechanisms intrinsic to scientific advance.

Ever since prehistoric antiquity one field of study after another has crossed the divide between what the historian might call its prehistory as a science and its history proper. These transitions to maturity have seldom been so sudden or so unequivocal as my necessarily schematic discussion may have implied. But neither have they been historically gradual, coextensive, that is to say, with the entire development of the fields within which they occurred. Writers on electricity during the first four decades of the eighteenth century possessed far more information about electrical phenomena than had their sixteenth-century predecessors. During the half-century after 1740, few new sorts of electrical phenomena were added to their lists. Nevertheless, in important respects, the electrical writings of Cavendish, Coulomb, and Volta in the last third of the eighteenth century seem further removed from those of Gray, Du Fay, and even Franklin than are the writings of these early eighteenth-century electrical discoverers from those of the sixteenth century.[12] Sometime between 1740 and 1780, electricians were for the first time enabled to take the foundations of their field for granted. From that point they pushed on to more concrete and recondite problems, and increasingly they then reported their results in articles addressed to other electricians rather than in books addressed to the learned world at large. As a group they achieved what had been gained by astronomers in antiquity and by students of motion in the Middle Ages, of physical optics in the late seventeenth century, and of historical geology in the early nineteenth. They had, that is, achieved a paradigm that proved able to guide the whole group's research. Except with the advantage of hindsight, it is hard to find another criterion that so clearly proclaims a field a science.

[12] The post-Franklinian developments include an immense decrease in the sensitivity of charge detectors, the first reliable and generally diffused techniques for measuring charge, the evolution of the concept of capacity and its relation to a newly refined notion of electric tension, and the quantification of electrostatic force. On all of these see Roller and Roller, *op. cit.*, pp. 66–81; W.C. Walker, "The Detection and Estimation of Electric Charges in the Eighteenth Century," *Annals of Science*, I (1936), 66–100; and Edmund Hoppe, *Geschichte der Elektrizität* (Leipzig, 1884), Part I, chaps. iii–iv.

II. Classical Perspectives on Psychology

In this section on the classical writers, readings from four major philosophers are offered. While the four writers—Plato (427–347 BC), Aristotle (384–322 BC), Augustine (354–430), and Thomas Aquinas (1225–1274)—cover a vast time range of intellectual thought and represent a wide divergence of beliefs, they all played a key role in the attempt to define the nature of experience. In particular, they wrestled with how thought processes support understanding of ourselves and our world, and they proposed systems to account for how we acquire knowledge and how we use knowledge. Such questions seem to define the core of what it means to be human and represent the perplexing issues of epistemology, which have challenged philosophers since the dawn of recorded history.

In the first reading taken from Plato's *Republic*, written about 380, B.C., we are confronted with controversy about the origins of knowledge. Some philosophers insist that all knowledge must get into the mind through the senses, which assumes that the senses can reliably portray the external world accurately. The analogy of the cave succinctly expresses Plato's skepticism about sensory knowledge. Plato argued that knowledge of the external world relying solely on sensory information is distorted. He suggested that our sensory ability is similar to images that the prisoners, who are chained within a cave, experience when seeing shadows of the "real world" reflected on the cave's wall. If sensory knowledge is so distorted and unreliable, how can the mind gain truth and absolute knowledge? For Plato, the answer is in terms of the mind's innate capacity and its ability to act rationally.

Aristotle moved away from his teacher's dismissal of the value of sensory knowledge and rescued sensation's place in the acquisition of knowledge by suggesting that the senses are extensions of the soul; they are inseparable. Aristotle's teachings on psychology were contained in his book *De Anima*, reconstructed from notes estimated to have been written about 330, B.C. In the first line of this selection from *De Anima*, Aristotle sets the context for his belief in the power of sensory observations. Indeed, Aristotle's argument forms the justification for empirical science, which he very much advocated. If our senses are unreliable, we cannot learn of the external, natural world in ways that yield consensus from other observers.

Of course the major historical event in the Mediterranean world between Aristotle and Augustine was the advent of Christianity and its spread throughout the Roman Empire and beyond. Augustine seems to share a Platonic version of the senses, since he relegates the body and its functions to an imperfect level. In the selection from *The Confessions*, written about 400, Augustine asserts a kind of hierarchy with sensory knowledge relegated to a distinctly inferior level compared to the spiritual soul. Moreover, the good person is defined as the individual who is able to rise above the world of the flesh, and secure salvation in the spiritual realm of God. Thus, for Augustine, life is a struggle, and knowledge through the senses is not only to be treated with skepticism, as Plato suggested, but actually avoided as evil.

Thomas Aquinas, like Aristotle, rescues the world of sensory knowledge by recognizing the dependency of the intellect on sense information. In this selection from his monumental *Summa Theologiae*, set in its final form about 1272, Aquinas begins by outlining eight propositions that take issue with Plato's notion of distorted reality or "phantasm", which is illusory. Only four of the first five articles are reproduced here. In Articles 4 and 5, we see that Aquinas uses sensory knowledge to build a foundation for our understanding of general principles or universals. This complementary relationship of the soul's extension to the bodily senses, not their opposition, sets the stage for the acceptance of empiricism based upon observation. A secondary point to note in this selection is the methodology of Aquinas: An initial proposition is put forth in the form of a question, and then various possibilities are exhausted to lead the reader to the truth or falsity of the proposition. The logical underpinnings of this method permitted Aquinas to conceive of the person as the essential unity of body and soul, whereby the intellect interacts with the natural environment through the senses.

REFERENCES

AQUINAS, T. (ca. 1272, 1948). *Summa Theologiae.* In A.C. Pegis (ed.) *Introduction to Saint Thomas Aquinas.* New York: The Modern Library, Question LXXXV. The mode and order of understanding, 400–405, 408–416.

ARISTOTLE. (ca 330, B.C., 1941). *De Anima.* In *The basic works of Aristotle* (R. McKeon, ed.; J.A. Smith, transl.). New York: Random House, Book II, Ch. 2 (Second definition of the soul), 557–559; Ch. 3 (The faculties of the soul), 559–560; Ch. 5 (Sense-perception) 564–566.

AUGUSTINE. (ca. 400, 1948). *The Confessions.* In W.J. Oates (ed.) *Basic writings of Saint Augustine.* New York: Random House, Chs. IX–XII, 122–127.

PLATO. (ca. 380, B.C., 1974). Book VII. Story of the Cave. In *Plato's republic.* Indianapolis: Hackett Publishing, 168–177.

Plato, Excerpt from Book VII. "Story of the Cave" from *The republic* (ca. 380, B.C.).*

BOOK VII

Next, I said, compare the effect of education and the lack of it upon our human nature to a situation like this: imagine men to be living in an underground cave-like dwelling place, which has a way up to the light along its whole width, but the entrance is a long way up. The men have been there from childhood, with their neck and legs in fetters, so that they remain in the same place and can only see ahead of them, as their bonds prevent them turning their heads. Light is provided by a fire burning some way behind and above them. Between the fire and the prisoners, some way behind them and on a higher ground, there is a path across the cave and along this a low wall has been built, like the screen at a puppet show in front of the performers who show their puppets above it.—I see it.

See then also men carrying along that wall, so that they overtop it, all kinds of artifacts, statues of men, reproductions of other animals in stone or wood fashioned in all sorts of ways, and, as is likely, some of the carriers are talking while others are silent.—This is a strange picture, and strange prisoners.

They are like us, I said. Do you think, in the first place, that such men could see anything of themselves and each other [1] except the shadows which the fire casts upon the wall of the cave in front of them?—How could they, if they have to keep their heads still throughout life?

* Plato (ca. 380, B.C., 1974). Excerpts from Book VII. Story of the Cave. In *Plato's republic*. Indianapolis: Hackett Publishing, 168–177. Reprinted by permission of Hackett Publishing Co.

[1] These shadows of themselves and each other are never mentioned again. A Platonic myth or parable, like a Homeric simile, is often elaborated in considerable detail. These contribute to the vividness of the picture but often have no other function, and it is a mistake to look for any symbolic meaning in them. It is the general picture that matters.

And is not the same true of the objects carried along the wall?—Quite.

If they could converse with one another, do you not think that they would consider these shadows to be the real thing?—Necessarily.

What if their prison had an echo which reached them from in front of them? Whenever one of the carriers passing behind the wall spoke, would they not think that it was the shadow passing in front of them which was talking? Do you agree?—By Zeus I do.

Altogether then, I said, such men would believe the truth to be nothing else than the shadows of the artifacts?—They must believe that.

Consider then what deliverance from their bonds and the curing of their ignorance would be if something like this naturally happened to them. Whenever one of them was freed, had to stand up suddenly, turn his head, walk, and look up toward the light, doing all that would give him pain, the flash of the fire would make it impossible for him to see the objects of which he had earlier seen the shadows. When do you think he would say if he was told that what he saw then was foolishness, that he was not somewhat closer to reality and turned to things that existed more fully, that he saw more correctly? If one then pointed to each of the objects passing by, asked him what each was, and forced him to answer, do you not think he would be at a loss and believe that the things which he saw earlier were truer than the things now pointed out to him? Much truer.

If one then compelled him to look at the fire itself, his eyes would hurt, he would turn round and flee toward those things which he could see, and think that they were in fact clearer than those now shown to him.—Quite so.

And if one were to drag him thence by force up the rough and steep path, and did not let him go before he was dragged into the sunlight, would he not be in physical pain and angry as he was dragged along? When he came into the light, with the sunlight filling his eyes, he would not be able to see a single one of the things which are now said to be true.—Not at once, certainly.

I think he would need time to get adjusted before he could see things in the world above; at first he would see shadows most easily, then reflections of men and other things in water, then the things themselves. After this he would see objects in the sky and the sky itself more easily at night, the light of the stars and the moon more easily than the sun and the light of the sun during the day.—Of course.

Then, at last, he would be able to see the sun, not images of it in water or in some alien place, but the sun itself in its own place, and be able to contemplate it.—That must be so.

After this he would reflect that it is the sun which provides the seasons and the years, which governs everything in the visible world, and is also in some way the cause of those other things which he used to see.—Clearly that would be the next stage.

What then? As he reminds himself of his first dwelling place, of the wisdom there and of his fellow prisoners, would he not reckon himself happy for the change, and pity them?—Surely.

And if the men below had praise and honours from each other, and prizes for the man who saw most clearly the shadows that passed before them, and who could best remember which usually came earlier and which later, and which came together and thus could most ably prophesy the future, do you think our man would desire those rewards and envy those who were honoured and held power among the prisoners, or would he feel, as Homer put it, that he certainly wished to be "serf to another man without possessions upon the earth"[2] and go through any suffering, rather than share their opinions and live as they do?—Quite so, he said, I think he would rather suffer anything.

Reflect on this too, I said. If this man went down into the cave again and sat down in the same seat, would his eyes not be filled with darkness, coming suddenly out of the sunlight?—They certainly would.

And if he had to contend again with those who had remained prisoners in recognizing those shadows while his sight was affected and his eyes had not settled down—and the time for this adjustment would not be short—would he not be ridiculed? Would it not be said that he had returned from his upward journey with his eyesight spoiled, and that it was not worthwhile even to attempt to travel upward? As for the man who tried to free them and lead them upward, if they could somehow lay their hands on him and kill him, they would do so.—They certainly would.

This whole image, my dear Glaucon, I said, must be related to what we said before. The realm of the visible should be compared to the prison dwelling, and the fire inside it to the power of the sun. If you interpret the upward journey and the contemplation of things above as the upward journey of the soul to the intelligible realm, you will grasp what I surmise since you were keen to hear it. Whether it is true or not only the god knows, but this is how I see it, namely that in the intelligible world the Form of the Good is the last to be seen, and with difficulty; when seen it must be reckoned to be for all the cause of all that is right and beautiful, to have produced in the visible world both light and the fount of light, while in the intelligible world it is itself that which produces and controls truth and intelligence, and he who is to act intelligently in public or in private must see it.—I share your thought as far as I am able.

Come then, share with me this thought also: do not be surprised that those who have reached this point are unwilling to occupy themselves with human affairs, and that their souls are always pressing upward to spend their time there, for this is natural if things are as our parable indicates.—That is very likely.

Further, I said, do you think it at all surprising that anyone coming to the evils of human life from the contemplation of the divine behaves awk-

---

[2] Odyssey 11, 489–90, where Achilles says to Odysseus, on the latter's visit to the underworld, that he would rather be a servant to a poor man on earth than king among the dead.

wardly and appears very ridiculous while his eyes are still dazzled and before he is sufficiently adjusted to the darkness around him, if he is compelled to contend in court or some other place about the shadows of justice or the objects of which they are shadows, and to carry through the contest about these in the way these things are understood by those who have never seen Justice itself?—That is not surprising at all.

Anyone with intelligence, I said, would remember that the eyes may be confused in two ways and from two causes, coming from light into darkness as well as from darkness into light. Realizing that the same applies to the soul, whenever he sees a soul disturbed and unable to see something, he will not laugh mindlessly but will consider whether it has come from a brighter life and is dimmed because unadjusted, or has come from greater ignorance into greater light and is filled with a brighter dazzlement. The former he would declare happy in its life and experience, the latter he would pity, and if he should wish to laugh at it, his laughter would be less ridiculous than if he laughed at a soul that has come from the light above.—What you say is very reasonable.

We must then, I said, if these things are true, think something like this about them, namely that education is not what some declare it to be; they say that knowledge is not present in the soul and that they put it in, like putting sight into blind eyes.—They surely say that.

Our present argument shows, I said, that the capacity to learn and the organ with which to do so are present in every person's soul. It is as if it were not possible to turn the eye from darkness to light without turning the whole body; so one must turn one's whole soul from the world of becoming until it can endure to contemplate reality, and the brightest of realities, which we say is the Good.—Yes.

Education then is the art of doing this very thing, this turning around, the knowledge of how the soul can most easily and most effectively be turned around; it is not the art of putting the capacity of sight into the soul; the soul possesses that already but it is not turned the right way or looking where it should. This is what education has to deal with.—That seems likely.

Now the other so-called virtues of the soul seem to be very close to those of the body—they really do not exist before and are added later by habit and practice—but the virtue of intelligence belongs above all to something more divine, it seems, which never loses its capacity but, according to which way it is turned, becomes useful and beneficial or useless and harmful. Have you ever noticed in men who are said to be wicked but clever, how sharply their little soul looks into things to which it turns its attention? Its capacity for sight is not inferior, but it is compelled to serve evil ends, so that the more sharply it looks the more evils it works.—Quite so.

Yet if a soul of this kind had been hammered at from childhood and those excrescences had been knocked off it which belong to the world of becoming and have been fastened upon it by feasting, gluttony, and similar pleasures, and which like leaden weights draw the soul to look downward—if, being rid of these, it turned to look at things that are true, then the same soul of the same man would see these just as sharply as it now sees the things towards which it is directed.—That seems likely.

Further, is it not likely, I said, indeed it follows inevitably from what was said before, that the uneducated who have no experience of truth would never govern a city satisfactorily, nor would those who are allowed to spend their whole life in the process of educating themselves; the former would fail because they do not have a single goal at which all their actions, public and private, must aim; the latter because they would refuse to act, thinking that they have settled, while still alive, in the faraway islands of the blessed.—True.

It is then our task as founders, I said, to compel the best natures to reach the study which we have previously said to be the most important, to see the Good and to follow that upward journey. When they have accomplished their journey and seen it sufficiently, we must not allow them to do what they are allowed to do today.—What is that?

To stay there, I said, and to refuse to go down again to the prisoners in the cave, there to share both their labours and their honours, whether these be of little or of greater worth.[3]

Are we then, he said, to do them an injustice by making them live a worse life when they could live a better one?

You are again forgetting, my friend, I said, that it is not the law's concern to make some one group in the city outstandingly happy but to contrive to spread happiness throughout the city, by bringing the citizens into harmony with each other by persuasion or compulsion, and to make them share with each other the benefits which each group can confer upon the community. The law has not made men of this kind in the city in order to allow each to turn in any direction they wish but to make use of them to bind the city together.—You are right, I had forgotten.

Consider then, Glaucon, I said, that we shall not be doing an injustice to those who have become philosophers in our city, and that what we shall say to them, when we compel them to care for and to guard the others, is just. For we shall say: "Those who become philosophers in other cities are justified in not sharing the city's labours, for they have grown into philosophy of their own accord, against the will of the government in each of those cities, and it is right that what grows of its own accord, as it owes no debt to anyone for its upbringing, should not be keen to pay it to anyone. But we have made you in our city kings and leaders of the swarm, as it were, both to your own advantage and to that of the rest of the city; you are better and more completely educated than those others, and you are better able to share in both kinds of life. Therefore you must each in turn go down to live with other men and grow accustomed

---

3 Plato does indeed require his philosopher to go back into the cave to help those less fortunate than himself, but only as a duty, not because he loves his neighbour or gets any emotional satisfaction from helping him.

to seeing in the dark. When you are used to it you will see infinitely better than the dwellers below; you will know what each image is and of what it is an image, because you have seen the truth of things beautiful and just and good, and so, for you as for us, the city will be governed as a waking reality and not as in a dream, as the majority of cities are now governed by men who are fighting shadows and striving against each other in order to rule as if this were a great good." For this is the truth: a city in which the prospective rulers are least keen to the rule must of necessity be governed best and be most free from civil strife, whereas a city with the opposite kind of rulers is governed in the opposite way.—Quite so.

Do you think that those we have nurtured will disobey us and refuse to share the labours of the city, each group in turn, though they may spend the greater part of their time dwelling with each other in a pure atmosphere?

They cannot, he said, for we shall be giving just orders to just men, but each of them will certainly go to rule as to something that must be done, the opposite attitude from that of the present rulers in every city.

That is how it is, my friend, I said. If you can find a way of life which is better than governing for the prospective governors, then a well-governed city can exist for you. Only in that city will the truly rich rule, not rich in gold but in the wealth which the happy man must have, a life with goodness and intelligence. If beggars hungry for private goods go into public life, thinking that they must snatch their good from it, the well-governed city cannot exist, for then office is fought for, and such a war at home inside the city destroys them and the city as well.—Very true.

Can you name, I said, any other life than that of true philosophy which disdains political office?—No, by Zeus.

And surely it is those who are no lovers of governing who must govern. Otherwise, rival lovers of it will fight them.—Of course.

What other men will you compel to become guardians of the city rather than those who have the best knowledge of the principles that make for the best government of a city and who also know honours of a different kind, and a better life than the political?—No one else.

Do you want us to examine how such men will come to be in our city, and how one will lead them to the light, as some are said to have gone up from the underworld to join the gods?—Of course I want it.

This is not a matter of spinning a coin[4] but of turning a soul from a kind of day that is night to the true day, being the upward way to reality which we say is true philosophy.—Quite so.

---

[4] A proverbial saying, referring to a children's game in which the players were divided into two groups. A shell or potsherd, white on one side and black on the other, was then thrown in the space between them to the cry of "night or day" (note the reference to night and day which immediately follows) and, according as the white or black fell uppermost, one group ran away pursued by the other. The meaning here is much the same as in our expression "spinning a coin," namely that this was not a matter to be settled in a moment or by chance.

We must therefore examine what study has the power to do so.—Of course.

What study would it be, Glaucon, which draws the soul from the world of that which becomes to the world of that which is? This occurs to me as I am speaking; did we not say that these men, in youth, must be athletes in war?—We did say that.

The study we seek must therefore also have this characteristic, besides the other.—Which characteristic?

It must not be useless to men at war.—That must be so, if possible.

We educated them before this in the arts and physical culture.—We did.

Now physical culture is concerned with what comes to be and dies, since it oversees the growth and decay of the body.—So it seems.

It could not therefore be the study we seek.—No.

Is it then that education in the arts which we described?

But that, he said, was the counterpart of physical training. It educated the guardians through habits; its melodies gave them a certain inner harmony, not knowledge, and its rhythms gave them a certain grace; moreover its stories, whether fictional or nearer the truth, cultivated certain habits akin to those, but there was no knowledge in it which would lead to what you are looking for now.

You remind me most precisely, I said. In fact it has nothing of the sort. But, my good Glaucon, what would such a study be? For all the crafts seemed to be too base.

Of course. Yet what study is there left, apart from the arts and physical training and the crafts?

Come, I said, if we can find nothing outside these, let us take something which bears upon them all.—What kind of thing?

For example, the common thing which is used by all crafts, all modes of thought, and all sciences, and which everybody of necessity must learn to begin with.—What is it?

That trifling thing, said I, namely to distinguish one and two and three, or, to give it one name, I call it number and calculation. Is it not true that every craft and science must have a share in this?—Certainly.

War then also shares in it?—It cannot avoid it.

Palamedes[5] in the tragedies shows up Agamemnon every time as a quite ridiculous general, or have you not noticed that he says he invented numbers which men did not know before, then arrayed the companies in the camp in Ilium and counted the ships and everything else. Agamemnon apparently did not even know how many feet he had, since he did not know how to count. What sort of a general do you think that made him?

A very strange one, he said, in my opinion, if that was true.

---

[5] In legend a clever Greek hero of the Trojan war. The invention of the alphabet and of arithmetic was credited to him. When Odysseus feigned madness to avoid going to Troy, Palamedes exposed him. In revenge Odysseus faked evidence of treason against him and he was put to death.

Shall we say then, I said, that this study is very necessary for a warrior, that is, to be able to count and calculate?

More necessary than anything else, he said, if he is to understand anything about marshalling troops, indeed if he is to be a man at all.

Do you think the same as I do about this study?—What?

It is likely to be one of those we are seeking, which leads to intelligent thought, but no one uses it correctly, though in every way it draws one to reality.—How do you mean?

I will try, I said, to make clear what I think. As I distinguish for myself the studies which lead in the direction we mentioned and those that do not, you must observe them along with me and agree or disagree, so that we may know more clearly whether it is as I surmise.—Show me.

Among our sense impressions there are some that do not call upon the intelligence to examine them because the decision of our perception is sufficient, while others certainly summon the help of intelligence to examine them because the sensation does not achieve a sensible result.

You are, he said, obviously referring to things appearing in the distance and to shadow-painting.

You are not quite getting my meaning, I said.—What is it then?

They do not call for help, I said, if they do not at the same time give a contrary impression; I describe those that do as calling for help whenever the sense perception does not point to one thing rather than its opposite, whether its object be far or near. You will understand my meaning better if I put it this way: here, we say, are three fingers, the smallest, the second, and the middle finger.—Quite so.

Assume that I am talking about them as being seen quite close. Now examine this about them.—What?

Each of them equally appears to be a finger, and in this respect it makes no difference whether it is seen to be at the end or in the middle, whether it is white or black, thick or thin, and all that sort of thing. In all this the soul of the many is not compelled to ask the intelligence what a finger is, for the sense of sight does not indicate to it that the finger is the opposite of a finger.—Certainly not.

Therefore this sense perception would not be likely to call on the intelligence or arouse it.—Not likely.

What about their bigness or smallness? Does the sense of sight have a sufficient perception of them, and does it make no difference to it whether the finger is in the middle or at one end? or their thickness and thinness, their hardness or softness in the case of the sense of touch? And do our other senses not lack clearness in their perception of these qualities? Does not each sense behave in the following way: in the first place the sense concerned with the hard is of necessity also concerned with the soft and it declares to the soul that it perceives the same object to be both hard and soft.[6]—That is so.

---

[6] What is big or hard in comparison with one thing can be small or soft in comparison with another. It appears therefore to have opposite qualities, and this is true of all the objects of sense.

Then in those cases the soul in turn is puzzled as to what this perception means by hard, if it says that the same thing is also soft; and so with the perception of the light and the heavy, the soul is puzzled as to what is the meaning of the light and the heavy, if sense perception indicates that what is light is also heavy, and what is heavy, light.

Yes, he said, these indications are strange to the soul, and need investigation.

It is likely then, I said, that in these cases the soul will attempt, by calling up calculation and intelligence, to examine whether each of the things announced to it is one or two.—Of course.

Then if they appear to be two, each appears as different and one.—Yes.

If each is one while both are two, it will think of the two as separate, for if they were not separate, it would not be thinking of them as two, but as one.—Correct.

But we say that the sense of sight saw big and small not as separate but as commingled. Is that not so?—Yes.

So in order to clarify this, intelligence is compelled to see big and small not as commingled but as separate, the opposite way from sight.—True.

And it is from some such circumstances that it first occurs to us to ask: "What is the nature of bigness, and again of smallness?"—That is surely true.

And so we called the one intelligible and the other visible.—Quite correct.

This is what I was trying to express before when I said that some things call upon thought, and others do not. Those which affect the senses in contrary ways at the same time I defined as calling on thought, while those which do not I described as not rousing the intelligence.—I understand now and I think that is right.

Well then, to which of these two classes do number and the unit seem to belong?—I do not know.

Reason it out from what was said before. If the unit, in and by itself, is adequately seen or perceived by any other sense, then, as we were saying in the case of the fingers, it would not draw one toward reality. If, however, something contrary to it is always seen at the same time so that it does not appear to be one more than the opposite, it would stand in need of a judge. The soul would then be at a loss, search for an answer, stir up intelligence within itself, and ask what is the nature of the unit in itself, and so the study of the unit would be one of those which leads the soul and turns it toward the contemplation of reality.

Certainly, he said, the sight of the unit possesses this characteristic to a remarkable degree, for we see the same object to be both one and an infinite number.

Then if the one has this quality, every number has it too.—Of course.

Now calculation and arithmetic are wholly concerned with number.—Definitely.

Then indeed they appear to lead one to the truth.—Remarkably so.

They would then belong, it seems to the studies we seek. The warrior must learn them to marshal his troops, and also the philosopher because he must emerge from the world of becoming and grasp reality, or never be a rational thinker.—That is so.

And our guardian must be both a warrior and a philosopher.—Definitely.

This study would then be a suitable one, Glaucon. We should legislate and persuade those who will share the highest offices in our city to turn to arithmetic and to pursue it in no amateur spirit, but until they reach by pure thought the contemplation of the nature of numbers. They do not pursue this study for the sake of buying and selling like merchants and retailers, but both for the sake of war and to attain ease in turning the soul itself from the world of becoming to truth and reality.—A fine statement.

Moreover it occurs to me, since the study of calculation has been mentioned, what a subtle study it is and in how many ways it is useful to our purpose, if one studies it for the sake of knowledge and not to buy and sell.—In what way?

In the way we were mentioning. It forcibly leads the soul upward and compels it to discuss the numbers themselves. Nor does the soul allow one to discuss them by presenting numbers with visible and touchable bodies.[7] You know how experts in these matters, if someone tries to divide the unit in argument, laugh at him and do not allow it; if you divide it, they multiply, taking care that the unit should never appear to be many parts and not to be one.—Very true indeed.

---

[7] The difference is between one material body, an apple for instance, which can be divided into a number of parts, and the concept of oneness or unity, which has no parts and remains the same. If you divide a physical unit into parts these parts multiply it in the sense that they multiply the number of units, i.e. each part is one or a unit, and the concept of one remains the same, without parts.

⇐ 4 ⇒

Aristotle, Excerpts from Book II, Ch. 2, "Second definition of the soul", Ch. 3, "The faculties of the soul", Ch. 5 "Sense-perception" from *De Anima* (ca. 330, B.C.).*

From this it indubitably follows that the soul is inseparable from its body, or at any rate that certain parts of it are (if it has parts)—for the actuality of some of them is nothing but the actualities of their bodily parts. Yet some may be separable because they are not the actualities of any body at all. Further, we have no light on the problem whether the soul may not be the actuality of its body in the sense in which the sailor is the actuality of the ship.

This must suffice as our sketch or outline determination of the nature of soul.

2   Since what is clear or logically more evident emerges from what in itself is confused but more observable by us, we must reconsider our results from this point of view. For it is not enough for a definitive formula to express as most now do the mere fact; it must include and exhibit the ground also. At present definitions are given in a form analogous to the conclusion of a syllogism; e.g. What is squaring? The construction of an equilateral rectangle equal to a given oblong rectangle. Such a definition is in form equivalent to a conclusion. One that tells us that squaring is the discovery of a line which is a mean proportional between the two unequal sides of the given rectangle discloses the ground of what is defined.

We resume our inquiry from a fresh starting-point by calling attention to the fact that what has soul in it differs from what has not in that the former displays life. Now this word has more than one sense, and provided any one alone of these is found in a thing we say that thing is living. Living, that is, may mean thinking or perception or local movement and rest, or movement in the

* From *Basic Works of Aristotle* by Aristotle, edited by R. McKeon and translated by J.A. Smith. Copyright (c) 1941 and renewed 1969 by Random House, Inc. Reprinted by permission of Random House, Inc.

sense of nutrition, decay and growth. Hence we think of plants also as living, for they are observed to possess in themselves an originative power through which they increase or decrease in all spatial directions; they grow up *and* down, and everything that grows increases its bulk alike in both directions or indeed in all, and continues to live so long as it can absorb nutriment.

This power of self-nutrition can be isolated from the other powers mentioned, but not they from it—in mortal beings at least. The fact is obvious in plants; for it is the only psychic power they possess.

This is the originative power the possession of which leads us to speak of things as *living* at all, but it is the possession of sensation that leads us for the first time to speak of living things as animals; for even those beings which possess no power of local movement but do possess the power of sensation we call animals and not merely living things.

The primary form of sense is touch, which belongs to all animals. Just as the power of self-nutrition can be isolated from touch and sensation generally, so touch can be isolated from all other forms of sense. (By the power of self-nutrition we mean that departmental power of the soul which is common to plants and animals: all animals whatsoever are observed to have the sense of touch.) What the explanation of these two facts is, we must discuss later. At present we must confine ourselves to saying that soul is the source of these phenomena and is characterized by them, viz. by the powers of self-nutrition, sensation, thinking, and motivity.

Is each of these a soul or a part of a soul? And if a part, a part in what sense? A part merely distinguishable by definition or a part distinct in local situation as well? In the case of certain of these powers, the answers to these questions are easy, in the case of others we are puzzled what to say. Just as in the case of plants which when divided are observed to continue to live though removed to a distance from one another (thus showing that in *their* case the soul of each individual plant before division was actually one, potentially many), so we notice a similar result in other varieties of soul, i.e. in insects which have been cut in two; each of the segments possesses both sensation and local movement; and if sensation, necessarily also imagination and appetition; for, where there is sensation, there is also pleasure and pain, and, where these, necessarily also desire.

We have no evidence as yet about mind or the power to think; it seems to be a widely different kind of soul, differing as what is eternal from what is perishable; it alone is capable of existence in isolation from all other psychic powers. All the other parts of soul, it is evident from what we have said, are, in spite of certain statements to the contrary, incapable of separate existence though, of course, distinguishable by definition. If opining is distinct from perceiving, to be capable of opining and to be capable of perceiving must be distinct, and so with all the other forms of living above enumerated. Further, some animals possess all these parts of soul, some certain of them only, others one only (this is what enables us to classify animals); the cause must be considered later. A similar arrangement is found also within the field of the sens-es; some classes of animals have all the senses, some only certain of them, others only one, the most indispensable, touch.

Since the expression 'that whereby we live and perceive' has two mean-ings, just like the expression 'that whereby we know' —that may mean either (*a*) knowledge or (*b*) the soul, for we can speak of knowing *by* or *with* either, and similarly that whereby we are in health may be either (*a*) health or (*b*) the body or some part of the body; and since of the two terms thus contrasted knowledge or health is the name of a form, essence, or ratio, or if we so express it an actu-ality of a recipient matter—knowledge of what is capable of knowing, health of what is capable of being made healthy (for the operation of that which is capa-ble of originating change terminates and has its seat in what is changed or altered); further, since it is the soul by or with which primarily we live, perceive, and think:—it follows that the soul must be a ratio or formulable essence, not a matter or subject. For, as we said, the word substance has three meanings—form, matter, and the complex of both—and of these three what is called mat-ter is potentiality, what is called form actuality. Since then the complex here is the living thing, the body cannot be the actuality of the soul; it is the soul which is the actuality of a certain kind of body. Hence the rightness of the view that the soul cannot be without a body, while it cannot *be* a body; it is not a body but something relative to a body. That is why it is *in* a body, and a body of a definite kind. It was a mistake, therefore, to do as former thinkers did, merely to fit it into a body without adding a definite specification of the kind or character of that body. Reflection confirms the observed fact; the actuality of any given thing can only be realized in what is already potentially that thing, i.e. in a matter of its own appropriate to it. From all this it follows that soul is an actuality or for-mulable essence of something that possesses a potentiality of being besouled.

3　　Of the psychic powers above enumerated some kinds of living things, as we have said, possess all, some less than all, others one only. Those we have mentioned are the nutritive, the appetitive, the sensory, the locomotive, and the power of thinking. Plants have none but the first, the nutritive, while another order of living things has this *plus* the sensory. If any order of living things has the sensory, it must also have the appetitive; for appetite is the genus of which desire, passion, and wish are the species; now all animals have one sense at least, viz. touch, and whatever has a sense has the capacity for pleasure and pain and therefore has pleasant and painful objects present to it, and wherever these are present, there is desire, for desire is just appetition of what is pleasant. Further, all animals have the sense for food (for touch is the sense for food); the food of all living things consists of what is dry, moist, hot, cold, and these are the qualities apprehended by touch; all other sensi-ble qualities are apprehended by touch only indirectly. Sounds, colours, and odours contribute nothing to nutriment; flavours fall within the field of tan-gible qualities. Hunger and thirst are forms of desire, hunger a desire for what is dry and hot, thirst a desire for what is cold and moist; flavour is a sort of seasoning added to both. We must later clear up these points, but at present it may be enough to say that all animals that possess the sense of touch have also appetition. The case of imagination is obscure; we must examine it later. Certain kinds of animals possess in addition the power of locomotion, and still another order of animate beings, i.e. man and possibly another order like man or superior to him, the power of thinking, i.e. mind. It is now evident that a single definition can be given of soul only in the same sense as one can be given of figure. For, as in that case there is no figure distinguishable and apart from triangle, & c., so here there is no soul apart from the forms of soul just enumerated. It is true that a highly general definition can be given for figure which will fit all figures without expressing the peculiar nature of any figure. So here in the case of soul and its specific forms. Hence it is absurd in this and similar cases to demand an absolutely general definition, which will fail to express the peculiar nature of anything that *is*, or again, omitting this, to look for separate definitions corresponding to each *infima species*. The cases of figure and soul are exactly parallel; for the particulars subsumed under the common name in both cases—figures and living beings—constitute a series, each successive term of which potentially contains its predecessor, e.g. the square the triangle, the sensory power the self-nutritive. Hence we must ask in the case of each order of living things, What is its soul, i.e. What is the soul of plant, animal, man? Why the terms are related in this serial way must form the subject of later examination. But the facts are that the power of perception is never found apart from the power of self-nutrition, while—in plants—the latter is found isolated from the former. Again, no sense is found apart from that of touch, while touch *is* found by itself; many animals have neither sight, hearing, nor smell. Again, among living things that possess sense some have the power of locomotion, some not. Lastly, certain living beings—a small minority—possess calculation and thought, for (among mortal beings) those which possess calculation have all the other powers above mentioned, while the converse does not hold—indeed some live by imagination alone, while others have not even imagination. The mind that knows with immediate intuition presents a different problem.

It is evident that the way to give the most adequate definition of soul is to seek in the case of *each* of its forms for the most appropriate definition.

5   Having made these distinctions let us now speak of sensation in the widest sense. Sensation depends, as we have said, on a process of movement or affection from without, for it is held to be some sort of change of quality. Now some thinkers assert that like is affected only by like; in what sense this is possible and in what sense impossible, we have explained in our general discussion of acting and being acted upon.

Here arises a problem: why do we not perceive the senses themselves as well as the external objects of sense, or why without the stimulation of external objects do they not produce sensation, seeing that they contain in themselves fire, earth, and all the other elements, which are the direct or indirect

objects of sense? It is clear that what is sensitive is so only potentially, not actually. The power of sense is parallel to what is combustible, for that never
ignites itself spontaneously, but requires an agent which has the power of
starting ignition; otherwise it could have set itself on fire, and would not have
needed actual fire to set it ablaze.

In reply we must recall that we use the word 'perceive' in two ways, for
we say (a) that what has the power to hear or see, 'sees' or 'hears', even
though it is at the moment asleep, and also (b) that what is actually seeing or
hearing, 'sees' or 'hears'. Hence 'sense' too must have two meanings, sense
potential, and sense actual. Similarly 'to be a sentient' means either (a) to
have a certain power or (b) to manifest a certain activity. To begin with, for a
time, let us speak as if there were no difference between (i) being moved or
affected, and (ii) being active, for movement is a kind of activity—an imperfect kind, as has elsewhere been explained. Everything that is acted upon or
moved is acted upon by an agent which is actually at work. Hence it is that in
one sense, as has already been stated, what acts and what is acted upon are
like, in another unlike, i.e. prior to and during the change the two factors are
unlike, after it like.

But we must now distinguish not only *between* what is potential and what
is actual but also different senses in which things can be said to be potential
or actual; up to now we have been speaking as if each of these phrases had
only one sense. We can speak of something as 'a knower' either (a) as when
we say that man is a knower, meaning that man falls within the class of beings
that know or have knowledge, or (b) as when we are speaking of a man who
possesses a knowledge of grammar; each of these is so called as having in him
a certain potentiality, but there is a difference between their respective potentialities, the one (a) being a potential knower, because his kind or matter is
such and such, the other (b), because he can in the absence of any external
counteracting cause realize his knowledge in actual knowing at will. This
implies a third meaning of 'a knower' (c), one who is already realizing his
knowledge—he is a knower in actuality and in the most proper sense is knowing, e.g. this A. Both the former are potential knowers, who realize their
respective potentialities, the one (a) by change of quality, i.e. repeated transitions from one state to its opposite under instruction, the other (b) by the
transition from the inactive possession of sense or grammar to their active
exercise. The two kinds of transition are distinct.

Also the expression 'to be acted upon' has more than one meaning; it
may mean either (a) the extinction of one of two contraries by the other, or
(b) the maintenance of what is potential by the agency of what is actual and
already like what is acted upon, with such likeness as is compatible with one's
being actual and the other potential. For what possesses knowledge becomes
an actual knower by a transition which is either not an alteration of it at all
(being in reality a development into its true self or actuality) or at least an
alteration in a quite different sense from the usual meaning.

Hence it is wrong to speak of a wise man as being 'altered' when he uses his wisdom, just as it would be absurd to speak of a builder as being altered when he is using his skill in building a house.

What in the case of knowing or understanding leads from potentiality to actuality ought not to be called teaching but something else. That which starting with the power to know learns or acquires knowledge through the agency of one who actually knows and has the power of teaching either (*a*) ought not to be said 'to be acted upon' at all *or* (*b*) we must recognize two senses of alteration, viz. (i) the substitution of one quality for another, the first being the contrary of the second, or (ii) the development of an existent quality from potentiality in the direction of fixity or nature.

In the case of what is to possess sense, the first transition is due to the action of the male parent and takes place before birth so that at birth the living thing is, in respect of sensation, at the stage which corresponds to the *possession* of knowledge. Actual sensation corresponds to the stage of the exercise of knowledge. But between the two cases compared there is a difference; the objects that excite the sensory powers to activity, the seen, the heard, & c., are outside. The ground of this difference is that what actual sensation apprehends is individuals, while what knowledge apprehends is universals, and these are in a sense within the soul. That is why a man can exercise his knowledge when he wishes, but his sensation does not depend upon himself—a sensible object must be there. A similar statement must be made about our *knowledge* of what is sensible—on the same ground, viz. that the sensible objects are individual and external.

A later more appropriate occasion may be found thoroughly to clear up all this. At present it must be enough to recognize the distinctions already drawn; a thing may be said to be potential in either of two senses, (*a*) in the sense in which we might say of a boy that he may become a general or (*b*) in the sense in which we might say the same of an adult, and there are two corresponding senses of the term 'a potential sentient'. There are no separate names for the two stages of potentiality; we have pointed out that they are different and how they are different. We cannot help using the incorrect terms 'being acted upon or altered' of the two transitions involved. As we have said, what has the power of sensation is potentially like what the perceived object is actually; that is, while at the beginning of the process of its being acted upon the two interacting factors are dissimilar, at the end the one acted upon is assimilated to the other and is identical in quality with it.

6   In dealing with each of the senses we shall have first to speak of the objects which are perceptible by each. The term 'object of sense' covers three kinds of objects, two kinds of which are, in our language, directly perceptible, while the remaining one is only incidentally perceptible. Of the first two kinds one (*a*) consists of what is perceptible by a single sense, the other (*b*) of what is perceptible by any and all of the senses. I call by the name of special object of this or that sense that which cannot be perceived by any other sense than that one and in respect of which no error is possible; in this sense colour is the special object of sight, sound of hearing, flavour of taste. Touch, indeed, discriminates more than one set of different qualities. Each sense has one kind of object which it discerns, and never errs in reporting that what is before it is colour or sound (though it may err as to what it is that is coloured or where that is, or what it is that is sounding or where that is). Such objects are what we propose to call the special objects of this or that sense.

'Common sensibles' are movement, rest, number, figure, magnitude; these are not peculiar to any one sense, but are common to all. There are at any rate certain kinds of movement which are perceptible both by touch and by sight.

We speak of an incidental object of sense where e.g. the white object which we see is the son of Diares; here because 'being the son of Diares' is incidental to the directly visible white patch we speak of the son of Diares as being (incidentally) perceived or seen by us. Because this is only incidentally an object of sense, it in no way as such affects the senses. Of the two former kinds, both of which are in their own nature perceptible by sense, the first kind—that of special objects of the several senses—constitute *the* objects of sense in the strictest sense of the term and it is to them that in the nature of things the structure of each several sense is adapted.

≈ 5 ≈

Augustine, Excerpt from *The confessions* (ca. 310, B.C.).*

CHAPTER IX

That the Wind Commands the Mind, But it Wills Not Entirely

Whence is this monstrous thing? And why is it? Let Thy mercy shine on me, that I may inquire, if the hiding-places of man's punishment and the darkest contritions of the sons of Adam may perhaps answer me. Whence is this monstrous thing? and why is it? The mind commands the body, and it obeys forthwith; the mind commands itself, and is resisted. The mind commands the hand to be moved, and such readiness is there that the command is scarce to be distinguished from the obedience. Yet the mind is mind, and the hand is body. The mind commands the mind to will, and yet, though it be itself, it obeys not. Whence this monstrous thing? and why is it? I repeat, it commands itself to will, and would not give the command unless it willed; yet is not that done which it commands. But it wills not entirely; therefore it commands not entirely. For so far forth it commands, as it wills; and so far forth is the thing commanded not done, as it wills not. For the will commands that there be a will—not another, but itself. But it does not command entirely, therefore that is not which it commands. For were it entire, it would not even command it to be, because it would already be. It is, therefore, no monstrous thing partly to will, partly to be unwilling, but an infirmity of the mind, that it does not wholly rise, sustained by truth, pressed down by custom. And so there are two wills, because one of them is not entire; and the one is supplied with what the other needs.

*From *Basic writings of Saint Augustine* by Saint Augustine, edited by Whitney Oates. Copyright 1948 and renewed 1976 by Random House, Inc. Reprinted by permission of Random House, Inc.

CHAPTER X

He Refutes the Opinion of the Manichaeans as to Two Kinds of Minds—One Good and the Other Evil

Let them perish from Thy presence, O God, as vain talkers and deceivers of the soul do perish, who, observing that there were two wills in deliberating, affirm that there are two kinds of minds in us—one good, the other evil. They themselves truly are evil when they hold these evil opinions, and they shall become good when they hold the truth, and shall consent unto the truth, that Thy apostle may say unto them, "Ye were sometimes darkness, but now are ye light in the Lord." But they, desiring to be light, not in the Lord, but in themselves, conceiving the nature of the soul to be the same as that which God is, are made more gross darkness; since through a shocking arrogance they went farther from Thee, the true Light, which lighteth every man that cometh into the world. Take heed what you say, and blush for shame; draw near unto Him and be lightened, and your faces shall not be ashamed. I, when I was deliberating upon serving the Lord my God now, as I had long purposed—I it was who willed, I who was unwilling. It was I, even I myself. I neither willed entirely, nor was entirely unwilling. Therefore I was at war with myself, and destroyed by myself. And this destruction overtook me against my will, and yet showed not the presence of another mind, but the punishment of my own. Now, then, it is no more I that do it, but sin that dwelleth in me—the punishment of a more unconfined sin, in that I was a son of Adam.

For if there be as many contrary natures as there are conflicting wills, there will not now be two natures only, but many. If any one deliberate whether he should go to their conventicle, or to the theatre, those men at once cry out, "Behold, here are two natures—one good, drawing this way, another bad, drawing back that way; for whence else is this indecision between conflicting wills?" But I reply that both are bad—that which draws to them, and that which draws back to the theatre. But they believe not that will to be other than good which draws to them. Supposing, then, one of us should deliberate, and through the conflict of his two wills should waver whether he should go to the theatre or to our church, would not these also waver what to answer? For either they must confess, which they are not willing to do, that the will which leads to our church is good, as well as that of those who have received and are held by the mysteries of theirs, or they must imagine that there are two evil natures and two evil minds in one man, at war one with the other; and that will not be true which they say, that there is one good and another bad; or they must be converted to the truth, and no longer deny that where any one deliberates, there is one soul fluctuating between conflicting wills.

Let them no more say, then, when they perceive two wills to be antagonistic to each other in the same man, that the contest is between two opposing minds, of two opposing substances, from two opposing principles, the one good and the other bad. For Thou, O true God, dost disprove, check, and convince them; as when both wills are bad, one deliberates whether he should kill a man by poison, or by the sword; whether he should take possession of this or that estate of another's, when he cannot both; whether he should purchase pleasure by prodigality, or retain his money by covetousness; whether he should go to the circus or the theatre, if both are open on the same day; or thirdly, whether he should rob another man's house, if he have the opportunity; or, fourthly, whether he should commit adultery, if at the same time he have the means of doing so—all these things concurring in the same point of time, and all being equally longed for, although impossible to be enacted at one time. For they rend the mind amid four, or even (among the vast variety of things men desire) more antagonistic wills, nor do they yet affirm that there are so many different substances. Thus also is it in wills which are good. For I ask them is it a good thing to have delight in reading the apostle, or good in have delight in a sober psalm, or good to discourse on the gospel? To each of these they will answer, "It is good." What, then, if all equally delight us, and all at the same time? Do not different wills distract the mind, when a man is deliberating which he should rather choose? Yet are they all good, and are at variance until one be fixed upon, whither the whole united will may be borne, which before was divided into many. Thus, also, when eternity delights us above, and the pleasure of temporal good holds us down below, it is the same soul which wills not that or this with an entire will, and is therefore torn asunder with grievous perplexities, while out of truth it prefers that, but out of custom does not lay aside this.

CHAPTER XI

In What Manner the Spirit Struggled with the Flesh, that it Might be Freed from the Bondage of Vanity

Thus was I sick and tormented, accusing myself far more severely than was my wont, tossing and turning me in my chain till that was utterly broken, whereby I now was but slightly, but still was held. And Thou, O Lord, pressedst upon me in my inward parts by a severe mercy, redoubling the lashes of fear and shame, lest I should again give way, and that same slender remaining tie not being broken off, it should recover strength, and enchain me the faster. For I said mentally, "Lo, let it be done now, let it be done now." And as I spoke, I all but came to a resolve. I all but did it, yet I did it not. Yet I fell not back to my old condition, but took up my position hard by, and drew breath. And I tried again, and wanted but very little of reaching it, and somewhat less, and then all but touched and grasped it; and yet came not at it, nor touched, nor grasped it, hesitating to die to death, and to live to life; and the worse, to which I had been habituated, prevailed more with me than the better, which I had not tried. And the very moment in which I was to become another man, the nearer it approached me, the greater horror did it strike into me; but it did not strike me back, nor turn me aside, but kept me in suspense.

The very toys of toys, and vanities of vanities, my old mistresses, still enthralled me; they shook my fleshly garment, and whispered softly, "Dost thou part with us? And from that moment shall we no more be with thee for ever? And from that moment shall not this or that be lawful for thee for ever?" And what did they suggest to me in the words "this or that?" What is it that they suggested, O my God? Let Thy mercy avert it from the soul of Thy servant. What impurities did they suggest! What shame! And now I far less than half heard them, not openly showing themselves and contradicting me, but muttering, as it were, behind my back, and furtively plucking me as I was departing, to make me look back upon them. Yet they did delay me, so that I hesitated to burst and shake myself free from them, and to leap over whither I was called—an unruly habit saying to me, "Dost thou think thou canst live without them?"

But now it said this very faintly; for on that side towards which I had set my face, and whither I trembled to go, did the chaste dignity of Continence appear to me, cheerful, but not dissolutely gay, honestly alluring me to come and doubt nothing, and extending her holy hands, full of a multiplicity of good examples, to receive and embrace me. There were there so many young men and maidens, a multitude of youth and every age, grave widows and ancient virgins, and Continence herself in all, not barren, but a fruitful mother of children of joys, by Thee, O Lord, her Husband. And she smiled on me with an encouraging mockery, as if to say, "Canst not thou do what these youths and maidens can? Or can one or other do it of themselves, and not rather in the Lord their God? The Lord their God gave me to them. Why standest thou in thine own strength, and so standest not? Cast thyself upon Him; fear not, He will not withdraw that thou shouldest fall; cast thyself upon Him without fear, He will receive thee, and heal thee." And I blushed beyond measure, for I still heard the muttering of those toys, and hung in suspense. And she again seemed to say, "Shut up thine ears against those unclean members of thine upon the earth, that they may be mortified. They tell thee of delights, but not as doth the law of the Lord thy God." This controversy in my heart was naught but self against self. But Alypius, sitting close by my side, awaited in silence the result of my unwanted emotion.

CHAPTER XII

Having Prayed to God, He Pours Forth a Shower of Tears, and, Admonished by a Voice, He Opens the Book and Reads the Words in Rom. XIII. 13; by Which, Being Changed in His Whole Soul, He Discloses the Divine Favor to His Friend and His Mother

But when a profound reflection had, from the secret depths of my soul, drawn together and heaped up all my misery before the sight of my heart, there arose a mighty storm accompanied by as mighty a shower of tears.

Which, that I might pour it forthfully, with its natural expressions, I stole away from Alypius; for it suggested itself to me that solitude was fitter for the business of weeping. So I retired to such a distance that even his presence could not be oppressive to me. Thus it was with me at that time, and he perceived it; for something, I believe, I had spoken, wherein the sound of my voice appeared choked with weeping, and in that state had I risen up. He then remained where we had been sitting, most completely astonished. I flung myself down, how, I know not, under a certain fig-tree, giving free course to my tears, and the streams of mine eyes gushed out, an acceptable sacrifice unto Thee. And, not indeed in these words, yet to this effect, spake I much unto Thee—"But Thou, O Lord, how long?" "How long, Lord? Wilt Thou be angry for ever? Oh, remember not against us former iniquities;" for I felt that I was enthralled by them. I sent up these sorrowful cries—"How long, how long? To-morrow, and to-morrow? Why not now? Why is there not this hour an end to my uncleanness?"

I was saying these things and weeping in the most bitter contrition of my heart, when, lo, I heard the voice as of a boy or girl, I know not which, coming from a neighboring house, chanting, and oft repeating, "Take up and read; take up and read." Immediately my countenance was changed, and I began most earnestly to consider whether it was usual for children in any kind of game to sing such words; nor could I remember ever to have heard the like. So, restraining the torrent of my tears, I rose up, interpreting it no other way than as a command to me from Heaven to open the book, and to read the first chapter I should light upon. For I had heard of Antony, that, accidentally coming in while the gospel was being read, he received the admonition as if what was read were addressed to him, "Go and sell that thou hast, and give to the poor, and thou shalt have treasure in heaven; and come and follow me." And by such oracle was he forthwith converted unto Thee. So quickly I returned to the place where Alypius was sitting; for there had I put down the volume of the apostles, when I rose thence. I grasped, opened, and in silence read that paragraph on which my eyes first fell—"Not in rioting and drunkenness, not in chambering and wantonness, not in strife and envying; but put ye on the Lord Jesus Christ, and make not provision for the flesh, to fulfil the lusts thereof." No further would I read, nor did I need; for instantly, as the sentence ended—by a light, as it were, of security infused into my heart—all the gloom of doubt vanished away.

Closing the book, then, and putting either my finger between, or some other mark, I now with a tranquil countenance made it known to Alypius. And he thus disclosed to me what was wrought in him, which I knew not. He asked to look at what I had read. I showed him; and he looked even further than I had read, and I knew not what followed. This it was, "Him that is weak in the faith, receive ye;" which he applied to himself, and discovered to me. By this admonition was he strengthened; and by a good resolution and purpose, very much in accord with his character (in which, for the better, he was always far different from me), without any restless delay he joined me. Thence we go in to my mother. We make it known to her—she rejoices. We relate how it came to pass—she leaps for joy, and triumphs, and blesses Thee, who art able to do exceeding abundantly above all that we ask or think; for she perceived Thee to have given her more for me than she used to ask by her pitiful and most doleful groanings. For Thou didst so convert me unto Thyself, that I sought neither a wife, nor any other of this world's hopes—standing in that rule of faith in which Thou, so many years before, had showed me unto her in a vision. And thou didst turn her grief into a gladness, much more plentiful than she had desired, and much dearer and chaster than she used to crave, by having grandchildren of my body.

6

Thomas Aquinas, Excerpts from *Summa Theologiae* (ca. 1272).*

Question LXXXV

THE MODE AND ORDER OF UNDERSTANDING

(In Eight Articles)

WE COME now to consider the mode and order of understanding. Under this head there are eight points of inquiry: (1) Whether our intellect understands by abstracting species from the phantasms? (2) Whether the intelligible species abstracted from the phantasms are what our intellect understands, or that whereby it understands? (3) Whether our intellect naturally first understands the more universal? (4) Whether our intellect can know many things at the same time? (5) Whether our intellect understands by composition and division? (6) Whether the intellect can err? (7) Whether one intellect can understand the same thing better than another? (8) Whether our intellect understands the indivisible before the divisible?

First Article

Whether Our Intellect Understands Corporeal and Material Things by Abstraction from Phantasms?

We proceed thus to the First Article:—

Objection 1. It would seem that our intellect does not understand corporeal and material things by abstraction from the phantasms. For the intellect

*Aquinas, T. (ca. 1272, 1948). Excerpts from *Summa Theologiae*. In A.C. Pegis (ed.) *Introduction to Saint Thomas Aquinas*. New York: The Modern Library, Question LXXXV. The mode and order of understanding, 400–405, 408–416. Reprinted by permission of the Estate of Anton Pegis.

is false if it understands a thing otherwise than as it is. Now the forms of material things do not exist in abstraction from the particular things represented by the phantasms. Therefore, if we understand material things by the abstraction of species from phantasms, there will be error in the intellect.

Obj. 2. Further, material things are those natural things which include matter in their definition. But nothing can be understood apart from that which enters into its definition. Therefore material things cannot be understood apart from matter. Now matter is the principle of individuation. Therefore material things cannot be understood by the abstraction of the universal from the particular; and this is to abstract intelligible species from the phantasm.

Obj. 3. Further, the Philosopher says that the phantasm is to the intellectual soul what color is to the sight. But seeing is not caused by abstraction of species from color, but by color impressing itself on the sight. Therefore neither does the act of understanding take place by the abstraction of something from the phantasms, but by the phantasms impressing themselves on the intellect.

Obj. 4. Further, the Philosopher says that there are two things in the intellectual soul—the possible intellect and the agent intellect. But it does not belong to the possible intellect to abstract the intelligible species from the phantasm, but to receive them already abstracted. Neither does it seem to be the function of the agent intellect, which is related to phantasms as light is to colors; since light does not abstract anything from colors, but rather acts on them. Therefore in no way do we understand by abstraction from phantasms.

Obj. 5. Further, the Philosopher says that *the intellect understands the species in the phantasms*, and not, therefore, by abstraction.

On the contrary, The Philosopher says that *things are intelligible in proportion as they are separable from matter.* Therefore material things must needs be understood according as they are abstracted from matter and from material images, namely, phantasms.

I answer that, As stated above, the object of knowledge is proportionate to the power of knowledge. Now there are three grades of the cognitive powers. For one cognitive power, namely, the sense, is the act of a corporeal organ. And therefore the object of every sensitive power is a form as existing in corporeal matter; and since such matter is the principle of individuation, therefore every power of the sensitive part can have knowledge only of particulars. There is another grade of cognitive power which is neither the act of a corporeal organ, nor in any way connected with corporeal matter. Such is the angelic intellect, the object of whose cognitive power is therefore a form existing apart from matter; for though angels know material things, yet they do not know them save in something immaterial, namely, either in themselves or in God. But the human intellect holds a middle place; for it is not the act of an organ, and yet it is a power of the soul, which is the form of the body, as is clear from what we have said above. And therefore it is proper to it to know a form existing individually in corporeal matter, but not as existing in this individual matter. But to know what is in individual matter, yet not as existing in such matter, is to abstract the form from individual matter which is represented by the phantasms. Therefore we must needs say that our intellect understands material things by abstracting from phantasms; and that through material things thus considered we acquire some knowledge of immaterial things, just as, on the contrary, angels know material things through the immaterial.

But Plato, considering only the immateriality of the human intellect, and not that it is somehow united to the body, held that the objects of the intellect are separate Ideas, and that we understand, not by abstraction, but rather by participating in abstractions, as was stated above.

Reply Obj. 1. Abstraction may occur in two ways. First, by way of composition and division, and thus we may understand that one thing does not exist in some other, or that it is separate from it. Secondly, by way of a simple and absolute consideration; and thus we understand one thing without considering another. Thus, for the intellect to abstract one from another things which are not really abstract from one another, does, in the first mode of abstraction, imply falsehood. But, in the second mode of abstraction, for the intellect to abstract things which are not really abstract from one another, does not involve falsehood, as clearly appears in the case of the senses. For if we said that color is not in a colored body, or that it is separate from it, there would be error in what we thought or said. But if we consider color and its properties, without reference to the apple which is colored, or if we express in word what we thus understand, there is no error in such an opinion or assertion; for an apple is not essential to color, and therefore color can be understood independently of the apple. In the same way, the things which belong to the species of a material thing, such as a stone, or a man, or a horse, can be thought without the individual principles which do not belong to the notion of the species. This is what we mean by abstracting the universal from the particular, or the intelligible species from the phantasm; in other words, this is to consider the nature of the species apart from its individual principles represented by the phantasms. If, therefore, the intellect is said to be false when it understands a thing otherwise than as it is, that is so, if the word *otherwise* refers to the thing understood; for the intellect is false when it understands a thing to be otherwise than as it is. Hence, the intellect would be false if it abstracted the species of a stone from its matter in such a way as to think that the species did not exist in matter, as Plato held. But it is not so, if the word *otherwise* be taken as referring to the one who understands. For it is quite true that the mode of understanding, in one who understands, is not the same as the mode of a thing in being; since the thing understood is immaterially in the one who understands, according to the mode of the intellect, and not materially, according to the mode of a material thing.

Reply Obj. 2. Some have thought that the species of a natural thing is a form only, and that matter is not part of the species. If that were so, matter would not enter into the definition of natural things. Therefore we must disagree and say that matter is twofold, common and *signate*, or individual: common, such as flesh and bone; individual, such as this flesh and these bones. The intellect therefore abstracts the species of a natural thing from the individual sensible matter, but not from the common sensible matter. For example, it abstracts the species of *man* from *this flesh and these bones*, which do not belong to the species as such, but to the individual, and need not be considered in the species. But the species of man cannot be abstracted by the intellect from *flesh and bones*.

Mathematical species, however, can be abstracted by the intellect not only from individual sensible matter, but also from common sensible matter. But they cannot be abstracted from common intelligible matter, but only from individual intelligible matter. For sensible matter is corporeal matter as subject to sensible qualities, such as being cold or hot, hard or soft, and the like; while intelligible matter is substance as subject to quantity. Now it is manifest that quantity is in substance before sensible qualities are. Hence quantities, such as number, dimension, and figures, which are the terminations of quantity, can be considered apart from sensible qualities, and this is to abstract them from sensible matter. But they cannot be considered without understanding the substance which is subject to the quantity, for that would be to abstract them from common intelligible matter. Yet they can be considered apart from this or that substance, and this is to abstract them from individual intelligible matter.

But some things can be abstracted even from common intelligible matter, such as *being, unity, potency, act*, and the like, all of which can exist without matter, as can be verified in the case of immaterial substances. And because Plato failed to consider the twofold kind of abstraction, as above explained, he held that all those things which we have stated to be abstracted by the intellect, are abstract in reality.

Reply Obj. 3. Colors, as being in individual corporeal matter, have the same mode of being as the power of sight; and therefore they can impress their own image on the eye. But phantasms, since they are images of individuals, and exist in corporeal organs, have not the same mode of being as the human intellect, as is clear from what we have said, and therefore they have not the power of themselves to make an impression on the possible intellect. But through the power of the agent intellect, there results in the possible intellect a certain likeness produced by the turning of the agent intellect toward the phantasms. This likeness represents what is in the phantasms, but includes only the nature of the species. It is thus that the intelligible species is said to be abstracted from the phantasm; not that the identical form which previously was in the phantasm is subsequently in the possible intellect, as a body transferred from one place to another.

Reply Obj. 4. Not only does the agent intellect illumine phantasms, it does more; by its power intelligible species are abstracted from phantasms. It illumines phantasms because, just as the sensitive part acquires a greater power by its conjunction with the intellectual part, so through the power of the agent intellect phantasms are made more fit for the abstraction of intelligible intentions from them. Now the agent intellect abstracts intelligible species from phantasms inasmuch as by its power we are able to take into our consideration the natures of species without individual conditions. It is in accord with their likenesses that the possible intellect is informed.

Reply Obj. 5. Our intellect both abstracts the intelligible species *from* phantasms, inasmuch as it considers the natures of things universally, and yet understands these natures *in* the phantasms, since it cannot understand the things, of which it abstracts the species, without turning to phantasms, as we have said above.

Third Article

Whether the More Universal Is First in Our Intellectual Cognition?
We proceed thus to the Third Article:—

Objection 1. It would seem that the more universal is not first in our intellectual cognition. For what is first and more known in its own nature is secondarily and less known in relation to ourselves. But universals come first as regards their nature, because *that is first which does not involve the existence of its correlative.* Therefore universals are secondarily known by our intellect.

Obj. 2. Further, the composite precedes the simple in relation to us. But universals are the more simple. Therefore they are known secondarily by us.

Obj. 3. Further, the Philosopher says that the object defined comes in our knowledge before the parts of its definition. But the more universal is part of the definition of the less universal, as *animal* is part of the definition of *man.* Therefore universals are secondarily known by us.

Obj. 4. Further, we know causes and principles by their effects. But universals are principles. Therefore universals are secondarily known by us.

On the contrary, We must proceed from the universal to the singular.

I answer that, In our knowledge there are two things to be considered. First, that intellectual knowledge in some degree arises from sensible knowledge. Now because sense has singular and individual things for its object, and intellect has the universal for its object, it follows that our knowledge of the former comes before our knowledge of the latter. Secondly, we must consider that our intellect proceeds from a state of potentiality to a state of actuality; and that every power thus proceeding from potentiality to actuality comes first to an incomplete act, which is intermediate between potentiality and actuality, before accomplishing the perfect act. The perfect act of the intellect is complete knowledge, when the object is distinctly and determinately known; whereas the incomplete act is imperfect knowledge, when the object is known indistinctly, and as it were confusedly. A thing thus imperfectly known is known partly in act and partly in potentiality. Hence the Philosopher says that *what is manifest and certain is known to us at first confusedly; afterwards we know it by distinguishing its principles and elements.* Now it is evident that to know something that comprises many things, without a proper knowledge of each thing contained in it, is to know that thing confusedly. In this way we can have knowledge not only of the universal whole, which contains parts potentially, but also of the integral whole; for each whole can be known confusedly, without its parts being known distinctly. But to know distinctly what is contained in the universal whole is to know the less common; and thus to know *animal* indistinctly is to know it as *animal,* whereas to know *animal* distinctly is to know it as *rational* or *irrational animal,* that is, to know a man or a lion. And so our intellect knows *animal* before it knows man; and the same reason holds in comparing any more universal concept with the less universal.

Moreover, as sense, like the intellect, proceeds from potentiality to act, the same order of knowledge appears in the senses. For by sense we judge of the more common before the less common, in reference both to place and time. In reference to place, when a thing is seen afar off it is seen to be a body before it is seen to be an animal, and to be an animal before it is seen to be a man, and to be a man before it is seen to be Socrates or Plato. The same is true as regards time, for a child can distinguish man from not-man before he distinguishes this man from that, and therefore *children at first call all men fathers, and later on distinguish each one from the others.* The reason of this is clear: he who knows a thing indistinctly is in a state of potentiality as regards its principle of distinction; just as he who knows *genus* is in a state of potentiality as regards *difference.* Thus it is evident that indistinct knowledge is midway between potentiality and act.

We must therefore conclude that knowledge of the singular and individual is prior, as regards us, to the knowledge of the universal, just as sensible knowledge is prior to intellectual knowledge. But in both sense and intellect the knowledge of the more common precedes the knowledge of the less common.

Reply Obj. 1. The universal can be considered in two ways. First, the universal nature may be considered together with the intention of universality. And since the intention of universality—viz., the relation of one and the same to many—is due to intellectual abstraction, the universal thus considered is subsequent in our knowledge. Hence it is said that the *universal animal is either nothing or something subsequent.* But according to Plato, who held that universals are subsistent, the universal considered thus would be prior to the particular, for the latter, according to him, are mere participation in the subsistent universals which he called Ideas.

Secondly, the universal can be considered according to the nature itself (for instance, *animality* or *humanity*) as existing in the individual. And thus we must distinguish two orders of nature: one, by way of generation and time; and thus the imperfect and the potential come first. In this way the more common comes first in the order of nature. This appears clearly in the generation of man and animal; for *the animal is generated before man*, as the Philosopher says. The other order is the order of perfection or of the intention of nature. For instance, act considered absolutely is naturally prior to potentiality, and the perfect to the imperfect; and thus the less common comes naturally before the more common, as man comes before animal. For the intention of nature does not stop at the generation of animal, but aims at the generation of man.

Reply Obj. 2. The more common universal may be compared to the less common as a whole, and as a part. As a whole, inasmuch as in the more universal there is potentially contained not only the less universal, but also other things; as in *animal* is contained not only *man* but also *horse*. As a part, inasmuch as the less common universal contains in its notion not only the more common, but also more; as *man* contains not only *animal* but also *rational*. Therefore *animal* considered in itself is in our knowledge before *man*; but *man* comes before *animal* considered as a part of the notion of man.

Reply Obj. 3. A part can be known in two ways. First, absolutely considered in itself; and thus nothing prevents the parts from being known before the whole, as stones are known before a house is known. Secondly, as belonging to a certain whole; and thus we must needs know the whole before its parts. For we know a house confusedly before we know its different parts. So, likewise, that which defines is known before the thing defined is known; otherwise the thing defined would not be made known by the definition. But as parts of the definition they are known after. For we know man confusedly as man before we know how to distinguish all that belongs to human nature.

Reply Obj. 4. The universal, as understood with the intention of universality, is, in a certain manner, a principle of knowledge, in so far as the intention of universality results from the mode of understanding, which is by way of abstraction. But that which is a principle of knowledge is not of necessity a principle of being, as Plato thought, since at times we know a cause through its effect, and substance through accidents. Therefore the universal thus considered, according to the opinion of Aristotle, is neither a principle of being, nor a substance, as he makes clear. But if we consider the generic or specific nature itself as existing in the singular, thus in a way it has the character of a formal principle in regard to singulars; for the singular is the result of matter, while the nature of the species is from the form. But the generic nature is compared to the specific nature rather after the fashion of a material principle, because the generic nature is taken from that which is material in a thing, while the nature of the species is taken from that which is formal. Thus the notion of animal is taken from the sensitive part, whereas the notion of man is taken from the intellectual part. Thus it is that the ultimate intention of nature is towards the species and not the individual, or the genus; because the form is the end of generation, while matter is for the sake of the form. Neither is it necessary that the knowledge of any cause or principle should be subsequent in relation to us, since through sensible causes we sometimes become acquainted with unknown effects, and sometimes conversely.

Fourth Article

Whether We Can Understand Many Things at the Same Time?

We proceed thus to the Fourth Article:—

Objection 1. It would seem that we can understand many things at the same time. For intellect is above time, whereas the succession of before and after belongs to time. Therefore the intellect does not understand different things in succession, but at the same time.

Obj. 2. Further, there is nothing to prevent different forms not opposed to each other from actually being in the same subject, as, for instance, color and smell are in the apple. But intelligible species are not opposed to each other. Therefore there is nothing to prevent the same intellect from being in act as regards different intelligible species. Thus it can understand many things at the same time.

Obj. 3. Further, the intellect understands a whole at the same time, such as a man or a house. But a whole contains many parts. Therefore the intellect understands many things at the same time.

Obj. 4. Further, we cannot know the difference between two things unless we know both at the same time; and the same is to be said of any other comparison. But our intellect knows the difference between one thing and another. Therefore it knows many things at the same time.

On the contrary, It is said that *understanding is of one thing only, science is of many.*

I answer that, The intellect can, indeed, understand many things as one, but not as many, that is to say, by *one* but not by *many* intelligible species. For the mode of every action follows the form which is the principle of that action. Therefore whatever things the intellect can understand under one species, it can understand together. Hence it is that God sees all things at the same time, because He sees all in one, that is, in His essence. But whatever things the intellect understands under different species, it does not understand at the same time. The reason for this is that it is impossible for one and the same subject to be perfected at the same time by many forms of one genus and diverse species, just as it is impossible for one and the same body at the same time to have different colors or different shapes. Now all intelligible species belong to one genus, because they are the perfections of one intellectual power even though the things which the species represent belong to different genera. Therefore it is impossible for one and the same intellect to be perfected at the same time by different intelligible species so as actually to understand different things.

Reply Obj. 1. The intellect is above that time which is the measure of the movement of corporeal things. But the multitude itself of intelligible species causes a certain succession of intelligible operations, according as one operation is prior to another. And this succession is called time by Augustine, who says that *God moves the spiritual creature through time.*

Reply Obj. 2. Not only is it impossible for opposite forms to exist at the same time in the same subject, but neither can any forms belonging to the same genus, although they be not opposed to one another, as is clear from the examples of colors and shapes.

Reply Obj. 3. Parts can be understood in two ways. First, in a confused way, as existing in the whole; and thus they are known through the one form of the whole, and so are known together. In another way, they are known distinctly; and thus each is known by its species, and hence they are not understood at the same time.

Reply Obj. 4. If the intellect sees the difference or comparison between one thing and another, it knows both in relation to their difference or comparison; just as it knows the parts in the whole, as we said above.

Fifth Article

Whether Our Intellect Understands by Composition and Division?
We proceed thus to the Fifth Article:—

Objection 1. It would seem that our intellect does not understand by composition and division. For composition and division are only of many, whereas the intellect cannot understand many things at the same time. Therefore it cannot understand by composition and division.

Obj. 2. Further, every composition and division implies past, present, or future time. But the intellect abstracts from time, as also from other particular conditions. Therefore the intellect does not understand by composition and division.

Obj. 3. Further, the intellect understands things by an assimilation to them. But composition and division are not in things; for nothing is in things but the thing which is signified by the predicate and the subject, and which is one and the same thing, provided that the composition be true; for *man* is truly what *animal* is. Therefore the intellect does not act by composition and division.

On the contrary, Words signify the conceptions of the intellect, as the Philosopher says. But in words we find composition and division, as appears in affirmative and negative propositions. Therefore the intellect acts by composition and division.

I answer that, The human intellect must of necessity understand by composition and division. For since the intellect passes from potentiality to act, it has a likeness to generable things, which do not attain to perfection all at once but acquire it by degrees. In the same way, the human intellect does not acquire perfect knowledge of a thing by the first apprehension; but it first apprehends something of the thing, such as its quiddity, which is the first and proper object of the intellect; and then it understands the properties, accidents, and various dispositions affecting the essence. Thus it necessarily relates one thing with another by composition or division; and from one composition and division it necessarily proceeds to another, and this is *reasoning*.

But the angelic and the divine intellects, like all incorruptible beings, have their perfection at once from the beginning. Hence the angelic and the divine intellect have the entire knowledge of a thing at once and perfectly; and hence, in knowing the quiddity of a thing, they know at once whatever we can know by composition, division and reasoning. Therefore the human intellect knows by composition, division and reasoning. But the divine and the angelic intellects have a knowledge of composition, division, and reasoning, not by the process itself, but by understanding the simple essence.

Reply Obj. 1. Composition and division of the intellect are made by differentiating and comparing. Hence the intellect knows many things by composition and division, by knowing the difference and comparison of things.

Reply Obj. 2. Although the intellect abstracts from phantasms, it does not understand actually without turning to the phantasms, as we have said. And in so far as the intellect turns to phantasms, composition and division involve time.

Reply Obj. 3. The likeness of a thing is received into the intellect according to the mode of the intellect, not according to the mode of the thing. Hence, although something on the part of the thing corresponds to the composition and division of the intellect, still, it does not exist in the same way in the intellect and in the thing. For the proper object of the human intellect is the quiddity of a material thing, which is apprehended by the senses and the imagination. Now in a material thing there is a twofold composition. First, there is the composition of form with matter. To this corresponds that composition of the intellect whereby the universal whole is predicated of its part: for the genus is derived from common matter, while the difference that completes the species is derived from the form, and the particular from individual matter. The second composition is of accident with subject; and to this composition corresponds that composition of the intellect whereby accident is predicated of subject, as when we say *the man is white*. Nevertheless, the composition of the intellect differs from the composition of things; for the components in the thing are diverse, whereas the composition of the intellect is a sign of the identity of the components. For the above composition of the intellect was not such as to assert that *man is whiteness*; but the assertion, *the man is white*, means that *the man is something having whiteness*. In other words, *man* is identical in subject with the *being having whiteness*. It is the same with the composition of form and matter. For *animal* signifies that which has a sensitive nature; *rational*, that which has an intellectual nature; *man*, that which has both; and *Socrates*, that which has all these things together with individual matter. And so, according to this kind of identity our intellect composes one thing with another by means of predication.

III. The Emergence of Psychology

The readings of this section represent primary source materials that defined the scope of Psychology as it emerged from the Renaissance into modern times. Descartes and Spinoza, the two most important writers in psychology of the 17th Century, begin these readings because of their contrasting views on the nature of the individual either in terms of a clear dualism, in the case of Descartes, or the more monistic and unified interpretation proposed by Spinoza. The remainder of this section's readings follow in order the national movements of 18th and 19th Century philosophical themes in France, England, and Germany.

René Descartes (1596–1650) is one of those pivotal writers in the history of psychology who seemed to set a context or framework for the way in which subsequent scholars thought about psychology. Descartes is also a transition figure, because he took the Greek notion of dualism between body and soul—the physical and spiritual aspects of human experience—which had been affirmed by the Christian writers, particularly Thomas Aquinas, and defined the soul part of the dualism as the province of psychology. Thus, from Descartes at the beginning of the emergence of modern science, psychology was placed in sharp distinction to the natural or physical sciences. According to Descartes, psychology deals with the mental, spiritual world, and physiology deals with the bodily or sensory aspects of the physical world. In this passage from *The passions of the soul* (1649), Descartes uses the first six articles to distinguish between those human activities that can be attributed to the body and those attributed to the soul. In Articles

7–16, Descartes gives us a quick lesson in his understanding of physiology, emphasizing a construct for the nervous system, which he called "animal spirits". In Articles 17–26, Descartes defines the psychological activities of the soul, ending in Article 27 with his famous statement on the passions. The first part of *The passions of the soul* contains another 23 articles, not reproduced here, which articulate specific passions and emotions and the ways in which body and soul interact. While some of what may be considered psychological within the present-day boundaries of the discipline were attributed to the body, it is clear that for Descartes physiology and psychology were quite distinct arenas for considering the two aspects of experience.

For Baruch Spinoza (1632–1677), human experience elicited thoughts of unity, rather than distinctions. In the piece excerpted from *The emendation of the intellect* (1677), Spinoza presents his definition of the intellect and its activities. In so doing, he also shows us a bit of the precision of his logic in arriving at an emphasis on the fundamental role of the intellect in accounting for experience. That is, the psychological processes that contribute to the intellect are intimately bound up in it, as are the products of the intellect, including the emotions or passions. This principle was underscored by Spinoza's assertion that removal of the intellect takes away all other aspects of experience, which is the point that ends the passage.

Following the initial writings of Descartes and Spinoza, philosophical writings on psychology began to take on a national character or theme. In France, the dualism of Descartes was reduced to the view that the mind can more or less be understood by its input, and so psychology was reduced to that input, termed "sensationalism". Étienne Bonnot de Condillac (1715–1780) was a major exponent of sensationalism. In this passage from his *Treatise on sensation* (1754), Condillac describes mental or cognitive abilities through his analogy of human experience, which uses a statue endowed with only the single sense of smell. Condillac tries to show how higher mental abilities can develop from this sense capacity.

Three readings from British philosophers are included because of the important antecedents of British thought in the emergence of American psychology during the late 19th and 20th centuries. Pursuing ideas initially put forth by Thomas Hobbes (1588–1679), the British tradition of empiricism and mental passivity received full expression in the writings of John Locke (1632–1704). Shunning the direction that led Condillac to reduce mental activity from Descartes' dualism to sensations, Locke preserved the need for the mind, but made it almost completely dependent upon environmental stimuli. In this passage from *An essay concerning human understanding* (1689), Locke explores how ideas originate and develop.

Extending Locke's model, the dependency on sense experience and importance of perception were themes developed by a philosopher close to Locke, George Berkeley (1685–1753). In the passage from *An essay towards a new theory of vision* (1709), Berkeley describes many perceptual experiences in terms of transposing sensations to ideas. A later representative of the British empiricist movement, John Stuart Mill (1806–1873) describes in this excerpt from *A system of logic* (1843) the principles of active associations as the mental process that acts upon environmental stimuli, justifying the need for a mind construct within Locke's model. Collectively, psychology was readily accommodated within the British philosophical tradition of mental passivity studied through the observed products of the mind.

In Germany, a somewhat different configuration of the mind emerged by emphasizing its essential activity, and this interpretation owed more to Spinoza than to Descartes. Immanuel Kant (1724–1804) is perhaps the most famous representative of this tradition within 18th and 19th Century German philosophy. In this passage from his *Critique of pure reason* (1781), Kant explores the distinction between knowledge derived from the senses and knowledge derived from the mind acting upon itself, which he termed "pure reason". In his psychological writings, Kant set the context of German emphases on the mind as dynamic and the depository for innate predispositions toward the environment.

REFERENCES

BERKELEY, G. (1709, 1963). *An essay towards a new theory of vision.* In C.M. Turbayne (ed.) *Works on Vision, George Berkeley.* New York: Bobbs-Merrill Co., 19–27.

CONDILLAC, É.B. DE (1754, 1930). Condillac's *Treatise on Sensations* (G. Carr, transl.). Los Angeles: University of Southern California Press, Part I, Chs. i, ii, 3–22.

DESCARTES, R. (1649, 1989). Part I. About the passions in general, and incidently about the entire nature of man. In S. Voss (transl.) *The passions of the soul.* Indianapolis: Hackett Publishing Co., 18–49.

KANT, I. (1781) in Kemp Smith, N. (1961). *Immanuel Kant's critique of pure reason.* New York: St. Martin's Press.

LOCKE, J. (1689, 1975). Book II, *An essay concerning human understanding.* (P.H. Nidditch, ed). Oxford: Clerendon Press, Ch. 1, 104–118.

MILL, J.S. (1843, 1870). *A system of logic, ratiocinative and inductive, being a connected view of the principles of evidence and methods of scientific investigation.* New York: Harper and Row. Book VI, Ch. IV, 530–537.

SPINOZA, B. (1677, 1985). The emendation of the intellect. In E. Curley (ed. and transl.) *The chief collected works of Spinoza.* Princeton, New Jersey: Princeton University Press, 39–45.

René Descartes, Excerpt from Part I, "About the passions in general, and incidently about the entire nature of man" from *The passions of the soul (1649).**

ABOUT THE PASSIONS IN GENERAL, AND INCIDENTALLY ABOUT THE ENTIRE NATURE OF MAN

Article 1. That What Is a Passion with Respect to a Subject Is Always an Action in Some Other Respect.[1]

The defectiveness of the sciences we inherit from the ancients is nowhere more apparent than in what they wrote about the Passions. For even though this is a topic about which knowledge has always been vigorously sought, and though it does not seem to be one of the most difficult—because,

*Descartes, R. (1649, 1989). Part I. About the passions in general, and incidently about the entire nature of man. In S. Voss (transl.) *The passions of the soul.* Indianapolis: Hackett Publishing Co., 18-49. Reprinted by permission of Hackett Publishing Co.

[1]In the first six articles, Descartes begins his study by developing a general principle: the first step in coming to understand anything that goes on within people should be to determine whether to attribute it to the soul or to the body. Then, in aa. 7–16, 17–29, and 30–50, he successively considers the nature of the body, the soul, and their union, insofar as they must be understood if we are to understand the nature of the passions of the soul: see notes 8, 18, and 31 below, and see the passages cited in note 29 below.

Descartes can be seen here as consciously applying the second rule of the method he had urged in Part Two of the *Discourse on Method*: "to divide each of the difficulties I examined into as many parts as possible and as may be required in order to resolve them better" (AT VI, 18: CSM I, 120); or the earlier *Rules for the Direction of the Mind*, Rules 5 and 6: AT X, 379–387: CSM I, 20–24. He begins both the *Treatise on Man* and the *Description of the Human Body* with similar applications of this rule: see AT XI, 119–120: Hall 1; and AT XI, 223–226; CSM I, 314–315. Elsewhere he suggests that there are three options, not just two, for locating what takes place within people: see to Elisabeth, 21 May 1643: AT III, 665–666: K 138; *Principles of Philosophy* I, a. 48: AT VIII, 23: CSM I, 208–209.

as everyone feels them in himself, one need not borrow any observation from elsewhere to discover their nature—nevertheless what the Ancients taught about them is so little, and for the most part so little believable, that I cannot hope to approach the truth unless I forsake the paths[2] they followed. For this reason I shall be obliged to write here as though I were treating a topic which no one before me had ever described. To begin with, I take into consideration that whatever is done or happens afresh is generally called by the Philosophers a Passion with respect to the subject it happens to, and an Action with respect to what makes it happen. Thus, even though the agent and the patient are often quite different, the Action and the Passion are always a single thing, which has these two names in accordance with the two different subjects it may be referred to.[3]

Article 2. That in Order to Understand the Passions of the Soul We Need to Distinguish Its Functions from Those of the Body.

Then I also take into consideration that we notice no subject that acts more immediately upon our soul than the body it is joined to, and that consequently we ought to think that what is a Passion in the former is commonly an Action in the latter. So there is no better path for arriving at an understanding of our Passions than to examine the difference between the soul and the body, in order to understand to which of the two each of the functions within us should be attributed.

Article 3. What Rule Must Be Followed to Achieve This End.

One will find no great difficulty in doing that if one bears this in mind: everything we find by experience to be in us which we see can also be in entirely inanimate bodies must be attributed to our body alone; on the other hand, everything in us which we conceive entirely incapable of belonging to a body must be attributed to our soul.[4]

---

[2] *Chermins.* As Rodis-Lewis hints (RL 65, n. 2), Descartes uses this word to distinguish his method from false ones. See *Discourse*, Parts 1 and 3: AT VI, 3.5–7 and 28.2: CSM I, 112 and 124–125; to Reneri for Pollot, April or May 1638: AT II, 38; and a. 2 below: 328.23. *Pace* AT (which—see note at XI, 719–720—retains dozens of trivial inaccuracies), Descartes's first use of *anciens* in a. 1 is lowercase.

[3] See to Hyperaspistes, August 1641: AT III, 428: K 115. What is an action in the body may not be a mode or modification of the body; a mode of the soul will qualify if it is caused when the body acts on the soul.

[4] Here "attribute" translates *attribuer,* and "belong", below, translates *appartenir.* When a person "attributes" a function to a thing, that person might be maintaining either that it is a mode of that thing, present in it, or that it is caused by that thing. That distinction must be kept in mind in the course of reading and assessing the argument in aa. 3–6.

Article 4. That the Heat and Movement of the Members Proceed from the Body, and Thoughts from the Soul.⁵

Thus, because we do not conceive the body to think in any way, we do right to believe that every kind of thought within us belongs to the soul. And because we have no doubt that there are inanimate bodies which can move in as many different ways as ours, or more, and which have as much heat, or more (experience shows this in [the case of] flame, which in itself has much more heat and motion than any of our members), we must believe that all the heat and all the movements which are in us, insofar as⁶ they do not depend on thought, belong to the body alone.

Article 5. That It Is an Error to Believe that the Soul Imparts Motion and Heat to the Body.

By means of this we shall avoid an error many have fallen into, a very serious one—so much so that I consider it the main reason why no one has yet been able to explain the Passions correctly, and the other things belonging to the soul. [The error] consists in this: on seeing that all dead bodies become devoid of heat and then movement, people have imagined that it was the absence of the soul that made the movements and the heat cease. And so they have groundlessly believed that our natural heat and all the movements of our body depended on the soul—whereas people ought to think, on the contrary, that the soul departs when someone dies only because that heat ceases and the organs used to move the body disintegrate.

Article 6. What the Difference Is Between a Living Body and a Dead Body.

Therefore, so that we may avoid this error, let us consider that death never occurs through the fault of the soul, but only because one of the prin-

---

⁵Articles 4-6 concern a central question about "the entire nature of man" (327.5–6): the explanation of life. Heat and movement mark off living bodies from dead ones, but since heat and movement are also found in inanimate bodies, they belong to and must be attributed to the body alone, and do not proceed from or depend on the soul. In this respect, life differs from thought. See to Regius, June 1642: AT III, 566: K 133; to More, 5 February 1649: AT V, 275–279: K 243–245. The serious error which Descartes identifies in a. 5 is considered in the Second Meditation: AT VII, 26: CSM II, 17–18, and is criticized in *Description of the Human Body:* AT XI, 224–226: CSM I, 314–315. When we learn (a. 29) that the passions are caused by movements within the body, we also discover one reason why the error is a serious one: thinking that those bodily movements depend on the soul would forestall explaining the passions as a physicist (Preface, 326).

⁶Descartes maintains a definite contrast between the phrase *en tant que*, which means "insofar as," and the phrase *autant que*, which means "inasmuch as." For example, his use of the former idiom here leaves open the possibility that the heat and movement within us may not always belong to the body alone—namely when they depend on thought. See however note 63 in Part II.

cipal parts of the body disintegrates. And let us judge that the body of a living man differs from that of a dead man as much as a watch or other automaton (that is, other self-moving machine), when it is wound and contains the bodily principle of the movements for which it is constructed, along with everything required for its action, [differs from] the same watch or other machine when it is broken and the principle of its movement ceases to act.[7]

Article 7. Brief Explanation of the Parts of the Body and Some of Its Functions.[8]

To render this more intelligible, I shall explain here in a few words all about the way in which the machine of our body is composed. There is no one who does not know by now that we have in us a heart, a brain, a stomach, muscles, nerves, arteries, veins, and similar things. It is known, too, that food that is eaten descends into the stomach and bowels, whence its juice, flowing into the liver and all of the veins, mingles with the blood they contain and thereby increases its quantity. Those who have heard even a little about Medicine know moreover the way the heart is composed, and how all the venous blood can easily flow from the vena cava into its right side, and pass from there into the lungs by the vessel that is named the arterial vein, then return from the lungs into the left side of the heart by the vessel named the venous artery, and finally pass from there into the great artery, whose branches spread out through the whole body.[9] Likewise, all those whom the authority of the Ancients has not entirely blinded, and who have been willing to open their eyes enough to examine Harvey's opinion concerning the circulation of the blood, do not doubt that all the body's veins and arteries are like streams through which the blood ceaselessly flows with great rapidity, making its way from the right chamber of the heart by the arterial vein, whose branches are dispersed all through the lungs and joined with those of the venous artery, by which it passes from the lungs into the left side of the heart; then from there it goes into the great artery, whose branches, dispersed through all the rest of

---

[7] The "principle" of the body's functions is thermodynamic (a. 8). And heat is itself explainable in terms of movement (see e.g. *The World*, ch. 2: AT XI, 7–10: CSM I, 83–84; *Meteorology*, Discourse 1: AT VI, 235–236: Olscamp 266; to Mersenne, 9 January 1639: AT II, 485; *Principles* IV, aa. 80, 92, and 198; AT VIII, 249, 255–256, 321–323: partially at CSM I, 284–285). Therefore it is accurate to describe the human body as a "machine" and to compare it to various automata (as Descartes does e.g. in *Treatise on Man*: AT XI, 120 and 130–132: Hall 2–5 and 21–22; in the Sixth Meditation: AT VII, 84–85: CSM II, 58–59; and here in aa. 6, 7, 13, 16, and 34).

[8] In articles 7-16 Descartes sketches the functions of the human body insofar as they can help us understand the passions of the soul, following the procedure recommended in a. 2. The sketch is filled out in *Treatise on Man* and *Description of the Human Body*, written respectively in 1632–1633 and 1648 but published posthumously, and also in *Discourse*, Part V, and *Dioptrics*. Articles 7-10 are anticipated in to [the Marques's of Newcastle], April 1645?: AT IV, 188–192.

[9] The "arterial vein" is the pulmonary artery, the "venous artery" is the set of four pulmonary veins, and the "great artery" is the aorta.

the body, are joined to the vena cava's branches, which carry the same blood anew into the right chamber of the heart: thus these two chambers are like sluices through each of which all the blood passes on every circuit it makes in the body.[10] Further, it is known that all the movements of the members depend on muscles, and that these muscles are opposed to one another in such a way that when one of them contracts it draws toward itself the part of the body it is attached to, which at the same time extends the muscle opposed to it. Then, if this latter happens to contract at another time, it extends the former, and draws back toward itself the part they are attached to. Finally, it is known that all these movements of the muscles, as well as all the senses, depend on nerves, which are like little filaments or little tubes which all come from the brain and which contain, just as it does, a certain very fine air or wind, called the animal spirits.

Article 8. What the Principle of All these Functions Is.

But the way in which these animal spirits and nerves contribute to the movements and senses is not commonly known, nor the bodily Principle that makes them act. This is why, although I have already described it somewhat in other writings,[11] I shall nevertheless say briefly here that while we live there is a continual heat in our heart, which is a species of fire that the venous blood maintains in it, and that this fire is the bodily principle of all the movements of our members.

Article 9. How the Movement of the Heart Takes Place.

Its first effect is to expand the blood with which the chambers of the heart are filled; this causes that blood, which needs a larger place to occupy, to pass forcefully from the right chamber into the arterial vein and from the left into the great artery.[12] Then, as this expansion ceases, blood immediately enters the right chamber of the heart afresh from the vena cava, and the left from the venous artery. For there are little membranes at the openings of these four vessels, so disposed that they prevent blood from entering the heart except by the latter two, and from leaving it except by the former two. The new blood that has entered the heart is immediately rarefied there in the same way as that which preceded it. And it is this alone in which the pulse or

[10] Descartes praised Harvey's discovery of the circulation of the blood, but wrongly defended his own thermodynamic explanation of the heartbeat against Harvey's nonthermodynamic account, e.g. in *Discourse*, Part 5: AT VI, 46–55: CSM I, 134–139, *Description of the Human Body*: AT XI, 231–244; partially in CSM I, 316–319. See also the passages cited in note 12 below and in note 46 in Part II. Concerning Harvey, see note 17 in the Preface, above.

[11] *Discourse*, Part 5: AT VI, 49–55: CSM I, 135–139; *Dioptrics*, Discourse 4: AT VI, 109–114: Olscamp 87–90.

[12] For dilation as the active phase of the heartbeat, see *Treatise on Man*: AT XI, 124–125: Hall 13–15; to Plempius for Fromondus, 3 October 1637: AT I, 416: French translation, Alquié I, 789. Cf. also a. 126, etc., below.

beating of the heart and arteries consists; so this beating recurs as often as blood enters the heart afresh. It is also this alone that gives the blood its motion, and makes it flow ceaselessly with great rapidity in all the arteries and veins, by means of which it carries the heat it acquires in the heart to all the other parts of the body, and serves as their sustenance.

Article 10. How the Animal Spirits Are Produced in the Brain.

But what matters more here is that all of the liveliest and finest parts of the blood that the heat has rarefied in the heart ceaselessly enter the cavities of the brain in great numbers. And the reason they go there rather than anywhere else is that all the blood leaving the heart by the great artery flows toward that place in a straight line, and, since they cannot all enter it, because there are only very narrow passages, only the most agitated and the finest of its parts get there while the rest spread out into all the other places in the body. Now these very fine parts of the blood compose the animal spirits. And to this end the only change they need to undergo in the brain is to be separated there from the other parts of the blood that are not so fine. For what I name spirits here are nothing but bodies; their only property is that they are bodies which are very small and which move very rapidly—just like the parts of the flame that emanates from a torch.[13] So they do not stop anywhere, and to the extent that some of them enter the brain's cavities, others leave through the pores in its substance; these pores guide them into nerves and thence into muscles, by means of which they move the body in all the different ways in which it can be moved.

Article 11. How the Movements of Muscles Take Place.

For the sole cause of all the members' movements is that some muscles contract and those opposing them become extended, as has already been said. And the sole cause making one muscle contract, rather than the opposing one, is that a slightly greater number of spirits come toward it from the brain than toward the other. Not that the spirits coming immediately from the brain suffice by themselves to move these muscles—but they make all the other spirits already in the two muscles leave one of them extremely rapidly and pass into the other, whence the one they leave becomes longer and slacker, and the one they enter, rapidly becoming swollen with them, contracts and pulls the member it is attached to. This is easy to understand, provided one knows that there are only very few animal spirits continually coming from the brain toward each muscle but that a great quantity of others are always

---

[13] The animal spirits are corporeal components of the blood; they are "spirits" as wine is, not as ghosts are, more spiritous than spiritual (see a. 15). They are therefore an appropriate resource for someone who wishes to treat the passions as a physicist (326), and, as we shall see, they play a central role in Descartes's treatment.

enclosed in the same muscle, moving very rapidly in it—sometimes merely whirling about where they are, when they find no open passages by which to leave it, and sometimes flowing into the opposing muscle. For there are little openings in each of these muscles through which these spirits can flow from one into the other, so disposed that when the spirits coming from the brain toward one of them have even a little more force than those going toward the other, they open all the openings through which the other muscle's spirits can pass into the first, and at the same time close all those through which its spirits can pass into the other one. By this means all the spirits heretofore contained in these two muscles collect very rapidly in one of them, swelling and contracting it, while the other becomes extended and relaxed.

Article 12. How Objects Outside Us Act upon the Sense Organs.

We still need to understand here the causes that keep the spirits from always flowing in the same way from the brain into the muscles, and at times make more of them come toward some than toward others. For, in addition to the action of the soul, which as I shall relate below[14] is truly one of these causes within us, two others besides, which depend only on the body, need to be noted. The first consists in the diversity of the movements excited in the sense organs by their objects, which I have already explained fully enough in the *Dioptrique*.[15] But, so that those who see this work may need to have read no others, I shall repeat here that there are three things to consider in the nerves, namely, their pith or internal substance, which extends in the form of little filaments from the brain, where it originates, to the ends of the other members these filaments are attached to; then the membranes which surround them and which, being continuous with the ones that envelop the brain, compose little tubes in which the little filaments are enclosed; then finally the animal spirits, which, carried by these same tubes from the brain to the muscles, cause the filaments therein to remain completely free and extended, in such a way that the least thing that moves the part of the body where the end of any of them is attached thereby makes the part of the brain it comes from move, in the same way in which, when we pull one end of a cord, we make the other move.

Article 13. That this Action of Objects Outside of Us Can Guide Spirits into the Muscles in Various Ways.

And I explained in the *Dioptrique*[16] how all the objects of vision are communicated to us in this way alone: by the mediation of transparent bodies between them and us, they locally move the little filaments of the optic nerves

[14] Articles 18, 31, 34 (centrally), and 43.

[15] Discourse 4: AT VI, 109–114: Olscamp 87–90.

[16] Discourses 5 and 6: AT VI, 128–147: Olscamp 100–113.

at the back of our eyes and then the parts of the brain these nerves come from—I said that they move them in as many different ways as there are diversities they make us see in things, and that it is not the movements occurring in the eye, but those occurring in the brain, that immediately represent those objects to the soul. From this example it is easy to understand that sounds, odors, tastes, hear, pain, hunger, thirst, and in general all the objects both of our other external senses and of our internal appetites also excite some movement in our nerves, which passes to the brain by means of them. In addition to the fact that these various movements of the brain make our soul have various sensations, they can also, apart from [the soul], make the spirits take their course toward certain muscles rather than others, and so [make them] move our members. I will prove this here by only one example. If someone were suddenly to thrust his hand near our eyes as if to strike us, even though we might know that he is our friend, that he is doing this only in jest, and that he will be very careful not to injure us, it would nevertheless be hard for us to keep from closing them. This shows that it is not by the mediation of our soul that they close, since it is against our volition—which is its only or at least its principal action—but that it is because the machine of our body is so composed that the movement of that hand toward our eyes excites another movement in our brain, which guides animal spirits into the muscles that make the eyelids lower.

Article 14. That the Diversity Existing among the Spirits Can Also Diversify Their Course.

The other cause serving to guide animal spirits into muscles in various ways is the unequal agitation of these spirits and the diversity of their parts. For when some of their parts are larger and more agitated than the rest, they pass further in a straight line into the brain's cavities and pores, and are thereby guided into other muscles than they would be if they had less force.

Article 15. What the Causes of Their Diversity Are.

And this inequality may originate from the varieties of stuff they are composed of, as we see in those who have drunk a lot of wine: the wine's vapors, suddenly entering the blood, rise from the heart to the brain, where they turn into spirits which, being stronger and more numerous than those commonly there, are capable of moving the body in many unusual ways. This inequality of the spirits may also originate from the diverse dispositions of the heart, liver, stomach, spleen, and all the other parts that contribute to their production. In this connection we must observe above all certain little nerves set into the upper part of the heart,[17] which serve to enlarge and contract the openings to its hollows, so that the blood as it expands more or less there pro-

---

[17] *La baze du coeur*: the broad upper part, not the bottom, of the heart.

duces spirits of diverse dispositions. We must also observe that even though the blood entering the heart arrives from all the other places in the body, it nevertheless often happens to be driven there from some parts more than others, because the nerves and muscles corresponding to the former parts press or agitate it more, and that according to the diversity of the parts most of it comes from, it expands in different ways in the heart, and then produces spirits having differing qualities. So, for example, [blood] that comes from the lower part of the liver, where the gall is, expands in the heart in a different way from that which comes from the spleen, and the latter otherwise from that which comes from the veins of the arms or legs, and finally this latter entirely otherwise from alimentary juice, when, having just left the stomach and bowels, it passes rapidly through the liver to the heart.

Article 16. How All the Members Can Be Moved by the Objects of the Senses and by the Spirits with No Help from the Soul.

Finally it must be noticed that the machine of our body is composed in such a way that all the changes taking place in the motion of the spirits can make them open some of the brain's pores more than others, and conversely that when one of these pores is open even slightly more than usual, through the action of the nerves serving the senses, this changes something in the motion of the spirits, and causes them to be led into the muscles serving to move the body in the manner in which it is commonly moved on the occasion of such an action. Thus all the movements we make without our will contributing (as often happens when we breathe, walk, eat, and in short do all the actions common to us and beasts) depend only on the arrangement of our members, and on the course which the spirits excited by the heat of the heart follow naturally in the brain, nerves, and muscles—in the same way in which a watch's movement is produced by the sheer force of its spring and the shape of its wheels.

Article 17. What the Functions of the Soul Are.[18]

After having thus taken into consideration all the functions that belong to the body alone, it is easy to understand that there remains nothing in us that we should attribute to our soul but our thoughts, which are principally of two genera—the first, namely, are the actions of the soul; the others are its passions. The ones I call its actions are all of our volitions, because we find by

---

[18]Articles 17–29 sketch the functions of the soul insofar as that will help provide an understanding of the passions. *Cf.* again note I. As Descartes had argued in Meditations 2 and 6 (AT VII, 25–29, 78, 85–86: CSM II, 17–19, 54, 59), it is precisely our thoughts (*pensées*)—in Descartes's consciously extended sense of that term—that can be attributed to our soul. The sketch here is a development of a passage in a letter to Elisabeth, 6 October 1645: AT IV, 310–311: K 177–178; it culminates, at aa. 27–29, in a definition of the passions of the soul.

experience[19] that they come directly from our soul and seem to depend only on it; as, on the other hand, all the sorts of cases of perception or knowledge to be found in us can generally be called its passions, because it is often not our soul that makes them such as they are, and because it always receives them from things that are represented by them.

Article 18. About Volition.

Again, our volitions are of two sorts. For the first are actions of the soul which have their terminus[20] in the soul itself, as when we will to love God or in general to apply our thought to some object that is not material. The others are actions which have their terminus in our body, as when, from the mere fact that we have the volition to take a walk, it follows that our legs move and we walk.

Article 19. About Perception.

Our perceptions are also of two sorts, and the first have the soul as cause, the others the body. Those which have the soul as cause are the perceptions of our volitions, and of all the imaginations or other thoughts that depend on them. For it is certain that we could not will anything unless we perceived by the same means that we willed it. And though with respect to our soul it is an action to will something, it can be said that it is also a passion within it to perceive that it wills. Nevertheless, because this perception and this volition are really only a single thing,[21] the denomination is always made by the loftier one, and so it is not usually named a passion, but an action only.

Article 20. About Imaginations and Other Thoughts that Are Formed by the Soul.

When our soul applies itself to imagine something which does not exist—as to represent to itself an enchanted palace or a chimera—and also when it applies to itself to attend to something which is solely intelligible and not imaginable—for example to attend to its own nature—the perceptions it

---

[19]*Nous experimentons que:* we find by experience that; we experience it to be true that. In this sense, we experience our own causality and can thereby distinguish our soul's actions from its passions. See Third Replies to the *Meditations:* AT VII, 191: CSM II, 134; Fifth Replies; AT VII, 377–378: CSM II, 259–260; *Principles* I, aa. 39 and 41: AT VIII, 19–20: CSM I, 209–206; to Mersenne, 28 January 1641: AT III, 295: K 93; to Regius, May 1641: AT III, 372: K 102; to Hyperaspistes, August 1641: AT III, 432: K 118; and aa. 153, 158, and 159 below.

[20] *Se Terminer.* Not "come to an end," but "have as an end, have their issue." We might even interpret "have as their intentional object," amplifying note 23 below. Here I simply give a neutral reproduction of the Latin that stood behind this unusual usage (the verb's only occurrences are in this article). For more, see Alquié 966–967, n. 3.

[21] Descartes suggests elsewhere as well that a thought and one's perception of that thought are identical: to Mersenne, 28 January 1641: AT III, 295: K 93; Third Objections and Replies: AT VII, 173–175: CSM II, 122–124; to Regius, May 1641: AT III, 372: K 102–103.

has of these things depend principally upon the volition that makes it perceive them. That is why they are usually regarded as actions rather than passions.

Article 21. About Imaginations that Have Only the Body as Cause.

Among perceptions caused by the body, most depend on the nerves, but are also some that do not depend on them, which are named imaginations, like those I just spoke of, but from which they differ in that our will is not employed in forming them—which disqualifies them from being numbered among the actions of the soul. And they only arise because the spirits, agitated in various ways and coming upon traces of various impressions which have preceded them in the brain, haphazardly take their course through certain of its pores rather than others. Such are the illusions of our dreams and likewise the waking reveries we often have, when our thought wanders carelessly without applying itself to anything of its own accord. Now even though some of these imaginations are passions of the soul, taking this word in its most fitting and particular sense, and though they can all be so named if it is taken in a more general sense, yet since they do not have so noteworthy and determinate a cause as the perceptions the soul receives by the mediation of the nerves, and since they seem to be only their shadow and picture, before we can distinguish them rightly it will be necessary to consider the difference among these other ones.[22]

Article 22. About the Difference Existing among the Other Perceptions.

All the perceptions I have not yet explained come to the soul by the mediation of the nerves, and there exists this difference among them: we refer some of them to objects outside us which strike our senses, others to our body or some of its parts, and finally others to our soul.[23]

[22] In order to locate those imaginations that are passions in the narrow sense, Descartes will first make the necessary distinction among perceptions that depend on the nerves (aa. 22–25); it will then emerge (a. 26) that there are both imaginations and neural perceptions which qualify as passions of the soul.

[23] *Nous les rapportons:* "we refer them" to external objects, to our body, and to our soul. Descartes uses the reflexive verb similarly, as at 350.16: our perceptions *se rapportent*—"have reference"—to various objects. He provides some materials for an account of the *content* or *intentionality* of passions in his use of these verbs and also (note 14, Part II) in his talk of the passions as "representing" things to us and in his talk of the "objects" of passions.

Descartes holds that we refer all our neural perceptions to some object (a. 22), and he regards it as a definitional truth that we refer the passions of the soul to our soul (aa. 27, 29). Since not all passions are neural perceptions, the possibility remains that some passions are *not* referred to the soul; see notes 22 and 26, and note 3 in Part II. When we refer a perception to some external object, we have the opinion that it is caused by that object, in such a way that we think we see or feel it (a. 23); when we refer a perception to an external object or to a part of our

Article 23. About Perceptions We Refer to Objects Outside Us.

Those we refer to things outside us, namely to the objects of our senses, are caused (at least when our opinion is not false) by those objects, which, exciting movements in the organs of the external senses, excite some in the brain too by the mediation of the nerves, which make the soul feel them.[24] So, when we see the light of a torch and hear the sound of a bell, the sound and the light are two different actions, which, solely by exciting two different movements in some of our nerves and thereby in the brain, impart to the soul two different sensations, which we refer to the subjects we suppose to be their causes in such a way that we think that we see the torch itself and hear the bell, and not that we only feel the movements proceeding from them.

---

body, we judge that the action that is making us feel some quality of that object is in that object (a. 24); when we refer a perception to our soul, however, we commonly know no proximate cause of that perception, and we feel its effects as in the soul itself (a. 25; to Elisabeth, 6 October 1645: AT IV, 311: K 178).

I propose this hypothesis about Descartes's conception of referring: we "refer" our perception to an object just in case we spontaneously judge that the action causing our perception is within that object. See Alquié 970, note 2.

Part II opens with an enumeration of the principal passions, based (a. 52) on the thesis that every sort of passion is normally caused, in part, by a judgment that some object is good or bad for us or at least matters to us in some way or other. (Thus note the descriptions of the six primitive passions in aa. 53, 56, 57, and 61, but note also the possibility of exceptions to the thesis, which is suggested in Part III, note 29.) We normally feel a passion only when we first judge that something is related to us in some such way. When we do feel the resulting passion, it is then understandable that we should spontaneously judge that that very passion is brought about by the fact that that object stands in that relation to us.

Now given the above hypothesis, to say that we make that spontaneous judgment about our passion is to say that we refer it to ourselves (and, of course, to the object which our judgment also concerns). But Descartes also holds that we are identical with our souls (see the texts from the *Meditations* cited in note 18 above). It is perhaps by such a line of thought that he might have concluded that, in general, we refer the passions of the soul to our souls themselves. Here is a simple example. Normally one of the causes of my love for X is my judgment that X is good for *me* (see a. 56). So I spontaneously judge that X's being good for me is the cause of the passion of love I now feel. In that way I "refer" my passion to myself. The apparent ubiquity of a word like "me," within our spontaneous judgments about the causes of our passions, may thus have led Descartes to the generalization that all the passions of the soul are referred to the soul itself. See notes 20 and 25, notes 6 and 14 in Part II, and notes 2 and 17 in Part III.

[24] The final clause is ambiguous in French. It may mean either that the nerves or that the brain movements make the soul feel either its own perceptions or the movements of the organs or the objects. But, given the context (a. 24) and a parallel passage (*Dioptrics*, Discourse 4: AT VI, 112–114: Olscamp 89–90), it probably means that the brain movements make the soul feel the objects. As the rest of a. 23 explains, the object the soul feels is not the torch or bell itself, but the movements which proceed from it—these being identical with the "actions" (aa. 23, 24) which, by the mediation of nerve and brain movements, give rise to these perceptions. As the Sixth Meditation explains more fully, while the senses indeed convey some truth to the mind, they cannot be counted on to inform it of the essential nature of external objects (AT VII, 78–83: CSM II, 54–58).

Article 24. About Perceptions We Refer to Our Body.

The perceptions we refer to our body or some of its parts are those we have of hunger, thirst, and our other natural appetites, to which may be added pain, heat, and the other affections that we feel as in our members and not as in objects outside us. So we may feel at the same time, and by the mediation of the same nerves, the coolness of our hand and the heat of the flame it approaches, or, on the contrary, the heat of the hand and the cold of the air it is exposed to—there being no difference between the actions making us feel the warmth or coolness in our hand and those making us feel that which is outside us except that, [now supposing that] one of these actions succeeds the other, we judge that the first is already in us and that the succeeding [action] is not there yet but in the object causing it.[25]

Article 25. About Perceptions We Refer to Our Soul.

The perceptions that are referred to the soul alone are those whose effects are felt as in the soul itself, and of which no proximate cause to which they may be referred is commonly known. Such are the sensations of joy, anger, and others like them, which are sometimes excited in us by objects that move our nerves and sometimes also by other causes.[26] Now even though all of our perceptions—those which are referred to objects outside us no less than those which are referred to various affections of our body—are truly passions with respect to our soul when this word is taken in its most general sense, nevertheless it is usually restricted to mean those only which have reference to the soul itself. And it is only these last which I have undertaken to explain here under the name of passions of the soul.

Article 26. That the Imaginations that Depend Only on the Haphazard Movements of Spirits May Be Passions as Truly as the Perceptions that Depend on the Nerves.

It remains here to observe that all the things the soul perceives by the mediation of nerves may also be represented to it by the haphazard course of spirits, the only difference being that impressions entering the brain through the nerves are usually more lively and more definite than those the spirits excite there—which led me to say in art. 21 that the latter are like the shadow or picture of the former. It must also be observed that this picture sometimes

---

[25] If we feel cold hand and warm air simultaneously, the actions causing our perceptions—movements in the air and hand—are identical. Perceptions referred to the external world differ from perceptions referred to our body not because different kinds of actions generate them but because we make different judgments about their causes; that is shown by the case in which we feel cold hand and warm air one after the other: in this case, similar actions produce perceptions about which we make different causal judgments. Recall the hypothesis suggested in note 23.

[26] These other causes are discussed in aa. 21, 26, 51, 93, and 94; cf. to Elisabeth, 6 October 1645: AT IV, 309–313: K 177–179.

happens to be so similar to the thing it represents that one can thereby be deceived, in connection with the perceptions which have reference to objects outside us, or those which have reference to some of the parts of our body, but that one cannot be [deceived] in the same manner in connection with the passions, inasmuch as they are so close and internal to our soul that it is impossible it should feel them without their truly being such as it feels them.[27] So, often when we are sleeping, and even sometimes when awake, we imagine certain things so forcefully that we think we see them before ourselves or feel them within our body, although they are not there at all. But even though we be asleep and dreaming, we cannot feel sad, or moved by any other passion, unless it be quite true that the soul has that passion within itself.[28]

Article 27. The Definition of the Passions of the Soul.

After having considered wherein the passions of the soul differ from all its other thoughts, it seems to me that they may generally be defined thus: perceptions or sensations or excitations of the soul which are referred to it in particular and which are caused, maintained, and strengthened by some movement of the spirits.

[27]A pervasive Cartesian conviction is that what is far away can deceive, while what is close at hand can give security. That is true not only of epistemic security (in addition to the present passage, see Meditations 1 and 3: AT VII, 18 and 37: CSM II, 12–13 and 26; and a. 1 above), but also of emotional security (see *Discourse*, Part 3: AT VI, 25–27: CSM I, 123–124, and aa. 147–148 below).

[28]The word "feel" (*sentir*) here must be read so that "we feel sad" means that we think we are sad, and not that we are sad, for the latter reading would render this sentence's argument pointless. Descartes invites a similar confusion in the passage from the Third Meditation cited in note 27. Yet the point—defended centrally in Meditation 2: AT VII, 28–29: CSM II, 19—is clear: I can perhaps be deceived about the cause of my thoughts, ideas, or passions, but not about their existence or specific nature.

~8~

Baruch Spinoza, Excerpt from "The emendation of the intellect" (1677).*

[94] So the right way of discovery is to form thoughts from some given definition. This will proceed the more successfully and easily, the better we have defined a thing. So the chief point of this second part of the Method is concerned solely with this: knowing the conditions of a good definition, and then, the way of finding good definitions. First, therefore, I shall deal with the conditions of definition.

[95] To be called perfect, a definition will have to explain the inmost essence of the thing, and to take care not to use certain *propria* in its place. So as not to seem bent on uncovering the errors of others, I shall use only the example of an abstract thing to explain this. For it is the same however it is defined. If a circle, for example, is defined as a figure in which the lines drawn from the center to the circumference are equal, no one fails to see that such a definition does not at all explain the essence of the circle, but only a property of it. And though, as I have said, this does not matter much concerning figures and other beings of reason, it matters a great deal concerning Physical and real beings, because the properties of things are not understood so long as their essences are not known. If we neglect them, we shall necessarily overturn the connection of the intellect, which ought to reproduce the connection of Nature, and we shall completely miss our goal.

[96] These are the requirements which must be satisfied in Definition, if we are to be free of this fault:

1. If the thing is created, the definition, as we have said, will have to include the proximate cause. E.g., according to this law, a circle would have to be defined as

*Spinoza, B. (1677, 1985). The emendation of the intellect. In E. Curley (ed. and transl.) *The chief collected works of Spinoza.* Copyright © by Princeton University Press. Reprinted by permission of Princeton University Press.

follows: it is the figure that is described by any line of which one end is fixed and the other movable. This definition clearly includes the proximate cause.[63]

2. We require a concept, *or* definition, of the thing such that when it is considered alone, without any others conjoined, all the thing's properties can be deduced from it (as may be seen in this definition of the circle). For from it we clearly infer that all the lines drawn from the center to the circumference are equal.

That this is a necessary requirement of a definition is so plain through itself to the attentive that it does not seem worth taking time to demonstrate it, nor to show also, from this second requirement, that every definition must be affirmative.

I mean intellectual affirmation—it matters little whether the definition is verbally affirmative; because of the poverty of language it will sometimes, perhaps, [only] be able to be expressed negatively, although it is understood affirmatively.

[97] These are the requirements for the definition of an uncreated thing:

1. That it should exclude every cause, i.e., that the object should require nothing else except its own being for its explanation.[64]

2. That, given the definition of this thing, there should remain no room for the Question—does it exist?

3. That (as far as the mind is concerned) it should have no substantives that could be changed into adjectives, i.e., that it should not be explained through any abstractions.

4. Finally (though it is not very necessary to note this) it is required that all its properties be inferred[65] from its definition.

All these things are evident to those who attend to them accurately.

[98] I have also said that the best conclusion will have to be drawn from a particular affirmative essence. For the more particular an idea is, the more distinct, and therefore the clearer it is. So we ought to seek knowledge of particulars as much as possible.

[99] As for order, to unite and order all our perceptions, it is required, and reason demands,[66] that we ask, as soon as possible, whether there is a cer-

---

[63]Cf. Hobbes, *De Corpore* I, i, 5, and his *Examinatio et emendatio mathematicae hodiernae*, second dialogue. See also Cassirer 2:98ff.

[64]According to Gueroult (1, 1:172–173), Spinoza later modified this requirement and came to regard his definition of God (E ID6) as a genetic, causal definition. It would still be true that God requires nothing else except his own being (i.e., the elements of his being, the attributes) for his explanation. But it would not be correct to say that a definition in terms of those elements excludes every cause. Whereas the notion of being *causa sui* is here treated as if equivalent to being without a cause, later it will be treated more positively. The key passage is in Letter 60 (IV/270–271).

[65]OP: "concludantur," NS: "verklaert worden" (literally: 'be explained').

[66]Accepting Leopold's emendation of the text. Cf. Joachim 2, 214 n.

tain being, and at the same time, what sort of being it is, which is the cause of all things, so that its objective essence may also be the cause of all our ideas, and then our mind will (as we have said)[67] reproduce Nature as much as possible. For it will have Nature's essence, order, and unity objectively.

From this we can see that above all it is necessary for us always to deduce all our ideas from Physical things, *or* from the real beings, proceeding, as far as possible, according to the series of causes, from one real being to another real being, in such a way that we do not pass over to abstractions and universals, neither inferring something real from them, nor inferring them from something real. For to do either interferes with the true progress of the intellect.

[100] But note that by the series of causes and of real beings I do not here understand the series of singular, changeable things, but only the series of fixed and eternal things. For it would be impossible for human weakness to grasp the series of singular, changeable things, not only because there are innumerably many of them, but also because of the infinite circumstances in one and the same thing, any of which can be the cause of its existence or nonexistence. For their existence has no connection with their essence, *or* (as we have already said) is not an eternal truth.

[101] But there is also no need for us to understand their series. The essences of singular, changeable things are not to be drawn from their series, *or* order of existing, since it offers us nothing but extrinsic denominations, relations, or at most, circumstances, all of which are far from the inmost essence of things. That essence is to be sought only from the fixed and eternal things, and at the same time from the laws inscribed in these things, as in their true codes, according to which all singular things come to be, and are ordered. Indeed these singular, changeable things depend so intimately, and (so to speak) essentially, on the fixed things that they can neither be nor be conceived without them. So although these fixed and eternal things are singular, nevertheless, because of their presence everywhere, and most extensive power, they will be to us like universals, *or* genera of the definitions of singular, changeable things, and the proximate causes of all things.

[102] But since this is so, there seems to be a considerable difficulty in our being able to arrive at knowledge of these singular things. For to conceive them all at once is a task far beyond the powers of the human intellect. But to understand one before the other, the order must be sought, as we have said, not from their series of existing, nor even from the eternal things. For there, by nature, all these things are at once. So other aids will have to be sought beyond those we use to understand the eternal things and their laws.

Nevertheless, this is not the place to treat them, nor is it necessary until after we have acquired a sufficient knowledge of the eternal things and their infallible laws, and the nature of our senses has become known to us. [103]

---

[67]Cf. §§ 42, 91, and 95.

Before we equip ourselves for knowledge of singular things, there will be time to treat those aids, all of which serve to help us know how to use our senses and to make, according to certain laws, and in order, the experiments that will suffice to determine the thing we are seeking, so that at last we may infer from them according to what laws of eternal things it was made, and its inmost nature may become known to us, as I shall show in its place.[68]

Here, to return to our theme, I shall only try to treat those things that seem necessary for us to be able to arrive at knowledge of eternal things, and for us to form their definitions according to the conditions laid down above. [104] To do this, we must recall what we said above:[69] when the mind attends to a thought—to weigh it, and deduce from it, in good order, the things legitimately to be deduced from it—if it is false, the mind will uncover the falsity; but if it is true, the mind will continue successfully, without any interruption, to deduce true things from it. This, I say, is required for our purpose. For our thoughts cannot be determined from any other foundation.[70] [105] If, therefore, we wish to investigate the first thing of all, there must be some foundation that directs our thoughts to it.

Next, because Method is reflexive knowledge itself, this foundation, which must direct our thoughts, can be nothing other than knowledge of what constitutes the form of truth, and knowledge of the intellect, and its properties and powers. For once we have acquired this [knowledge], we shall have the foundation from which we shall deduce our thoughts and the way by which the intellect, according to its capacity, will be able to reach the knowledge of eternal things, with due regard, of course, to its own powers.

[106] But if forming true ideas pertains to the nature of thought, as shown in the first part, here we must investigate what we understand by the powers of the intellect. Since the chief part of our Method is to understand as well as possible the powers of the intellect, and its nature, we are necessarily forced, by what I have taught in this second part of the Method, to deduce these from the very definition of thought and intellect.

[107] But so far we have had no rules for discovering definitions. And because we cannot give them unless the nature, *or* definition, of the intellect,

[68]Various scholars (Leopold, Appuhn, Joachim) have seen in this sentence a digression, probably added by Spinoza as a marginal note. Gebhardt, following both the OP and the NS, retains it in the text, rightly, I think.

[69]I take the reference to be § 61, as Gebhardt apparently does at II/337. But at II/338 he apparently takes it to be to § 70, as part of his case for his emendation of II/38/1–2.

[70]OP: "Nam ex nullo fundamento cogitationes nostrae terminari queunt." Elwes' translation of that text is as reasonable as any: "For our thoughts may be brought to a close by the absence of a foundation." Gebhardt (following the NS) emends to: "Nam ex nullo alio fundamento cogitationes nostrae determinari queunt," which is what I have translated. But Appuhn's conjecture is also plausible: "Nam ex nullo fundamento cogitationes nostrae determinari nequeunt" (= "for without a foundation our thoughts cannot be determined"). For a fuller discussion see Eisenberg 1, 103–105, or Gebhardt II/337–339. Cf. Aristotle, NE, 1098 b1–12.

and its power are known, it follows that either the definition of the intellect must be clear through itself, or else we can understand nothing. It is not, however, absolutely clear through itself; but because its properties (like all the things we have from intellect) cannot be perceived clearly and distinctly unless their nature is known, if we attend to the properties of the intellect that we understand clearly and distinctly, its definition will become known through itself. We shall, therefore, enumerate the properties of the intellect here, and consider them, and begin to deal with out innate tools.[g]

[108] The properties of the intellect which I have chiefly noted, and understand clearly, are these:

1. That it involves certainty, i.e., that the intellect knows that things are formally as they are contained objectively in itself.

2. That it perceives certain things, *or* forms certain ideas, absolutely, and forms certain ideas from others. For it forms the idea of quantity absolutely, without attending to other thoughts, but it forms the ideas of motion only by attending to the idea of quantity.

3. Those that it forms absolutely express infinity, but determinate ideas it forms from others. For if it perceives the idea of a quantity through a cause, then it determines [that idea] through [the idea] of a quantity,[71] as when it perceives that a body arises from the motion of some plane, a plane from the motion of a line, and finally, a line from the motion of a point. These perceptions do not help to understand the quantity, but only to determine it. This is evident from the fact that we conceive them as arising from the motion, although the motion is not perceived unless the quantity is perceived, and also because we can continue the motion to form a line to infinity, which we could not do at all, if we did not have the idea of infinite quantity.

4. It forms positive ideas before negative ones.

5. It perceives things not so much under duration as under a certain species of eternity, and in an infinite number—or rather, to perceive things, it attends neither to number nor to duration; but when it imagines things, it perceives them under a certain number, determinate duration and quantity.

6. The clear and distinct ideas that we form seem to follow so from the necessity of our nature alone that they seem to depend absolutely on our power alone. But with confused ideas it is quite the contrary—they are often formed against our will.

7. The mind can determine in many ways the ideas of things that the intellect forms from others—as, for example, to determine the plane of an ellipse, it feigns that a pen attached to a cord is moved around two centers, or conceives infinitely many points always having the same definite relation to some given straight line,

---

[g]Cf. above [II/13–14ff.].

[71]The text is evidently corrupt here. Gebhardt emends along lines suggested by the NS. I believe his version of the text makes sense if understood as I have translated it. For an alternative version and full discussion, see Eisenberg 1, 107–109.

or a cone cut by some oblique plane, so that the angle of inclination is greater than the angle of the cone's vertex, or in infinite other ways.

8. The more ideas express of the perfection of some object, the more perfect they are. For we do not admire the architect who has designed a chapel so much as one who has designed a notable temple.

[109] I shall not linger over the other things that are referred to thought, such as love, joy, etc. For they contribute nothing to our present purpose, nor can they be conceived unless the intellect is perceived. For if perception is altogether taken away, then all these are taken away.

[110] False and fictitious ideas have nothing positive (as we have shown abundantly) through which they are called false or fictitious, but they are considered as such only from a defect of our knowledge. So false and fictitious ideas, as such, can teach us nothing concerning the essence of thought. It is rather to be sought from the positive properties just surveyed, i.e., we must now establish something common from which these properties necessarily follow, *or* such that when it is given, they are necessarily given, and when it is taken away, they are taken away.

The rest is lacking.

≈ 9 ≈

Étienne Bonnot de Condillac, Excerpt from *Treatise on the Sensations* (1754).*

I THE FIRST COGNITIONS OF A MAN LIMITED TO THE SENSE OF SMELL

1 *The statue limited to the sense of smell can only know odours.* Our statue being limited to the sense of smell its cognitions cannot extend beyond smells. It can no more have ideas of extension, shape or of anything outside itself, or outside its sensations, than it can have ideas of colour, sound or taste.

2 *Only relatively to itself are odours smelled.* If we give the statue a rose to smell, to us it is a statue smelling a rose, to itself it is smell of rose.

The statue therefore will be rose smell, pink smell, jasmine smell, violet smell, according to the flower which stimulates its sense organ. In a word, in regard to itself smells are its modifications or modes. It cannot suppose itself to be anything else, since it is only susceptible to sensations.

3 *It has no idea of matter.* Let the philosophers, to whom it appears so evident that all is material, put themselves for a moment in its place, and then imagine how they could suspect the existence of anything which resembles what we call *matter*.

4 *It could not be more limited in its cognitions.* This is enough to prove that we have only to increase or diminish the number of senses, in order to make us pass quite different judgments from those which now seem natural to us; and our statue limited to the sense of smell, can give us the idea of a class of beings with extremely limited cognitions.

* Condillac, É. B. de (1754, 1930). Excerpts from Condillac's *Treatise on Sensations* (G. Carr, transl.). Los Angeles: University of Southern California Press, Part I, Chs. i, ii, 3–22. Reprinted by permission of the University of Southern California Press.

II HOW THE UNDERSTANDING WORKS IN A MAN LIMITED TO THE SENSE OF SMELL AND HOW THE DIFFERENT DEGREES OF PLEASURE AND PAIN ARE THE PRINCIPLE OF ITS COGNITIONS

1 *The statue capable of attention,* At the first smell our statue's capacity of feeling is entirely due to the impression which is made upon its sense organ. This is what I call attention.

2 *of enjoying and suffering,* From this moment it begins to enjoy or to suffer. For if the capacity of feeling is confined to a pleasant smell, there is enjoyment; and if it is confined to an unpleasant smell, there is suffering.

3 *powerless to form desires.* But our statue has yet no idea of the different changes it can undergo. Thus it is well without wishing to be better, or ill without wishing to be well. Suffering can no more make it desire a good it does not know than enjoyment can make it fear an ill it does not know. Consequently, however unpleasant the first sensation may be, were it to the point of wounding the sense organ and causing a violent pain, it would not give rise to desire.

If in us suffering is always accompanied with the desire not to suffer, this cannot be the case with the statue. Pain in us gives rise to this desire because we already know the different state. The habit we have contracted of looking upon pain as something which we have been without and might be again without, makes it impossible for us to suffer pain without wishing at once that we were not suffering, and in us this wish is inseparable from a painful state. But the statue, which in the first instance is only conscious of itself in the pain it is experiencing, is not aware that the pain can cease and become something else, or that there can be no pain at all. As yet it has no idea of change, succession, duration. It exists, then, without being able to form desires.

4 *Pleasure and pain the principles of its operations.* When it is able to notice that it can cease to be what it is, in order to be what it was, we shall see how a state of pain can give rise to desire, for it will compare a state of pleasure it can remember to the state of pain it is suffering. It is by this artifice that pleasure and pain become the unique principle which determines all the operations of its soul, and will raise it by degrees to all the cognitions of which it is capable. In order to discern the progress it can make, we have only to observe the pleasures it can desire, the pains it can fear, and the influence of each according to the circumstances.

5 *How it would be limited without memory.* If there remained no recollection of former modifications, then on the occasion of each sensation it would believe itself to be feeling for the first time. Whole years might be swallowed up in each present moment. Were its attention always limited to one mode of being it would never be able to take account of two together, and never be able to judge of their relations. It would enjoy or suffer without having yet either desire or fear.

6 *Dawn of memory.* The smell is not wholly forgotten when the odoriferous substance which caused it has ceased to act on the sense organ, for the attention retains it, and an impression remains stronger or weaker according as the attention has been more or less vivid. This is memory.

7 *Division of the capacity of feeling between smell and memory.* When our statue is a new smell, it has still present that which it had been the moment before. Its capacity of feeling is divided between the memory and the smell. The first of these faculties is attentive to the past sensation, whilst the second is attentive to the present sensation.

8 *Memory only a mode of feeling.* There are then in the statue two ways of feeling. They differ only in one being related to a present sensation and the other to a sensation which no longer exists but of which the impression still remains. Ignorant of any objects acting upon it, ignorant even of its own sense organ, it usually distinguishes the memory of a sensation from a present sensation only insofar as it feels the one feebly, the other vividly.

9 *The feeling of it can be more vivid than the sensation.* I say *usually* because memory is not always a feeble feeling, nor is sensation always a vivid feeling. For whenever the memory is recalling the past forcibly and the sense organ, on the contrary, is receiving only slight impressions, then the feeling of a present sensation is much less vivid than the memory of a sensation which no longer exists.

10 *The statue distinguishes in itself a succession.* Thus, whenever an odoriferous substance is making an impression on the sense organ itself, there is another smell present to the memory, because the impression of another odoriferous substance subsists in the brain, to which the sense organ has already transmitted it. By passing as it were through these two states the statue feels that it is no longer what it was. The knowledge of this change makes it relate the first smell to a different moment from that in which it is experiencing the second, and this makes it perceive a difference between existing in one state and remembering having existed in another.

11 *How it is active and passive.* It is active in regard to one of its states of feeling, and passive in regard to the other. It is active when it remembers a sensation, because it has in itself the cause which recalls it, that is to say memory. It is passive when it experiences a sensation, because the cause which produces it is outside it, that is to say, in the odoriferous substances which act on its sense organ.[1]

12 *It cannot differentiate the two states.* Being unable to imagine the action of external objects upon itself, it cannot differentiate between a cause which is within and a cause which is without. All its modifications are, in regard to itself, as if it owed them only to itself; and whether it experiences a sensation or whether it only recalls one, it never perceives anything which is not or has not been its own state of being. Consequently, it cannot notice any difference between the state in which it is active and that in which it is entirely passive.

13 *Memory becomes a habit.* The more the memory is exercised the more easily it acts. In this way the statue will acquire the habit of recalling without effort the changes

---

[1] There is in us a principle of our actions, which we feel but cannot define. We call it force. We are equally active with regard to what this *force* produces either within us, or outside us. For example, we are active either when we are reflecting or when we are making our body move. By analogy, in all objects which produce some change, we suppose a force which we know even less about than the objects which produce it, and are passive to the impressions which the objects make on us. Thus a being is active or passive, according as the cause of the effect produced is inside it or outside.

it has passed through, and of dividing its attention between what it is and what it has been. For habit is only a facility of repeating what we have already done, and this facility is acquired by going over the acts again.[1]

14 *It compares.* If after having repeatedly smelled rose and pink the statue then smells rose, the passive attention which is caused by the smell is entirely the present smell of rose, and the active attention which is caused by the memory is divided between the recollection which remains of the smells of rose and pink. Now modes of being can only divide the capacity of feeling insofar as they are compared; for comparing is nothing else but giving attention to two ideas at the same time.

15 *It judges.* When there is comparison there is judgment. Our statue cannot be at one and the same time attentive to the smell of rose and pink, without perceiving that the one is not the other, and it cannot be attentive to a rose which it smells, and a rose which it has smelled, without perceiving that the two are the same. A judgment is only the perception of a relation between two ideas which are compared.

16 *These operations turn into habits.* To the extent that comparisons and judgments are repeated, they are made by our statue with increased facility. Thus it contracts with greater force according as it is determined by the vividness of pleasure and pain. But when there has been a series of modifications, the statue, preserving the memory of a great number, will be inclined to retrace preferably those which are able to contribute most to its happiness. It will pass rapidly over the others, or will only stop because it cannot help itself. In order to bring this truth to light we must examine the different degrees of pleasure and pain to which we are susceptible, and the comparisons which we make of them.

22 *Two kinds of pleasures and pains.* Pleasures and pains are of two kinds. The one kind belong more particularly to the body; they are sensible. The other kind are in the memory and in all the faculties of the soul; they are intellectual or spiritual. But it is a difference which the statue is incapable of noticing.

This ignorance will guard it from an error which we have difficulty in avoiding: for these feelings do not differ as much as we imagine. Of a truth, they are all intellectual or spiritual, because, rightly understood, it is only the soul which feels. There is, indeed, a sense in which we can say they are all sensible or corporeal, because the body alone is their occasional cause. It is only according as they are related to the faculties of the body or to those of the soul that we distinguish them into two kinds.

23 *Different degrees in the one and in the other.* Pleasure can diminish or increase by degrees; in diminishing it tends to become extinguished, and it vanishes with the sensation. In increasing, on the contrary, it can lead even to pain, because the impression can become too strong for the organ. Thus there are two limits in pleasure. The weakest is where the sensation commences with least force. It is the first

---

[1]Here and throughout this work I am only speaking of habits which are naturally acquired; in the supernatural order everything is subject to other laws.

step from nothing to feeling. The strongest is where the sensation cannot increase without ceasing to be pleasant. It is the state nearest pain.

The impression of a feeble pleasure appears to be concentrated in the sense organ which transmits it to the soul. But if it attains a certain degree of vividness, it is accompanied by an emotion which is spread over the whole body. This emotion is a fact which is verified by experience.

Pain can equally increase or diminish. In increasing it tends to the total destruction of the animal, but in diminishing it does not, as with pleasure, lead to the privation of all feeling. On the contrary the moment which terminates pain is always one of pleasure.

24 *A state is only indifferent by comparison.* Among these different degrees there is no state of indifference. At the first sensation, however feeble it may be, the statue is necessarily either contented or discontented. When it has felt in succession the sharpest pains and the keenest pleasures, it will judge indifferent, or will cease to regard as agreeable or disagreeable, those feebler sensations which will appear feebler when compared with the strongest.

We can suppose then that it has agreeable and disagreeable modifications in different degrees and that there are modifications which it regards as indifferent.

25 *Origin of need.* Whenever it is ill at ease or less comfortable than it was, it recalls its past sensations and compares them with its present, and it feels the importance of becoming again what it was. From this arises the need, or the knowledge it has of a well-being which it judges necessary for its comfort.

It knows of needs only because it compares the pain which it suffers with the pleasure which it has enjoyed. Remove the remembrance of these pleasures, it will then be ill at ease without suspecting that it has any need, for in order to feel the need for a thing there must be some knowledge of it. Thus in the supposition we are making, the statue knows of no other state than that in which it finds itself. But when it recalls a happier state, its present state makes it immediately feel the need for that happier state. Thus it is that pleasure and pain will always determine the actions of its faculties.

26 *How need determines the operations of the soul.* Its need may be occasioned by a real pain or by a disagreeable sensation, or by a sensation less agreeable than some which have preceded, or finally by a state of apathy, in which it is reduced to one of the modifications it deems indifferent.

If its need is caused by an odour which gives it actual pain, it takes away almost all power to feel, and leaves to memory alone the power to recall that it has not always been so uncomfortable. In its present state it is incapable of comparing the different modes through which it has passed. It is incapable of judging which is the most agreeable. All its interest is in escaping from its present state, in order to enjoy another, whatsoever it be. If it knew a means which could put an end to its sufferings, it would employ all its faculties to make use of it. It is thus that in severe illness we cease to desire pleasures which we had sought before with ardour, and no longer think of anything but the recovery of health. If it is a less agreeable sensation which produces the need, we must distinguish two cases: either the pleasures with which the statue compares this sensation have been vivid, and accompanied by the strongest emotions, or else they have been less vivid and have scarcely affected it.

In the first case, the past happiness is awakened with the more force the more it differs from the present sensation. The emotion which accompanies it is partly reproduced and, absorbing almost all capacity of feeling, does not allow it to notice the agreeable feelings which followed or preceded. The statue, then, not being distracted, is better able to compare its past happiness with its present state; it is better able to judge how it differs from it; and depicting happiness is the most vivid manner, its privation causes a greater need, and the possession of happiness becomes a more necessary good.

In the second case, on the contrary, the past happiness is recalled with less force; other pleasures divide the attention; the advantage which it offers is less felt; it reproduces little or no emotion. The statue is then not so much interested in the return of the pleasure, and it does not apply its faculties to it.

Finally, if the need is caused by one of the sensations which it is accustomed to judge as indifferent, it regards it from the first without shewing either pleasure or pain. But this state, compared with the happy situations in which it had been, soon becomes disagreeable, and the pain which it suffers is then what we call *boredom*. But boredom endures, increases, becomes insupportable, and at last forcibly directs the faculties towards the recovery of the happiness of which it feels the loss.

This state of boredom can be as overpowering as pain. In this case, the statue has no other interest than to escape from it, and it turns indifferently to all modes of being likely to dissipate it. But if the weight of this irksomeness is lightened, then its state will be less unhappy and it will be less eager to escape from it. It will then be able to turn its attention to all the agreeable feelings which it retains in its memory, and the pleasure with which it will recall its most vivid idea will lead in the end to the use of all its faculties.

27 *Need makes memory active.* There are then two principles which determine the degree of the action of its faculties: the one is the lively feeling of a good which is no more, the other is the lack of pleasure in the present sensation, or the actual pain which accompanies it.

When these two principles are united, it makes more effort to recall what it has ceased to be, and it feels less what it is. For its capacity of feeling being necessarily limited, memory can draw its part only at the expense of sensation. If indeed the action of this faculty of memory is strong enough it will displace the whole capacity of feeling and the statue will then no longer notice the impression which is made upon its sense organ, and its vivid memory will seem to be its present sensation.[1]

28 *When the need ceases, the activity ceases.* If its present state is the happiest it has known, then the pleasure is enough to make it enjoy it by preference. There is no further cause which could make its memory work with sufficient force to overcome the sensation to the point of extinguishing the feeling of it. Pleasure, on the contrary, fixes at least the greatest part of attention, or of the capacity of feeling, on the present sensation. If the statue still recalls what it has been, it is because the comparison which it makes between the past and present, enables it the better to relish its happiness.

29 *Difference between memory and imagination.* There are then two effects of memory: one is a sensation which is recalled as vividly as an impression on the sense-organ, the other is a sensation of which only a slight remembrance remains.

We are able therefore to distinguish in the faculty of memory two degrees: the feebler is that in which it scarcely enjoys that which is past, the vivider that in which it enjoys it as if it were present.

We name the faculty *memory*, when it only recalls things as past, we name it *imagination* when it recalls them with so much force that they appear present. Imagination has then its place in our statue as well as memory, and these two faculties differ only as more and less. Memory is the commencement of an imagination which has yet little force; imagination is the same memory enriched with all the liveliness of which it is susceptible.

As we have distinguished two attentions in the statue, one caused by sensation, the other by memory, we can now add a third, caused by imagination. The characteristic of this last is to arrest the impressions of the senses in order to substitute for them a feeling independent of the action of external objects.[2]

30 *This difference is unnoticed by the statue.* When, however, the statue imagines a sensation which is past, and represents it as vividly as if it were present, it does not know that there is an inner cause producing the same effect as the odoriferous body acting on its sense-organ. It cannot, therefore, make the difference we make between imagining a sensation and having one.

---

[1] Our experience proves this. There is probably no one who has not sometimes recalled pleasures which he has enjoyed as vivid as those which he is still enjoying, or at least has recalled them with sufficient vividness to distract attention from his actual state however grievous.

[2] Many facts prove the power of imagination on the senses. A man deeply occupied in thought does not see the thousand objects around him, nor hear the noises which strike his ears. Everyone knows the story of Archimedes (absorbed in his geometrical problems when Syracuse was taken and the Roman soldiers broke in upon him and slew him). According as the imagination is applied with increased force to an object, one may be pricked or burned without feeling pain, and the soul appears to free itself from all the impressions of the senses. In order to understand the possibility of these phenomena it is enough to bear in mind that, our capacity of feeling being limited, we shall be absolutely insensible to the impressions on the senses whenever our imagination is completely engrossed in its object.

31 *Its imagination is more active than ours.* We may even presume that its imagination
is more active than ours. For its capacity of feeling being entirely confined to one
kind of sensation and its faculties being applied uniquely to smell, there is nothing which can distract it. We, on the contrary, divided between a multitude of sensations and ideas which are continually assailing us, and preserving in our imagination only a part of our forces, imagine but feebly. Our senses, always on guard,
keep us constantly warned against the objects we are trying to imagine. On the
other hand a perfectly free course is open to the imagination of our statue. It can
recall without difficulty a sensation it has once enjoyed, and it will then enjoy it as
if its organs were really affected by it. The ease with which we are able to avoid
objects hurtful to us, and secure those we want, brings about a still further weakening of our imagination. But since our statue can only escape a disagreeable feeling by vividly imagining a more pleasurable state, it will exercise its imagination to
procure effects which our imagination cannot procure.[1]

32 *Unique case in which the statue's imagination remains inactive.* Yet there is one circumstance in which the activity of its imagination, and that of its memory also, is
absolutely suspended. This is when a sensation is sufficiently vivid to take complete possession of its capacity of feeling. Then the statue is perfectly passive. For
it pleasure is a kind of intoxication, in which it is hardly aware of enjoyment; and
pain a kind of paroxysm in which it scarcely suffers.

33 *How imagination returns to activity.* But in proportion as the sensation loses some
degrees of vividness the faculties of the soul return, and need becomes again the
determining cause of action.

34 *How it gives a new order to ideas.* Our statue's most pleasing modifications are not
always the last it has received. They may as easily be found at the beginning or in
the middle of the chain of its cognitions as at the end. Imagination, therefore, is
often obliged to pass rapidly over intermediate ideas. It may have to go to the furthest off, change the memory order, and form an entirely new chain.

The connexion of ideas does not then follow the same order in the two
faculties. The more what it holds in the imagination becomes familiar, the less
it will keep what memory has given it. Thus ideas are connected in innumerable different ways, and often the statue will remember less of the order in
which it has experienced its sensations than of the order in which it has imagined them.

35 *Ideas are connected differently only because new comparisons are made.* But all these
chains have been formed only by comparisons of the link which precedes with
that which follows, and by judgments passed on their relations. The link becomes
stronger in proportion as the exercise of the faculties fortifies the habits of
remembering and imagining. By means of it we get the enormous advantage of
recognizing sensations which we have already had.

----

[1]However surprising may be the effects of imagination, there need be no doubt of them if
we reflect on what happens in dreaming. For then we see, hear, and touch bodies which are not
acting upon our senses; and there is every reason to believe that the imagination has this greater
force because we are not distracted by the multitude of ideas and sensations which occupy us in
waking.

36 *By means of this connexion the statue recognizes its past modifications.* In fact if we make our statue sense an odour already familiar to it, what we then have is a state of being which it has compared, on which it has passed judgments, and which it has linked to some of the parts of the chain its memory is in the habit of running over. This is how it comes to judge that the present state in which it is, is similar to one of its past states. But a smell which it has not yet sensed is in a different case, it will be a new smell.

37 *It cannot account for this phenomenon.* It is needless to say that, when the statue recognizes a mode of being, it is not able to give an account of it. The cause which makes one phenomenon like another is so difficult to discern, that it escapes all who have not learnt to observe and analyze what is taking place in themselves.

38 *How ideas are preserved and renewed in memory.* But when the statue is a long time without thinking of a mode of being, what becomes during that time, of the idea it has acquired of it? Where does it come from when afterwards it is recalled in the memory? Is it preserved in the soul or in the body? In neither.

It is not in the soul, since it is sufficient to have a derangement of the brain to take away the power to recall. It is not in the body. Only the physical cause is preserved in the body and for the idea to be preserved there we should have to suppose that the brain had remained absolutely in the state in which it had been left by the sensation which the statue recalls. How can such a supposition agree with the continual movement of the animal spirits? How can we make it agree, especially when we consider the multitude of ideas with which the memory is enriched? The phenomenon can be explained in a much simpler way.

I have a sensation when a movement in one of my sense organs is transmitted to the brain. If the movement begins in the brain and is extended to the sense organ, I believe that I have a sensation which in fact I have not: it is an illusion. But if the movement begins and ends in the brain, then I recall the sensation which I have had.

When an idea is recalled by the statue, it is not, then, because it is preserved either in the body or in the soul: it is because the movement which is the physical and occasional cause of the idea is reproduced in the brain. But this is not the place to hazard conjectures on the mechanism of memory. We preserve the remembrance of our sensations. We recall them to ourselves, after having been a long time without thinking of them. It is sufficient for this that they should have made a vivid impression on us, or that we should have experienced them on many occasions. These facts authorize me to suppose that our statue, being organized like ourselves, is like us, capable of memory.

⚈ 10 ⚈

John Locke, Excerpts from Book II, *An essay concerning human understanding* (1689).*

BOOK II

Chapter I

Of **Ideas** *in general, and their Original.*   § **1.** Every Man being conscious to himself, That he thinks, and that which his Mind is employ'd about whilst thinking, being *the Ideas,* that are there, 'tis past doubt, that Men have in their Minds several *Ideas,* such as are those expressed by the words, *Whiteness, Hardness, Sweetness, Thinking, Motion, Man, Elephant, Army, Drunkenness,* and others: It is in the first place then to be enquired, How he comes by them? I know it is a received Doctrine, That Men have native *Ideas,* and original Characters stamped upon their Minds, in their very first Being. This Opinion I have at large examined already; and, I suppose, what I have said in the foregoing Book, will be much more easily admitted, when I have shewn, whence the Understanding may get all the *Ideas* it has, and by what ways and degrees they may come into the Mind; for which I shall appeal to every one's own Observation and Experience.

§ **2.** Let us then suppose the Mind to be, as we say, white Paper, void of all Characters, without any *Ideas*; How comes it to be furnished? Whence comes it by that vast store, which the busy and boundless Fancy of Man has painted on it, with an almost endless variety? Whence has it all the materials of Reason and Knowledge? To this I answer, in one word, From *Experience:* In that, all our Knowledge is founded; and from that it ultimately derives it self.

*(c) Oxford University Press 1975. Reprinted from *An essay concerning human understanding* by John Locke edited by Peter H. Nidditch (1975) by permission of Oxford University Press.

§ 1. Idea *is the Object of Thinking.*

§ 2. *All* Ideas *come from Sensation or Reflection.*

Our Observation employ'd either about *external, sensible Objects; or about the internal Operations of our Minds, perceived and reflected on by our selves, is that, which supplies our Understandings with all the materials of thinking.* These two are the Fountains of Knowledge, from whence all the *Ideas* we have, or can naturally have, do spring.

§ **3.** First, *Our Senses,* conversant about particular sensible *Objects, do convey into the Mind,* several distinct *Perceptions* of things, according to those various ways, wherein those Objects do affect them: And thus we come by those *Ideas,* we have of *Yellow, White, Heat, Cold, Soft, Hard, Bitter, Sweet,* and all those which we call sensible qualities, which when I say the senses convey into the mind, I mean, they from external Objects convey into the mind what produces there those *Perceptions.* This great Source, of most of the *Ideas* we have, depending wholly upon our Senses, and derived by them to the Understanding, I call *SENSATION.*

§ **4.** Secondly, The other Fountain, from which Experience furnisheth the Understanding with *Ideas,* is the *Perception of the Operations of our own Minds* within us, as it is employ'd about the *Ideas* it has got; which Operations, when the Soul comes to reflect on, and consider, do furnish the Understanding with another set of *Ideas,* which could not be had from things without: and such are, *Perception, Thinking, Doubting, Believing, Reasoning, Knowing, Willing,* and all the different actings of our own Minds; which we being conscious of, and observing in our selves, do from these receive into our Understandings, as distinct *Ideas,* as we do from Bodies affecting our Senses. This Source of *Ideas,* every Man has wholly in himself: And though it be not Sense, as having nothing to do with external Objects; yet it is very like it, and might properly enough be call'd internal Sense. But as I call the other *Sensation,* so I call this *REFLECTION,* the *Ideas* it affords being such only, as the Mind gets by reflecting on its own Operations within it self. By *REFLECTION* then, in the following part of this Discourse, I would be understood to mean, that notice which the Mind takes of its own Operations, and the manner of them, by reason whereof, there come to be *Ideas* of these Operations in the Understanding. These two, I say, *viz.* External, Material things, as the Objects of *SENSATION;* and the Operations of our own Minds within, as the Objects of *REFLECTION,* are, to me, the only Originals, from whence all our *Ideas* take their beginnings. The term *Operations* here, I use in a large sence, as comprehending not barely the Actions of the Mind about its *Ideas,* but some sort of Passions arising sometimes from them, such as is the satisfaction or uneasiness arising from any thought.

§ **5.** The Understanding seems to me, not to have the least glimmering of any *Ideas,* which it doth not receive from one of these two. *External Objects furnish the Mind with the* Ideas *of sensible qualities,* which are all those different

---

§ 3. *The Objects of Sensation one Source of* Ideas.

§ 4. *The Operations of our Minds, the other Source of them.*

§ 5. *All our* Ideas *are of the one or the other of these.*

perceptions they produce in us: And the *Mind furnishes the Understanding with* Ideas *of its own Operations.*

These, when we have taken a full survey of them, and their several Modes, Combinations, and Relations, we shall find to contain all our whole stock of *Ideas*; and that we have nothing in our Minds, which did not come in, one of these two ways. Let any one examine his own Thoughts, and throughly search into his Understanding, and then let him tell me, Whether all the original *Ideas* he has there, are any other than of the Objects of his *Senses*; or of the Operations of his Mind, considered as Objects of his *Reflection*: and how great a mass of Knowledge soever he imagines to be lodged there, he will, upon taking a strict view, see, that he has *not any* Idea *in his Mind, but what one of these two have imprinted*; though, perhaps, with infinite variety compounded and enlarged by the Understanding, as we shall see hereafter.

§ 6. He that attentively considers the state of a *Child*, at his first coming into the World, will have little reason to think him stored with plenty of *Ideas*, that are to be the matter of his future Knowledge. 'Tis by degrees he comes to be furnished with them: And though the *Ideas* of obvious and familiar qualities, imprint themselves, before the Memory begins to keep a Register of Time and Order, yet 'tis often so late, before some unusual qualities come in the way, that there are few Men that cannot recollect the beginning of their acquaintance with them: And if it were worth while, no doubt a Child might be so ordered, as to have but a very few, even of the ordinary *Ideas*, till he were grown up to a Man. But all that are born into the World being surrounded with Bodies, that perpetually and diversly affect them, variety of *Ideas*, whether care be taken about it or no, are imprinted on the Minds of Children. *Light*, and *Colours*, are busie at hand every where, when the Eye is but open; *Sounds*, and some *tangible Qualities* fail not to solicite their proper Senses, and force an entrance to the Mind; but yet, I think, it will be granted easily, That if a Child were kept in a place, where he never saw any other but Black and White, till he were a Man, he would have no more *Ideas* of Scarlet or Green, than he that from his Childhood never tasted an Oyster, or a Pine-Apple, has of those particular Relishes.

§ 7. Men then come to be furnished with fewer or more simple *Ideas* from without, according as the *Objects*, they converse with, afford greater or less variety; and from the Operation of their Minds within, according as they more or less *reflect* on them. For, though he that contemplates the Operations of his Mind, cannot but have plain and clear *Ideas* of them; yet unless he turn his Thoughts that way, and considers them *attentively*, he will no more have clear and distinct *Ideas* of all the *Operations of his Mind*, and all that may be observed therein, than he will have all the particular *Ideas* of any Landscape, or of the Parts and Motions of a Clock, who will not turn his Eyes to it, and

---

§ 6. *Observable in Children.*

§ 7. *Men are differently furnished with these, according to the different Objects they converse with.*

with attention heed all the Parts of it. The Picture, or Clock may be so placed, that they may come in his way every day; but yet he will have but a confused *Idea* of all the Parts they are made up of, till he *applies himself with attention*, to consider them each in particular.

§ **8.** And hence we see the Reason, why 'tis pretty late, before most Children get *Ideas* of the Operations of their own Minds; and some have not any very clear, or perfect *Ideas* of the greatest part of them all their Lives. Because, though they pass there continually; yet like floating Visions, they make not deep Impressions enough, to leave in the Mind clear distinct lasting *Ideas*, till the Understanding turns inwards upon it self, *reflects* on its own *Operations*, and makes them the Object of its own Contemplation. Children, when they come first into it, are surrounded with a world of new things, which, by a constant solicitation of their senses, draw the mind constantly to them, forward to take notice of new, and apt to be delighted with the variety of changing Objects. Thus the first Years are usually imploy'd and diverted in looking abroad. Men's Business in them is to acquaint themselves with what is to be found without; and so growing up in a constant attention to outward Sensations, seldom make any considerable Reflection on what passes within them, till they come to be of riper Years; and some scarce ever at all.

§ **9.** To ask, *at what time a Man has first any* Ideas, is to ask, when he begins to perceive; having *Ideas*, and Perception being the same thing. I know it is an Opinion, that the Soul always thinks, and that it has the actual Perception of *Ideas* in it self constantly, as long as it exists; and that actual thinking is as inseparable from the Soul, as actual Extension is from the Body; which if true, to enquire after the beginning of a Man's *Ideas*, is the same, as to enquire after the beginning of his Soul. For by this Account, Soul and its *Ideas*, as Body and its Extension, will begin to exist both at the same time.

§ **10.** But whether the Soul be supposed to exist antecedent to, or coeval with, or some time after the first Rudiments of Organisation, or the beginnings of Life in the Body, I leave to be disputed by those, who have better thought of that matter. I confess my self, to have one of those dull Souls, that doth not perceive it self always to contemplate *Ideas*, nor can conceive it any more necessary for the *Soul always to think*, than for the Body always to move; the perception of *Ideas* being (as I conceive) to the Soul, what motion is to the Body, not its Essence, but one of its Operations: And therefore, though thinking be supposed never so much the proper Action of the Soul; yet it is not necessary, to suppose, that it should be always thinking, always in Action. That, perhaps, is the Privilege of the infinite Author and Preserver of things, *who never slumbers nor sleeps*; but is not competent to any finite Being, at least not to the Soul of Man. We know certainly by Experience, that we sometimes think, and thence draw this infallible Consequence, That there is something in us,

§ 8. Ideas *of Reflexion later, because they need Attention.*

§ 9. *The Soul begins to have* Ideas, *when it begins to perceive.*

§ 10. *The Soul thinks not always; for this wants Proofs.*

that has a Power to think: But whether that Substance perpetually thinks, or no, we can be no farther assured, than Experience informs us. For to say, that actual thinking is essential to the Soul, and inseparable from it, is to beg, what is in Question, and not to prove it by Reason; which is necessary to be done, if it be not a self-evident Proposition. But whether this, *That the Soul always thinks*, be a self-evident Proposition, that every Body assents to at first hearing, I appeal to Mankind. 'Tis doubted whether I thought all last night, or no; the Question being about a matter of fact, 'tis begging it, to bring, as a proof for it, an Hypothesis, which is the very thing in dispute: by which way one may prove any thing, and 'tis but supposing that all watches, whilst the balance beats, think, and 'tis sufficiently proved, and past doubt, that my watch thought all last night. But he, that would not deceive himself, ought to build his Hypothesis on matter of fact, and make it out by sensible experience, and not presume on matter of fact, because of his Hypothesis, that is, because he supposes it to be so: which way of proving, amounts to this, That I must necessarily think all last night, because another supposes I always think, though I my self cannot perceive, that I always do so.

But Men in love with their Opinions, may not only suppose what is in question, but alledge wrong matter of fact. How else could any one make it an *inference* of mine, *that a thing is not, because we are not sensible of it in our sleep.* I do not say there is no Soul in a Man, because he is not sensible of it in his sleep; But I do say, he cannot think at any time waking or sleeping, without being sensible of it. Our being sensible of it is not necessary to any thing, but to our thoughts; and to them it is; and to them it will always be necessary, till we can think without being conscious of it.

§ 11. I grant that the Soul in a waking Man is never without thought, because it is the condition of being awake: But whether sleeping without dreaming be not an Affection of the whole Man, Mind as well as Body, may be worth a waking Man's Consideration; it being hard to conceive, that any thing should think, and not be conscious of it. If the *Soul* doth *think in a sleeping Man*, without being conscious of it, I ask, whether, during such thinking, it has any Pleasure or Pain, or be capable of Happiness or Misery? I am sure the Man is not, no more than the Bed or Earth he lies on. For to be happy or miserable without being conscious of it, seems to me utterly inconsistent and impossible. Or if it be possible, that the Soul can, whilst the Body is sleeping, have its Thinking, Enjoyments, and Concerns, its Pleasure or Pain apart, which the Man is not conscious of, nor partakes in: It is certain, that *Socrates* asleep, and *Socrates* awake, is not the same Person; but his Soul when he sleeps, and *Socrates* the Man consisting of Body and Soul when he is waking, are two Persons: Since waking *Socrates*, has no Knowledge of, or Concernment for that Happiness, or Misery of his Soul, which it enjoys alone by it self whilst he sleeps, without perceiving any thing of it; no more than he has for the Happiness, or Misery of a Man in the *Indies*, whom he knows not. For if we take wholly away all Consciousness of our Actions and Sensations, especially

---

§ 11. *It is not always conscious of it.*

of Pleasure and Pain, and the concernment that accompanies it, it will be hard to know wherein to place personal Identity.

§ **12.** The Soul, during sound Sleep, thinks, say these Men. *Whilst it thinks* and perceives, it is capable certainly of those of Delight or Trouble, as well as any other Perceptions; and *it must necessarily be conscious of its own Perceptions*. But it has all this apart: The sleeping Man, 'tis plain, is conscious of nothing of all this. Let us suppose then the Soul of *Castor*, whilst he is sleeping, retired from his Body, which is no impossible Supposition for the Men I have here to do with, who so liberally allow Life, without a thinking Soul to all other Animals. These Men cannot then judge it impossible, or a contradiction, That the Body should live without the Soul; nor that the Soul should subsist and think, or have Perception, even Perception of Happiness or Misery, without the Body. Let us then, as I say, suppose the Soul of *Castor* separated, during his Sleep, from his Body, to think apart. Let us suppose too, that it chuses for its Scene of Thinking, the Body of another Man, *v.g. Pollux*, who is sleeping without a Soul: For if *Castor's* Soul can think whilst *Castor* is asleep, what *Castor* is never conscious of, 'tis no matter what Place it chuses to think in. We have here then the Bodies of two Men with only one Soul between them, which we will suppose to sleep and wake by turns; and the Soul still thinking in the waking Man, whereof the sleeping Man is never conscious, has never the least Perception. I ask then, Whether *Castor* and *Pollux*, thus, with only one Soul between them, which thinks and perceives in one, what the other is never conscious of, nor is concerned for, are not two as distinct Persons, as *Castor* and *Hercules*; or, as *Socrates* and *Plato* were? And whether one of them might not be very happy, and the other very miserable? Just by the same Reason, they make the Soul and the Man two Persons, who make the Soul think apart, what the Man is not conscious of. For, I suppose, no body will make Identity of Persons, to consist in the Soul's being united to the very same numerical Particles of matter: For if that be necessary to Identity, 'twill be impossible, in that constant flux of the Particles of our Bodies, that any Man should be the same Person, two days, or two moments together.

§ **13.** Thus, methinks, every drowsy Nod shakes their Doctrine, who teach, That the Soul is always thinking. Those, at least, who do at any time *sleep without dreaming*, can never be convinced, That their Thoughts are sometimes for four hours busy without their knowing of it; and if they are taken in the very act, waked in the middle of that sleeping contemplation, can give no manner of account of it.

§ **14.** 'Twill perhaps be said, That the *Soul thinks*, even *in* the soundest *Sleep, but the Memory retains it not*. That the Soul in a sleeping Man should be this moment busy a thinking, and the next moment in a waking Man, not remember, nor be able to recollect one jot of all those Thoughts, is very hard to be conceived, and would need some better Proof than bare Assertion, to

§ 12. *If a sleeping Man thinks without knowing it, the sleeping and waking Man are two Persons.*

§ 13. *Impossible to convince those that sleep without dreaming, that they think.*

§ 14. *That Men dream without remembering it, in vain urged.*

make it be believed. For who can without any more ado, but being barely told so, imagine, That the greatest part of Men, do, during all their Lives, for several hours every day, think of something, which if they were asked, even in the middle of these Thoughts, they could remember nothing at all of? Most Men, I think, pass a great part of their Sleep without dreaming. I once knew a Man, that was bred a Scholar, and had no bad Memory, who told me, he had never dream'd in his Life, till he had that Fever, he was then newly recovered of, which was about the Five or Six and Twentieth Year of his Age. I suppose the World affords more such Instances: At least every one's Acquaintance will furnish him with Examples enough of such, as pass most of their Nights without dreaming.

§ **15**. *To think often, and never to retain it so much as one moment, is a very useless sort of thinking:* and the Soul in such a state of thinking, does very little, if at all, excel that of a Looking-glass, which constantly receives variety of Images, or *Ideas,* but retains none; they disappear and vanish, and there remain no footsteps of them; the Looking-glass is never the better for such *Ideas,* nor the Soul for such Thoughts. Perhaps it will be said, that in a waking Man, the materials of the Body are employ'd, and made use of, in thinking; and that the memory of Thoughts, is retained by the impressions that are made on the Brain, and the traces there left after such thinking; but that in the *thinking of the Soul,* which is not perceived *in a sleeping Man,* there the Soul thinks apart, and *making no use* of the Organs of *the Body, leaves no impressions on it, and consequently no memory* of such Thoughts. Not to mention again the absurdity of two distinct Persons, which follows from this Supposition, I answer farther, That whatever *Ideas* the Mind can receive, and contemplate without the help of the Body, it is reasonable to conclude, it can retain without the help of the Body too, or else the Soul, or any separate Spirit, will have but little advantage by thinking. If it has no memory of its own Thoughts; if it cannot lay them up for its use, and be able to recal them upon occasion; if it cannot reflect upon what is past, and make use of its former Experiences, Reasonings, and Contemplations, to what purpose does it think? They, who make the Soul a thinking Thing at this rate, will not make it a much more noble Being, than those do, whom they condemn, for allowing it to be nothing but the subtilest parts of Matter. Characters drawn on Dust, that the first breath of wind effaces; or Impressions made on a heap of Atoms, or animal Spirits, are altogether as useful, and render the Subject as noble, as the Thoughts of a Soul that perish in thinking; that once out of sight, are gone for ever, and leave no memory of themselves behind them. Nature never makes excellent things, for mean or no uses: and it is hardly to be conceived, that our infinitely wise Creator, should make so admirable a Faculty, as the power of Thinking, that Faculty which comes nearest the Excellency of his own incomprehensible Being, to be so idlely and uselesly employ'd, at least 1/4 part of its time here, as to think constantly, without remembring any of

---

§ 15. *Upon this Hypothesis, the Thoughts of a sleeping Man ought to be most rational.*

those Thoughts, without doing any good to it self or others, or being any way useful to any other part of the Creation. If we will examine it, we shall not find, I suppose, the motion of dull and sensless matter, any where in the Universe, made so little use of, and so wholly thrown away.

§ **16**. 'Tis true, we have sometimes instances of Perception, whilst we are *asleep*, and retain the memory of those *Thoughts*: but how *extravagant* and incoherent for the most part they are; how little conformable to the Perfection and Order of a rational Being, those who are acquainted with Dreams, need not be told. This I would willingly be satisfied in, Whether the Soul, when it thinks thus apart, and as it were separate from the Body, acts less rationally than when conjointly with it, or no: If its separate Thoughts be less rational, then these Men must say, That the Soul owes the perfection of rational thinking to the Body: If it does not, 'tis a wonder that our Dreams should be, for the most part, so frivolous and irrational; and that the Soul should retain none of its more rational Soliloquies and Meditations.

§ **17**. Those who so confidently tell us, That the Soul always actually thinks, I would they would also tell us, what those *Ideas* are, that are in the Soul of a Child, before, or just at the union with the Body, before it hath received any by *Sensation*. The *Dreams* of sleeping Men, *are*, as I take it, all *made up of the waking Man's* Ideas, though, for the most part, oddly put together. 'Tis strange, if the Soul has *Ideas* of its own, that it derived not from *Sensation* or *Reflection*, (as it must have, if its thought before it received any impressions from the Body) that it should never, in its private thinking, (so private, that the Man himself perceives it not) retain any of them, the very moment it wakes out of them, and then make the Man glad with new discoveries. Who can find it reasonable, that the Soul should, in its retirement, during sleep, have so many hours thoughts, and yet never light on any of those *Ideas* it borrowed not from *Sensation* or *Reflection*, or at least preserve the memory of none, but such, which being occasioned from the Body, must needs be less natural to a Spirit? 'Tis strange, the Soul should never once in a Man's whole life, recal over any of its pure, native Thoughts, and those *Ideas* it had before it borrowed any thing from the Body; never bring into the waking Man's view, any other *Ideas*, but what have a tangue of the Cask, and manifestly derive their Original from that union. If it always thinks, and so had *Ideas* before it was united, or before it received any from the Body, 'tis not to be supposed, but that during sleep, it recollects its native *Ideas*, and during that retirement from communicating with the Body, whilst it thinks by it self, the *Ideas*, it is busied about, should be, sometimes at least, those more natural and congenial ones which it had in it self, underived from the Body or its own Operations about them: which since the waking Man never remembers, we must from this Hypothesis conclude, either that the Soul remembers some-

---

§ 16. *On this Hypothesis the Soul must have* Ideas *not derived from Sensation or Reflexion, of which there is no appearance.*

§17. *If I think when I know it not, no body else can know it.*

thing that the Man does not; or else that Memory belongs only to such *Ideas*, as are derived from the Body, or the Minds Operations about them.

§ **18.** I would be glad also to learn from these Men, who so confidently pronounce, that the humane Soul, or which is all one, that a Man always thinks, how they come to know it; nay, *how they come to know, that they themselves think, when they themselves do not perceive it*. This, I am afraid, is to be sure, without proofs; and to know, without perceiving: 'Tis, I suspect, a confused Notion, taken up to serve an Hypothesis; and none of those clear Truths, that either their own Evidence forces us to admit, or common Experience makes it impudence to deny. For the most that can be said of it, is, That 'tis possible the Soul may always think, but not always retain it in memory: And, I say, it is as possible, that the Soul may not always think; and much more probable, that it should sometimes not think, than that it should often think, and that a long while together, and not be conscious to it self the next moment after, that it had thought.

§ **19.** To suppose the Soul to think, and the Man not to perceive it, is, as has been said, to make two Persons in one Man: And if one considers well these Men's way of speaking, one should be led into a suspicion, that they do so. For they who tell us, that the Soul always thinks, do never, that I remember, say, That a Man always thinks. Can the Soul think, and not the Man? Or a Man think, and not be conscious of it? This, perhaps, would be suspected of *Fargon* in others. If they say, The Man thinks always, but is not always conscious of it; they may as well say, His Body is extended, without having parts. For 'tis altogether as intelligible to say, that a body is extended without parts, as that any thing *thinks without being conscious of it*, or perceiving, that it does so. They who talk thus, may, with as much reason, if it be necessary to their Hypothesis, say, That a Man is always hungry, but that he does not always feel it: Whereas hunger consists in that very sensation, as thinking consists in being conscious that one thinks. If they say, That a Man is always conscious to himself of thinking; I ask, How they know it? Consciousness is the perception of what passes in a Man's own mind. Can another Man perceive, that I am conscious of any thing, when I perceive it not my self? No Man's Knowledge here, can go beyond his Experience. Wake a Man out of a sound sleep, and ask him, What he was that moment thinking on. If he himself be conscious of nothing he then thought on, he must be a notable Diviner of Thoughts, that can assure him, that he was thinking: May he not with more reason assure him, he was not asleep? This is something beyond Philosophy; and it cannot be less than Revelation, that discovers to another, Thoughts in my mind, when I can find none there my self: And they must needs have a penetrating sight, who can certainly see, that I think, when I cannot perceive it my self, and when I

§ 18. *How knows any one that the Soul always thinks? For if it be not a self-evident Proposition, it needs proof.*

§ 19. *That a Man should be busie in thinking, and yet not retain it the next moment, very improbable.*

declare, that I do not; and yet can see, that Dogs or Elephants do not think, when they give all the demonstration of it imaginable, except only telling us, that they do so. This some may suspect to be a step beyond the *Rosecrucians*; it seeming easier to make ones self invisible to others, than to make another's thoughts visible to me, which are not visible to himself. But 'tis but defining the Soul to be a substance, that always thinks, and the business is done. If such a definition be of any Authority, I know not what it can serve for, but to make many Men suspect, That they have no Souls at all, since they find a good part of their Lives pass away without thinking. For no Definitions, that I know, no Suppositions of any Sect, are of force enough to destroy constant Experience; and, perhaps, 'tis the affectation of knowing beyond what we perceive, that makes so much useless dispute, and noise, in the World.

§ **20.** I see no Reason therefore to believe, that the *Soul thinks before the Senses have furnish'd it with Ideas* to think on; and as those are increased, and retained; so it comes, by Exercise, to improve its Faculty of thinking in the several parts of it, as well as afterwards, by compounding those *Ideas*, and reflecting on its own Operations, it increases its Stock as well as Facility, in remembering, imagining, reasoning, and other modes of thinking.

§ **21.** He that will suffer himself, to be informed by Observation and Experience, and not make his own Hypothesis the Rule of Nature, will find few Signs of a Soul accustomed to much thinking in a new born Child, and much fewer of any Reasoning at all. And yet it is hard to imagine, that the rational Soul should think so much, and not reason at all. And he that will consider, that Infants, newly come into the World, spend the greatest part of their time in Sleep, and are seldom awake, but when either Hunger calls for the Teat, or some Pain, (the most importunate of all Sensations) or some other violent Impression on the Body, forces the mind to perceive, and attend to it. He, I say, who considers this, will, perhaps, find Reason to imagine, That a *Fetus in the Mother's Womb, differs not much from the State of a Vegetable*; but passes the greatest part of its time without Perception or Thought, doing very little, but sleep in a Place, where it needs not seek for Food, and is surrounded with Liquor, always equally soft, and near of the same Temper; where the Eyes have no Light, and the Ears, so shut up, are not very susceptible of Sounds; and where there is little or no variety, or change of Objects, to move the Senses.

§ **22.** Follow a *Child* from its Birth, and observe the alterations that time makes, and you shall find, as the Mind by the Senses comes more and more to be furnished with *Ideas*, it comes to be more and more awake; thinks more, the more it has matter to think on. After some time, it begins to know the Objects, which being most familiar with it, have made lasting Impressions. Thus it comes, by degrees, to know the Persons it daily converses with, and distinguish them from Strangers; which are Instances and Effects of its coming to retain and distinguish the *Ideas* the Senses convey to it: And so we may

§§ 20–3. *No* Ideas *but from Sensation or Reflection, evident, if we observe Children.*

observe, how the Mind, *by degrees*, improves in these, and *advances* to the Exercise of those other Faculties of *Enlarging, Compounding*, and *Abstracting* its *Ideas*, and of reasoning about them, and reflecting upon all these, of which, I shall have occasion to speak more hereafter.

§ **23**. If it shall be demanded then, *When a Man begins to have any Ideas?* I think, the true Answer is, When he first has any *Sensation*. For since there appear not to be any *Ideas* in the Mind, before the Senses have conveyed any in, I conceive that *Ideas* in the Understanding, are coeval with *Sensation*; which is such an Impression or Motion, made in some part of the Body, as produces some Perception in the Understanding. 'Tis about these Impressions made on our Senses by outward Objects, that the Mind seems first to employ it self in such Operations as we call *Perception, Remembring, Consideration, Reasoning*, etc.

§ **24**. In time, the Mind comes to reflect on its own *Operations*, about the *Ideas* got by *Sensation*, and thereby stores it self with a new set of *Ideas*, which I call *Ideas* of *Reflection*. These are the *Impressions* that are made on our *Senses* by outward Objects, that are extrinsical to the Mind; and *its own Operations*, proceeding from Powers intrinsical and proper to it self, which when reflected on by it self, become also Objects of its contemplation, are, as I have said, *the Original of all Knowledge*. Thus the first Capacity of Humane Intellect, is, That the mind is fitted to receive the Impressions made on it; either, through the *Senses*, by outward Objects; or by its own Operations, when it *reflects* on them. This is the first step a Man makes towards the Discovery of any thing, and the Groundwork, whereon to build all those Notions, which ever he shall have naturally in this World. All those sublime Thoughts, which towre above the Clouds, and reach as high as Heaven it self, take their Rise and Footing here: In all that great Extent wherein the mind wanders, in those remote Speculations, it may seem to be elevated with, it stirs not one jot beyond those *Ideas*, which *Sense* or *Reflection*, have offered for its Contemplation.

§ **25**. In this Part, the *Understanding* is merely *passive*; and whether or no, it will have these Beginnings, and as it were materials of Knowledge, is not in its own Power. For the Objects of our Senses, do, many of them, obtrude their particular *Ideas* upon our minds, whether we will or no: And the Operations of our minds, will not let us be without, at least some obscure Notions of them. No Man, can be wholly ignorant of what he does, when he thinks. These *simple Ideas*, when offered to the mind, *the Understanding can* no more refuse to have, nor alter, when they are imprinted, nor blot them out, and make new ones in it self, than a mirror can refuse, alter, or obliterate the Images or *Ideas*, which, the Objects set before it, do therein produce. As the Bodies that surround us, do diversly affect our Organs, the mind is forced to receive the Impressions; and cannot avoid the Perception of those *Ideas* that are annexed to them.

§ 24. *The original of all our Knowledge.*

§ 25. *In the reception of simple* Ideas, *the Understanding is for the most part passive.*

11

George Berkeley, Excerpts from *An essay towards a new theory of vision* (1709).*

AN ESSAY TOWARDS A NEW THEORY OF VISION

1. My design is to show the manner wherein we perceive by sight the distance, magnitude, and situation of objects.[7] Also to consider the difference there is betwixt the ideas of sight and touch, and whether there be any idea common to both senses.[8]

2. It is, I think, agreed by all that distance, of itself and immediately, cannot be seen.[9] For, distance being a line directed endwise to the eye, it projects only one point in the fund of the eye, which point remains invariably the same, whether the distance be longer or shorter.[10]

3. I find it also acknowledged that the estimate we make of the distance of objects considerably remote is rather an act of judgment grounded on experience than

*Berkeley, G. (1709, 1963). Excerpts from *An essay towards a new theory of vision*. In C.M. Turbayne (ed.) *Works on Vision, George Berkeley*, 19–27. Reprinted by permission of the Editor and Greenwood Press, Inc.

[7][This "analysis" (*see Visual Language*, sec. 38) occupies secs. 2-120.]

[8][Both senses—I: both senses. In treating of all which, it seems to me, the writers of optics have proceeded on wrong principles.

Secs. 121–46. Berkeley reaches the conclusion of his analysis in secs. 147–48 and then draws a corollary in secs. 149–59.]

[9][How we perceive by sight the distance of objects is analyzed in secs. 2–51. Cf. *Alciphron*, Dial. IV, secs. 8–9; *Visual Language*, secs. 62–68; *Three Dialogues*, I.]

[10][The view that "distance, of itself and immediately, cannot be seen" is considered by some critics to be a central contribution of Berkeley, the premise of the conclusions of the theory of vision, and the argument for it—Berkeley's only one—invalid. See, e.g., Samuel Bailey's *Review of Berkeley's Theory of Vision* (London, 1842), pp. 38–43; Thomas K. Abbott's *Sight and Touch* (London, 1864), pp. 9–12; and David M. Armstrong's *Berkeley's Theory of Vision* (Melbourne, 1961), pp. xiii, 9–15. Mill defends it in his *Dissertations and Discussions* (London, 1859), II, 172–74. The view, however, is not Berkeley's own although he does accept this much of the received theory, summarized in secs. 2–7, most of it expressed in Molyneux's *New Dioptrics* (London, 1692), p. 113,

of sense. For example, when I perceive a great number of intermediate objects, such as houses, fields, rivers, and the like, which I have experienced to take up a considerable space, I thence form a judgment or conclusion that the object I see beyond them is at a great distance. Again, when an object appears faint and small which at a near distance I have experienced to make a vigorous and large appearance, I instantly conclude it to be far off. And this, it is evident, is the result of experience without which, from the faintness and littleness, I should not have inferred anything concerning the distance of objects.

4. But, when an object is placed at so near a distance as that the interval between the eyes bears any sensible proportion to it, the opinion of speculative men is[11] that the two optic axes (the fancy that we see only with one eye at once being exploded), concurring at the object, do there make an angle,[12] by means of which, according as it is greater or lesser, the object is perceived to be nearer or farther off.[13]

5. Betwixt which and the foregoing manner of estimating distance there is this remarkable difference: that whereas there was no apparent necessary connection between small distance and a large and strong appearance, or between great distance and a little and faint appearance, there appears a very necessary connection between an obtuse angle and near distance, and an acute angle and farther distance. It does not in the least depend upon experience, but may be evidently known by anyone before he had experienced it, that the nearer the concurrence of the optic axes, the greater the angle, and the remoter their concurrence is, the lesser will be the angle comprehended by them.

6. There is another way, mentioned by optic writers, whereby they will have us judge of those distances in respect of which the breadth of the pupil has any sensible bigness. And that is the greater or lesser divergency of the rays which, issuing from the visible point, do fall on the pupil—that point being judged nearest which is seen by most diverging rays, and that remoter which is seen by less diverging rays, and so on; the apparent distance still increasing, as the divergency of the rays decreases, till at length it becomes infinite, when the rays that fall on the pupil are to sense parallel. And after this manner it is said we perceive distance when we look only with one eye.[14]

e.g., "Distance of itself is not to be perceived. For it is a line (or a length) presented to our eye with its end toward us, which must therefore be only a point, and that is invisible." Berkeley and the optical theorists deny not that we can tell by sight the distance of objects but that we sense it (sec. 11). Berkeley's contribution here is his account of the manner in which we tell the distance of near objects by sight. The view, accepted both by Berkeley and his opponents, that distance is not immediately seen is a conclusion, not a premise, of his theory of vision.]

11[The opinion of speculative men is—I: it is the received opinion—II: it is the opinion of some.]

12[I.e., convergence. Cf. Descartes' *Dioptrics* (1637), Discourse VI, sec. 13, translated in note 3 to Appendix of *Essay*, p. 99. Others include Johannes Kepler (*Supplement to Witelo* [Frankfurt, 1604], III, 8) and Malebranche (*The Search*, Bk. I, chap. ix, sec. 3).]

13See what Descartes and others have written on this subject. [I and II omit this footnote.]

14[I.e., accommodation. Cf. Descartes' *Dioptrics*, Bk. VI, and Kepler's *Supplement*, III, ix: "In vision with one eye we are able to use the distance-measuring triangle (*triangulum distantiae mensorium*) which has its vertex in the point of the object and its base in the width of the pupil."]

7. In this case also it is plain we are not beholden to experience, it being a certain necessary truth that the nearer the direct rays falling on the eye approach to a parallelism, the farther off is the point of their intersection, or the visible point from whence they flow.

8. Now though the accounts here given of perceiving *near* distance by sight are received for true,[15] and accordingly made use of[16] in determining the apparent places of objects, they do nevertheless seem very unsatisfactory, and that for these following reasons:

9. It is evident that, when the mind perceives any idea not immediately and of itself, it must be by the means of some other idea. Thus, for instance, the passions which are in the mind of another are of themselves to me invisible. I may nevertheless perceive them by sight; though not immediately, yet by means of the colors they produce in the countenance. We often see shame or fear in the looks of a man by perceiving the changes of his countenance to red or pale.

10. Moreover, it is evident that no idea which is not itself perceived can be the means of perceiving any other idea.[17] If I do not perceive the redness or paleness of a man's face themselves, it is impossible I should perceive by them the passions which are in his mind.

11. Now, from sec. 2 it is plain that distance is in its own nature imperceptible, and yet it is perceived by sight.[18] It remains, therefore, that it be brought into view by means of some other idea that is itself immediately perceived in the act of vision.

12. But those lines and angles by means whereof some men[19] pretend to explain the perception of distance are themselves not at all perceived; nor are they in truth ever thought of by those unskillful in optics. I appeal to anyone's experience whether, upon sight of an object, he computes its distance by the bigness of the angle made by the meeting of the two optic axes? Or whether he ever thinks of the greater or lesser divergency of the rays which arrive from any point to his pupil?[20] Everyone is himself the best judge of what he perceives and what not. In vain shall any man[21] tell me that I perceive certain lines and angles which introduce into my mind the various ideas of distance so long as I myself am conscious of no such thing.

[15][Received for true—II: received for true by some.]

[16][8. Now though the accounts . . . made use of—I: 8. I have here set down the common, current accounts that are given of our perceiving near distances by sight, which though they are unquestionably received for true by mathematicians, and accordingly made use of by them.]

[17][The first implicit use of the language model which prescribes that signs are noticeable, contrary to the received theory in which the means need not be noticeable. *Cf. Alciphron*, Dial. IV, sec. 8, and Descartes' *Dioptrics*, Bk. VI.]

[18][Note here the systematic ambiguity of "to perceive" used throughout meaning (I) "to sense" or (2) "to perceive" in the etymological sense, viz., "to take (something) through (something else)."]

[19][Some men—I: mathematicians.]

[20][His pupil?—I: his pupil? Nay, whether it be not perfectly impossible for him to perceive by sense the various angles wherewith the rays according to their greater or less divergence do fall on his eye.]

[21][Any man—I: all the mathematicians in the world.]

13. Since, therefore, those angles and lines are not themselves perceived by sight, it follows, from sec. 10, that the mind does not by them judge of the distance of objects.

14. The truth of this assertion will be yet further evident to anyone that considers those lines and angles have no real existence in nature, being only a hypothesis[22] framed by the mathematicians, and by them introduced into optics that they might treat of that science in a geometrical way.

15. The last reason I shall give for rejecting that doctrine is that though we should grant the real existence of those optic angles, etc., and that it was possible for the mind to perceive them, yet these principles would not be found sufficient to explain the phenomena of distance, as shall be shown hereafter.

16. Now, it being already shown that distance is suggested[23] to the mind by the mediation of some other idea which is itself perceived in the act of seeing, it remains that we inquire what ideas or sensations there be that attend vision, unto which we may suppose the ideas of distance are connected and by which they are introduced into the mind. And, *first*, it is certain by experience that when we look at a near object with both eyes, according as it approaches or recedes from us, we alter the disposition of our eyes by lessening or widening the interval between the pupils. This disposition or turn of the eyes is attended with a sensation[24] which seems to me to be that which in this case brings the idea of greater or lesser distance into the mind.

17. Not that there is any natural or necessary connection between the sensation we perceive by the turn of the eyes and greater or lesser distance. But—because the mind has, by constant experience, found the different sensations corresponding to the different dispositions of the eyes to be attended each with a different degree of distance in the object—there has grown a habitual or customary connection between those two sorts of ideas so that the mind no sooner perceives the sensation arising from the different turn it gives the eyes, in order to bring the pupils nearer or farther asunder, but it withal perceives the different idea of distance which was wont to be connected with that sensation. Just as, upon hearing a certain sound, the idea is immediately suggested to the understanding which custom had united with it.

18. Nor do I see how I can easily be mistaken in this matter. I know evidently that distance is not perceived of itself; that, by consequence, it must be perceived by means of some other idea which is immediately perceived, and varies with the different degrees of distance. I know also that the sensation arising from the turn of the eyes is of itself immediately perceived; and various degrees thereof are connected with different distances, which never fail to accompany them into my mind, when I view an object distinctly with both eyes whose distance is so small that in respect of it the interval between the eyes has any considerable magnitude.

---

[22][Cf. *De Motu*, secs. 17, 18, 39, 66, etc.; *Alciphron*, Dial. VII, sec. 9: *Siris*, sec. 250: "Mechanic philosophers and geometricians . . . take mathematical hypotheses for real beings. . . ."]

[23][First use of this important term expressing the relation between the sign and the thing signified. *Cf. Alciphron*, Dial. IV, sec. 9: *Visual Language*, sec. 42.]

[24][I.e., of touch. Cf. *Essay*, sec. 145; *Visual Language*, sec. 66.]

19. I know it is a received opinion that, by altering the disposition of the eyes, the mind perceives whether the angle of the optic axes or the lateral angles comprehended between the interval of the eyes and the optic axes are[25] made greater or lesser; and that, accordingly, by a kind of natural geometry, it judges the point of their intersection to be nearer or farther off. But that this is not true I am convinced by my own experience; since I am not conscious that I make any such use of the perception I have by the turn of my eyes. And for me to make those judgments and draw those conclusions from it, without knowing that I do so, seems altogether incomprehensible.

20. From all which it follows that the judgment we make of the distance of an object viewed with both eyes is entirely the result of experience. If we had not constantly found certain sensations, arising from the various disposition of the eyes, attended with certain degrees of distance, we should never make those sudden judgments from them concerning the distance of objects; no more than we would pretend to judge of a man's thoughts by his pronouncing words we had never heard before.

21. *Secondly*, an object placed at a certain distance from the eye, to which the breadth of the pupil bears a considerable proportion, being made to approach, is seen more confusedly.[26] And the nearer it is brought the more confused appearance it makes. And this being found constantly to be so, there arises in the mind a habitual connection between the several degrees of confusion and distance, the greater confusion still implying the lesser distance and the lesser confusion the greater distance of the object.

22. This confused appearance of the object does therefore seem to be the medium whereby the mind judges of distance in those cases wherein the most approved writers of optics will have it judge by the different divergency with which the rays flowing from the radiating point fall on the pupil. No man, I believe, will pretend to see or feel those imaginary angles that the rays are supposed to form according to their various inclinations on his eye. But he cannot choose seeing whether the object appear more or less confused. It is therefore a manifest consequence from what has been demonstrated that, instead of the greater or lesser divergency of the rays, the mind makes use of the greater or lesser confusedness of the appearance, thereby to determine the apparent place of an object.

23. Nor does it avail to say there is not any necessary connection between confused vision and distance great or small. For I ask any man what necessary connection he sees between the redness of a blush and shame? And yet no sooner shall he behold that color to arise in the face of another but it brings into his mind the idea of that passion which has been observed to accompany it.

24. What seems to have misled the writers of optics in this matter is that they imagine men judge of distance as they do of a conclusion in mathematics; betwixt which and the premises it is indeed absolutely requisite there be an apparent necessary connection. But it is far otherwise in the sudden judgments men make of distance. We are not to think that brutes and children, or even grown reasonable

[25][Or the lateral angles . . . optic axes are—I, II: is.]
[26][Cf. sec. 35.]

men, whenever they perceive an object to approach or depart from them, do it by virtue of geometry and demonstration.

25. That one idea may suggest another to the mind, it will suffice that they have been observed to go together, without any demonstration of the necessity of their coexistence or without so much as knowing what makes them so to coexist. Of this there are innumerable instances, of which no one can be ignorant.

26. Thus, greater confusion having been constantly attended with nearer distance, no sooner is the former idea perceived but it suggests the latter to our thoughts. And, if it had been the ordinary course of nature that the farther off an object were placed the more confused it should appear, it is certain the very same perception that now makes us think an object approaches would then have made us to imagine it went farther off, that perception, abstracting from custom and experience, being equally fitted to produce the idea of great distance, or small distance, or no distance at all.

27. *Thirdly*, an object being placed at the distance above specified, and brought nearer to the eye, we may nevertheless prevent, at least for some time, the appearance's growing more confused by straining the eye. In which case that sensation supplies the place of confused vision in aiding the mind to judge of the distance of the object, it being esteemed so much the nearer by how much the effort or straining of the eye in order to distinct vision is greater.

28. I have here set down those sensations or ideas that seem to be the constant and general occasions of introducing into the mind the different ideas of near distance. It is true, in most cases, that divers other circumstances contribute to frame our idea of distance, viz., the particular number, size, kind, etc., of the things seen. Concerning which, as well as all other the forementioned occasions which suggest distance, I shall only observe, they have none of them, in their own nature, any relation or connection with it; nor is it possible they should ever signify the various degrees thereof otherwise than as by experience they have been found to be connected with them.

☞ **12** ☜

Mill, J. S. Excerpt from Book VI of *A system of logic, ratiocinative and inductive, being a connected view of the principles of evidence and methods of scientific investigation* (1843).*

CHAPTER IV.

Of the Laws of Mind.

§1. WHAT the Mind is, as well as what Matter is, or any other question respecting Things in themselves, as distinguished from their sensible manifestations, it would be foreign to the purposes of this Treatise to consider. Here, as throughout our inquiry, we shall keep clear of all speculations respecting the Mind's own nature, and shall understand by the Laws of Mind, those of mental Phenomena; of the various feelings or states of consciousness of sentient beings. These according to the classification we have uniformly followed, consist of Thoughts, Emotions, Volitions, and Sensations: the last being as truly States of Mind as the three *former*. It is usual indeed to speak of Sensations as states of body, not of mind. But this is the common confusion of giving one and the same name to a phenomenon and to the proximate cause or conditions of the phenomenon. The immediate antecedent of a Sensation is a state of Body, but the sensation itself a state of Mind. If the word Mind means anything, it means that which feels. If we allow ourselves to use language implying that the Body feels, there is no reason against being consistent in that language, after saying that the Body also thinks.

The phenomena of Mind, then, are the various feelings of our nature, both those called physical, and those peculiarly designated as Mental: and by the Laws of Mind, I mean the laws according to which those feelings generate one another.

*Mill, J. S. (1843, 1870). Excerpts from *A system of logic, ratiocinative and inductive, being a connected view of the principles of evidence and methods of scientific investigation*. New York: Harper and Row, Book VI, Ch. IV, 530–537. Reprinted by permission of Harper and Row Publishers.

§ 2. All states of mind are immediately caused either by other states of mind, or by states of body. When a state of mind is produced by a state of mind, I call the law concerned in the case, a law of Mind. When a state of mind is produced directly by a state of body, the law is a law of Body, and belongs to physical science.

With regard to those states of mind which are called Sensations, all are agreed that these have for their immediate antecedents, states of body. Every sensation has for its proximate cause some affection of the portion of our frame called the nervous system; whether this affection originate in the action of some external object, or in some pathological condition of the nervous organization itself. The laws of this portion of our nature—the varieties of our sensations, and the physical conditions on which they proximately depend—manifestly fall under the province of Physiology.

Whether any other portion of our mental states are similarly dependent on physical conditions, is one of those scientific questions respecting human nature which are still in abeyance. It is yet undecided whether our thoughts, emotions, and volitions are generated through the intervention of material mechanism; whether we have organs of thought and of emotion, in the same sense in which we have organs of sensation. Many eminent physiologists hold the affirmative. These contend, that a thought (for example) is as much the result of nervous agency, as a sensation: that some particular state of our nervous system, in particular of that central portion of it called the brain, invariably precedes, and is presupposed by, every state of our consciousness. According to this theory, one state of mind is never really produced by another: all are produced by states of body. When one thought seems to call up another by association, it is not really a thought which recalls a thought; the association did not exist between the two thoughts, but between the two states of the brain or nerves which preceded the thoughts; one of those states recalls the other, each being attended, in its passage, by the particular mental state which is consequent upon it. On this theory, the uniformities of succession among states of mind would be mere derivative uniformities, resulting from the laws of succession of the bodily states which cause them. There would be no original mental laws, no Laws of Mind in the sense in which I use the term, at all; but Mental Science would be a mere branch, though the highest and most recondite branch, of the Science of Physiology. This is what M. Comte must be understood to mean, when he claims the scientific cognizance of moral and intellectual phenomena exclusively for physiologists; and not only denies to Psychology, or Mental Philosophy properly so called, the character of a science, but places it, in the chimerical nature of its objects and pretensions, almost on a par with Astrology.

But, after all has been said which can be said, it remains incontestable by M. Comte and by all others, that there do exist uniformities of succession among states of mind, and that these can be ascertained by observation and experiment. Moreover, even if it were rendered far more certain than I believe it as yet to be, that every mental state has a nervous state for its immediate antecedent and proximate cause; yet every one must admit that we are wholly ignorant of the characteristics of these nervous states; we know not, nor can hope to know, in what respect one of them differs from another; and our only mode of studying their successions or coexistences must be by observing the successions and coexistences of the mental states of which they are supposed to be the generators or causes. The successions, therefore, which obtain among mental phenomena, do not admit of being deduced from the physiological laws of our nervous organization; and all real knowledge of them must continue, for a long time at least, if not for ever, to be sought in the direct study, by observation and experiment, of the mental successions themselves. Since therefore the order of our mental phenomena must be studied in those phenomena, and not inferred from the laws of any phenomena more general, there is a distinct and separate Science of Mind. The relations, indeed, of that science to the Science of Physiology must never be overlooked or undervalued. It must by no means be forgotten that the laws of mind may be derivative laws resulting from laws of animal life, and that their truth, therefore, may ultimately depend upon physical conditions; and the influence of physiological states or physiological changes in altering or counteracting the mental successions, is one of the most important departments of psychological study.

§3. The subject, then, of Psychology, is the uniformities of succession, the laws, whether ultimate or derivative, according to which one mental state succeeds another; is caused by, or at the least, is caused to follow, another. Of these laws, some are general, others more special. The following are examples of the most general laws.

First: Whenever any state of consciousness has once been excited in us, no matter by what cause; an inferior degree of the same state of consciousness, a state of consciousness resembling the former, but inferior in intensity, is capable of being reproduced in us, without the presence of any such cause as excited it at first. Thus, if we have once seen or touched an object, we can afterwards think of the object although it be absent from our sight or from our touch. If we have been joyful or grieved at some event, we can think of, or remember, our past joy or grief, although no new event of a happy or a painful nature has taken place. When a poet has put together a mental picture of an imaginary object, a Castle of Indolence, a Una, or a Juliet, he can afterwards think of the ideal object he has created, without any fresh act of intellectual combination. This law is expressed by saying, in the language of Hume, that every mental *impression* has its *idea*.

Secondly: These Ideas, or secondary mental states, are excited by our impressions, or by other ideas, according to certain laws which are called Laws of Association. Of these laws the first is, that similar ideas tend to excite one another. The second is, that when two impressions have been frequently experienced (or even thought of) either simultaneously or in immediate succession, then whenever either of these impressions or the idea of it recurs, it tends to excite the idea of the other. The third law is, that greater intensity, in either or both of the impressions, is equivalent, in rendering them excitable by one another, to a greater frequency of conjunction. These are the laws of Ideas: upon which I shall not enlarge in this place, but refer the reader to works professedly psychological, in particular to Mr. Mill's *Analysis of the Phenomena of the Human Mind*, where the principal laws of association, both in themselves and in many of their applications, are copiously exemplified, and with a masterly hand.

These simple or elementary Laws of Mind have long been ascertained by the ordinary methods of experimental inquiry; nor could they have been ascertained in any other manner. But a certain number of elementary laws having thus been obtained, it is a fair subject of scientific inquiry how far those laws can be made to go in explaining the actual phenomena. It is obvious that complex laws of thought and feeling not only may, but must, be generated from these simple laws. And it is to be remarked, that the case is not always one of Composition of Causes: the effect of concurring causes is not always precisely the sum of the effects of those causes when separate, nor even always an effect of the same kind with them. Reverting to the distinction which occupies so prominent a place in the theory of induction; the laws of the phenomena of mind are sometimes analogous to mechanical, but sometimes also to chemical laws. When many impressions or ideas are operating in the mind together, there sometimes takes place a process of a similar kind to chemical combination. When impressions have been so often experienced in conjunction, that each of them calls up readily and instantaneously the ideas of the whole group, those ideas sometimes melt and coalesce into one another, and appear not several ideas but one; in the same manner as when the seven prismatic colors are presented to the eye in rapid succession, the sensation produced is that of white. But as in this last case it is correct to say that the seven colors when they rapidly follow one another *generate* white, but not that they actually *are* white; so it appears to me that the Complex Idea, formed by the blending together of several simpler ones, should, when it really appears simple, (that is when the separate elements are not consciously distinguishable in it,) be said to *result from*, or be *generated by*, the simple ideas, not to *consist* of them. Our idea of an orange really *consists* of the simple ideas of a certain color, a certain form, a certain taste and smell, &c., because we can by interrogating our consciousness, perceive all these elements in the idea. But we cannot perceive, in so apparently simple a feeling as our perception of the shape of an object by the eye, all that multitude of ideas derived from other senses, without which it is well ascertained that no such visual perception would ever have had existence; nor, in our idea of Extension, can we discover those elementary ideas of resistance, derived from our muscular frame, in which Dr. Brown has rendered it highly probable that the idea originates. These therefore are cases of mental chemistry: in which it is proper to say that the simple ideas generate, rather than that they compose, the complex ones.

With respect to all the other constituents of the mind, its beliefs, its abstruser conceptions, its sentiments, emotions, and volitions; there are some (among whom are Hartley, and the author of the *Analysis*) who think that the whole of these are generated from simple ideas of sensation, by a chemistry similar to that which we have just exemplified. I am unable to satisfy myself that this conclusion is, in the present state of our knowledge, fully made out. In many cases I cannot even perceive, that the line of argument adopted has much tendency to establish it. The philosophers to whom I have referred have, indeed, conclusively shown that there is such a thing as mental chemistry; that the heterogeneous nature of a feeling, A, considered in relation to B and C, is no conclusive argument against its being generated from B and C. Having proved this, they proceed to show, that where A is found, B and C were, or may have been, present, and why therefore, they say, should not A have been generated from B and C. But even if this evidence were carried to the highest degree of completeness which it admits of; if it were shown that certain groups of associated ideas not only might have been, but actually were, present whenever the more recondite mental feeling was experienced; this would amount only to the Method of Agreement, and could not prove causation until confirmed by the more conclusive evidence of the Method of Difference. If the question be whether Belief is a mere case of close association of ideas, it would be necessary to examine experimentally if it be true that any ideas whatever, provided they are associated together with the required degree of closeness, are sufficient to give rise to belief. If the inquiry be into the origin of moral feelings, the feelings for example of moral reprobation, the first step must be to compare all the varieties of actions or states of mind which are ever morally disapproved, and see whether in all these cases it can be shown that the action or state of mind had become connected by association, in the disapproving mind, with some particular class of hateful or disgusting ideas; and the method employed is, thus far, that of Agreement. But this is not enough. Supposing this proved, we must try further, by the Method of Difference, whether this particular kind of hateful or disgusting ideas, when it becomes associated with an action previously indifferent, will render that action a subject of moral disapproval. If this question can be answered in the affirmative, it is shown to be a law of the human mind, that an association of that particular description is the generating cause of moral reprobation. But these experiments have either never been tried, or never with the degree of precision indispensable for conclusiveness; and, considering the difficulty of accurate experimentation upon the human mind, it will probably be long before they are so.

It is further to be remembered, that even if all which this theory of mental phenomena contends for could be proved, we should not be the more enabled to resolve the laws of the more complex feelings into those of the simpler ones. The generation of one class of mental phenomena from another, whenever it can be made out, is a highly interesting fact in psychological chemistry; but it no more supersedes the necessity of an experimental study of the generated phenomenon, than a knowledge of the properties of oxygen and sulphur enables us to deduce those of sulphuric acid without specific observation and experiment. Whatever, therefore, may be the final issue of the attempt to account for the origin of our judgments, our desires, or our volitions, from simpler mental phenomena, it is not the less imperative to ascertain the sequences of the complex phenomena themselves, by special study in conformity to the canons of Induction. Thus, in respect of Belief, the psychologist will always have to inquire, what beliefs we have intuitively, and according to what laws one belief produces another; what are the laws in virtue of which one thing is recognized by the mind, either rightly or erroneously, as evidence of another thing. In regard to Desire, he will examine what objects we desire naturally, and by what causes we are made to desire things originally indifferent or even disagreeable to us; and so forth. It may be remarked, that the general laws of association prevail among these more intricate states of mind, in the same manner as among the simpler ones. A desire, an emotion, an idea of the higher order of abstraction, even our judgments and volitions when they have become habitual, are called up by association, according to precisely the same laws as our simple ideas.

§4. In the course of these inquiries it will be natural and necessary to examine, how far the production of one state of mind by another is influenced by any assignable state of body. The commonest observation shows that different minds are susceptible in very different degrees to the action of the same psychological causes. The idea, for example, of a given desirable object, will excite in different minds very different degrees of intensity of desire. The same subject of meditation, presented to different minds, will excite in them very unequal degrees of intellectual action. These differences of mental susceptibility in different individuals may be, *first,* original and ultimate facts, or, *secondly,* they may be consequences of the previous mental history of those individuals, or, thirdly and lastly, they may depend upon varieties of physical organization. That the previous mental history of the individuals must have some share in producing or in modifying the whole of their present mental character, is an inevitable consequence of the laws of mind; but that differences of bodily structure also coöperate, in the assertion not only of phrenologists, but, to a greater or less extent, of all physiologists who lay any stress upon the magnitude of the hemispheres of the brain, indicated by the facial angle, as a measure of natural intelligence, or upon temperament as a source of moral and emotional peculiarities.

What portion of these assertions the physiological school of psychologists, whether phrenologists or otherwise, have either succeeded in establishing, or shown ground for supposing it possible to establish hereafter, I would not undertake to say. Nor do I believe that the inquiry will be brought to a satisfactory issue, while it is abandoned, as unfortunately it has hitherto been, to physiologists who have no adequate knowledge of mental laws, or psychologists who have no sufficient acquaintance with physiology.

It is certain that the natural differences which really exist in the mental predispositions or susceptibilities of different persons, are often not unconnected with diversities in their organic constitution. But it does not therefore follow that these organic differences must in all cases influence the mental phenomena directly and immediately. They may often affect them through the medium of their psychological causes. For example, the idea of some particular pleasure may excite in different persons, even independently of habit or education, very different strengths of desire, and this may be the effect of their different degrees or kinds of nervous susceptibility; but these organic differences, we must remember, will render the pleasurable sensation itself more intense in one of these persons than in the other; so that the idea of the pleasure will also be an intenser feeling, and will, by the operation of mere mental laws, excite an intenser desire, without its being necessary to suppose that the desire itself is directly influenced by the physical peculiarity. As in this, so in many cases, such differences in the kind or in the intensity of the physical sensations as much necessarily result from differences of bodily organization, will of themselves account for many differences not only in the degree, but even in the kind, of the other mental phenomena. So true is this, that even different *qualities* of mind, different types of mental character, will naturally be produced by mere differences of *intensity* in the sensations generally. This truth is so well exemplified, and in so short a compass, in a very able essay on Dr. Priestley, mentioned in a former chapter, that I think it right to quote the passage:—

"The sensations which form the elements of all knowledge are received either simultaneously or successively; when several are received simultaneously, as the small, the taste, the color, the form, & c. of a fruit, their association together constitutes our idea of an *object*; when received successively, their association makes up the idea of an *event*. Anything, then, which favors the associations of synchronous ideas, will tend to produce a knowledge of objects, a perception of qualities; while anything which favors association in the successive order, will tend to produce a knowledge of events, of the order of occurrences, and of the connexion of cause and effect: in other words, in the one case a perceptive mind, with a discriminative feeling of the pleasurable and painful properties of things, a sense of the grand and the beautiful, will be the result: in the other, a mind attentive to the movements and phenomena, a ratiocinative and philosophic intellect. Now it is an acknowledged principle, that all sensations experienced during the presence of any vivid impression, become strongly associated with it, and with each other; and does it not follow, that the synchronous feelings of a sensitive constitution (*i.e.* the one which has vivid impressions) will be more intimately blended than in a differently formed mind? If this suggestion has any foundation in truth, it leads to an inference not unimportant; that where nature has endowed an individual with great original susceptibility, he will probably be distinguished by fondness for natural history, a relish for the beautiful and great, and moral enthusiasm; where there is but a mediocrity of sensibility, a love of science, of abstract truth, with a deficiency of taste and of fervor, is likely to be the result."

We see from this example, that when the general laws of mind are more accurately known, and above all, more skillfully applied to the detailed explanation of mental peculiarities, they will account for many more of those peculiarities than is ordinarily supposed. I by no means seek to imply from this that they will account for all; but that which remains to be otherwise accounted for is merely a residual phenomenon; and the amount of the residue can only be determined by persons already familiar with the explanation of phenomena by psychological laws.

On the other hand, it is equally clear that when physiologists, taking into account the whole animal creation, attempt, by a judicious application of the Method of Concomitant Variations, grounded chiefly on extreme cases, to establish a connexion between the strength of different mental propensities or capacities and the proportional or absolute magnitudes of different regions of the brain; the evidences which are or may be produced in support of this pretension, ought to be taken into serious consideration by psychologists. Nor will this part of the science of mind be ever cleared up, until those evidences shall be not only sifted and analyzed, but, when necessary, added to and completed, by persons sufficiently versed in psychological laws to be capable of discriminating how much of each phenomenon such laws will suffice to explain.

Even admitting the influence of cerebral conformation to be as great as is contended for, it would still be a question how far the cerebral development determined the propensity itself, and how far it only acted by modifying the nature and degrees of the sensations on which the propensity may be psychologically dependent. And it is certain that, in human beings at least, differences in education and in outward circumstances, together with physical differences in the sensations produced in different individuals by the same external or internal cause, are capable of accounting for a far greater portion of character than is supposed even by the most moderate phrenologists. There are, however, many mental facts which do not seem to admit of this mode of explanation. Such, to take the strongest case, are the various instincts of animals, the portion of human nature which corresponds to those instincts. No mode has been suggested, even by way of hypothesis, in which these can receive any satisfactory, or even plausible, explanation from psychological causes alone; and they may probably be found to have as positive, and even perhaps as direct and immediate, a connexion with physical conditions of the brain and nerves, as any of our mere sensations have.

How much further this remark might be extended, I do not pretend to determine. My object is not to establish the doctrines, but to discriminate the true Method, of mental science; and this, so far as regards the establishment of the general and elementary laws, may be considered to be sufficiently accomplished.

⚞ 13 ⚟

Immanuel Kant, Excerpt from Critique of Pure Reason (1781).*

INTRODUCTION

I. The Distinction Between Pure and Empirical Knowledge

THERE can be no doubt that all our knowledge begins with experience. For how should our faculty of knowledge be awakened into action did not objects affecting our senses partly of themselves produce representations, partly arouse the activity of our understanding to compare these representations, and, by combining or separating them, work up the raw material of the sensible impressions into that knowledge of objects which is entitled experience? In the order of time, therefore, we have no knowledge antecedent to experience, and with experience all our knowledge begins.

But though all our knowledge begins with experience, it does not follow that it all arises out of experience. For it may well be that even our empirical knowledge is made up of what we receive through impressions and of what our own faculty of knowledge (sensible impressions serving merely as the occasion) supplies from itself. If our faculty of knowledge makes any such addition, it may be that we are not in a position to distinguish it from the raw material, until with long practice of attention we have become skilled in separating it.

This, then, is a question which at least calls for closer examination, and does not allow of any off-hand answer:—whether there is any knowledge that is thus independent of experience and even of all impressions of the senses.

*Kant, I. (1781) in Kemp Smith, N. (1961). *Immanuel Kant's Critique of Pure Reason*. New York: St. Martin's Press, 41–48. Reprinted by permission of Macmillan Press, Ltd.

Such knowledge is entitled *a priori*, and distinguished from the *empirical*, which has its sources *a posteriori*, that is, in experience.

The expression '*a priori*' does not, however, indicate with sufficient precision the full meaning of our question. For it has been customary to say, even of much knowledge that is derived from empirical sources, that we have it or are capable of having it *a priori*, meaning thereby that we do not derive it immediately from experience, but from a universal rule—a rule which is itself, however, borrowed by us from experience. Thus we would say of a man who undermined the foundations of his house, that he might have known *a priori* that it would fall, that is, that he need not have waited for the experience of its actual falling. But still he could not know this completely *a priori*. For he had first to learn through experience that bodies are heavy, and therefore fall when their supports are withdrawn.

In what follows, therefore, we shall understand by *a priori* knowledge, not knowledge independent of this or that experience, but knowledge absolutely independent of all experience. Opposed to it is empirical knowledge, which is knowledge possible only *a posteriori*, that is, through experience. *A priori* modes of knowledge are entitled pure when there is no admixture of anything empirical. Thus, for instance, the proposition, 'every alteration has its cause', while an *a priori* proposition, is not a pure proposition, because alteration is a concept which can be derived only from experience.[1]

II. We are in Possession of certain Modes of *A Priori* Knowledge, and even the Common Understanding is never without them

What we here require is a criterion[2] by which to distinguish with certainty between pure and empirical knowledge. Experience teaches us that a thing is so and so, but not that it cannot be otherwise. First, then, if we have a proposition which in being thought is thought as *necessary*, it is an *a priori* judgment; and if, besides, it is not derived from any proposition except one which also has the validity of a necessary judgment, it is an absolutely *a priori* judgment. Secondly, experience never confers on its judgments true or strict, but only assumed and comparative *universality*, through induction. We can properly only say, therefore, that, so far as we have hitherto observed, there is no exception to this or that rule. If, then, a judgment is thought with strict universality, that is, in such manner that no exception is allowed as possible, it is not derived from experience, but is valid absolutely *a priori*. Empirical universality is only an arbitrary extension of a validity holding in most cases to one which holds in all, for instance, in the proposition, 'all bodies are heavy'. When, on the other hand, strict universality is essential to a judgment, this indicates a special source of knowledge, namely, a faculty of *a priori* knowl-

---

[1][Cf. below, pp. 44, 76, 216-7.]
[2][*Merkmal.*]

edge. Necessity and strict universality are thus sure criteria of *a priori* knowledge, and are inseparable from one another. But since in the employment of these criteria the contingency of judgments is sometimes more easily shown than their empirical limitation,[1] or, as sometimes also happens, their unlimited universality can be more convincingly proved than their necessity, it is advisable to use the two criteria separately, each by itself being infallible.

Now it is easy to show that there actually are in human knowledge judgments which are necessary and in the strictest sense universal, and which are therefore pure *a priori* judgments. If an example from the sciences be desired, we have only to look to any of the propositions of mathematics; if we seek an example from the understanding in its quite ordinary employment, the proposition, 'every alteration must have a cause', will serve our purpose. In the latter case, indeed, the very concept of a cause so manifestly contains the concept of a necessity of connection with an effect and of the strict universality of the rule, that the concept would be altogether lost if we attempted to derive it, as Hume has done, from a repeated association of that which happens with that which precedes, and from a custom of connecting representations, a custom originating in this repeated association, and constituting therefore a merely subjective necessity. Even without appealing to such examples, it is possible to show that pure *a priori* principles are indispensable for the possibility of experience, and so to prove their existence *a priori*. For whence could experience derive its certainty, if all the rules, according to which it proceeds, were always themselves empirical, and therefore contingent? Such rules could hardly be regarded as first principles. At present, however, we may be content to have established the fact that our faculty of knowledge does have a pure employment, and to have shown what are the criteria of such an employment.

Such *a priori* origin is manifest in certain concepts, no less than in judgments. If we remove from our empirical concept of a body, one by one, every feature in it which is [merely] empirical, the colour, the hardness or softness, the weight, even[2] the impenetrability, there still remains the space which the body (now entirely vanished) occupied, and this cannot be removed. Again, if we remove from our empirical concept of any object, corporeal or incorporeal, all properties which experience has taught us, we yet cannot take away that property through which the object is thought as substance or as inhering in a substance (although this concept of substance is more determinate than that of an object in general). Owing, therefore, to the necessity with which this concept of substance forces itself upon us, we have no option save to admit that it has its seat in our faculty of *a priori* knowledge.

---

[1] [Reading, with Vaihinger, *die Zufälligkeit in den Urteilen als die empirische Beschränktheit derselben* for *die empirische Beschränktheit derselben als die Zufälligkeit in den Urteilen.*]

[2] [*selbst* omitted in the 4th edition.]

III. Philosophy Stands in Need of a Science which shall determine the Possibility, the Principles, and the Extent of all *a priori* Knowledge

But what is still more extraordinary than all the preceding[1] is this, that certain modes of knowledge leave the field of all possible experiences and have the appearance of extending the scope of our judgments beyond all limits of experience, and this by means of concepts to which no corresponding object can ever be given in experience.

It is precisely by means of the latter modes of knowledge, in a realm beyond the world of the senses, where experience can yield neither guidance nor correction, that our reason carries on those enquiries which owing to their importance we consider to be far more excellent, and in their purpose far more lofty, than all that the understanding can learn in the field of appearances. Indeed we prefer to run every risk of error rather than desist from such urgent enquiries, on the ground of their dubious character, or from disdain and indifference.[2] These unavoidable problems set by pure reason itself are *God, freedom,* and *immortality.* The science which, with all its preparations, is in its final intention directed solely to their solution is metaphysics; and its procedure is at first dogmatic, that is, it confidently sets itself to this task without any previous examination of the capacity or incapacity of reason for so great an undertaking.

Now it does indeed seem natural that, as soon as we have left the ground of experience, we should, through careful enquiries, assure ourselves as to the foundations of any building that we propose to erect, not making use of any knowledge that we possess without first determining whence it has come, and not trusting to principles without knowing their origin. It is natural, that is to say, that the question should first be considered, how the understanding can arrive at all this knowledge *a priori,* and what extent, validity, and worth it may have. Nothing, indeed, could be more natural, if by the term 'natural'[3] we signify what fittingly and reasonably ought to happen. But if we mean by 'natural' what ordinarily happens, then on the contrary nothing is more natural and more intelligible than the fact that this enquiry has been so long neglected. For one part of this knowledge, the mathematical, has long been of established reliability, and so gives rise to a favourable presumption as regards the other part, which may yet be of quite different nature. Besides, once we are outside the circle of experience, we can be sure of not being *contradicted* by experience. The charm of extending our knowledge is so great that nothing short of encountering a direct contradiction can suffice to arrest us in our course; and this can be avoided, if we are careful in our fabrications—which

---

[1] [*als alle vorige* added in B.]

[2] ["These unavoidable . . ." to end of paragraph added in B.]

[3] [In A *unter diesem Wort:* in B *unter dem Wort natürlich.*]

none the less will still remain fabrications. Mathematics gives us a shining example of how far, independently of experience, we can progress in *a priori* knowledge. It does, indeed, occupy itself with objects and with knowledge solely in so far as they allow of being exhibited in intuition. But this circumstance is easily overlooked, since this intuition can itself be given *a priori*, and is therefore hardly to be distinguished from a bare and pure concept. Misled[1] by such a proof of the power of reason, the demand for the extension of knowledge recognises no limits. The light dove, cleaving the air in her free flight, and feeling its resistance, might imagine that its flight would be still easier in empty space. It was thus that Plato left the world of the senses, as setting too narrow limits to[2] the understanding, and ventured out beyond it on the wings of the ideas, in the empty space of the pure understanding. He did not observe that with all his efforts he made no advance—meeting no resistance that might, as it were, serve as a support upon which he could take a stand, to which he could apply his powers, and so set his understanding in motion. It is, indeed, the common fate of human reason to complete its speculative structures as speedily as may be, and only afterwards to enquire whether the foundations are reliable. All sorts of excuses will then be appealed to, in order to reassure us of their solidity, or rather indeed[3] to enable us to dispense altogether with so late and so dangerous an enquiry. But what keeps us, during the actual building, free from all apprehension and suspicion, and flatters us with a seeming thoroughness, is this other circumstance, namely, that a great, perhaps the greatest, part of the business of our reason consists in analysis[4] of the concepts which we already have of objects. This analysis supplies us with a considerable body of knowledge, which, while nothing but explanation or elucidation of what has already been thought in our concepts, though in a confused manner, is yet prized as being, at least as regards its form, new insight. But so far as the matter or content is concerned, there has been no extension of our previously possessed concepts, but only an analysis of them. Since this procedure yields real knowledge *a priori*, which progresses in an assured and useful fashion, reason is so far misled as surreptitiously to introduce, without itself being aware of so doing, assertions of an entirely different order, in which it attaches to given concepts others completely foreign to them, and moreover attaches them *a priori*.[5] And yet it is not known how reason can be in position to do this. Such a question[6] is never so much as thought of. I shall therefore at once proceed to deal with the difference between these two kinds of knowledge.

[1] [In A: Encouraged.]

[2] [In A: placing such manifold hindrances in the way of.]

[3] [*lieber gar* added in B.]

[4] [Reading, with the 5th edition. *Zergliederung* for *Zergliederungen*.]

[5] [In A: attaches a priori to given concepts others completely foreign to them.]

[6] [In A: This question.]

IV. The Founding of Modern Psychology

From the national movements articulating the competing interpretations of the nature of human experience and the related assumptions about psychological processes, two expressions of psychology emerged somewhat simultaneously. In the writings of Wilhelm Wundt (1832–1920), psychology studied the elements of immediate experience through the method of introspection, which defined psychology as a natural science in the same tradition as the physical sciences. Alternatively for Franz Brentano (1838–1917), psychological events were mental acts, which have both coherence and integrity. If analyzed or reduced to elements or components, the unity of psychic acts is lost. While both perspectives overlap and Wundt's theory evolved considerably over the course of his long career, the definitions of psychology proposed by Wundt and Brentano nevertheless hold some fundamental differences about the nature of people, which have obvious and profound implications for psychology.

The passage taken from *Grundriss der psychologie* (*Outlines of psychology,* 1897) offers Wundt's definition of the problem and method of psychology. In presenting these distinctions, Wundt also specified the level of experience that is appropriately psychological. He insisted that experience must be analyzed independent of subjective feelings and attitudes accumulated over time by a person. The passage also reflects the very deliberate character of Wundt's analysis and his careful attention to subtle distinctions in the experience as it is happening. Recent scholarship (e.g., Blumenthal, 1985) has pointed out that the historical evaluation of Wundt's theory has been seen through Titchener's influence in America and Titchener's student, Boring's (1950) *History of psychology.* This interpretation has tended to ignore Wundt's reliance on the German philosophical emphasis on mental activity, portraying more of an empirical Wundt than perhaps was the case. At any rate,

Wundt's psychology was quite comprehensive and included a "folk" psychology that emerged toward the end of his life.

Brentano's Act Psychology is less well developed than Wundt's theory. In this passage from his major psychological work, *Psychology from an empirical standpoint* (1874), Brentano offers four reasons to study psychology. Basic to this justification and his definition of psychological acts is Brentano's focus on phenomena, which are known only through the wholeness and unity of experience. It is interesting to observe Brentano's reliance on the tradition of mental activity in his citations from Aristotle to Kant, as well as his broad appreciation of contemporary psychological views of late 19th Century European thought.

The final selection in this section is Titchener's 1925 paper on "Experimental psychology: A retrospect". Edward Bradford Titchener (1867–1927) received most of his education in England and was influenced by the prevailing British model of mental passivity. After studying under Wundt, he went to Cornell University and became one of the earliest pioneers of American psychology. The selection was written toward the end of his life on the occasion of the dedication of a building at Princeton University, and Titchener offered three influences, albeit negative, on the development of experimental psychology. The influence that dominates the article is that of empirical psychology, especially represented by Brentano. Thus, this selection offers a comparison, from the eyes of Titchener, of the two dominant figures in the emergence of modern psychology: Wundt and Brentano.

REFERENCES

BORING, E.G. (1950). *A history of experimental psychology* (2nd ed). Englewood Cliffs, N.J.: Prentice Hall.

BLUMENTHAL, A.L. (1985). Wilhelm Wundt: Psychology as the propaedeutic science. In C. Buxton (ed.) *Points of view in the modern history of psychology.* New York: Academic Press, 19–50.

BRENTANO, F. (1874, 1973). The concept and purpose of psychology. In L. McAlister (ed). *Psychology from an empirical standpoint.* London: Routledge & Kegan Paul, 3–27.

TITCHENER, E.B. (1925). Experimental psychology: A retrospect. *The American Journal of Psychology, 36,* 313–323.

WUNDT, W. (1897, 1969). *Grundriss der Psychologie.* Leipzig: Englemann. From C.H. Judd (translator) (1902). *Outlines of psychology.* St. Claires Shores, MI: Scholarly Press, 1–6, 18–24.

⤳ 14 ⤲

Wilhelm Wundt, Excerpt from *Grundriss der Psychologie (Outlines of psychology) (1897, 1902).* *

INTRODUCTION

§ 1. Problem of Psychology.

1. Two definitions of psychology have been the most prominent in the history of this science. According to one, psychology is the "science of mind": psychical processes are regarded as phenomena from which it is possible to infer the nature of an underlying metaphysical mind-substance. According to the other, psychology is the "science of inner experience": psychical processes are here looked upon as belonging to a specific form of experience, which is readily distinguished by the fact that its contents are known through "introspection", or the "inner sense" as it has been called to distinguish it from sense-perception through the outer senses.

Neither of these definitions, however, is satisfactory to the psychology of to-day. The first, or metaphysical, definition belongs to a period of development that lasted longer in this science than in others. But it is here too forever left behind, since psychology has developed into an empirical discipline, operating with methods of its own; and since the "mental sciences" have gained recognition as a great department of scientific investigation, distinct from the sphere of the natural sciences, and requiring as a general groundwork an independent psychology, free from all metaphysical theories.

The second, or empirical, definition, which sees in psychology a "science of inner experience", is inadequate because it may give rise to the misunder-

*Wundt, W. (1897, 1969). Excerpt from *Grundriss der psychologie.* Leipzig: Englemann. From C.H. Judd (translator) (1902). *Outlines of psychology.* St. Claires Shores, MI: Scholarly Press, 1–6, 18–24.

standing that psychology has to do with objects totally different from those of the so-called "outer experience". It is, indeed, true that there are contents of experience which belong in the sphere of psychological investigation, but are not to be found among the objects and processes studied by natural science: such are our feelings, emotions, and decisions. On the other hand, there is not a single natural phenomenon that may not, from a different point of view, become an object of psychology. A stone, a plant, a tone, a ray of light, are, as natural phenomena, objects of mineralogy, botany, physics, etc.; but in so far as they arouse in us *ideas*, they are at the same time objects of psychology. For psychology seeks to account for the genesis of these ideas, and for their relations both to other ideas and to those psychical processes not referred to external objects, such as feelings, volitions, etc. There is, then, no such thing as an "inner sense" which can be regarded as an organ of introspection, and thus distinct from the outer senses, or organs of objective perception. Ideas, whose attributes psychology seeks to investigate, arise through the outer senses no less than do the sense-perceptions on which natural science is based; while the subjective activities of feeling, emotion, and volition, which are neglected in natural science, are not known through special organs, but are directly and inseparably connected with the ideas referred to external objects.

2. It follows, then, that the expressions outer and inner experience do not indicate different objects, but *different points of view* from which we start in the consideration and scientific treatment of a unitary experience. We are naturally led to these points of view, because every concrete experience immediately divides into *two factors*: into a *content* presented to us, and our *apprehension* of this content. We call the first of these factors *objects of experience*, the second *experiencing subject*. This division points out two directions for the treatment of experience. One is that of the *natural sciences*, which concern themselves with the *objects* of experience, thought of as independent of the subject. The other is that of *psychology*, which investigates the whole content of experience in its relations to the subject and in its attributes derived directly from the subject. The standpoint of natural science may, accordingly, be designated as that of *mediate experience*, since it is possible only after abstracting from the subjective factor present in all actual experience; the standpoint of psychology, on the other hand, may be designated as that of *immediate experience*, since it purposely does away with this abstraction and all its consequences.

3. The assignment of this problem to psychology, making it an empirical science coordinate with natural science and supplementary to it, is justified by the method of all the *mental sciences*, for which psychology furnishes the basis. All of these sciences, philology, history, and political and social science, have for their subject-matter immediate experience as determined by the interaction of objects with the knowing and acting subject. None of the mental sciences employs the abstractions and hypothetical supplementary concepts of natural science; quite otherwise, they all accept ideas and the accompanying subjective activities as immediate reality. The effort is then made to explain the single components of this reality through their mutual interconnections. This method of psychological

interpretation employed in the mental sciences, must also be the mode of procedure in psychology itself, being the method required by the subject-matter of psychology, the immediate reality of experience.

3a. Since natural science investigates the content of experience after
abstracting from the experiencing subject, its problem is usually stated as the
acquirement of "knowledge of the outer world". By the expression outer world
is meant the sum total of all the objects presented in experience. The problem
of psychology has sometimes been correspondingly defined as "self-knowledge
of the subject". This definition is, however, inadequate because the interaction
of the subject with the outer world and with other similar subjects is just as much
a problem of psychology as are the attributes of the single subject. Furthermore,
the expression can easily be interpreted to mean that outer world and subject
are separate components of experience or that they can at least be distinguished
as independent contents of experience, whereas, in truth, outer experience is
always connected with the apprehending and knowing functions of the subject,
and inner experience always contains ideas from the outer world as indispensable components. This interconnection is the necessary result of the fact that in
reality experience is not a mere juxtaposition of different elements, but a single
organized whole which requires in each of its components the subject that
apprehends the content, and the objects that are presented as content. For this
reason natural science can not abstract from the knowing subject entirely, but
only from those attributes of the subject which either disappear entirely when we
remove the subject in thought, as, the feelings, or from those which, on the
ground of physical researches, must be regarded as belonging to the subject, as,
the qualities of sensations. Psychology, on the contrary, has as its subject of treatment the *total* content of experience in its immediate character.

The only ground, then, for the division between natural science on the
one hand, and psychology and the mental sciences on the other, is to be
found in the fact that all experience contains as its factors a content objectively presented, and an experiencing subject. Still, it is by no means necessary
that *logical* definitions of these two factors should precede the separation of
the sciences from one another, for it is obvious that such definitions are possible only after they have a basis in the investigations of natural science and of
psychology. All that it is necessary to presuppose from the first, is the consciousness which accompanies all experience, that in this experience objects
are being presented to a subject. There can be no assumption of a knowledge
of the conditions upon which the distinction is based, or of the definite characteristics by which one factor can be distinguished from the other. Even the
use of the terms object and subject in this connection must be regarded as the
application to the first stage of experience, of distinctions which are reached
only by developed logical reflection.

The forms of interpretation in natural science and psychology are supplementary not only in the sense that the first considers objects after abstracting, as far as possible, from the subject, while the second has to do with the
part the subject plays in the rise of experience; but they are also supplemen-

tary in the sense that each takes a different point of view in considering the single contents of experience. Natural science seeks to discover the nature of objects without reference to the subject. The knowledge that it produces is therefore *mediate* or *conceptual.* In place of the immediate objects of experience, it sets concepts gained from these objects by abstracting from the subjective components of our ideas. This abstraction makes it necessary, continually to supplement reality with hypothetical elements. Scientific analysis shows that many components of experience—as, for example, sensations—are subjective effects of objective processes. These objective processes in their objective character, independent of the subject, can therefore never be a part of experience. Science makes up for this lack by forming supplementary hypothetical concepts of the objective properties of matter. Psychology, on the other hand, investigates the contents of experience in their complete and actual form, both the ideas that are referred to objects, and all the subjective processes that cluster about them. Its knowledge is, therefore, *immediate* and *perceptual:* perceptual in the broad sense of the term in which not only sense-perceptions, but all *concrete reality* is distinguished from all that is abstract and conceptual in thought. Psychology can exhibit the interconnection of the contents of experience as actually presented to the subject, only by avoiding entirely the abstractions and supplementary concepts of natural science. Thus, while natural science and psychology are both empirical sciences in the sense that they aim to explain the contents of experience, though from different points of view, still it is obvious that, in consequence of the character of its problem, psychology is the *more strictly empirical.*

§ 3. Methods of Psychology.

1. Since psychology has for its object, not specific contents of experience, but *general experience in its immediate character,* it can make use of no methods except such as the empirical sciences in general employ for the determination, analysis, and causal synthesis of facts. The circumstance, that natural science abstracts from the subject, while psychology does not, can be no ground for modifications in the essential character of the methods employed in the two fields, though it does modify the way in which these methods are applied.

The natural sciences, which may serve as an example for psychology in this respect, since they were developed earlier, make use of *two* chief methods: *experiment* and *observation. Experiment* is observation connected with an intentional interference on the part of the observer, in the rise and course of the phenomena observed. *Observation,* in its proper sense, is the investigation of phenomena without such interference, just as they are naturally presented to the observer in the continuity of experience. Wherever experiment is possible, it is always used in the natural sciences: for under all circumstances, even when the phenomena in themselves present the conditions for sufficiently exact observation, it is an advantage to be able to control at will their rise and progress, or to isolate the various components of a composite phenomenon.

Still, even in the natural sciences the two methods have been distinguished according to their spheres of application. It is held that the experimental methods are indispensable for certain problems, while in others the desired end may not infrequently be reached through mere observation. If we neglect a few exceptional cases due to special relations, these two classes of problems correspond to the general division of natural phenomena into *processes* and *objects.*

Experimental interference is required in the exact determination of the course, and in the analysis of the components, of any natural *process,* such as, for example, light-waves or sound-waves, an electric discharge, the formation or disintegration of a chemical compound, and stimulation and metabolism in plants and animals. As a rule, such interference is desirable because exact observation is possible only when the observer can determine the moment at which the process shall commence. It is also indispensable in separating the various components of a complex phenomenon from one another. As a rule, this is possible only through the addition or subtraction of certain conditions, or a quantitative variation of them.

The case is different with *objects* of nature. They are relatively constant; they do not have to be produced at a particular moment, but are always at the observer's disposal and ready for examination. Here, then, experimental investigation is generally necessary only when the production and modification of the objects are to be inquired into. In such a case, they are regarded either as products or components of natural processes and come under the head of processes rather than objects. When, on the contrary, the only question is the actual nature of these objects, without reference in their origin or modification, mere observation is generally enough. Thus, mineralogy, botany, zoology, anatomy, and geography, are pure sciences of observation so long as they are kept free from the physical, chemical, and physiological problems that are, indeed, frequently brought into them, but have to do with processes of nature, not with the objects in themselves.

2. If we apply these considerations to psychology, it is obvious at once, from the very nature of its subject-matter, that exact observation is here possible only in the form of *experimental* observation, and that psychology can never be a *pure* science of observation. The contents of this science are exclusively *processes,* not permanent objects. In order to investigate with exactness the rise and progress of these processes, their composition out of various components, and the interrelations of these components, we must be able first of all to bring about their beginning at will, and purposely to vary the conditions of the same. This is possible here, as in all cases, only through experiment, not through pure introspection. Besides this general reason there is another, peculiar to psychology, that does not apply at all to natural phenomena. In the latter case we purposely abstract from the perceiving subject, and under circumstances, especially when favored by the regularity of the phenomena, as in astronomy, mere observation may succeed in determining with adequate certainty the objective contents of the processes. Psychology, on the contrary, is debarred from this abstraction by its fundamental principles, and the

conditions for chance observation can be suitable only when the same objective components of immediate experience are frequently repeated in connection with the same subjective states. It is hardly to be expected, in view of the great complexity of psychical processes, that this will ever be the case. The coincidence is especially improbable since the very *intention to observe*, which is a necessary condition of all observation, modifies essentially the rise and progress of psychical processes. Observation of nature is not disturbed by this intention on the part of the observer, because here we purposely abstract from the state of the subject. The chief problem of psychology, however, is the exact observation of the rise and progress of subjective processes, and it can be readily seen that under such circumstances the intention to observe either essentially modifies the facts to be observed, or completely suppresses them. On the other hand, psychology, by the very way in which psychical processes originate, is led, just as physics and physiology are, to employ the experimental mode of procedure. A sensation arises in us under the most favorable conditions for observation when it is caused by an external sense-stimulus, as, for example, a tone-sensation from an external tone-vibration, or a light-sensation from an external light-impression. The idea of an object is always caused originally by the more or less complicated cooperation of external sense-stimuli. If we wish to study the way in which an idea is formed, we can choose no other method than that of imitating this natural process. In doing this, we have at the same time the great advantage of being able to modify the idea itself by changing at will the combination of the impressions that cooperate to form it, and of thus learning what influence each single condition exercises on the product. Memory-images, it is true, can not be directly aroused through external sense impressions, but follow them after a longer or shorter interval. Still, it is obvious that their attributes and especially their relation to the primary ideas aroused through direct impressions, can be most accurately learned, not by waiting for their chance arrival, but by using such memory-ideas as may be aroused in a systematic, experimental way, through immediately preceding impressions. The same is true of feelings and volitions: they will be presented in the form best adapted to exact investigation when those impressions are purposely produced which experience has shown to be regularly connected with affective and volitional reactions. There is, then, no fundamental psychical process to which experimental methods can not be applied, and therefore none in whose investigation they are not logically required.

3. *Pure observation*, such as is possible in many departments of natural science, is, from the very character of psychical phenomena, impossible in *individual* psychology. Such a possibility would be conceivable only under the condition that there existed permanent psychical objects, independent of our attention, similar to the relatively permanent objects of nature, which remain unchanged by our observation of them. There are, indeed, certain facts at the disposal of psychology, which, although they are not real objects, still have the character of psychical objects inasmuch as they possess these attributes of relative permanence, and independence of the observer. Connected with these characteristics is the further fact that they are unapprochable by means of experiment in the common acceptance of the term. These facts are the *mental products* that have been developed in the course of history, such as language, mythological ideas, and customs. The origin and development of these products depend in every case on general psy-

chical conditions which may be inferred from their objective attributes. Psychological analysis can, consequently, explain the psychical processes operative in their formation and development. All such mental products of a general character presuppose as a condition the existence of a mental *community* composed of many individuals, though, of course, their deepest sources are the psychical attributes of the individual. Because of this dependence on the community, in particular the social community, this whole department of psychological investigation is designated as *social psychology*, and distinguished from individual, or as it may be called because of its predominating method, *experimental* psychology. In the present stage of the science these two branches of psychology are generally taken up in different treatises: still, they are not so much different departments as different *methods*. So-called social psychology corresponds to the method of pure observation, the objects of observation in this case being the mental products. The necessary connection of these products with social communities, which has given to social psychology its name, is due to the fact that the mental products of the individual are of too variable a character to be the subjects of objective observation. The phenomena gain the necessary degree of constancy only when they become collective.

Thus psychology has, like natural science, *two* exact methods: the experimental method, serving for the analysis of simpler psychical processes, and the observation of general mental products, serving for the investigation of the higher psychical processes and developments.

3a. The introduction of the experimental method into psychology was originally due to the modes of procedure in physiology, especially in the physiology of the sense-organs and the nervous system. For this reason experimental psychology is also commonly called "physiological psychology"; and works treating it under this title regularly contain those supplementary facts from the physiology of the nervous system and the sense-organs, which require special discussion with a view to the interests of psychology, though in themselves they belong to physiology alone. "Physiological psychology" is, accordingly, an intermediate discipline which is, however, as the name indicates, primarily *psychology*, and is, apart from the supplementary physiological facts that it presents, just the same as "experimental psychology" in the sense above defined. The attempt sometimes made, to distinguish psychology proper from physiological psychology, by assigning to the first the psychological interpretation of inner experience, and to the second the derivation of this experience from physiological processes, is to be rejected as inadmissible. There is only *one* kind of causal explanation in psychology, and that is the derivation of more complex psychical processes from simpler ones. In this method of interpretation physiological elements can be used only as supplementary aids, because of the relation between natural science and psychology as above defined (§ 2, 4). Materialistic psychology denies the existence of psychical causality, and substitutes for this problem the other, of explaining psychical processes by brain-physiology. This tendency, which has been shown (§ 2, 10a) to be epistemologically and psychologically untenable, appears among the representatives of both "pure" and "physiological" psychology.

⮠ 15 ⮡

Franz Brentano, Excerpt from *Psychology from an empirical standpoint* (1874).*

I THE CONCEPT AND PURPOSE OF PSYCHOLOGY

There are certain phenomena which once seemed familiar and obvious and appeared to provide an explanation for things which had been obscure. Subsequently, however, these phenomena began to seem quite mysterious themselves and began to arouse astonishment and curiosity. These phenomena, above all others, were zealously investigated by the great thinkers of antiquity. Yet little agreement or clarity has been reached concerning them to this day. It is these phenomena which I have made my object of study. In this work I shall attempt to sketch in general terms an accurate picture of their characteristics and laws. There is no branch of science that has borne less fruit for our knowledge of nature and life, and yet there is none which holds greater promise of satisfying our most essential needs. There is no area of knowledge, with the single exception of metaphysics, which the great mass of people look upon with greater contempt. And yet there is none to which certain individuals attribute greater value and which they hold in higher esteem. Indeed, the entire realm of truth would appear poor and contemptible to many people if it were not so defined as to include this province of knowledge. For they believe that the other sciences are only to be esteemed insofar as they lead the way to this one. The other sciences are, in fact, only the foundation; psychology is, as it were, the crowning pinnacle. All the other sciences are a preparation for psychology; it is dependent on all of them. But it is said to exert a most powerful reciprocal influence upon them. It is supposed to renew man's

*Brentano, F. (1874, 1973). The concept and purpose of psychology. In L. McAlister (ed). *Psychology from an empirical standpoint*. London: Routledge & Kegan Paul, 3–27. Reprinted by permission of Routledge & Kegan Paul.

entire life and hasten and assure progress. And if, on the one hand, it appears to be the pinnacle of the towering structure of science, on the other hand, it is destined to become the basis of society and of its noblest possessions, and, by this very fact, to become the basis of all scientific endeavor as well.

1. The word "psychology" means *science of the soul.* In fact, Aristotle, who was the first to make a classification of science and to expound its separate branches in separate essays, entitled one of his works περι ψυχης. He meant by "soul" the nature, or, as he preferred to express it, the form, the first activity, the first actuality of a living being.* And he considers something a living being if it nourishes itself, grows and reproduces and is endowed with the faculties of sensation and thought, or if it possesses at least one of these faculties. Even though he is far from ascribing consciousness to plants, he nevertheless considered the vegetative realm as living and endowed with souls. And thus, after establishing the concept of the soul, the oldest work on psychology goes on to discuss the most general characteristics of beings endowed with vegetative as well as sensory or intellectual faculties.

This was the range of problems which psychology originally encompassed. Later on, however, its field was narrowed substantially. Psychologists no longer discussed vegetative activities. On the assumption that it lacked consciousness, the entire realm of vegetative life ceased to be considered within the scope of their investigations. In the same way, the animal kingdom, insofar as it, like plants and inorganic things is an object of external perception,[1] was excluded from their field of research. This exclusion was also extended to phenomena closely associated with sensory life, such as the nervous system and muscles, so that their investigation became the province of the physiologist rather than the psychologist.

This narrowing of the domain of psychology was not an arbitrary one. On the contrary, it appears to be an obvious correction necessitated by the nature of the subject matter itself. In fact, only when the unification of related fields and the separation of unrelated fields is achieved can the boundaries between the sciences be correctly drawn and their classification contribute to the progress of knowledge. And the phenomena of consciousness are related to one another to an extraordinary degree. The same mode of perception gives us all our knowledge of them, and numerous analogies relate higher and lower phenomena to one another.[2] The things which external perception has shown us about living beings are seen as if from a different angle or even in a completely different form, and the general truths which we find here are

---

*The Greek expressions are: ψυσις, μορfh, πrwthe nergeia, πρωτη εντελεχεια.

[1]"External perception" is to be understood in its extended, inexact sense here. Cp. Book Two, p. 91.

[2]According to Brentano the concept of consciousness is perfectly uniform; the individual species of consciousness are analogous to one another. For example, judgement is either affirmation or denial, emotive activity is either love or hate. Love is analogous to affirmation, hate to denial.

sometimes the same principles which we see governing inorganic nature, and sometimes analogous ones.

It could be said, and not without some justification, that Aristotle himself suggests this later and more correct delimitation of the boundaries of psychology. Those who are acquainted with him know how frequently, while expounding a less advanced doctrine, he sets forth the rudiments of a different and more correct viewpoint. His metaphysics as well as his logic and ethics provides examples of this. In the third book of his treatise *On the Soul*, where he deals with voluntary actions, he dismisses the thought of investigating the organs that serve as intermediaries between a desire and the part of the body toward whose movement the desire is directed. For, he says, sounding exactly like a modern psychologist, such an investigation is not the province of one who studies the soul, but of one who studies the body.* I say this only in passing so as perhaps to make it easier to convince some of the enthusiastic followers of Aristotle who still exist even in our own times.

We have seen how the field of psychology became circumscribed. At the same time, and in quite an analogous manner, the concept of life was also narrowed, or, if not this concept—for scientists still ordinarily use this term in its broad original sense—at least the concept of the soul.

In modern terminology the word "soul" refers to the substantial bearer of presentations (*Vorstellungen*) and other activities which are based upon presentations and which, like presentations, are only perceivable through inner perception. Thus we usually call soul the substance which has sensations such as fantasy images, acts of memory, acts of hope or fear, desire or aversion.[3]

We, too, use the word "soul" in this sense. In spite of the modification in the concept, then, there seems to be nothing to prevent us from defining psychology in the terms in which Aristotle once defined it, namely as the science of the soul. So it appears that just as the natural sciences study the properties and laws of physical bodies, which are the objects of our external perception,[4] psychology is the science which studies the properties and laws of the soul, which we discover within ourselves directly by means of inner perception, and which we infer, by analogy, to exist in others.

Thus delimited, psychology and the natural sciences appear to divide the entire field of the empirical sciences between them, and to be distinguished from one another by a clearly defined boundary.

But this first claim, at least, is not true. There are facts which can be demonstrated in the same way in the domain of inner perception or external perception. And precisely because they are wider in scope, these more com-

De Anima, III, 10, 433 b 21.

[3] By "substance" we are to understand an entity in which other things subsist but which does not subsist in anything itself: the ultimate subject. The question as to whether the subject of consciousness is spiritual or material is not prejudged by assuming a "substantial substrate."

[4] Cp. above. note 1.

prehensive principles belong exclusively neither to the natural sciences nor to psychology. The fact that they can be ascribed just as well to the one science as to the other shows that it is better to ascribe them to neither. They are, however, numerous and important enough for there to be a special field of study devoted to them. It is this field of study which, under the name metaphysics, we must distinguish from both the natural sciences and psychology.

Moreover, even the distinction between the two less general of these three great branches of knowledge is not an absolute one. As always happens when two sciences touch upon one another, here too borderline cases between the natural and mental sciences are inevitable. For the facts which the physiologist investigates and those which the psychologist investigates are most intimately correlated, despite their great differences in character. We find physical and mental properties united in one and the same group. Not only may physical states be aroused by physical states and mental states by mental, but it is also the case that physical states have mental consequences and mental states have physical consequences.

Some thinkers have distinguished a separate science which is supposed to deal with these questions. One in particular is Fechner, who named this branch of science "psychophysics" and called the famous law which he established in this connection the "Psychophysical Law." Others have named it, less appropriately, "physiological psychology."*

Such a science is supposed to eliminate all boundary disputes between psychology and physiology. But would not new and even more numerous disputes arise in their place between psychology and psychophysics on the one hand and between psychophysics and physiology on the other? Or† is it not obviously the task of the psychologist to ascertain the basic elements of mental phenomena?[5] Yet the psychophysicist must study them too, because sensations are aroused by physical stimuli. Is it not the task of the physiologist to trace voluntary as well as reflex actions back to the origins through an uninterrupted causal chain? Yet the psychophysicist, too, will have to investigate the first physical effects of mental causes.

---

*Recently Wundt adopted this expression in his important work *Principles of Physiological Psychology* [trans. E. B. Titchener (London and New York, 1904)]. Even though it may not be the case in this context, such an expression could be misunderstood, and the term "physiological" taken to refer to the method used. As we shall soon see, some people have wanted to base all of psychology on physiological investigations. Cp. also F. W. Hagen, *Psychologische Studien* (Braunschweig, 1847), p. 7.

†[Translators' note: Reading "oder" with the 1874 edition.]

[5]The task of "ascertaining the basic elements of mental phenomena" Brentano later assigned to "descriptive psychology," and the laws governing their coming into existence, duration, and passing away, to the investigations of "genetic psychology," which is then predominantly physiological in character. But before he had separated the two *disciplines*, he had already sharply discriminated between descriptive and genetic *questions*. Cp. Chap. 3, Sect. 2, p. 44.

Let us not, then, be unduly disturbed by the inevitable encroachment of physiology upon psychology and vice versa. These encroachments will be no greater than those which we observe, for example, between physics and chemistry. They do nothing to refute the correctness of the boundary line we have established; they only show that, justified as it is, this distinction, like every other distinction between sciences, is somewhat artificial. Nor will it be in any way necessary to treat the whole range of so-called psychophysical questions twice, i.e. once in physiology and once in psychology. In the case of each of these problems we can easily show which field contains the essential difficulty. Once this difficulty is solved, the problem itself is as good as solved. For example, it will definitely be the task of the psychologist to ascertain the first mental phenomena which are aroused by a physical stimulus, even if he cannot dispense with looking at physiological facts in so doing. By the same token, in the case of voluntary movements of the body, the psychologist will have to establish the ultimate and immediate mental antecedents of the whole series of physical changes which are connected with them, but it will be the task of the physiologist to investigate the ultimate and immediate physical causes of sensation, even though in so doing he must obviously also look at the mental phenomenon. Likewise, with reference to movements that have mental causes, the physiologist must establish within his own field their ultimate and proximate effects.

Concerning the demonstration that there is a proportional relationship between increases in physical and mental causes and effects, i.e. the investigation of the so-called "Psychophysical Law," it seems to me that the problem has two parts, one of which pertains to the physiologist, while the other is the task of the psychologist. The first is to determine which relative differences in the intensity of physical stimuli correspond to the smallest noticeable differences in the intensity of mental phenomena. The second consists in trying to discover the relations which these smallest noticeable differences bear to one another. But is not the answer to the latter question immediately and completely evident? Is it not clear that all the smallest noticeable differences must be considered equal to one another? This is the view which has been generally accepted. Wundt himself, in his *Physiological Psychology* (p. 295), offers the following argument: "A difference in intensity which is just barely noticeable is . . . a psychic value of constant magnitude. In fact, if one just noticeable difference were greater or smaller than another, *then it would be greater or smaller than the just noticeable,* which is a contradiction." Wundt does not realize that this is a circular argument. If someone doubts that all differences which are just noticeable are equal, then as far as he is concerned, being "just noticeable" is no longer a characteristic property of a constant magnitude. The only thing that is correct and evident *a priori* is that all just noticeable differences are equally noticeable, but not that they are equal. If that were so, every increase which is equal would have to be equally noticeable and every increase which equally noticeable would have to be equal. But this remains to be investigated, and the investigation of this question, which is the job of the psychologist because it deals with laws of comparative judgement, could yield a result quite different from what was expected. The moon does seem to change position more noticeably when it is nearer the horizon than when it is high in the sky, when in fact it changes the same amount in the same amount of time in either case. On the other hand, the first task mentioned above undoubtedly belongs to the psychologist. Physical observations have more extensive application here. And it is certainly no coincidence that we have to thank a physiologist of the first rank such as E. H. Weber for paving the way for this law, and a philosophically trained physicist such as Fechner for establishing it in a more extended sphere.*

So the definition of psychology which was given above appears to be justified, and its position among its neighboring sciences to have been clarified.

2. Nevertheless, not all psychologists would agree to defining psychology as the science of the soul, in the sense indicated above. Some define it, rather, as the science of mental phenomena,[6] thereby placing it on the same level as its sister sciences. Similarly, in their opinion, natural science is to be defined as the science of physical phenomena, rather than as the science of bodies.

Let us clarify the basis of this objection. What is meant by "science of mental phenomena" or "science of physical phenomena"? The words "phenomenon" or "appearance" are often used in opposition to "things which really and truly exist." We say, for example, that the objects of our senses, as revealed in sensation, are merely phenomena; color and sound, warmth and taste do not really and truly exist outside of our sensations, even though they may point to objects which do so exist. John Locke once conducted an experiment in which, after having warmed one of his hands and cooled the other, he immersed both of them simultaneously in the same basin of water. He experienced warmth in one hand and cold in the other, and thus proved that neither warmth nor cold really existed in the water. Likewise, we know that pressure on the eye can arouse the same visual phenomena as would be caused by rays emanating from a so-called colored object. And with regard to determinations of spatial location, those who take appearances for true reality can easily be convinced of their error in a similar way. From the same distance away, things which are in different locations can appear to be in the same location, and from different distances away, things which are in the same location can

---

*In this connection Gustav Fachner says: "From physics outer psychophysics borrows aids and methodology; inner psychophysics leans more to physiology and anatomy, particularly of the nervous system . . ." *Elements of Psychophysics* [trans. Helmut E. Adler (New York, 1966)], p. 10. And again he says in the preface (p. xxix) "that this work would particularly interest physiologists, even though I would at the same time like to interest philosophers."

6On this point, cp. Introduction, p. 402 ff.

appear to be in different locations. A related point is that movement may appear as rest and rest as movement. These facts prove beyond doubt that the objects of sensory experience are deceptive.[7] But even if this could not be established so clearly, we would still have to doubt their veracity because there would be no guarantee for them as long as the assumption that there is a world that exists in reality which causes our sensations and to which their content bears certain analogies, would be sufficient to account for the phenomena.

We have no right, therefore, to believe that the objects of so-called external perception really exist as they appear to us. Indeed, they demonstrably do not exist outside of us. In contrast to that which really and truly exists, they are mere phenomena.

What has been said about the objects of external perception does not, however, apply in the same way to objects of inner perception. In their case, no one has ever shown that someone who considers these phenomena to be true would thereby become involved in contradictions. On the contrary, of their existence we have that clear knowledge and complete certainty which is provided by immediate insight. Consequently, no one can really doubt that a mental state which he perceives in himself exists, and that it exists just as he perceives it. Anyone who could push his doubt this far would reach a state of absolute doubt, a skepticism which would certainly destroy itself, because it would have destroyed any firm basis upon which it could endeavor to attack knowledge.

Defining psychology as the science of mental phenomena in order to make natural science and mental science resemble each other in this respect, then, has no reasonable justification.*

There is another, quite different reason which generally motivates those who advocate such a definition, however. These people do not deny that thinking and willing really exist. And they use the expression "mental phenomena" or "mental appearances" as completely synonymous with "mental

---

[7]That is to say, it can be proved that the qualitatively extended thing which appears to us does not exist *as what it appears to us to be* (cp. Introduction, p. 392 ff.). Below (Book Two, Chap. 1, Sect. 9) it is maintained that the external world is not really "spatial" and "temporal" but "quasi-spatial" and "quasi-temporal."—Brentano expresses himself more clearly in his 1869 essay on Comte (reprinted) and in later essays. That the external world is "quasi-spatial" and "quasi-temporal" can only mean that it is *analogous* to what our perception of space and time shows us. "Analogous," means that the spatial and temporal world exhibits the *same relations* as those exhibited by the object of our perceptions of space and time. That this is how the terms "quasi-spatial" and "quasi-temporal" are to be understood can be seen in the lines that follow, which mention the fact that the real world displays "certain analogies" to the world of our perception, i.e. exhibits the same relationships. Cp. below Sect. 3, p. 19, end of the first paragraph and my note to it, and Chap. 3, Sect. 6, p. 60, Book Two, Chap. 2, p. 107.

*Kant has certainly done this, and it is a mistake which has often been reproved, in particular by Überweg in his *System der Logik*.

states", "mental processes," and "mental events," as inner perception reveals them to us. Nevertheless, their objection to the old definition, too, is related to the fact that on such a definition the limits of knowledge are misunderstood. If someone says that natural science is the science of bodies, and he means by "body" a substance which acts on our sense organs and produces presentations of physical phenomena, he assumes that substances are the cause of external appearances. Likewise, if someone says that psychology is the science of the soul, and means by "soul" the substantial bearer of mental states, then he is expressing his conviction that mental events are to be considered properties of a substance. But what entitles us to assume that there are such substances? It has been said that such substances are not objects of experience; neither sense perception nor inner experience reveal substances to us.[8] Just as in sense perception we encounter phenomena such as warmth, color and sound, in inner perception we encounter manifestations of thinking, feeling and willing. But we never encounter that something of which these things are properties. It is a fiction to which no reality of any sort corresponds, or whose existence could not possibly be proved, even if it did exist. Obviously, then, it is not an object of science. Hence natural science may not be defined as the science of bodies nor may psychology be defined as the science of the soul. Rather, the former should be thought of simply as the science of physical phenomena, and the latter, analogously, as the science of mental phenomena. There is no such thing as the soul, at least not as far as we are concerned, but psychology can and should exist nonetheless, although, to use Albert Lange's paradoxical expression, it will be a psychology without a soul.*

We see that the idea is not as absurd as the expression makes it seem. Even viewed in this way psychology still retains a wide area for investigation.

A glance at natural science makes this clear. For all the facts and laws which this branch of inquiry investigates when it is conceived of as the science

---

[8]Brentano maintains the opposite view: according to his theory, which follows Aristotle, both sensation and inner perception exhibit *substances* to us. In inner perception we apprehend ourselves as "thinking things" (thinking in the Cartesian sense = consciousness) or "*res cogitans.*" In external perception we apprehend something as a subject which has accidents, for example, something extended which has a color. The assumption that there is a substance is not a fiction, but the assumption that there is an attribute without any subject supporting it is an immediately absurd fiction. (Cp. Condillac, cited in Vaihinger's *Philosophie des Als Ob*, p. 383.) But for quite a while—even in the study of "mental phenomena"—this fiction proves to be harmless, very much as one can study scientifically the transcendent "physical phenomena" of the external world and leave the question of their subject in doubt.—This comfortable fiction is not only harmless, but advantageous insofar as it eliminates a point of controversy in broad stretches of a large area of investigation.

The History of Materialism [trans. Ernest Chester Thomas, 3rd ed. (London, 1892)], Book II, Sect. iii, Chap. 3, p. 168. "Calmly assume, then, a psychology without a soul! And yet the name will still be useful so long as we have something to study that is not completely covered by any other science."

of bodies will continue to be investigated by it when it is viewed only as the science of physical phenomena. This is how it is actually viewed at present by many famous natural scientists who have formed opinions about philosophical questions, thanks to the noteworthy trend which is now bringing philosophy and the natural sciences closer together. In so doing, they in no way restrict the domain of the natural sciences. All of the laws of coexistence and succession which these sciences encompass according to others, fall within their domain according to these thinkers, too.

The same thing is true of psychology. The phenomena revealed by inner perception are also subject to laws. Anyone who has engaged in scientific psychological research recognizes this and even the layman can easily and quickly find confirmation for it in his own inner experience. The laws of the coexistence and succession of mental phenomena remain the object of investigation even for those who deny to psychology any knowledge of the soul. And with them comes a vast range of important problems for the psychologist, most of which still await solution.

In order to make more intelligible the nature of psychology as he conceived it, John Stuart Mill, one of the most decisive and influential advocates of this point of view, has given in his *System of Logic** a synopsis of the problems with which psychology must be concerned.

In general, according to Mill, psychology investigates the laws which govern the succession of our mental states, i.e. the laws according to which one of these states produces another.†

In his opinion, some of these laws are general, others more special. A general law, for example, would be the law according to which, "whenever any state of consciousness has once been excited in us, no matter by what cause . . . a state of consciousness resembling the former but inferior in intensity, is capable of being reproduced in us, without the presence of any such cause as excited it at first." Every impression, he says, using the language of Hume, has its idea. Similarly, there would also be certain general laws which determine the actual appearance of such an idea. He mentions three such Laws of Association of Ideas. The first is the Law of Similarity: "Similar ideas tend to excite one another." The second is the Law of Contiguity: "When two impressions have been frequently experienced . . . either simultaneously or in immediate succession, then when one of these impressions, or the idea of it recurs,

---

*VI, Chap. 4, Sect. 3.

†Certainly sensations are also mental states. Their succession, however, is the same as the succession of the physical phenomena which they represent. Therefore, it is the task of the natural scientist to establish the laws of this succession insofar as it is dependent upon the physical stimulation of the sense organs.[9]

[9]The note means that the study of the *genetic* laws governing sensations is the business of the physiologist or the "psycho-physicist." Cp. p. 7. Just above Brentano proved that it is inevitable for both psychology and the natural sciences to mutually interact in the areas. Cp. also p. 98.

it tends to excite the idea of the other." The third is the Law of Intensity: "Greater intensity in either or both of the impressions, is equivalent, in rendering them excitable by one another, to a greater frequency of conjunction."

The further task of psychology, according to Mill, is to derive from these general and elementary laws of mental phenomena more specific and more complex laws of thought. He says that since several mental phenomena often work concurrently, the question arises whether or not every such case is a case of a combination of causes—in other words, whether or not effects and initial conditions are always related in the same way, as they are in the field of mechanics, where a motion is always the result of motion, homogeneous with its causes and in a certain sense the sum of its causes; or whether the mental realm also exhibits cases similar to the process of chemical combination, where you see in water none of the characteristics of hydrogen and oxygen, and in cinnabar none of the characteristics of mercury and sulphur. Mill himself believed it to be an established fact that both types of case exist in the domain of inner phenomena. Sometimes the processes are analogous to those in mechanics and sometimes to those in chemical reactions. For it may happen that several ideas coalesce in such a way that they no longer appear as several but seem to be a single idea of a completely different sort. Thus, for example, the idea of extension and three dimensional space develops from kinesthetic sensations.

A series of new investigations is linked with this point. In particular the question will be raised as to whether belief and desire are cases of mental chemistry, i.e. whether they are the product of a fusion of ideas. Mill thinks that perhaps we must answer this question negatively. In whatever way it should be decided, perhaps even affirmatively, it would nevertheless be certain that entirely different fields of investigation are opened here. And so there emerges the new task of ascertaining, by means of special observations, the laws of succession of these phenomena, i.e. of ascertaining whether or not they are the products of such psychological chemistry, so to speak. In respect to belief, we would inquire what we believe directly; according to what laws one belief produces another; and what are the laws in virtue of which one thing is taken, rightly or erroneously, as evidence for another thing. In regard to desire, the primary task would consist in determining what objects we desire naturally and originally, and then we must go on to determine by what causes we are made to desire things originally indifferent or even disagreeable to us.

In addition, there is yet another rich area for investigation, one in which psychological and physiological research become more closely involved with one another than elsewhere. The psychologist, according to Mill, has the task of investigating how far the production of one mental state by others is influenced by confirmable physical states. Individual differences in susceptibility to the same psychological causes can be conceived as having a threefold basis. They could be an original and ultimate fact, they could be consequences of the previous mental history of those individuals, and they could be the result of differences in physical organization. The attentive and critical observer will recognize, Mill thinks, that by far the greatest portion of a person's character can be adequately explained in terms of his education and outward circumstances. The remainder can, by and large, only be explained indirectly in terms of organic differences. And obviously this holds true not merely for the commonly recognized tendency of the deaf toward mistrustfulness, of the congenitally blind toward lustfulness, of the physically handicapped toward irritability, but also for many other, less easily intelligible phenomena. If there are still, as Mill grants, other phenomena, instincts in particular, which cannot be explained in any other way except directly in terms of one's particular physical organization, we see that a wide field of investigation is assured for psychology in the area of ethology, i.e. formulating the laws of the formation of character.

This is a survey of psychological problems from the point of view of one of the most important advocates of psychology as a purely phenomenalistic science. It is really true that in none of the above-mentioned respects is psychology harmed by this new conception of it or by the point of view which leads to such a conception. As a matter of fact, in addition to the questions raised by Mill and those implicit in them, there are still others which are equally significant. Thus there is no shortage of important tasks for psychologists of this school, among whom are, at the present time, men who have made themselves preeminently of service to the advancement of science.

Nevertheless, the above conception of psychology seems to exclude at least one question which is of such importance that its absence alone threatens to leave a serious gap in this science. The very investigation which the older conception of psychology considered its main task, the very problem which gave the first impetus to psychological research can, apparently, no longer be raised on this view of psychology. I mean the question of continued existence after death. Anyone familiar with Plato knows that above all else it was the desire to ascertain the truth about this problem which led him to the field of psychology. His *Phaedo* is devoted to it, and other dialogues such as the *Phaedrus, Timaeus* and the *Republic* come back to the question time and again. And the same thing is true of Aristotle. Admittedly he sets forth his proofs for the immortality of the soul in less detail than Plato, but it would be a mistake to conclude from this that the problem was any less important to him. In his logical works, where the doctrine of apodictic or scientific demonstration was necessarily the most important issue, he still discusses the problem, condensed into a few pages in the *Posterior Analytics*, in striking contrast to other long, extended discussions. In the *Metaphysics* he speaks of the deity only in a few short sentences in the last book,* yet this study was avowedly so essential to him that he actually applied the name "theology" to the entire science, as

---

*I mean, of course, Book Lambda.

well as the names "wisdom" and "first philosophy." In the same way, in his treatise *On the Soul*, he discusses man's soul and its immortality only very briefly,
even when he is doing more than merely mentioning it in passing. Yet the classification of psychological problems at the beginning of this work clearly indicates that this question seemed to him to be the most important object of psychology. We are told there that the psychologist has the task, first of all, of
investigating what the soul is, and then of investigating its properties, some of
which appear to inhere in it alone and not in the body, and, as such, are spiritual. Furthermore he must investigate whether the soul is composed of parts
or whether it is simple, and whether all the parts are bodily states or whether
there are some which are not, in which case its immortality would be assured.
The various *aporiai* which are linked with these questions show that we have
hit upon the point which aroused this great thinker's thirst for knowledge
most of all. This is the task to which psychology first devoted itself, and which
gave it its first impetus for development. And it is precisely this task which
appears, at the present time, to have fallen into disrepute and to have become
impossible, at least from the standpoint of those who reject psychology as the
science of the soul. For if there is no soul, then, of course, the immortality of
the soul is out of the question.

This conclusion appears to be so immediately obvious that we cannot be
surprised if some partisans of the conception here developed, A. Lange, for
one, consider it to be self-evident.[†] And so psychology offers us a drama similar to the one which occurred in the natural sciences. The alchemists' striving
to produce gold from mixtures of elements first instigated chemical research,
but the mature science of chemistry abandoned such ambitions as impossible.
And somewhat in the manner of the well-known parable about the promise of
the dying father, here too the heirs of earlier investigators have fulfilled the
predictions of their predecessors. In the parable the sons industriously dug up
the vineyard in which they believed a treasure was hidden, and if they did not
find the buried gold, they reaped the fruit of the well-tilled soil instead.
Something similar has happened to chemists, and would be happening to psychologists too. The mature science would have to abandon the question of
immortality, but we could say that, as consolation, the zealous efforts which
stemmed from a desire for the impossible have led to the solution of other
questions whose far-reaching significance cannot be called into question.

Nevertheless, these two cases are not wholly identical. In place of the
alchemists' dreams, reality offered a higher substitute. But in comparison with
Plato's and Aristotle's hopes of reaching certainty concerning the continued
existence of our better part after the dissolution of the body, the laws of association of ideas, of the development of convictions and opinions, and of the origin and growth of desire and love, would hardly be real compensation. The
loss of this hope would appear to be far more regrettable. Consequently, if the

---

[†]*History of Materialism*, trans. Thomas, 3rd ed., Book II, Sect. i, Chap. 1, p. 162.

opposition between these two conceptions of psychology really implied the acceptance or rejection of the question of immortality, this issue would become of paramount importance and would compel us to undertake metaphysical research concerning the existence of substance as the bearer of mental states.

Yet, whatever appearance of necessity there is for restricting the range of inquiry in this connection, it may still be no more than an appearance. In his time David Hume strongly opposed the metaphysicians who claimed to have found within themselves a substance which was the bearer of mental states. "For my part," he says, "when I enter most intimately into what I call *myself*, I always stumble on some particular perception or other, of heat or cold, light or shade, love or hatred, pain or pleasure. I never can catch *myself* at any time without a perception, and never can observe anything but the perception. When my perceptions are removed for any time, as by sound sleep; so long am I insensible of myself, and may truly be said not to exist." If certain philosophers claim that they perceive *themselves* as something simple and permanent, Hume does not want to contradict them, but of himself and of everyone else (this sort of metaphysician alone excepted), he is convinced "that they are nothing but a bundle or collection of different perceptions, which succeed each other with an inconceivable rapidity, and are in a perpetual flux and movement."* We see, therefore, that Hume ranks unequivocally among the opponents of a substantial soul. Nevertheless, Hume himself remarks that in a conception such as his, all the proofs of immortality retain absolutely the same strength as in the traditional conception to which it is opposed. Of course, Albert Lange interprets this declaration as a mockery,** and he may very likely be right, for it is known that Hume did not elsewhere scorn the use of malicious irony as a weapon.† What Hume says, however, is not so obviously ridiculous as Lange and perhaps Hume himself might think. For even though it is self-evident that those who deny the existence of a substantial soul cannot speak of the immortality of the soul in the proper sense of the word, it still does not follow that the question of the immortality of the soul loses all meaning because we deny the existence of a substantial bearer of mental phenomena. This becomes evident as soon as you recognize that with or without a substantial soul you cannot deny that there is a certain continuity of our mental life here on earth. If someone rejects the existence of a substance, he must assume that such a continuity does not require a substantial bearer. And the question whether our mental life somehow continues even after the destruction of the body will be no more meaningless for him than for anyone else. It is wholly inconsistent for thinkers of this persuasion to reject, for the

*Treatise on Human Nature, Book I, IV, Sect. 6.

**History of Materialism, trans. Thomas, 3rd ed., Book II, Sect. i, Chap. 1, p. 162.

†Alexander Bain says of him, "As he was a man fond of literary effects, as well as of speculation, we do not always know when he is in earnest." Mental Science, 3rd ed., p. 207.

reasons mentioned, the question of immortality even in this, its essential sense, though it certainly would be more appropriate to call it immortality of life than immortality of the soul.

This was fully recognized by John Stuart Mill. In the passage from his *Logic* cited earlier, it is true that we do not find the question of immortality listed among those problems to be dealt with by psychology. In his work on Hamilton, however, he has developed with utmost clarity the very idea that we have just formulated.*

Likewise, at the present time in Germany no important thinker has expressed his rejection of a substantial substrate for both mental and physical states as often and as categorically as Theodor Fechner. In his *Psychophysics*, in his *Atomenlehre* and in other writings, he criticizes this doctrine, sometimes in earnest, sometimes humorously. Nevertheless, he candidly acknowledges his belief in immortality. It is clear, therefore, that even if one accepts the metaphysical view which led modern thinkers to substitute the definition of psychology as the science of mental phenomena for the traditional definition as the science of the soul, the field of psychology would not thereby be narrowed in any way, and, above all, it would not suffer any essential loss.

It would appear to be just as inadmissible, however, to accept this view without a thorough metaphysical investigation, as it is to reject it without a test. Just as there are eminent men who have questioned and denied that phenomena have a substantial bearer there also have been and still are other very famous scientists who firmly believe that they do. H. Lotze agrees with Aristotle and Leibniz on this point, as does Herbert Spencer, among contemporary English empiricists.** And, with his characteristic frankness, even John Stuart Mill has recognized, in his work on Hamilton, that the rejection of substance as the bearer of phenomena is not entirely free from difficulties and uncertainties, especially in the mental realm.† If, then, the new definition of psychology were connected with the new metaphysics just as inseparably as the old definition was with the old, we would be forced either to look for a third definition, or to descend into the fearful depths of metaphysics.

Happily, the opposite is true. There is nothing in the new definition of psychology which would not have to be accepted by adherents of the older school as well. For whether or not there are souls, the fact is that there are mental phenomena. And no one who accepts the theory of the substantiality of the soul will deny that whatever can be established with reference to the soul is also related to mental phenomena. Nothing, therefore, stands in our

---

*An Examination of Sir William Hamilton's Philosophy, Chap. XII: "As to immortality, it is precisely as easy to conceive that a succession of feelings, a thread of consciousness, may be prolonged to eternity, as that a spiritual substance forever continues to exist; and any evidence which proves the one, will prove the other."

**See his *First Principles*.

†*Exam. of Sir Wm. Hamilton's Philo.*, Chap. XII.

way if we adopt the modern definition instead of defining psychology as the science of the soul. Perhaps both are correct. The differences which still exist between them are that the old definition contains metaphysical presuppositions[10] from which the modern one is free; that the latter is accepted by opposing schools of thought, while the former already bears the distinctive mark of one particular school; and the one, therefore, frees us from general preliminary researches which the other would oblige us to undertake. Consequently, the adoption of the modern conception simplifies our work. Furthermore, it offers an additional advantage: any exclusion of an unrelated question not only simplifies, but also reinforces the work. It shows that the results of our investigation are dependent on fewer presuppositions, and thus lends greater certainty to our convictions.

We, therefore, define psychology as the science of mental phenomena, in the sense indicated above. The preceding discussion should be sufficient to clarify the general meaning of this definition. Our subsequent investigation of the difference between mental and physical phenomena will provide whatever further clarification is needed.

3. If someone wanted to compare the relative value of the scientific field which we have just described with that of the natural sciences, using as a measuring stick only and exclusively the interest aroused at the present time by these two types of investigations, psychology would undoubtedly be overshadowed. It is a different matter if we compare the goals which each of the two sciences pursue. We have seen what kind of knowledge the natural scientist is able to attain. The phenomena of light, sound, heat, spatial location and locomotion which he studies are not things which really and truly exist.[11] They are signs of something real, which, through its causal activity, produces presentations of them. They are not, however, an adequate representation of this reality, and they give us knowledge of it only in a very incomplete sense. We can say that there exists something which, under

---

[10]The assumption that there is a substantial substrate of mental activities is not really a metaphysical, i.e., a transcendent assumption, according to Brentano's later doctrine, for a presentation without a subject is an absurd fiction. The subject of the presentation, or its subsistent substrate which does not subsist in anything further, is the only thing which deserves the name "substance." Cp. above Note 3 and the introduction.

[11]This passage is misleading; in order to understand it correctly, one must read and interpret it in connection with Chap. I, Sect. 2, p. 9, Chap. III, Sect. 4, pp. 47, 48, and Book Two, Chap. I, Sect. 9, p. 97 ff. In the sentence as it reads in the text "light" is to be understood as meaning the colored, "sound" as meaning the heard sound, just as in the beginning of Sect. 2 and repeatedly, for example pp. 69, 70, i.e. the *sense-quality* which we somehow perceive with relative spatial determination. Natural science, especially physics, has to do with these "mere phenomena" insofar as it (1) shows us that color and sound, etc., are merely appearances and so do not exist, and (2) investigates the transcendent causes of the perceptions (sensations) in which these qualities appear to us. This comes out unambiguously from pp. 10, 47, 48, 60, 98, 107. It also emerges from the immediately following sentences, moreover. In Chap. III, p. 44, and in other passages light and sound are spoken of in the physical sense, i.e. as the transcendent vibrations of the ether or air.

certain conditions, causes this or that sensation. We can probably also prove that there must be relations among these realities similar to those which are manifested by spatial phenomena shapes and sizes. But this is as far as we can go. We have no experience of that which truly exists, in and of itself, and that which we do experience is not true. The truth of physical phenomena is, as they say, only a relative truth.[12]

The phenomena of inner perception are a different matter. They are true in themselves. As they appear to be, so they are in reality, a fact which is attested to by the evidence with which they are perceived. Who could deny, then, that this constitutes a great advantage of psychology over the natural sciences?

The high theoretical value of psychological knowledge is obvious in still another respect. The worthiness of a science increases not only according to the manner in which it is known, but also with the worthiness of its object. And the phenomena the laws of which psychology investigates are superior to physical phenomena not only in that they are true and real in themselves,[13] but also in that they are incomparably more beautiful and sublime. Color and sound, extension and motion are contrasted with sensation and imagination, judgement and will, with all the grandeur these phenomena exhibit in the ideas of the artist, the research of a great thinker, and the self-dedication of the virtuous man. So we have revealed in a new way how the task of the psychologist is higher than that of the natural scientist.

It is also true that things which directly concern us claim our attention more readily than things foreign to us. We are more eager to know the order and origin of our own solar system than that of some more remote group of heavenly bodies. The history of our own country and of our ancestors attracts our attention more than that of other people with whom we have no close ties. And this is another reason for conferring the higher value upon the science of mental phenomena. For our mental phenomena are the things which are most our own. Some philosophers have even identified the self with a collection of mental phenomena, others with the substantial bearer of such a collection of phenomena. And in ordinary language we say that physical changes are external to us while mental changes take place within us.

---

[12]Cp. Book Two, Chap. I, p. 98.

[13]This passage is also misleading; in Brentano's opinion the physicist, too, is concerned with "things which are true and real in themselves," namely certain transcendent causes of sensations. Cp. Note 7 and pp. 95, 60. Of course, he also deals with the "color," the "sound," but this is primarily in order to study the causes of seeing the color, hearing the sound and, insofar as he is not a phenomenalist like Mach, to establish that colors and sounds are "mere phenomena," i.e. cannot be proved to exist. What exists is, on the one hand, the person who sees colors, hears sounds, and, on the other hand, the event which happens in the ether and is one of the causes of seeing and hearing. Psychology is distinguished by the fact that it has to do with phenomena which *are known immediately as true and real in themselves*. This, and nothing else, was and is Brentano's doctrine.

These very simple observations can easily convince anyone of the great theoretical significance of psychological knowledge. But even from the point of view of practical significance—and perhaps this is what is most surprising—psychological questions are in no way inferior to those which occupy the natural sciences. Even in this respect there is hardly another branch of science which can be placed on the same level with psychology unless perhaps it is one which merits the same consideration on the grounds that it is an indispensable preparatory step toward the attainment of psychological knowledge.

Let me point out merely in passing that psychology contains the roots of aesthetics, which, in a more advanced stage of development, will undoubtedly sharpen the eye of the artist and assure his progress. Likewise, suffice it to say that the important art of logic, a single improvement in which brings about a thousand advances in science, also has psychology as its source.[14] In addition, psychology has the task of becoming the scientific basis for a theory of education, both of the individual and of society. Along with aesthetics and logic, ethics and politics also stem from the field of psychology. And so psychology appears to be the fundamental condition of human progress in precisely those things which, above all, constitute human dignity. Without the use of psychology, the solicitude of the father as well as that of the political leader, remains an awkward groping. It is because there has been no systematic application of psychological principles in the political field until now, and even more because the guardians of the people have been, almost without exception, completely ignorant of these principles, that we can assert along with Plato and with many contemporary thinkers that, no matter how much fame individuals have attained, no truly great statesman has yet appeared in history. Even before physiology was systematically applied to medicine, there was no lack of famous physicians, as shown by the great confidence they won and by the astonishing cures attributed to them. But anyone who is acquainted with medicine today knows how impossible it would have been for there to have been a single truly great physician prior to the last few decades. The others were all merely blind empiricists, more or less skillful, and more or less lucky. They were not, and could not have been what a trained and discerning physician must be. Up to the present time the same thing holds true of statesmen. The extent to which they, too, are merely blind empiricists is demonstrated every time that an extraordinary event suddenly changes the political situation, and even more clearly every time one of them finds himself in a foreign country where conditions are different. Forsaken by their empirically derived maxims, they become completely incompetent and helpless.

How many evils could be remedied, both on the individual and social level, by the correct psychological diagnosis, or by knowledge of the laws

[14]Concerning the charge of psychologism which was raised against Brentano because of this and other views, see the supplementary essays and the editor's introduction.

according to which a mental state can be modified! What an increase in mental power mankind would achieve if the basic mental conditions which determine the different aptitudes for being a poet, a scientist, or a man of practical ability could be fully ascertained beyond any doubt by means of psychological analysis! If this were possible, we could recognize the tree, not from its fruit, but from its very first budding leaves, and could transplant it immediately to a place suited to its nature. For aptitudes are themselves very complex phenomena; they are the remote consequences of forces whose original activity suggests these consequences no more than the shape of the first buds suggests the fruit which the tree will bear. In both cases, however, we are dealing with relationships that are subject to similar laws. And just as botany can make accurate predictions, a sufficiently developed psychology must be able to do the same. In this and in a thousand other different ways, its influence would become most beneficial. Perhaps it alone will be in a position to provide us the means to counteract the decadence which sadly interrupts the otherwise steadily ascending cultural development from time to time.[15] It has long been noted, and correctly so, that the often-used metaphorical expressions, "old nation," and "old civilization," are not strictly appropriate, because, while organisms only partially regenerate themselves, society renews itself completely in each successive generation; we can speak of peoples and epochs becoming sick, but not old. There are, however, such sicknesses which have always appeared periodically up to now, and which, because of our lack of medical skill, have regularly led to death. Hence, even though the really essential analogy is missing, the similarity to old age in external appearance is undeniable.

It is apparent that the practical tasks I assign to psychology are far from insignificant. But is it conceivable that psychology will ever really approach this ideal? Doubt on this point seems to be well-founded. From the fact that up to now, for thousands of years, psychology has made practically no progress, many would like to believe that they are justified in concluding with certainty that it will also do little in the future to further the practical interests of mankind.

The answer to this objection is not far to seek. It is revealed by a simple consideration of the place which psychology occupies in the system of sciences.

The general theoretical sciences form a kind of hierarchy in which each higher step is erected on the basis of the one below it. The higher sciences investigate more complex phenomena, the lower ones phenomena that are simpler, but which contribute to the complexity. The progress of the sciences which stand higher in the scale naturally presupposes that of the lower ones. It is, therefore, evident that, apart from certain weak empirical antecedents, the higher sciences will attain their development later than the lower. In par-

[15]See the title essay in Franz Brentano's *Die Vier Phasen der Philosophie und ihr augenblicklicher Stand*, ed. Oskar Kraus (Leipzig, 1926) and Kraus's book, *Franz Brentano*, p. 18.

ticular, they will not be able to reach that state of maturity in which they can meet the vital needs of life at the same time as the lower sciences. Thus we saw that mathematics had long been turned to practical applications, while physics still lay dozing in its cradle and did not give the slightest sign of its capacity, subsequently so brilliantly proved, to be of service to the needs and desires of life. Similarly, physics had long attained fame and multiple practical applications when, through Lavoisier, chemistry discovered the first firm basis upon which it could stand, in the next few decades, in order to revolutionize, if not the earth, at least the cultivation of the earth, and with it so many other spheres of practical activity. And once again, chemistry had already achieved many splendid results while physiology was yet to be born. And it is not necessary to go back too many years to find the beginnings of a more satisfactory development in physiology, and attempts at practical application followed immediately. They were incomplete perhaps, but nonetheless served to demonstrate that only from physiology is a re-birth of medicine to be expected. It is easy to explain why physiology developed so late. The phenomena it studies are much more complex than those studied by the earlier sciences and are dependent upon them, just as the phenomena of chemistry are dependent upon those of physics and the phenomena of physics are dependent upon those of mathematics. But it is just as easy to understand, then, why psychology has not borne more abundant fruit up until now.[16] Just as physical phenomena are under the influence of mathematical laws, and chemical phenomena are under the influence of physical laws, and those of physiology under the influence of all these laws, so psychological phenomena are influenced by the laws governing the forces which shape and renew the bodily organs involved. Consequently, if someone knew from direct experience absolutely nothing about the state of psychology up to the present time, and were acquainted only with the history of the other theoretical sciences and with the recent birth of physiology and indeed even chemistry, he could affirm, without in any way being a skeptic about psychological matters, that psychology has achieved nothing as yet, or that it has achieved very little, and that at best it is only recently that it has shown a tendency toward a more substantial development. This implies that the most important fruits which psychology may bear for practical life, lie in the future. So, should this person turn his attention to the history of psychology, he would merely find in its barrenness confirmation of his expectations; and he would find himself in no way committed to an unfavorable judgement as to its future accomplishments.

[16]On this point, see Brentano's inaugural lecture in Vienna, "Ueber die Gründe der Entmutigung auf philosophischem Gebiete," reprinted in *Ueber die Zukunft der Philosophie*, ed. Oskar Kraus (Leipzig, 1929). Brentano arranges the sciences in order somewhat as Comte does. Of course Comte leaves psychology out, while according to Brentano it is to be placed after physiology and prior to sociology. But it is only *genetic* and *physiological* psychology which presupposes the development of scientific knowledge of nature for its complete development. Descriptive-phenomenological psychology is independent of it to a great extent.

We see that the backward condition in which psychology has remained appears to be a necessity, even if we do not doubt the possibility of a rich development in the future. That there is such a possibility is shown by the promising, though weak, beginning it has already in fact made. Once a certain level of its possible development has been reached, the practical consequences will not fail to materialize. For the individual and even more for the masses, where the imponderable circumstances which impede and promote progress balance each other out, psychological laws will afford a sure basis for action.

We may, therefore, confidently hope that psychology will not always lack both inner development and useful applications. Indeed the needs which it must satisfy have already become pressing. Social disorders cry out more urgently for redress than do the imperfections in navigation and railway commerce, agriculture and hygiene. Questions to which we might give less attention, if it were up to us to choose, force themselves upon everyone's attention. Many people have already seen this to be the most important task of our time. We could mention several great scientists who are devoting themselves, with this end in view, to the investigation of psychological laws and to methodological inquiries concerning the derivation and confirmation of conclusions to be applied in practice.

It cannot possibly be the task of political economy to put an end to the present confusion and to re-establish the peace in society which has been increasingly lost amid the clash of conflicting interests. Political economy has a role to play, but neither the whole task nor the major part depends upon it. And indeed even the growing interest which is being accorded to it can serve to corroborate these statements. In the introduction to his *Principles of Political Economy,* John Stuart Mill has touched upon the relation between this science and psychology. The differences in the production and distribution of goods by different peoples and at different times, in his opinion, would depend to a certain extent on differences in the states of their knowledge of physical matters, but would also have psychological causes. "Insofar as the economic condition of nations turns upon the state of physical knowledge," he continues, "it is a subject for the physical sciences, and the arts founded on them. But insofar as the causes are moral or psychological, dependent on institutions and social relations or on the principles of human nature, their investigation belongs not to physical, but to moral and social science, and is the object of what is called Political Economy."*

It seems beyond doubt, therefore, that in the future—and to a certain extent perhaps the not too distant future—psychology will exert a consider-

*P. 26.

able influence upon the practical aspects of life. In this sense we could characterize psychology, as others have already done, as the science of the future, i.e. as the science to which, more than any other, the future belongs; the science which, more than any other, will mould the future; and the science to which, in the future, other sciences will be of service and to which they will be subordinate in their practical application. For this will be the position of psychology once it reaches maturity and is capable of effective action. Aristotle called politics the master art to which all others serve as subsidiaries. As we have seen, however, in order to be what it should be, it is necessary that politics pay heed to psychology, just as the lesser arts must heed the teachings of natural science. Its theory, I would like to suggest, will merely be a different arrangement and further development of psychological principles directed toward the attainment of a practical goal.

We have advanced four reasons which appear to be sufficient to show the outstanding importance of the science of psychology: the inner truth of the phenomena it studies, the sublimity of these phenomena, the special relationship they have to us, and finally, the practical importance of the laws which govern it. To these we must add the special and incomparable interest which psychology possesses insofar as it instructs us about immortality and thus becomes, in another sense, the science of the future. The question concerning the hope of a hereafter and our participation in a more perfect state of the world falls to psychology. As we have noted, psychology has already made attempts to solve this problem, and it does not seem that all its efforts in that direction have been without success. If this really is the case, we have here, without doubt, its highest theoretical achievement, which would be of the greatest practical importance as well,[17] besides lending new value to psychology's other theoretical achievements. When we depart from this life we separate ourselves from all that is subject to the laws of natural science. The laws of gravitation, of sound, of light and electricity disappear along with the

---

[17]Immortality, i.e. survival after death, is probable only if we assume an optimistic *Weltanschauung,* i.e. if we assume that the universe is subject to a rational necessity. Without such an assumption there would be no reason to suppose that, in some other mode of life, the subject would have an organ of consciousness such as the brain is in this life. In a world of blind necessity, as pessimists have realized, continued life is not worth desiring at all. Now psychology as such can very well initiate inquiries about the spirituality and indestructibility of the subject of consciousness and affirm both, but the question of immortality is really a metaphysical problem. The belief that the mental dispositions acquired in this world will be retained in the next can exert a powerful influence upon our behavior, and the "practical significance" of the problem of immortality lies in this fact. See Brentano's *The Origin of our Knowledge of Right and Wrong* (London and New York, 1969), pp. 40–41 n., 130. When we conjecture what the next world is going to be like, we need not limit ourselves to a three-dimensional world. See *Die vier Phasen,* p. 45.

phenomena[18] for which experience has established them. Mental laws, on the other hand, hold true for our life to come as they do in our present life, insofar as this life is immortal.[19]

So Aristotle had good reason for placing psychology above all the other sciences, as he did at the beginning of his treatise *On the Soul*, even though in so doing he took into consideration its theoretical advantages exclusively. He says,

> Holding as we do that, while knowledge of any kind is a thing to be honoured and prized, one kind of it may, either by reason of its greater exactness or of a higher dignity and greater wonderfulness in its objects, be more honourable and precious than another, on both counts we should naturally be led to place in the front rank the study of the soul.*

What undoubtedly causes surprise is the fact that Aristotle here asserts that even with respect to its exactitude psychology is superior to the other sciences. For him the exactitude of knowledge is bound up with the imperishability of the object. According to him, that which changes continuously and in every respect evades scientific investigation, whereas that which is most permanent possesses the most abiding truth. Be that as it may, we, too, cannot deny that the laws of psychology at least possess a permanent important truth.

---

[18]Here "phenomenon" is used for the transcendent event in nature, contrary to p. 95.

[19]In saying this, Brentano can only have been thinking of the laws of descriptive psychology, not the ultimate laws of genetic psychology. For the latter, insofar as they are physiological in nature, must be different in another sort of world (one of 3 + n dimensions, for example).

*[Editor's note: *De Anima*, 402 a 1–3, trans. J. A. Smith, in *The Works of Aristotle*, ed. W. D. Ross (Oxford, 1931), III.]

≈ 16 ≈

Edward Bradford Titchener, "Experimental psychology: A retrospect" (1925).*

Experimental psychology, as we all know, took shape against a background of physics and of a physiology informed by physics. Fechner was a physicist; Helmholtz was physicist and physiologist; Weber and Hering and Wundt were physiologists. The new science, then, was to be a science of the type of experimental physiology; Wundt called his great compendium of 1874 Principles of Physiological Psychology; and in all sorts of ways—in choice of subjects for investigation, in the manner of presentation of published results, in the psychologist's general mode of approach to experimental problems— the influence of physiology was manifest. Think of the early problems!—sensory quality and sensory intensity, the reaction experiment in its various complications, the time sense, the range and fluctuations of attention, the perception of tactual and visual space; they were one and all of them problems that had a physiological aspect and that suggested an experimental control by instruments of physiological type. Wundt's Physiological Psychology is a tremendous advance upon the Lectures of eleven years before; yet a very great deal of it is anticipated in the third edition of Wundt's own Physiology.

These things, in the large, are known to all of us, and I do not wish to spend time on the familiar. We cannot, however, if we are taking an historical view, omit facts simply because they are obvious; and besides, the facts of which I am reminding you are, in my judgment, of quite first-rate importance.

*Titchener, E. B. (1925). Experimental psychology: A retrospect. *The American Journal of Psychology, 36*, 313–323. Reprinted with the permission of the University of Illinois Press.

[1]This paper contains the substance of an address delivered before the twenty-second annual meeting of Experimental Psychologists, April 9, 1925, at the dedication of Eno Hall, Princeton University.

I believe that experimental psychology had an extraordinarily fortunate birth. No doubt, the early investigators set to work too hastily and too confidently. No doubt, we have wasted an immense amount of energy on Weber's Law and Helmholtz' theory of visual sensations and the windinesses of nativism and empiricism. No doubt. But when all is said it remains true that the initial impulse was sound and the initial perspective correct. If physics and physiology and psychology—let us rather use the more general word, and say: if physics and biology and psychology cannot be housed under one roof, as members of a single family, then the term science can have no stable meaning. The accomplishment seems more difficult to us than it did to the mid nineteenth century; our store of facts is more bewildering, and we put less trust in our coordinating concepts. The ideal, nevertheless, of a biology modelled upon physics, the mother of the sciences, and of a psychology modelled upon that physically informed biology holds for us no less than it held for our fathers.

So experimental psychology, as it started on its course, was impelled by the inner urge to be a science in the manner of experimental physiology. What, now, were the external influences that bore upon it, and under what environmental conditions did it grow up? The environment, I need not say, was hostile; and if we are to 'know ourselves' as we are today,[2] we must take some account of the kind and degree of that hostility.

The first of the three major influences that wrought against the establishment of experimental psychology—for as I look back on our history, I distinguish three such influences—was local and temporal; it was the influence of Herbart and the Herbartian psychology. To most of us, I suppose, Herbart is little more than an historical name; to Wundt in the seventies Herbart was an all-pervading institutional opponent.[3] Leipzig, in particular, the university to which Wundt was called in 1875, had long been the head and centre of the Herbartian movement. Hartenstein, Herbart's editor, had it is true given up his chair some fifteen years earlier. But Ziller was still there,—Ziller, who was one of the original editors of the *Zeitschrift für exacte Philosophie*, the technical organ of the Herbartian school, and who in 1868 had founded the hardly less important *Verein für wissenschaftliche Pädagogik*. Drobisch and Strümpell, two of the greatest names among the Herbartians, still held their Leipzig chairs,—and were to hold them for some time to come, since Drobisch lived to 1896 and Strümpell to 1899. In 1875 Lazarus and Steinthal, the founders of the *Zeitschrift für Völkerpsychologie und Sprachwissenschaft* (Wundt had already had a tilt with them in 1863) were professors in Berlin; Volkmann and Lindner were at Prag,—the whole of Austria, indeed, had been Herbartianised by Bonitz and Exner; Waitz was at Marburg; Stoy was at Jena. To us, truly, these men are

---

[2]The Delphic maxim γνωθι σαυτον is carved above the door of Eno Hall.

[3]It is worth remembering that the lives of the two men overlapped; Wundt was nine years old when Herbart died.

just a list of names and dates; to a nascent experimental psychology they represented a highly formidable opposition.

It would, of course, be a very foolish critic who should say that Wundt became a voluntarist because Herbart had been an intellectualist, or that Wundt made psychology the basis of the *Geisteswissenschaften* because Herbart had severed theoretical from practical philosophy and had derived his psychology in part from metaphysics. Yes, but it would be a foolish reader, too, who should forget that all through the second part of the Physiological Psychology Wundt has Herbart steadily in mind; that the improvised doctrine of apperception is meant as a counterblast to Herbart; that the whole of Wundt's psychology beyond the chapter on perception is shaped with polemical reference to Herbart. That, you see, is the sort of trick that history plays upon us; a good many of the later Wundtians have been anti-Herbartians without realising it. So that the effect of Herbartianism upon experimental psychology was in reality twofold, internal and external. The Herbartians were in possession; they must be dislodged, superseded, discredited, if experimental psychology was to grow to power; that was the external side of things. Internally, meantime, the very fact of having to combat a well-rounded and critically tested system tinged and moulded the doctrines of experimental psychology itself. I shall not try to give you further details; let me only remind you, before we leave Herbart, that the struggle lasted over into the present century; Wundt's rejoinder to Delbrück appeared in 1901.[4]

The second unfavorable influence which I have to note is of far greater importance,—partly because of its antiquity and perennial vitality, partly because of its seeming innocence and the guise of kinship with experimental psychology which it often assumes, so that it works insidiously from within rather than openly from without. It is the influence of empirical psychology, a mode of psychology that goes back to Aristotle and Thomas Aquinas, and that forms the staple contents of most psychologies, down to and including our twentieth-century textbooks. The empirical psychologist professes to take mind as he finds it: I use the term 'mind' without prejudice, for the subject-matter of empirical psychology; in point of fact, the definition of that subject-matter has varied very greatly: always, however, the empirical psychologist professes to take mind as he finds it. And, like everybody else, he finds mind in use, whether in a man's converse with himself or in his intercourse with his fellow-men. This subject-matter, then, mind in use, the empirical psychologist seeks to reduce to order and arrangement; and empirical psychology thus becomes a rationalisation of practice, a 'description and explanation' of mental uses. Our sister-science of biology suffers from the same sort of contamination: I have read textbooks of physiology that were in essence nothing else than rationalisations of the art of medicine, and I have read textbooks of biol-

[4] *Sprachgeschichte und Sprachpsychologie, mit Rücksicht auf B. Delbrücks "Grundfragen der Sprachforschung,"* esp. I. and II.

ogy that contained little more than a 'description and explanation' of the practice of adaptation. Biology, fortunately for her, stands nearer than we to physics, and has that great example more closely before her eyes; none the less, biology has suffered. Experimental psychology has suffered immensely more.

It happened that the year 1874, which saw the publication of the Physiological Psychology, was also the year of the appearance of Brentano's Psychology from the Empirical Standpoint,—a masterly and masterful work which shows the temper of the empirical psychologist in exemplary form. Brentano's book made from the first a deep impression upon psychology, and this impression has but deepened and widened as the years have passed. It did not, however, come on the scene as a third combatant, opposed equally to the Herbartians and to experimental psychology; things were not as simple as that. On the one hand, Brentano did not think it worth while to challenge Herbart on even terms. His teacher Trendelenburg had already disposed polemically of the Herbartian metaphysics; and Brentano, when he has to speak of the Herbartian psychology, dismisses it in a few polite but very decided sentences as an obvious failure. Though, then, the Empirical Psychology gives a round dozen references to Herbart and the leading Herbartians, it deals with them only in matters of detail; it looks on the dominance of the Herbartian school as an historical accident, of no intrinsic importance; it shows nothing of the obsession that we have noted in the Physiological Psychology. Wundt, in this regard, had found an ally; but the ally showed a certain aristocratic indifference toward the common enemy. On the other hand,—and this was the real danger for experimental psychology,—neither Brentano nor Wundt saw that his own conception of psychology refused and denied the conception of his rival: that an empirical psychology, a rationalisation of mental practice, was utterly at variance with an experimental psychology that should be a science of fact and law coordinate with experimental physiology and experimental physics. Wundt still had one foot, so to say, in the empirical camp; and Brentano was ready, subject to his own view of psychological method, to adapt the procedures of experiment to his empirical purposes.

You will expect me, now, to compare and contrast the two books, the Physiological and the Empirical Psychologies. You will realise, from what I have just said, that the contrast will not be clean and sharp; there is in Wundt a great deal of empirical psychology. That apart, however, there is still a preliminary point to be made, before we can draw our parallels. Empirical psychology is not to be defined by the contents of any single book. I have called Brentano's work exemplary; but that does not mean that his doctrines would find universal acceptance, even among his fellow empiricists. For it is of the very essence of empiricism, you remember, to classify and explain the uses of mind; and that is a task which calls less for facts than for ingenuity; and where ingenuities are in play, systems will differ individually. Let me take an illustration; and I choose one in which both the men of whom I am speaking are involved. We find that the Wundt of 1874 tends to delimit psychology, as the later Wundt overtly delimits it, by point of view and not by subject-matter; there are for Wundt no psychical, there are only psychological phenomena. We find that Brentano, on the contrary, recognises psychical phenomena as a special and distinct field of subject-matter. But on this point Brentano is at one with Herbart, the metaphysical psychologist, while Wundt represents a tendency that first appears among the empirical psychologists of purest blood. The definition by point of view has its source in the empirical psychology of Locke; and it has been adopted, in our own day, by Ward and (in his later years) by James,—by the two most distinguished and most representative empirical psychologists of the English-speaking world. Should we not have expected that Brentano, steeped as he was in the traditional British psychology, would work out to the position of Ward and James rather than range himself with Herbart? The question plainly asks too much; we must not forget Brentano's training; but at any rate the illustration shows that Brentano is not 'typical of his kind'. Or let me take another instance: we tend to think of the doctrine of association of ideas as 'typically' empirical. Here again, however, Brentano would have gone his own way. He would, we know, have discussed association when he came to deal with the laws and properties of ideas,—and what he would have made of it we may, perhaps, guess in part from the treatment accorded it by Stumpf; but he would have left it behind when he was dealing with judgments and with feeling and will. Wundt, too, revolts from associationism; but the revolt is not experimentally motived. On the contrary, the doctrine of apperception is no less empirical than that of association; it bases on the 'feeling of activity'; and since activity is not a psychological quality, the 'feeling of activity' already implies a rationalisation of psychological experience, quite in the empirical manner. In this instance, therefore, both Brentano and Wundt diverge, within empiricism itself, from what we are tempted to call the empirical 'type'. It is clear that not everything that Brentano says is characteristically empirical, as I have also shown you that not every difference between Brentano and Wundt is a difference between empirical and experimental psychology.

When we put the two books side by side, we find, indeed, far too much agreement. Wundt, like Brentano, accepts from the older empiricists a whole array of classificatory and explanatory terms: consciousness, attention, association,—perception, emotion, memory, imagination. If only he had had the insight to throw them all away! Wundt possessed, in fact, just one clear concept, the concept of sensation as composed of intensity and quality; and that concept was neither happily chosen nor, after its adoption, adequate to support a whole experimental psychology. All the rest were foggy from much argument; and though Wundt made heroic efforts to clarify some of them— notably in the instance of consciousness, which he sought to redefine in a strictly experimental atmosphere—they were in the end too much for him;

empirical they had been, and empirical they remained. From our point of later vantage we can see that a tremendous opportunity was lost; but we have no right to think either that Wundt should have seen that opportunity or, if he had, should have thought himself strong enough or privileged enough to seize it. At any rate, nobody has been strong enough since; we ourselves are getting rid of the equivocal and theory-ridden terms piecemeal, a little at a time; and it will be long before experimental psychology is finally free of them.

The acceptance of these concepts meant, naturally, the acceptance of certain positions with which they were historically connected; and so, for example, we find Wundt as ready as Brentano to make psychology the basis of the mental sciences. It is true that Brentano is looking particularly toward logic, while Wundt has rather in mind disciplines like history, ethics, jurisprudence. It is true also that Wundt puts experimental psychology at the lower end of the psychological scale, nearest to natural science and furthest from the mental sciences. All the same, he makes psychology continuous throughout, and does not see that he changes his attitude—from experimental to empirical—as he travels upward; that is one of the reasons why the later *Völkerpsychologie* is psychologically unsatisfactory. We can only regret, once more, that his vision was not clearer, and try to take care ourselves, now that our eyes are opened, to avoid the sort of confusion of thought that this example betrays. The task for us is very far from easy.

What, then, of the differences between the books? The differences are unmistakable. Let me remind you, to begin with, of the difference in treatment of psychological method. Three of Brentano's thirteen chapters are given over to the discussion of method. Wundt does not discuss method at all; he names it in passing, and gets on at once to the account of experimental procedures, the description of available apparatus.[5] Surely, that single difference would be enough to prove that Wundt, however imperfectly he realises what he is about, has in fact attained to a new standpoint in psychology. A science is concerned to set forth its facts and uniformities; it has no call and, as science, it has no competence to treat of method. The textbooks of the pattern sciences, experimental physics and experimental physiology, do not dream of introducing chapters on method; they leave all such preliminaries to logic, which has a place reserved for methodology; and Wundt's own *Methodenlehre* appears, accordingly, not in the Psychology of 1874, but in the Logic of 1883. Brentano, on his side, was entirely consistent. Since empirical psychology is, as I have pointed out, a work of ingenuity, since logical argumentation is of its very texture and substance, it involves a special methodology as an integral part of its construction; science is transformed into an applied logic. There is the difference; and in the effecting of the difference

---

[5]Cf. the references to "innere Beobachtung," "reine Selbstbeobachtung," *Phys. Psych.*, 1874, 5, 8. The discussion of Kant's second objection is, evidently, methodological; but even here the argument turns on the possibility of recourse to an experimental procedure.

experimental psychology had chosen the right scientific road. Would that we might have been allowed to walk in it! But controversies began; Wundt was presently beguiled into discussing method within his psychological system; and our experimental textbooks, ever since, have done homage to logic. Remember, nevertheless, that we were started aright, and that if we ever succeed in ousting empiricism and in banishing method to its proper limbo we shall only be recovering the position that Wundt once occupied for us.

This difference, the stressing of logical method and the stressing of experimental procedure, is perhaps the most salient single difference between the two books. There are, however, plenty of other differences. Brentano, for instance, gives a long programme of psychological applications, a programme that has an extraordinarily modern tone; Wundt says not a word about applications. This difference, again, is characteristic. Brentano starts out from mind in use, and his general psychology is, one might almost say, a theoretical applied psychology; it is, at any rate, a rationalising of general mental application; it was but natural, then, that he should look forward to special fields of application. Moreover, Brentano's general psychology is, for him, a completed psychology; however much remains to be done in detail, the principles are established,—established internationally, for psychology as a whole, now and for ever; and such a psychology is fit and ready for application. Wundt, however, does not share the confidence that is natural to the empirical psychologist; for him, psychology is just beginning; he foresees long years of patient experimentation to be spent on the establishment of principle; and application simply does not occur to him, does not show above his horizon. Or consider, again, the use that the two men make of physiology. Brentano appeals to physiology for purposes of explanation, under the principle of sufficient reason; Wundt is, in 1874, a thorough-going parallelist. And so the list might be lengthened. In sum, however, all differences may be traced back to the fundamental ground of divergence: Brentano is an empirical psychologist, Wundt is trying, however blindly, to escape from empiricism, and to inaugurate an experimental psychology. Brentano offers us a logical construction, built of argument and counter-argument; his bricks are the opinions of authorities, which he accepts, rejects, reshapes, in accordance with his design. Wundt seeks to put together a psychology of experimentally determined fact, and is ready to give as much space to the description of an experimental set-up as to the view of some influential empiricist. The resulting structure is ricketty enough, and is patched out all too freely with borrowed or improvised empirical materials; it represents, nevertheless, a new kind of psychology; the design, for all its hesitancies and concessions, is the design of experimental physics and experimental physiology.

I have spoken of this second influence upon our science, the influence of empirical psychology, as if it were unmitigatedly bad. So, abstractly regarded, I take it to have been. But that does not mean, let me add, that empirical psychology in and for itself is unmitigatedly bad. Not only has it shown itself, historically, the necessary forerunner of experimental psychology, but even in the days of experimental psychology it may do good service as an intermediary between science and special application. I am not here concerned with that question,[6] any more than I am with the intrinsic merits of particular empiricists,—some of whom have done sheerly first-rate work. I am concerned with the effect of empiricism upon experimentalism; and in the abstract that effect has been wholly bad. Only, we live in the concrete; and in the concrete there are always mitigating circumstances. It was very much to the good, I said just now, that experimental psychology takes its descent from experimental physiology. Yes, but the 'psychology' of the physicist and the physiologist is almost universally an empirical psychology; that is why we see distinguished physicists running to spiritism; and you can hardly imagine a follower of Helmholtz, for example, approaching psychology in any other than empirical terms. It may well be, therefore, that the admixture of empirical psychology, which I have been condemning, was of practical utility—not only in holding Wundt's reports of experiments together in a quasi-systematic way, but also in securing friends for the new movement among the representatives of the other sciences.[7]

Such friendship, even if based in part upon misunderstanding, would help the new science in its struggle with the third environmental influence,—the hostility of philosophy. I have spoken of the Herbartians: but while in the early seventies the Herbartian psychology was dominant in Germany, it cannot be said that the Herbartian philosophy was similarly dominant. Think, for instance, of the more important men who derive from Hegel,—Erdmann at Halle (I am afraid that we do not nowadays read his delightful *Psychologische Briefe* as widely as we should), Kuno Fischer at Heidelberg, Michelet and Zeller at Berlin; and there were other schools and other distinguished and influential men. All these philosophers were, so to say on principle, opposed to experimental psychology, and Wundt's choice of the title *Philosophische Studien* for his laboratory studies reminds one of nothing so much as the small boy with thumb to nose. The philosophers were shocked at the mere idea of subjecting mind to the color-mixer and the chronoscope; and they were shocked the more as the sacrilege threatened one of their vested rights. So the controversies began,—and, really, there is a good deal in them of childish wrangling. Wundt in 1905 thought that the main battle was won, and changed to

---

[6] I do not myself believe that empirical psychology is adequate to this mediating function; I believe that we should be on firmer ground in logic and should also get better results in practice if we looked for mediation to a phenomenology of the 'psychophysical' organism, the entire man (cf. my *Thought-Processes*, 1909, 75). But the question is not in point here,—and obviously a footnote is not the place for its discussion.

[7] I need hardly remark that if I had been tracing the history of experimental psychology in its material rather than in its formal aspects I should have had a great deal to say of the positive contributions that physiologists have made to our science.

the title *Psychologische Studien.* Perhaps he was right; though the field of battle has not by any means been cleared up, and local conflicts are still going merrily on. Good time and valuable energy have, at all events, been wasted upon an intrinsically foolish quarrel; and there is no countervailing gain save a certain solidarity of front, a certain esprit de corps, that we should have attained in any case, under the other two hostile influences, without the added spur of philosophical antagonism. The struggle with Herbart was incidental; Herbartianism would have died a natural death in due course, and the coming of experimental psychology merely hastened the end. The struggle with empirical psychology was inevitable and has inevitably been long drawn out; for the experimental movement was, in fact, a revolutionary movement,—and, like other revolutionary movements, could grow to power and to clear vision only by way of actual conflict. The struggle with philosophy was on a lower plane than either of these others; it reflects on the one side the over-assurance of youth, and on the other the unwillingness of high priori prejudice to face the trend of events.

I have now set forth, in the oversimplified outline that is all that an address of this sort permits, what I take to be the most important facts regarding the nature and nurture of our young science. Experimental psychology came of excellent stock: a stock that had not only attained prestige in matters of the intellect, but that had also learned to frame ideals and to bear responsibilities; the birth of the science was auspicious. Its bringing up was variously chequered. The hostile influences of which I have spoken have, obviously, been unable to throttle it; otherwise we should not be here today. But indeed, its growth has been, on the whole, steady and assured. There were a few years, in the nineties of the last century, when it seemed to be outgrowing its strength; but that danger passed; and no one can now doubt that the infant of the sixties and seventies has proved itself viable. The question that remains is—What, in the year of grace 1925, is its mental age?

The question is one, I take it, that has attracted us all; and we have answered it differently, according as our mood happened to be depressed or cheerful. It is, of course, a question that we cannot properly answer at all, because—if I may use the figure—we stand somewhere within our own perspective, and therefore cannot judge either how far we have come or how far, to attain the status of the adult, we have yet to go. On the whole, I daresay that we tend to overrate our progress, perhaps on the principle that a space of time variously filled looks long in retrospect. Still, there are signs and symptoms; and we may as well pluck up our courage and try to read them. We have, I think without question, passed from infancy into childhood. Our independence of physiology is a guarantee of that: we no longer feel any necessity of consulting physiology when we lay out our investigations; we do not necessarily borrow physiological apparatus and procedures; it does not occur to us to imitate physiology in the presentation of results; in a word, we are out of our physiological leading-strings. It is pleasant and reassuring, certainly, if while an enquiry is in course or after it has been brought to completion we can make a cross-correlation with physiology; but we feel ourselves, none the less, to be independent; we do not lean upon physiology. That sign, then, seems unequivocal; and there is another, which a bold spirit might interpret to the effect that we are approaching adolescence—I mean the radical change that has been wrought over the whole field of the science since it turned to phenomenology. We can trace the impulse to this change directly to Hering; and if Hering has had to wait a long time before coming to his own, that is partly because he was overshadowed, for almost the whole of his working life, by the counter-influence of Helmholtz, and partly because he was himself otherwise entangled in a rather crude form of empirical psychology. Phenomenology is not yet, is not of itself, experimental psychology; but it provides today a safe and sure mode of approach to the analysis of our psychological subject-matter; and our recourse to it, our realisation of its promise, may perhaps be taken as a sign of adolescence. If, then, Godfrey Thomson is right, and the intellect is most alert and most capable at the age of sixteen, we may congratulate ourselves that experimental psychology is nearing that critical point, and may expect far better things from it in the near future than have been accomplished in the past.[8]

---

[8]Several friendly critics among my hearers have told me that this concluding paragraph is too optimistic. I am afraid they are right; I can only plead in excuse that the occasion of the address—the dedication of the first independent building in the western hemisphere planned and erected exclusively for psychological teaching and psychological research—naturally disposed one toward optimism.

V. American Functional Psychology

As psychology began to take on a particularly American flavor, the combined spirits of pragmatism and utilitarianism provided a standard. That is, questions of use and application determined the value of serious research into psychological issues. The more abstract, theoretical arguments that had dominated the European debate about the nature of the mind gave way to considerations of the workings of the mind, and American psychology shied away from blind adherence to any theoretical preconception and opted for an eclectic approach.

The philosopher William James (1842–1910) became the best known American psychologist and wrote his influential text, *The Principles of Psychology* (1890), which is excerpted here. James's psychology drew on all of the European traditions, but he blended them into an integration tempered by common sense and pragmatism. In this selection, James' vision of psychology is clearly expressed. His psychology emphasized the process of consciousness, not unlike Brentano's formulation, and he added purpose to give consciousness coherence and direction. James was neither a systematic theorist nor a rigorous experimenter, but he was open to varieties of opinion, and he was instrumental to establishing a receptive context for psychology in the United States.

John Dewey (1859–1952) was another great figure of early American psychology, and participated at the two great centers of American Functional Psychology, the University of Chicago and

Columbia University. His paper, "The reflex arc concept in psychology" (1896) was a major break from the Wundt-Titchener definition of psychology, since he argued for the importance of motor activity viewed as smooth, coordinated and flowing—that movement was something more than the sum of its constituent muscle reactions and reflexes. This paper is important because it states a clearly functional standard and responds to the prevailing European notions of dualism.

Perhaps the closest that functionalism ever came to being defined within its contemporary context was attempted in the paper by James Rowland Angell (1869–1949). In this 1907 paper, a portion of which is reproduced here, Angell justified the biological foundations of mental adaptation and placed psychology clearly in support of Darwin's theory of evolution by natural selection. Thus, psychological activity had survival value for the organism, which in Angell's judgment is the ultimate standard of value.

It has often been remarked that functional psychology was less a formal system than a type of consensus about the value of psychology. Perhaps more importantly, functionalism in psychology provided a vehicle for the new science to be introduced in the United States, while also giving it a distinctive American imprint. Although it was a fairly short-lived movement, functionalism did establish the discipline of psychology within American academia, and it contributed to American leadership in psychology which continued throughout the 20th Century.

REFERENCES

ANGELL, J. R. (1907). The province of functional psychology. *Psychological Review, 14,* 61–71.

DEWEY, J. (1896). The reflex arc concept in psychology. *Psychological Review, 3,* 357–370.

JAMES, W. (1890). The scope of psychology. In *The principles of psychology.* Cambridge, MA: Harvard University Press, 15–24.

❧ 17 ❧

William James, Excerpt from *The principles of psychology* (1890).*

THE SCOPE OF PSYCHOLOGY

Psychology is the Science of Mental Life, both of its phenomena and of their conditions. The phenomena are such things as we call feelings, desires, cognitions, reasonings, decisions, and the like; and, superficially considered, their variety and complexity is such as to leave a chaotic impression on the observer. The most natural and consequently the earliest way of unifying the material was, first, to classify it as well as might be, and, secondly, to affiliate the diverse mental modes thus found, upon a simple entity, the personal Soul, of which they are taken to be so many facultative manifestations. Now, for instance, the Soul manifests its faculty of Memory, now of Reasoning, now of Volition, or again its Imagination or its Appetite. This is the orthodox 'spiritualistic' theory of scholasticism and of common-sense. Another and a less obvious way of unifying the chaos is to seek common elements *in* the divers mental facts rather than a common agent behind them, and to explain them constructively by the various forms of arrangement of these elements, as one explains houses by stones and bricks. The 'associationist' schools of Herbart in Germany, and of Hume, the Mills and Bain in Britain, have thus constructed a *psychology without a soul* by taking discrete 'ideas,' faint or vivid, and showing how, by their cohesions, repulsions, and forms of succession, such things as reminiscences, perceptions, emotions, volitions, passions, theories, and all the other furnishings of an individual's mind may be engendered. The

*Reprinted by permission of the publishers from William James, *The Principles of psychology*, Volume I, Frederick Burkhardt, General Editor, Fredson Bowers, Textual Editor, Cambridge, Mass: Harvard University Press, 15–24, Copyright (c) 1981 by the President and Fellows of Harvard College.

very Self or *ego* of the individual comes in this way to be viewed no longer as the pre-existing source of the representations, but rather as their last and most complicated fruit.

Now, if we strive rigorously to simplify the phenomena in either of these ways, we soon become aware of inadequacies in our method. Any particular cognition, for example, or recollection, is accounted for on the soul-theory by being referred to the spiritual faculties of Cognition or of Memory. These faculties themselves are thought of as absolute properties of the soul; that is, to take the case of memory, no reason is given why we should remember a fact as it happened, except that so to remember it constitutes the essence of our Recollective Power. We may, as spiritualists, try to explain our memory's failures and blunders by secondary causes. But its *successes* can invoke no factors save the existence of certain objective things to be remembered on the one hand, and of our faculty of memory on the other. When, for instance, I recall my graduation-day, and drag all its incidents and emotions up from death's dateless night, no mechanical cause can explain this process, nor can any analysis reduce it to lower terms or make its nature seem other than an ultimate *datum*, which, whether we rebel or not at its mysteriousness, must simply be taken for granted if we are to psychologize at all. However the associationist may represent the present ideas as thronging and arranging themselves, still, the spiritualist insists, he has in the end to admit that *something*, be it brain, be it 'ideas,' be it 'association,' *knows* past time *as* past, and fills it out with this or that event. And when the spiritualist calls memory an 'irreducible faculty,' he says no more than this admission of the associationist already grants.

And yet the admission is far from being a satisfactory simplification of the concrete facts. For why should this absolute god-given faculty retain so much better the events of yesterday than those of last year, and, best of all, those of an hour ago? Why, again, in old age should its grasp of childhood's events seem firmest? Why should illness and exhaustion enfeeble it? Why should repeating an experience strengthen our recollection of it? Why should drugs, fevers, asphyxia, and excitement resuscitate things long since forgotten? If we content ourselves with merely affirming that the faculty of memory is so peculiarly constituted by nature as to exhibit just these oddities, we seem little the better for having invoked it, for our explanation becomes as complicated as that of the crude facts with which we started. Moreover there is something grotesque and irrational in the supposition that the soul is equipped with elementary powers of such an ingeniously intricate sort. Why *should* our memory cling more easily to the near than the remote? Why should it lose its grasp of proper sooner than of abstract names? Such peculiarities seem quite fantastic; and might, for aught we can see *a priori*, be the precise opposites of what they are. Evidently, then, *the faculty does not exist absolutely, but works under conditions*; and *the quest of the conditions* becomes the psychologist's most interesting task.

However firmly he may hold to the soul and her remembering faculty, he must acknowledge that she never exerts the latter without a *cue*, and that something must always precede and *remind* us of whatever we are to recollect. "An *idea!*" says the associationist, "an idea associated with the remembered thing; and this explains also why things repeatedly met with are more easily recollected, for their associates on the various occasions furnish so many distinct avenues of recall." But this does not explain the effects of fever, exhaustion, hypnotism, old age, and the like. And in general, the pure associationist's account of our mental life is almost as bewildering as that of the pure spiritualist. This multitude of ideas, existing absolutely, yet clinging together, and weaving an endless carpet of themselves, like dominoes in ceaseless change, or the bits of glass in a kaleidoscope,—whence do they get their fantastic laws of clinging, and why do they cling in just the shapes they do?

For this the associationist must introduce the order of experience in the outer world. The dance of the ideas is a copy, somewhat mutilated and altered, of the order of phenomena. But the slightest reflection shows that phenomena have absolutely no power to influence our ideas until they have first impressed our senses and our brain. The bare existence of a past fact is no ground for our remembering it. Unless we have seen it, or somehow *undergone* it, we shall never know of its having been. The experiences of the body are thus one of the conditions of the faculty of memory being what it is. And a very small amount of reflection on facts shows that one part of the body, namely, the brain, is the part whose experiences are directly concerned. If the nervous communication be cut off between the brain and other parts, the experiences of those other parts are non-existent for the mind. The eye is blind, the ear deaf, the hand insensible and motionless. And conversely, if the brain be injured, consciousness is abolished or altered, even although every other organ in the body be ready to play its normal part. A blow on the head, a sudden subtraction of blood, the pressure of an apoplectic hemorrhage, may have the first effect; whilst a very few ounces of alcohol or grains of opium or hasheesh, or a whiff of chloroform or nitrous oxide gas, are sure to have the second. The delirium of fever, the altered self of insanity, are all due to foreign matters circulating through the brain, or to pathological changes in that organ's substance. The fact that the brain is the one immediate bodily condition of the mental operations is indeed so universally admitted nowadays that I need spend no more time in illustrating it, but will simply postulate it and pass on. The whole remainder of the book will be more or less of a proof that the postulate was correct.

Bodily experiences, therefore, and more particularly brain-experiences, must take a place amongst those conditions of the mental life of which Psychology need take account. *The spiritualist and the associationist must both be 'cerebralists,'* to the extent at least of admitting that certain peculiarities in the way of working of their own favorite principles are explicable only by the fact that the brain laws are a codeterminant of the result.

Our first conclusion, then, is that a certain amount of brain-physiology must be presupposed or included in Psychology.[1]

In still another way the psychologist is forced to be something of a nerve-physiologist. Mental phenomena are not only conditioned *a parte ante* by bodily processes; but they lead to them *a parte post*. That they lead to *acts* is of course the most familiar of truths, but I do not merely mean acts in the sense of voluntary and deliberate muscular performances. Mental states occasion also changes in the calibre of blood-vessels, or alteration in the heart-beats, or processes more subtle still, in glands and viscera. If these are taken into account, as well as acts which follow at some *remote period* because the mental state was once there, it will be safe to lay down the general law that *no mental modification ever occurs which is not accompanied or followed by a bodily change*. The ideas and feelings, e.g., which these present printed characters excite in the reader's mind not only occasion movements of his eyes and nascent movements of articulation in him, but will some day make him speak, or take sides in a discussion, or give advice, or choose a book to read, differently from what would have been the case had they never impressed his retina. Our psychology must therefore take account not only of the conditions antecedent to mental states, but of their resultant consequences as well.

But actions originally prompted by conscious intelligence may grow so automatic by dint of habit as to be apparently unconsciously performed. Standing, walking, buttoning and unbuttoning, piano-playing, talking, even saying one's prayers, may be done when the mind is absorbed in other things. The performances of animal *instinct* seem semi-automatic, and the *reflex acts* of self-preservation certainly are so. Yet they resemble intelligent acts in bringing about the *same ends* at which the animals' consciousness, on other occasions, deliberately aims. Shall the study of such machine-like yet purposive acts as these be included in Psychology?

The boundary-line of the mental is certainly vague. It is better not to be pedantic, but to let the science be as vague as its subject, and include such phenomena as these if by so doing we can throw any light on the main business in hand. It will ere long be seen, I trust, that we can; and that we gain much more by a broad than by a narrow conception of our subject. At a certain stage in the development of every science a degree of vagueness is what best consists with fertility. On the whole, few recent formulas have done more real service of a rough sort in psychology than the Spencerian one that the essence of mental life and of bodily life are one, namely, 'the adjustment of inner to outer relations.' Such a formula is vagueness incarnate: but because it takes into account the fact that minds inhabit environments which act on them and on which they in turn react; because, in short, it takes mind in the midst of all its concrete relations, it is immensely more fertile than the old-fashioned 'rational psychology,' which treated the soul as a detached existent,

[1]Cf. George T. Ladd: *Elements of Physiological Psychology* (1887), pt. III, chap. III. §§ 9, 12.

sufficient unto itself, and assumed to consider only its nature and properties. I shall therefore feel free to make any sallies into zoology or into pure nerve-physiology which may seem instructive for our purposes, but otherwise shall leave those sciences to the physiologists.

Can we state more distinctly still the manner in which the mental life seems to intervene between impressions made from without upon the body, and reactions of the body upon the outer world again? Let us look at a few facts.

If some iron filings be sprinkled on a table and a magnet brought near them, they will fly through the air for a certain distance and stick to its surface. A savage seeing the phenomenon explains it as the result of an attraction or love between the magnet and the filings. But let a card cover the poles of the magnet, and the filings will press forever against its surface without its ever occurring to them to pass around its sides and thus come into more direct contact with the object of their love. Blow bubbles through a tube into the bottom of a pail of water, they will rise to the surface and mingle with the air. Their action may again be poetically interpreted as due to a longing to recombine with the mother-atmosphere above the surface. But if you invert a jar full of water over the pail, they will rise and remain lodged beneath its bottom, shut in from the outer air, although a slight deflection from their course at the outset, or a re-descent towards the rim of the jar when they found their upward course impeded, would easily have set them free.

If now we pass from such actions as these to those of living things, we notice a striking difference. Romeo wants Juliet as the filings want the magnet; and if no obstacles intervene he moves towards her by as straight a line as they. But Romeo and Juliet, if a wall be built between them, do not remain idiotically pressing their faces against its opposite sides like the magnet and the filings with the card. Romeo soon finds a circuitous way, by scaling the wall or otherwise, of touching Juliet's lips directly. With the filings the path is fixed; whether it reaches the end depends on accidents. With the lover it is the end which is fixed, the path may be modified indefinitely.

Suppose a living frog in the position in which we placed our bubbles of air, namely, at the bottom of a jar of water. The want of breath will soon make him also long to rejoin the mother-atmosphere, and he will take the shortest path to his end by swimming straight upwards. But if a jar full of water be inverted over him, he will not, like the bubbles, perpetually press his nose against its unyielding roof, but will restlessly explore the neighborhood until by re-descending again he has discovered a path round its brim to the goal of his desires. Again the fixed end, the varying means!

Such contrasts between living and inanimate performances end by leading men to deny that in the physical world final purposes exist at all. Loves and desires are to-day no longer imputed to particles of iron or of air. No one supposes now that the end of any activity which they may display is an ideal purpose presiding over the activity from its outset and soliciting or drawing it into being by a sort of *vis a fronte*. The end, on the contrary, is deemed a mere passive result, pushed into being *a tergo,* having had, so to speak, no voice in its own production. Alter the pre-existing conditions, and with inorganic materials you bring forth each time a different apparent end. But with intelligent agents, altering the conditions changes the activity displayed, but not the end reached; for here the idea of the yet unrealized end co-operates with the conditions to determine what the activities shall be.

The pursuance of future ends and the choice of means for their attainment are thus the mark and criterion of the presence of mentality in a phenomenon. We all use this test to discriminate between an intelligent and a mechanical performance. We impute no mentality to sticks and stones, because they never seem to move for *the sake of* anything, but always when pushed, and then indifferently and with no sign of choice. So we unhesitatingly call them senseless.

Just so we form our decision upon the deepest of all philosophic problems: Is the Kosmos an expression of intelligence rational in its inward nature, or a brute external fact pure and simple? If we find ourselves, in contemplating it, unable to banish the impression that it is a realm of final purposes, that it exists for the sake of something, we place intelligence at the heart of it and have a religion. If, on the contrary, in surveying its irremediable flux, we can think of the present only as so much mere mechanical sprouting from the past, occurring with no reference to the future, we are atheists and materialists.

In the lengthy discussions which psychologists have carried on about the amount of intelligence displayed by lower mammals, or the amount of consciousness involved in the functions of the nerve-centres of reptiles, the same test has always been applied: Is the character of the actions such that we must believe them to be performed *for the sake* of their result? The result in question, as we shall hereafter abundantly see, is as a rule a useful one,—the animal is, on the whole, safer under the circumstances for bringing it forth. So far the action has a teleological character; but such mere outward teleology as this might still be the blind result of *vis a tergo.* The growth and movements of plants, the processes of development, digestion, secretion, etc., in animals, supply innumerable instances of performances useful to the individual which may nevertheless be, and by most of us are supposed to be, produced by automatic mechanism. The physiologist does not confidently assert conscious intelligence in the frog's spinal cord until he has shown that the useful result which the nervous machinery brings forth under a given irritation *remains the same when the machinery is altered.* If, to take the stock-instance, the right knee of a headless frog be irritated with acid, the right foot will wipe it off. When, however, this foot is amputated, the animal will often raise the *left* foot to the spot and wipe the offending material away.

Pflüger and Lewes reason from such facts in the following way: If the first reaction were the result of mere machinery, they say; if that irritated portion of the skin discharged the right leg as a trigger discharges its own barrel of a shotgun; then amputating the right foot would indeed frustrate the wiping, but would not make the *left* leg move. It would simply result in the right stump moving through the empty air (which is in fact the phenomenon sometimes observed). The right trigger makes no effort to discharge the left barrel if the right one be unloaded; nor does an electrical machine ever get restless because it can only emit sparks, and not hem pillow-cases like a sewing-machine.

If, on the contrary, the right leg originally moved for the *purpose* of wiping the acid, then nothing is more natural than that, when the easiest means of effecting that purpose prove fruitless, other means should be tried. Every failure must keep the animal in a state of disappointment which will lead to all sorts of new trials and devices; and tranquility will not ensue till one of these, by a happy stroke, achieves the wished-for end.

In a similar way Goltz ascribes intelligence to the frog's optic lobes and cerebellum. We alluded above to the manner in which a sound frog imprisoned in water will discover an outlet to the atmosphere. Goltz found that frogs deprived of their cerebral hemispheres would often exhibit a like ingenuity. Such a frog, after rising from the bottom and finding his farther upward progress checked by the glass bell which has been inverted over him, will not persist in butting his nose against the obstacle until dead of suffocation, but will often re-descend and emerge from under its rim as if, not a definite mechanical propulsion upwards, but rather a conscious desire to reach the air by hook or crook were the mainspring of his activity. Goltz concluded from this that the hemispheres are not the seat of intellectual power in frogs. He made the same inference from observing that a brainless frog will turn over from his back to his belly when one of his legs is sewed up, although the movements required are then very different from those excited under normal circumstances by the same annoying position. They seem determined, consequently, not merely by the antecedent irritant, but by the final end,—though the irritant of course is what makes the end desired.

Another brilliant German author, Liebmann,[2] argues against the brain's mechanism accounting for mental action, by very similar considerations. A machine as such, he says, will bring forth right results when it is in good order, and wrong results if out of repair. But both kinds of result flow with equally fatal necessity from their conditions. We cannot suppose the clock-work whose structure fatally determines it to a certain rate of speed, noticing that this speed is too slow or too fast and vainly trying to correct it. Its conscience, if it have any, should be as good as that of the best chronometer, for both alike obey equally well the same eternal mechanical laws—laws from behind. But if the *brain* be out of order and the man says "Twice four are two," instead of "Twice four are eight," or else "I must go to the coal to buy the wharf," instead of "I must go to the wharf to buy the coal," instantly there arises a consciousness of error. The wrong performance, though it obey the same mechanical

[2]Zur *Analysis der Wirklichkeit,* p. 489.

law as the right, is nevertheless condemned,—condemned as contradicting the inner law—the law from in front, the purpose or ideal for which the brain *should* act, whether it do so or not.

We need not discuss here whether these writers in drawing their conclusion have done justice to all the premises involved in the cases they treat of. We quote their arguments only to show how they appeal to the principle that *no actions but such as are done for an end, and show a choice of means, can be called indubitable expressions of Mind.*

I shall then adopt this as the criterion by which to circumscribe the subject-matter of this work so far as action enters into it. Many nervous performances will therefore be unmentioned, as being purely physiological. Nor will the anatomy of the nervous system and organs of sense be described anew. The reader will find in H. N. Martin's *Human Body*, in G. T. Ladd's *Physiological Psychology*, and in all the other standard Anatomies and Physiologies, a mass of information which we must regard as preliminary and take for granted in the present work.[3] Of the functions of the cerebral hemispheres, however, since they directly subserve consciousness, it will be well to give some little account.

[3]Nothing is easier than to familiarize one's self with the mammalian brain. Get a sheep's head, a small saw, chisel, scalpel and forceps (all three can best be had from a surgical instrument maker), and unravel its parts either by the aid of a human dissecting book, such as Holden's *Manual of Anatomy*, or by the specific directions *ad hoc* given in such books as Foster and Langley's *Practical Physiology* (Macmillan) or Morrell's *Comparative Anatomy, and Guide to Dissection* (Longman & Co.).

⇒18⇐

John Dewey,
"The reflex arc concept
in psychology" (1896).*

That the greater demand for a unifying principle and controlling work-ing hypothesis in psychology should come at just the time when all general-izations and classifications are most questioned and questionable is natural enough. It is the very cumulation of discrete facts creating the demand for unification that also breaks down previous lines of classification. The materi-al is too great in mass and too varied in style to fit into existing pigeon-holes, and the cabinets of science break of their own dead weight. The idea of the reflex arc has upon the whole come nearer to meeting this demand for a gen-eral working hypothesis than any other single concept. It being admitted that the sensori-motor apparatus represents both the unit of nerve structure and the type of nerve function, the image of this relationship passed over into psy-chology, and became an organizing principle to hold together the multiplici-ty of fact.

In criticising this conception it is not intended to make a plea for the principles of explanation and classification which the reflex arc idea has replaced; but, on the contrary, to urge that they are not sufficiently displaced, and that in the idea of the sensori-motor circuit, conceptions of the nature of sensation and of action derived from the nominally displaced psychology are still in control.

The older dualism between sensation and idea is repeated in the current dualism of peripheral and central structures and functions; the older dualism of body and soul finds a distinct echo in the current dualism of stimulus and response. Instead of interpreting the character of sensation, idea and action from their place and function in the sensori-motor circuit, we still incline to

*Dewey, J. (1896). The reflex arc concept in psychology. *Psychological Review, 3*, 357–370. Reprinted by permission of the American Psychological Association.

interpret the latter from our preconceived and preformulated ideas of rigid distinctions between sensations, thoughts and acts. The sensory stimulus is one thing, the central activity, standing for the idea, is another thing, and the motor discharge, standing for the act proper, is a third. As a result, the reflex arc is not a comprehensive, or organic unity, but a patchwork of disjointed parts, a mechanical conjunction of unallied processes. What is needed is that the principle underlying the idea of the reflex arc as the fundamental psychical unity shall react into and determine the values of its constitutive factors. More specifically, what is wanted is that sensory stimulus, central connections and motor responses shall be viewed, not as separate and complete entities in themselves, but as divisions of labor, functioning factors, within the single concrete whole, now designated the reflex arc.

What is the reality so designated? What shall we term that which is not sensation-followed-by-idea-followed-by-movement, but which is primary; which is, as it were, the psychical organism of which sensation, idea and movement are the chief organs? Stated on the physiological side, this reality may most conveniently be termed coördination. This is the essence of the facts held together by and subsumed under the reflex arc concept. Let us take, for our example, the familiar child-candle instance. (James, Psychology, Vol. I, p. 25.) The ordinary interpretation would say the sensation of light is a stimulus to the grasping as a response, the burn resulting is a stimulus to withdrawing the hand as response and so on. There is, of course, no doubt that is a rough practical way of representing the process. But when we ask for its psychological adequacy, the case is quite different. Upon analysis, we find that we begin not with a sensory stimulus, but with a sensori-motor coördination, the optical-ocular, and that in a certain sense it is the movement which is primary, and the sensation which is secondary, the movement of body, head and eye muscles determining the quality of what is experienced. In other words, the real beginning is with the act of seeing; it is looking, and not a sensation of light. The sensory quale gives the value of the act, just as the movement furnishes its mechanism and control, but both sensation and movement lie inside, not outside the act.

Now if this act, the seeing, stimulates another act, the reaching, it is because both of these acts fall within a larger coördination; because seeing and grasping have been so often bound together to reinforce each other, to help each other out, that each may be considered practically a subordinate member of a bigger coördination. More specifically, the ability of the hand to do its work will depend, either directly or indirectly, upon its control, as well as its stimulation, by the act of vision. If the sight did not inhibit as well as excite the reaching, the latter would be purely indeterminate, it would be for anything or nothing, not for the particular object seen. The reaching, in turn, must both stimulate and control the seeing. The eye must be kept upon the candle if the arm is to do its work; let it wander and the arm takes up another task. In other words, we now have an enlarged and transformed coördination; the act is seeing no less than before, but it is now seeing-for-reaching purposes. There is still a sensori-motor circuit, one with more content or value, not a substitution of a motor response for a sensory stimulus.[1]

Now take the affairs at its next stage, that in which the child gets burned. It is hardly necessary to point out again that this is also a sensori-motor coördination and not a mere sensation. It is worth while, however, to note especially the fact that it is simply the completion, or fulfillment, of the previous eye-arm-hand coördination and not an entirely new occurrence. Only because the heat-pain quale enters into the same circuit of experience with the optical-ocular and muscular quales, does the child learn from the experience and get the ability to avoid the experience in the future.

More technically stated, the so-called response is not merely *to* the stimulus; it is *into* it. The burn is the original seeing, the original optical-ocular experience enlarged and transformed in its value. It is no longer mere seeing; it is seeing-of-a light-that-means-pain-when-contact-occurs. The ordinary reflex arc theory proceeds upon the more or less tacit assumption that the outcome of the response is a totally new experience; that it is, say, the substitution of a burn sensation for a light sensation through the intervention of motion. The fact is that the sole meaning of the intervening movement is to maintain, reinforce or transform (as the case may be) the original quale; that we do not have the replacing of one sort of experience by another, but the development (or as it seems convenient to term it) the mediation of an experience. The seeing, in a word, remains to control the reaching, and is, in turn, interpreted by the burning.[2]

The discussion up to this point may be summarized by saying that the reflex arc idea, as commonly employed, is defective in that it assumes sensory stimulus and motor response as distinct psychical existences, while in reality they are always inside a coördination and have their significance purely from the part played in maintaining or reconstituting the coördination; and (secondly) in assuming that the quale of experience which precedes the 'motor' phase and that which succeeds it are two different states, instead of the last being always the first reconstituted, the motor phase coming in only for the sake of such mediation. The result is that the reflex arc idea leaves us with a disjointed psychology, whether viewed from the standpoint of development in the individual or in the race, or from that of the analysis of the mature consciousness. As to the former, in its failure to see that the arc of which it talks is virtually a circuit, a continual reconstitution, it breaks continuity and leaves us nothing but a series of jerks, the origin of each jerk to be sought outside the process of experience itself, in either an external pressure of 'environ-

---

[1]See THE PSYCHOLOGICAL REVIEW for May, 1896, p. 253, for an excellent statement and illustration, by Messrs. Angell and Moore, of this mutuality of stimulation.

[2]See, for a further statement of mediation, my *Syllabus of Ethics*, p. 15.

ment,' or else in an unaccountable spontaneous variation from within the 'soul' or the 'organism.'[1] As to the latter, failing to see the unity of activity, no matter how much it may prate of unity, it still leaves us with sensation or peripheral stimulus; idea, or central process (the equivalent of attention); and motor response, or act, as three disconnected existences, having to be somehow adjusted to each other, whether through the intervention of an extra-experimental soul, or by mechanical push and pull.

Before proceeding to a consideration of the general meaning for psychology of the summary, it may be well to give another descriptive analysis, as the value of the statement depends entirely upon the universality of its range of application. For such an instance we may conveniently take Baldwin's analysis of the reactive consciousness. In this there are, he says (Feeling and Will, p. 60), "three elements corresponding to the three elements of the nervous arc. First, the receiving consciousness, the stimulus—say a loud, unexpected sound; second, the attention involuntarily drawn, the registering element; and, third, the muscular reaction following upon the sound—say flight from fancied danger." Now, in the first place, such an analysis is incomplete; it ignores the status prior to hearing the sound. Of course, if this status is irrelevant to what happens afterwards, such ignoring is quite legitimate. But is it irrelevant either to the quantity or the quality of the stimulus?

If one is reading a book, if one is hunting, if one is watching in a dark place on a lonely night, if one is performing a chemical experiment, in each case, the noise has a very different psychical value; it is a different experience. In any case, what proceeds the 'stimulus' is a whole act, a sensori-motor coördination. What is more to the point, the 'stimulus' emerges out of this coördination; it is born from it as its matrix; it represents as it were an escape from it. I might here fall back upon authority, and refer to the widely accepted sensation continuum theory, according to which the sound cannot be absolutely *ex abrupto* from the outside, but is simply a shifting of focus of emphasis, a redistribution of tensions within the former act; and declare that unless the sound activity had been present to some extent in the prior coördination, it would be impossible for it now to come to prominence in consciousness. And such a reference would be only an amplification of what has already been said concerning the way in which the prior activity influences the value of the sound sensation. Or, we might point to cases of hypnotism, mono-ideaism and absent-mindedness, like that of Archimedes, as evidences that if the previous coördination is such as rigidly to lock the door, the auditory disturbance will knock in vain for admission to consciousness. Or, to speak more truly in the

---

[1] It is not too much to say that the whole controversy in biology regarding the source of variation, represented by Weismann and Spencer respectively, arises from beginning with stimulus or response instead of with the coördination with reference to which stimulus and response are functional divisions of labor. The same may be said, on the psychological side, of the controversy between the Wundtian 'apperceptionists' and their opponents. Each has a *disjectum membrum* of the same organic whole, whichever is selected being an arbitrary matter of personal taste.

metaphor, the auditory activity must already have one foot over the threshold, if it is ever to gain admittance.

But it will be more satisfactory, probably, to refer to the biological side of the case, and point out that as the ear activity has been evolved on account of the advantage gained by the whole organism, it must stand in the strictest histological and physiological connection with the eye, or hand, or leg, or whatever other organ has been the overt center of action. It is absolutely impossible to think of the eye center as monopolizing consciousness and the ear apparatus as wholly quiescent. What happens is a certain relative prominence and subsidence as between the various organs which maintain the organic equilibrium.

Furthermore, the sound is not a mere stimulus, or mere sensation; it again is an act, that of hearing. The muscular response is involved in this as well as sensory stimulus; that is, there is a certain definite set of the motor apparatus involved in hearing just as much as there is in subsequent running away. The movement and posture of the head, the tension of the ear muscles, are required for the 'reception' of the sound. It is just as true to say that the sensation of sound arises from a motor response as that the running away is a response to the sound. This may be brought out by reference to the fact that Professor Baldwin, in the passage quoted, has inverted the real order as between his first and second elements. We do not have first a sound and then activity of attention, unless sound is taken as mere nervous shock or physical event, not as conscious value. The conscious sensation of sound depends upon the motor response having already taken place; or, in terms of the previous statement (if stimulus is used as a conscious fact, and not as a mere physical event) it is the motor response or attention which constitutes that, which finally becomes the stimulus to another act. Once more, the final 'element,' the running away, is not merely motor, but is sensori-motor, having its sensory value and its muscular mechanism. It is also a coördination. And, finally, this sensori-motor coördination is not a new act, supervening upon what preceded. Just as the 'response' is necessary to constitute the stimulus, to determine it as sound and as this kind of sound, of wild beast or robber, so the sound experience must persist as a value in the running, to keep it up, to control it. The motor reaction involved in the running is, once more, into, not merely to, the sound. It occurs to change the sound, to get rid of it. The resulting quale, whatever it may be, has its meaning wholly determined by reference to the hearing of the sound. It is that experience mediated.[1] What we have is

---

[1]In other words, every reaction is of the same type as that which Professor Baldwin ascribes to imitation alone, viz., circular. Imitation is simply that particular form of the circuit in which the 'response' lends itself to comparatively unchanged maintainance of the prior experience. I say comparatively unchanged, for as far as this maintainance means additional control over the experience, it is being psychically changed, becoming more distinct. It is safe to suppose, moreover, that the 'repetition' is kept up only so long as this growth or mediation goes on. There is the new-in-the-old, if it is only the new sense of power.

a circuit, not an arc or broken segment of a circle. This circuit is more truly termed organic than reflex, because the motor response determines the stimulus, just as truly as sensory stimulus determines movement. Indeed, the movement is only for the sake of determining the stimulus, of fixing what kind of a stimulus it is, of interpreting it.

I hope it will not appear that I am introducing needless refinements and distinctions into what, it may be urged, is after all an undoubted fact, that movement as response follows sensation as stimulus. It is not a question of making the account of the process more complicated, though it is always wise to beware of that false simplicity which is reached by leaving out of account a large part of the problem. It is a question of finding out what stimulus or sensation, what movement and response mean; a question of seeing that they mean distinctions of flexible function only, not of fixed existence; that one and the same occurrence plays either or both parts, according to the shift of interest; and that because of this functional distinction and relationship, the supposed problem of the adjustment of one to the other, whether by superior force in the stimulus or an agency *ad hoc* in the center or the soul, is a purely self-created problem.

We may see the disjointed character of the present theory, by calling to mind that it is impossible to apply the phrase 'sensori-motor' to the occurrence as a simple phrase of description; it has validity only as a term of interpretation, only, that is, as defining various functions exercised. In terms of description, the whole process may be sensory or it may be motor, but it cannot be sensori-motor. The 'stimulus,' the excitation of the nerve ending and of the sensory nerve, the central change, are just as much, or just as little, motion as the events taking place in the motor nerve and the muscles. It is one uninterrupted, continuous redistribution of mass in motion. And there is nothing in the process, from the standpoint of description, which entitles us to call this reflex. It is redistribution pure and simple; as much so as the burning of a log, or the falling of a house or the movement of the wind. In the physical process, as physical, there is nothing which can be set off as stimulus, nothing which reacts, nothing which is response. There is just a change in the system of tensions.

The same sort of thing is true when we describe the process purely from the psychical side. It is now all sensation, all sensory quale; the motion, as psychically described, is just as much sensation as is sound or light or burn. Take the withdrawing of the hand from the candle flame as example. What we have is a certain visual-heat-pain-muscular-quale, transformed into another visual-touch-muscular-quale—the flame now being visible only at a distance, or not at all, the touch sensation being altered, etc. If we symbolize the original visual quale by v, the temperature by h, the accompanying muscular sensation by m, the whole experience may be stated as vhm-vh$m$-vhm'; m being the quale of withdrawing, m' the sense of the status after the withdrawal. The motion is not a certain kind of existence; it is a sort of sensory experience interpreted, just as is candle flame, or burn from candle flame. All are on a par.

But, in spite of all this, it will be urged, there is a distinction between stimulus and response, between sensation and motion. Precisely; but we ought now to be in a condition to ask of what nature is the distinction, instead of taking it for granted as a distinction somehow lying in the existence of the facts themselves. We ought to be able to see that the ordinary conception of the reflex arc theory, instead of being a case of plain science, is a survival of the metaphysical dualism, first formulated by Plato, according to which the sensation is an ambiguous dweller on the border land of soul and body, the idea (or central process) is purely psychical, and the act (or movement) purely physical. Thus the reflex arc formulation is neither physical (or physiological) nor psychological; it is a mixed materialistic-spiritualistic assumption.

If the previous descriptive analysis has made obvious the need of a reconsideration of the reflex arc idea, of the nest of difficulties and assumptions in the apparently simple statement, it is now time to undertake an explanatory analysis. The fact is that stimulus and response are not distinctions of existence, but teleological distinctions, that is, distinctions of function, or part played, with reference to reaching or maintaining an end. With respect to this teleological process, two stages should be discriminated, as their confusion is one cause of the confusion attending the whole matter. In one case, the relation represents an organization of means with reference to a comprehensive end. It represents an accomplished adaptation. Such is the case in all well developed instincts, as when we say that the contact of eggs, is a stimulus to the hen to set; or the sight of corn a stimulus to pick; such also is the case with all thoroughly formed habits, as when the contact with the floor stimulates walking. In these instances there is no question of consciousness of stimulus *as* stimulus, of response *as* response. There is simply a continuously ordered sequence of acts, all adapted in themselves and in the order of their sequence, to reach a certain objective end, the reproduction of the species, the preservation of life, locomotion to a certain place. The end has got thoroughly organized into the means. In calling one stimulus, another response we mean nothing more than that such an orderly sequence of acts is taking place. The same sort of statement might be made equally well with reference to the succession of changes in a plant, so far as these are considered with reference to their adaptation to, say, producing seed. It is equally applicable to the series of events in the circulation of the blood, or the sequence of acts occurring in a self-binding reaper.[1]

Regarding such cases of organization viewed as already attained, we may say, positively, that it is only the assumed common reference to an inclusive end which marks each member off as stimulus and response, that apart from

---

[1]To avoid misapprehension, I would say that I am not raising the question as to how far this teleology is real in any one of these cases; real or unreal, my point holds equally well. It is only when we regard the sequence of acts as *if* they were adapted to reach some end that it occurs to us to speak of one as stimulus and the other as response. Otherwise, we look at them as a *mere* series.

such reference we have only antecedent and consequent;[1] in other words, the distinction is one of interpretation. Negatively, it must be pointed out that it is not legitimate to carry over, without change, exactly the same order of considerations to cases where it is a question of *conscious* stimulation and response. We may, in the above case, regard, if we please, stimulus and response each as an entire act, having an individuality of its own, subject even here to the qualification that individuality means not an entirely independent whole, but a division of labor as regards maintaining or reaching an end. But in any case, it is an act, a sensori-motor coördination, which stimulates the response, itself in turn sensori-motor, not a sensation which stimulates a movement. Hence the illegitimacy of identifying, as is so often done, such cases of organized instincts or habits with the so-called reflex arc, or of transferring, without modification, considerations valid of this serial coördination of acts to the sensation-movement case.

The fallacy that arises when this is done is virtually the psychological or historical fallacy. A set of considerations which hold good only because of a completed process, is read into the content of the process which conditions this completed result. A state of things characterizing an outcome is regarded as a true description of the events which led up to this outcome; when, as a matter of fact, if this outcome had already been in existence, there would have been no necessity for the process. Or, to make the application to the case in hand, considerations valid of an attained organization or coördination, the orderly sequence of minor acts in a comprehensive coördination, are used to describe a process, viz., the distinction of mere sensation as stimulus and of mere movement as response, which takes place only because such an attained organization is no longer at hand, but is in process of constitution. Neither mere sensation, nor mere movement, can ever be either stimulus or response; only an act can be that; the *sensation* as stimulus means the lack of and search for such an objective stimulus, or orderly placing of an act; just as mere movement as response means the lack of and search for the right act to complete a given coördination.

A recurrence to our example will make these formulae clearer. As long as the seeing is an unbroken act, which is as experienced no more mere sensation than it is mere motion (though the on-looker or psychological observer can interpret it into sensation and movement), it is in no sense the sensation which stimulates the reaching; we have, as already sufficiently indicated, only the serial steps in a coördination of *acts*. But now take a child who, upon reaching for bright light (that is, exercising the seeing-reaching coördination) has sometimes had a delightful exercise, sometimes found something good to eat and sometimes burned himself. *Now the response is not only uncertain, but the stimulus is equally uncertain; one is uncertain only in so far as the other*

---

[1]Whether, even in such a determination, there is still not a reference of a more latent kind to an end is, of course, left open.

is. The real problem may be equally well stated as either to discover the right stimulus, to constitute the stimulus, or to discover, to constitute, the response. The question of whether to reach or to abstain from reaching is the question what sort of a bright light have we here? Is it the one which means playing with one's hands, eating milk, or burning one's fingers? The stimulus must be constituted for the response to occur. Now it is at precisely this juncture and because of it that the distinction of sensation as stimulus and motion as response arises.

The sensation or conscious stimulus is not a thing or existence by itself; it is that phase of a coördination requiring attention because, by reason of the conflict within the coördination, it is uncertain how to complete it. It is to doubt as to the next act, whether to reach or no, which gives the motive to examining the act. The end to follow is, in this sense, the stimulus. It furnishes the motivation to attend to what has just taken place; to define it more carefully. From this point of view the discovery of the stimulus is the 'response' to possible movement as 'stimulus.' We must have an anticipatory sensation, an image, of the movements that may occur, together with their respective values, before attention will go to the seeing to break it up as a sensation of light, and of light of this particular kind. It is the initiated activities of reaching, which, inhibited by the conflict in the coördination, turn round, as it were, upon the seeing, and hold it from passing over into further act until its quality is determined. Just here the act as objective stimulus becomes transformed into sensation as possible, as conscious, stimulus. Just here also, motion as conscious response emerges.

In other words, sensation as stimulus does not mean any particular psychical *existence*. It means simply a function, and will have its value shift according to the special work requiring to be done. At one moment the various activities of reaching and withdrawing will be the sensation, because they are that phase of activity which sets the problem, or creates the demand for, the next act. At the next moment the previous act of seeing will furnish the sensation, being, in turn, that phase of activity which sets the pace upon which depends further action. Generalized, sensation as stimulus, is always that phase of activity requiring to be defined in order that a coördination may be completed. What the sensation will be in particular at a given time, therefore, will depend entirely upon the way in which an activity is being used. It has no fixed quality of its own. The search for the stimulus is the search for exact conditions of action; that is, for the state of things which decides how a beginning coördination should be completed.

Similarly, motion, as response, has only a functional value. It is whatever will serve to complete the disintegrating coördination. Just as the discovery of the sensation marks the establishing of the problem, so the constitution of the response marks the solution of this problem. At one time, fixing attention, holding the eye fixed, upon the seeing and thus bringing out a certain quale of light is the response, because that is the particular act called for just then; at another time, the movement of the arm away from the light is the response. There is nothing in itself which may be labelled response. That one certain set of sensory quales should be marked off by themselves as 'motion' and put in antithesis to such sensory quales as those of color, sound and contact, as legitimate claimants to the title of sensation, is wholly inexplicable unless we keep the difference of function in view. It is the eye and ear sensations which fix for us the problem; which report to us the conditions which have to be met if the coördination is to be successfully completed; and just the moment we need to know about our movements to get an adequate report, just that moment, motion miraculously (from the ordinary standpoint) ceases to be motion and become 'muscular sensation.' On the other hand, take the change in values of experience, the transformation of sensory quales. Whether this change will or will not be interpreted as movement, whether or not any consciousness of movement will arise, will depend upon whether this change is satisfactory, whether or not it is regarded as a harmonious development of a coördination, or whether the change is regarded as simply a means in solving a problem, an instrument in reaching a more satisfactory coördination. So long as our experience runs smoothly we are no more conscious of motion as motion than we are of this or that color or sound by itself.

To sum up: the distinction of sensation and movement as stimulus and response respectively is not a distinction which can be regarded as descriptive of anything which holds of psychical events or existences as such. The only events to which the terms stimulus and response can be descriptively applied are to minor acts serving by their respective positions to the maintenance of some organized coördination. The conscious stimulus or sensation, and the conscious response or motion, have a special genesis or motivation, and a special end or function. The reflex arc theory, by neglecting, by abstracting from, this genesis and this function gives us one disjointed part of a process as if it were the whole. It gives us literally an arc, instead of the circuit; and not giving us the circuit of which it is an arc, does not enable us to place, to center, the arc. This arc, again, falls apart into two separate existences having to be either mechanically or externally adjusted to each other.

The circle is a coördination, some of whose members have come into conflict with each other. It is the temporary disintegration and need of reconstitution which occasions, which affords the genesis of, the conscious distinction into sensory stimulus on one side and motor response on the other. The stimulus is that phase of the forming coördination which represents the conditions which have to be met in bringing it to a successful issue; the response is that phase of one and the same forming coördination which gives the key to meeting these conditions, which serves as instrument in effecting the successful coördination. They are therefore strictly correlative and contemporaneous. The stimulus is something to be discovered; to be made out; if the activity affords its own adequate stimulation, there is no stimulus save in the objective sense already referred to. As soon as it is adequately determined, then and then only is the response also complete. To attain either, means that the coördination has completed itself. Moreover, it is the motor response which assists in discovering and constituting the stimulus. It is the holding of the movement at a certain stage which creates the sensation, which throws it into relief.

It is the coördination which unifies that which the reflex arc concept gives us only in disjointed fragments. It is the circuit within which fall distinctions of stimulus and response as functional phases of its own mediation or completion. The point of this story is in its application; but the application of it to the question of the nature of psychical evolution, to the distinction between sensational and rational consciousness, and the nature of judgment must be deferred to a more favorable opportunity.

≈19≈

James Angell, Excerpt from "The province of functional psychology" (1907).*

Functional psychology is at the present moment little more than a point of view, a program, an ambition. It gains its vitality primarily perhaps as a protest against the exclusive excellence of another starting point for the study of the mind, and it enjoys for the time being at least the peculiar vigor which commonly attaches to Protestantism of any sort in its early stages before it has become respectable and orthodox. The time seems ripe to attempt a somewhat more precise characterization of the field of functional psychology than has as yet been offered. What we seek is not the arid and merely verbal definition which to many of us is so justly anathema, but rather an informing appreciation of the motives and ideals which animate the psychologist who pursues this path. His status in the eye of the psychological public is unnecessarily precarious. The conceptions of his purposes prevalent in non-functionalist circles range from positive and dogmatic misapprehension, through frank mystification and suspicion up to moderate comprehension. Nor is this fact an expression of anything peculiarly abstruse and recondite in his intentions. It is due in part to his own ill-defined plans, in part to his failure to explain lucidly exactly what he is about. Moreover, he is fairly numerous and it is not certain that in all important particulars he and his confrères are at one in their beliefs. The considerations which are herewith offered suffer inevitably from this personal limitation. No psychological council of Trent has as yet pronounced upon the true faith. But in spite of probable failure it seems worth while to hazard an attempt at delineating the scope of functionalist principles.

*Angell, J.R. (1907). Excerpt from The province of functional psychology. *Psychological Review, 14*, 61–71. Reprinted by permission of the American Psychological Association.

[1]Delivered in substantially the present form as the President's Annual Address before the American Psychological Association at its fifteenth annual meeting held at Columbia University, New York City, December 27, 28 and 29, 1906.

I formally renounce any intention to strike out new plans; I am engaged in what is meant as a dispassionate summary of actual conditions.

Whatever else it may be, functional psychology is nothing wholly new. In certain of its phases it is plainly discernible in the psychology of Aristotle and in its more modern garb it has been increasingly in evidence since Spencer wrote his *Psychology* and Darwin his *Origin of Species*. Indeed, as we shall soon see, its crucial problems are inevitably incidental to any serious attempt at understanding mental life. All that is peculiar to its present circumstances is a higher degree of self-consciousness than it possessed before, a more articulate and persistent purpose to organize its vague intentions into tangible methods and principles.

A survey of contemporary psychological writing indicates, as was intimated in the preceding paragraph, that the task of functional psychology is interpreted in several different ways. Moreover, it seems to be possible to advocate one or more of these conceptions while cherishing abhorrence for the others. I distinguish three principal forms of the functional problem with sundry subordinate variants. It will contribute to the clarification of the general situation to dwell upon these for a moment, after which I propose to maintain that they are substantially but modifications of a single problem.

I.

There is to be mentioned first the notion which derives most immediately from contrast with the ideals and purposes of structural psychology so-called.[1] This involves the identification of functional psychology with the effort to discern and portray the typical *operations* of consciousness under actual life conditions, as over against the attempt to analyze and describe its elementary and complex *contents*. The structural psychology of sensation, *e. g.*, undertakes to determine the number and character of the various unanalyzable sensory materials, such as the varieties of color, tone, taste, etc. The functional psychology of sensation would on the other hand find its appropriate sphere of interest in the determination of the character of the various sense activities as differing in their *modus operandi* from one another and from other mental processes such as judging, conceiving, willing and the like.

In this its older and more pervasive form functional psychology has until very recent times had no independent existence. No more has structural psychology for that matter. It is only lately that any motive for the differentiation of the two has existed and structural psychology—granting its claims and pretensions of which more anon—is the first, be it said, to isolate itself. But in so far as functional psychology is synonymous with descriptions and theories of

[1]The most lucid exposition of the structuralist position still remains, so far as I know, Titchener's paper, 'The Postulates of a Structural Psychology,' *Philosophical Review*, 1898 [VII.], p. 499. Cf. also the critical-controversial papers of Caldwell, *Psychological Review*, 1899, p. 187, and Titchener, *Philosophical Review*, 1899 [VIII.], p. 290.

mental action as distinct from the materials of mental constitution, so far it is everywhere conspicuous in psychological literature from the earliest times down.

Its fundamental intellectual prepossessions are often revealed by the classifications of mental process adopted from time to time. Witness the Aristotelian bipartite division of intellect and will and the modern tripartite division of mental activities. What are cognition, feeling and will but three basally distinct modes of mental action? To be sure this classification has often carried with it the assertion, or at least the implication, that these fundamental attributes of mental life were based upon the presence in the mind of corresponding and ultimately distinct mental elements. But so far as concerns our momentary interest this fact is irrelevant. The impressive consideration is that the notion of definite and distinct forms of mental action is clearly in evidence and even the much-abused faculty psychology is on this point perfectly sane and perfectly lucid. The mention of this classic target for psychological vituperation recalls the fact that when the critics of functionalism wish to be particularly unpleasant, they refer to it as a bastard offspring of the faculty psychology masquerading in biological plumage.

It must be obvious to any one familiar with psychological usage in the present year of grace that in the intent of the distinction herewith described certain of our familiar psychological categories are primarily structural—such for instance as affection and image—whereas others immediately suggest more explicit functional relationships—for example, attention and reasoning. As a matter of fact it seems clear that so long as we adhere to these meanings of the terms structural and functional every mental event can be treated from either point of view, from the standpoint of describing its detectable contents and from the standpoint of characteristic mental activity differentiable from other forms of mental process. In the practice of our familiar psychological writers both undertakings are somewhat indiscriminately combined.

The more extreme and ingenuous conceptions of structural psychology seem to have grown out of an unchastened indulgence in what we may call the 'states of consciousness' doctrine. I take it that this is in reality the contemporary version of Locke's 'idea.' If you adopt as your material for psychological analysis the isolated 'moment of consciousness,' it is very easy to become so absorbed in determining its constitution as to be rendered somewhat oblivious to its artificial character. The most essential quarrel which the functionalist has with structuralism in its thoroughgoing and consistent form arises from this fact and touches the feasibility and worth of the effort to get at mental process as it *is* under the conditions of actual experience rather than as it *appears* to a merely postmortem analysis. It is of course true that for introspective purposes we must in a sense always work with vicarious representatives of the particular mental processes which we set out to observe. But it makes a great difference even on such terms whether one is directing attention primarily to the discovery of the way in which such a mental process operates, and what the conditions are under which it appears, or whether one is engaged simply in teasing apart the fibers of its tissues. The latter occupation is useful and for certain purposes essential, but it often stops short of that which is as a life phenomenon the most essential, *i. e.*, the *modus operandi* of the phenomenon.

As a matter of fact many modern investigations of an experimental kind largely dispense with the usual direct form of introspection and concern themselves in a distinctly functionalistic spirit with a determination of what work is accomplished and what the conditions are under which it is achieved. Many experiments in memory and association, for instance, are avowedly of this character.

The functionalist is committed *vom Grunde auf* to the avoidance of that special form of the psychologist's fallacy which consists in attributing to mental states without due warrant, as part of their overt constitution in the moment of experience, characteristics which subsequent reflective analysis leads us to suppose they must have possessed. When this precaution is non-scrupulously observed we obtain a sort of *pâte de foie gras* psychology in which the mental conditions portrayed contain more than they ever naturally would or could hold.

It should be added that when the distinction is made between psychic structure and psychic function, the anomalous position of structure as a category of mind is often quite forgotten. In mental life the sole appropriateness of the term structure hinges on the fact that any moment of consciousness can be regarded as a complex capable of analysis, and the terms into which our analyses resolve such complexes are the analogues—and obviously very meager and defective ones at that—of the structures of anatomy and morphology.

The fact that mental contents are evanescent and fleeting marks them off in an important way from the relatively permanent elements of anatomy. No matter how much we may talk of the preservation of psychical dispositions, nor how many metaphors we may summon to characterize the storage of ideas in some hypothetical deposit chamber of memory, the obstinate fact remains that when we are not experiencing a sensation or an idea it is, strictly speaking, non-existent. Moreover, when we manage by one or another device to secure that which we designate the same sensation or the same idea, we not only have no guarantee that our second edition is really a replica of psychology, but phrasing itself somewhat differently, is the view which regards the functional problem as concerned with discovering how and why conscious processes are what they are, instead of dwelling as the structuralist is supposed to do upon the problem of determining the irreducible elements of consciousness and their characteristic modes of combination. I have elsewhere defended the view that however it may be in other sciences dealing with life phenomena, in psychology at least the answer to the question 'what' implicates the answer to the questions 'how' and 'why.'[1]

---

[1]'The Relations of Structural and Functional Psychology to Philosophy,' *Philosophical Review*, 1903 [XII.], p. 203 ff.

Stated briefly the ground on which this position rests is as follows: In so far as you attempt to analyze any particular state of consciousness you find that the mental elements presented to your notice are dependent upon the particular exigencies and conditions which call them forth. Not only does the affective coloring of such a psychical moment depend upon one's temporary condition, mood and aims, but the very sensations themselves are determined in their qualitative texture by the totality of circumstances subjective and objective within which they arise. You cannot get a fixed and definite color sensation for example, without keeping perfectly constant the external and internal conditions in which it appears. The particular sense quality is in short functionally determined by the necessities of the existing situation which it emerges to meet. If you inquire then deeply enough what particular sensation you have in a given case, you always find it necessary to take account of the manner in which, and the reasons why, it was experienced at all. You may of course, if you will, abstract from these considerations, but in so far as you do so, your analysis and description is manifestly partial and incomplete. Moreover, even when you do so abstract and attempt to describe certain isolable sense qualities, your descriptions are of necessity couched in terms not of the experienced quality itself, but in terms of the conditions which produced it, in terms of some other quality with which it is compared, or in terms of some more overt act to which the sense stimulation led. That is to say, the very description itself is functionalistic and must be so. The truth of this assertion can be illustrated and tested by appeal to any situation in which one is trying to reduce sensory complexes, *e. g.*, colors or sounds, to their rudimentary components.

II.

A broader outlook and one more frequently characteristic of contemporary writers meets us in the next conception of the task of functional psychology. This conception is in part a reflex of the prevailing interest in the larger formulae of biology and particularly the evolutionary hypotheses within whose majestic sweep is nowadays included the history of the whole stellar universe; in part it echoes the same philosophical call to new life which has been heard as pragmatism, as humanism, even as functionalism itself. I should not wish to commit either party by asserting that functional psychology and pragmatism are ultimately one. Indeed, as a psychologist I should hesitate to bring down on myself the avalanche of metaphysical invective which has been loosened by pragmatic writers. To be sure pragmatism has slain its thousands, but I should cherish scepticism as to whether functional psychology would the more speedily slay its tens of thousands by announcing an offensive and defensive alliance with pragmatism. In any case I only hold that the two movements spring from similar logical motivation and rely for their vitality and propagation upon forces closely germane to one another.

The functional psychologist then in his modern attire is interested not alone in the operations of mental process considered merely of and by and for itself, but also and more vigorously in mental activity as part of a larger stream of biological forces which are daily and hourly at work before our eyes and which are constitutive of the most important and most absorbing part of our world. The psychologist of this stripe is wont to take his cue from the basal conception of the evolutionary movement, *i. e.*, that for the most part organic structures and functions possess their present characteristics by virtue of the efficiency with which they fit into the extant conditions of life broadly designated the environment. With this conception in mind he proceeds to attempt some understanding of the manner in which the psychical contributes to the furtherance of the sum total of organic activities, not alone the psychical in its entirety, but especially the psychical in its particularities—mind as judging, mind as feeling, etc.

This is the point of view which instantly brings the psychologist cheek by jowl with the general biologist. It is the presupposition of every philosophy save that of outright ontological materialism that mind plays the stellar role in all the environmental adaptations of animals which possess it. But this persuasion has generally occupied the position of an innocuous truism or at best a jejune postulate, rather than that of a problem requiring, or permitting, serious scientific treatment. At all events, this was formerly true.

This older and more complacent attitude toward the matter is, however, being rapidly displaced by a conviction of the need for light on the exact character of the accommodatory service represented by the various great modes of conscious expression. Such an effort if successful would not only broaden the foundations for biological appreciation of the intimate nature of accommodatory process, it would also immensely enhance the psychologist's interest in the exact portrayal of conscious life. It is of course the latter consideration which lends importance to the matter from our point of view. Moreover, not a few practical consequences of value may be expected to flow from this attempt, if it achieves even a measurable degree of success. Pedagogy and mental hygiene both await the quickening and guiding counsel which can only come from a psychology of this stripe. For their purposes a strictly structural psychology is as sterile in theory as teachers and psychiatrists have found it in practice.

As a concrete example of the transfer of attention from the more general phases of consciousness as accommodatory activity to the particularistic features of the case may be mentioned the rejuvenation of interest in the quasi-biological field which we designate animal psychology. This movement is surely among the most pregnant with which we meet in our own generation. Its problems are in no sense of the merely theoretical and speculative kind, although, like all scientific endeavor, it possesses an intellectual and methodological background on which such problems loom large. But the frontier upon which it is pushing forward its explorations is a region of definite, concrete fact, tangled and confused and often most difficult of access, but nevertheless a region of fact, accessible like all other facts to persistent and intelligent interrogation.

That many of the most fruitful researches in this field have been achievements of men nominally biologists rather than psychologists in no wise affects the merits of the case. A similar situation exists in the experimental psychology of sensation where not a little of the best work has been accomplished by scientists not primarily known as psychologists.

It seems hardly too much to say that the empirical conceptions of the consciousness of the lower animals have undergone a radical alteration in the past few years by virtue of the studies in comparative psychology. The splendid investigations of the mechanism of instinct, of the facts and methods of animal orientation, of the scope and character of the several sense processes, of the capabilities of education and the range of selective accommodatory capacities in the animal kingdom, these and dozens of other similar problems have received for the first time drastic scientific examination, experimental in character wherever possible, observational elsewhere, but observational in the spirit of conservative non-anthropomorphism as earlier observations almost never were. In most cases they have to be sure but shown the way to further and more precise knowledge, yet there can be but little question that the trail which they have blazed has success at its farther end.

One may speak almost as hopefully of human genetic psychology which has been carried on so profitably in our own country. As so often in psychology, the great desideratum here, is the completion of adequate methods which will insure really stable scientific results. But already our general psychological theory has been vitalized and broadened by the results of the genetic methods thus far elaborated. These studies constantly emphasize for us the necessity of getting the longitudinal rather than the transverse view of life phenomena and they keep immediately in our field of vision the basic significance of growth in mental process. Nowhere is the difference more flagrant between a functional psychology and the more literal minded type of structural psychology. One has only to compare with the better contemporary studies some of the pioneer work in this field, conceived in the more static and structuralistic manner, as Preyer's for example was, to feel at once the difference and the immensely greater significance both for theory and for practice which issues from the functional and longitudinal descriptions.

The assertions which we have permitted ourselves about genetic psychology are equally applicable to pathological psychology. The technique of scientific investigation is in the nature of the case often different in this field of work from that characteristic of the other ranges of psychological research. But the attitude of the investigator is distinctly functionalistic. His aim is one of a thoroughly vital and generally practical kind leading him to emphasize precisely those considerations which our analysis of the main aspects of functional psychology disclose as the goal of its peculiar ambitions.

VI. German Dynamic Psychology

The German tradition of mental activity within psychology, descendent from the line of scholarship beginning with Spinoza and culminating in Brentano's Act Psychology, found divergent expression. The two movements selected to represent this trend are Gestalt Psychology and Psychoanalysis. Both evolved to address quite different issues within psychology, yet they share a common heritage in assuming a central organization that predisposes the person to interact with the environment in dynamic ways.

Influenced by the prevailing German philosophical views of mental activity, several scholars of the early 20th Century extended Brentano's conceptualization to react to some of the basic tenets of Wundt's system. Carl Stumpf (1848–1936) and Christian von Ehrenfels (1859–1932) supported Brentano's Act Psychology for a generation of students during their long careers, and Oswald Külpe (1862–1915) established a research program at Würzburg University, which resolved a number of experimental questions that had challenged Wundt's system. However, it was Max Wertheimer (1880–1943) who wrote a very influential paper on apparent movement, the phi phenomenon, which marked the foundation of the Gestalt system in psychology. Briefly, the Gestalt movement is characteristically anti-reductionistic, arguing that people are predisposed to recognize the essential unity and coherence of the environment. Psychology appropriately belongs at this level of person-environment interaction, and the reduction of this level to components or stimuli destroys the phenomenal level.

The reading selections were written by Wertheimer's important students and collaborators, Kurt Koffka (1886–1941) and Wolfgang

Köhler (1887–1967). Koffka's paper, "Perception: An introduction to Gestalt-theorie" (1922), was an attempt to attract an American audience to the movement. The part reproduced here defines several psychological processes from a Gestalt perspective. The excerpt from Köhler's writings, *The mentality of apes* (1938), was derived from Köhler's observations of problem solving in primates undertaken while he was detained on the Canary Islands during World War I. From both the theoretical and experimental perspectives, Gestalt Psychology provided a means of broadening the prevailing functional-behavioral orientation of American psychologists, but did not replace it.

Psychoanalysis and especially the writings of its founder, Sigmund Freud (1856–1939), have exerted a most profound influence on the intellectual climate of the 20th Century. Freud's preconception of mental activity, at both conscious and unconscious levels, represents the strongest statement of the mind's acting upon environmental events and, more importantly, upon itself. The reading from Freud's writings was selected because of its revolutionary character. That is, the admission of dreams as legitimate psychological events, and the interpretation of their symbols extended psychology's definition in ways not accommodated by any other system. Freud gathered his material from keen observations of his patient's recollections, which admitted a whole new data base to psychology.

The German dynamic tradition in psychology recognized and accounted for the individuality of experience. Accordingly, mental contents are not reducible or explained by environmental input only. Emphasizing consciousness as the central fact of psychology, the German tradition of dynamic interaction between the person and the environment draws inspiration from the variability of human experience.

REFERENCES

FREUD, S. (1933, 1965). Revision of the theory of dreams. In J. Strachey (editor & translator) *New introductory lectures on psychoanalysis*. New York: W.W. Norton & Co., 7–30.

KOFFKA, K. (1922). Perception: An introduction to Gestalt-theorie. *Psychological Bulletin, 19*, 531–586.

KÖHLER, W. (1938). *The mentality of apes*. London: Routledge & Kegan Paul, Ch. VII, 215–222.

⌇20⌇

Kurt Koffka, Excerpt from "Perception: An introduction to Gestalt-theorie" (1922).*

When it was suggested to me that I should write a general critical review of the work recently carried on in the field of perception, I saw an opportunity of introducing to American readers a movement in psychological thought which has developed in Germany during the last ten years. In 1912 Wertheimer stated for the first time the principles of a *Gestalt-Theorie* which has served as the starting point of a small number of German psychologists. Wherever this new method of thinking and working has come in touch with concrete problems, it has not only showed its efficiency, but has also brought to light startling and important facts, which, without the guidance of this theory, could not so easily have been discovered.

The *Gestalt-Theorie* is more than a theory of perception: it is even more than a mere psychological theory. Yet it originated in a study of perception, and the investigation of this topic has furnished the better part of the experimental work which has been done. Consequently, an introduction to this new theory can best be gained, perhaps, by a consideration of the facts of perception.

Since the new point of view has not yet won its way in Germany, it is but fair to state at the outset that the majority of German psychologists still stands aloof. However, much of the work done by other investigators contains results that find a place within the scope of our theory. Accordingly I shall refer to these results as well as to those secured by the *Gestalt*-psychologists proper; for I wish to demonstrate the comprehensiveness of our theory by showing how readily it embraces a number of facts hitherto but imperfectly explained. For

*Koffka, K. (1922). Excerpts from Perception: An introduction to Gestalt-theorie. *Psychological Bulletin*, *19*, 531–537. Reprinted by permission of the American Psychological Association. Numbers in parentheses refer to citations not included in this excerpt.

the same reason I shall occasionally go farther back and refer to older investigations. On the other hand, I cannot hope to give a complete survey of the work on perception, and I shall therefore select my facts with reference to my primary purpose.

Since my chief aim is to invite a consideration of the new theory, I shall try first of all to make my American readers understand what the theory purports to be. So far there exists no general presentation of the theory which marshals all the facts upon which it rests; indeed, the general field of psychology has not, as yet, been treated from this point of view. For this reason the understanding of the theory has met with serious difficulties, and numerous misunderstandings have occasioned a great deal of the disapprobation which the theory has met. And yet, a theory which has admittedly inspired so many successful investigations may surely claim the right to be at least correctly understood.

My plan in detail is the following: After giving a short sketch of the chief concepts of current psychology as they present themselves to the mind of a *Gestalt*-psychologist, I shall introduce the newer concepts by demonstrating how appropriate they are in the solution of a very old psychological problem. I shall then proceed by developing a fundamental distinction made by the new theory which is quite contrary to the traditional view, and I shall also show the wide application of this distinction. This is all I shall attempt in this paper. In a second one I shall hope to be able to review the rest of the experimental evidence in support of the theory which has been gained in the various fields of perception, such as movement, form, etc. The reader, therefore, will have the complete case before him only after reading the second paper. I have preferred to write the essay in English in order to avoid the misunderstandings which always result from translation; and Professor Ogden has kindly undertaken to correct my manuscript.

When I speak of perception in the following essay, I do not mean a specific psychical function; all I wish to denote by this term is the realm of experiences which are not merely "imagined," "represented," or "thought of." Thus, I would call the desk at which I am now writing a perception, likewise the flavor of the tobacco I am now inhaling from my pipe, or the noise of the traffic in the street below my window. That is to say, I wish to use the term perception in a way that will exclude all theoretical prejudice; for it is my aim to propose a theory of these everyday perceptions which has been developed in Germany during the last ten years, and to contrast this theory with the traditional views of psychology. With this purpose in mind, I need a term that is quite neutral. In the current textbooks of psychology the term perception is used in a more specific sense, being opposed to sensation, as a more complex process. Here, indeed, is the clue to all the existing theories of perception which I shall consider in this introductory section, together with a glance at the fundamental principles of traditional psychology. Thus I find three concepts, involving three principles of psychological theory, in every current psychological system. In some systems these are the only fundamental concepts, while in others they are supplemented by additional conceptions; but for a long time the adequacy of these three has been beyond dispute. The three concepts to which I refer are those of *sensation, association,* and *attention.* I shall formulate the theoretical principles based upon these concepts and indicate their import in a radical manner so as to lay bare the methods of thinking which have been employed in their use. I am fully aware, of course, that most, if not all, the writers on this subject have tried to modify the assertions which I am about to make; but I maintain, nevertheless, that in working out concrete problems these principles have been employed in the manner in which I shall state them.

I

Sensation: All present or existential consciousness consists of a finite number of real, separable (though not necessarily separate) elements, each element corresponding to a definite stimulus[1] or to a special memory-residuum (see below). Since a conscious unit is thus taken to be a bundle of such elements, Wertheimer, in a recent paper on the foundations of our new theory, has introduced the name "bundle-hypothesis" for this conception (65). These elements, or rather, some of them, are the sensations,[2] and it is the first task of psychology to find out their number and their properties.

The elements, once aroused in the form of sensations, may also be experienced in the form of images. The images are also accepted as elements or atoms of psychological textures and are distinguishable from sensations by certain characteristic properties. They are, however, very largely a dependent class, since every image presupposes a corresponding sensation. Thus the concept of image, though not identical with that of sensation, rests upon the same principle, namely, the bundle-hypothesis.

In accordance with the method by which sensations have been investigated, it has been necessary to refer to the stimulus-side in defining the principle which underlies this concept. More explicitly, this relation of the sensation to its stimulus is expressed by a generally accepted rule, termed by Köhler the "constancy-hypothesis" (34); that the sensation is a direct and definite function of the stimulus. Given a certain stimulus and a normal sense-organ, we know what sensation the subject must have, or rather, we know its intensity and quality, while its "clearness" or its "degree of consciousness" is dependent upon still another factor, namely, *attention.*

[1]The exceptions to this universal rule occasioned by factors such as fatigue, practice, etc., do not affect the general interpretation and may here be neglected.

[2]We shall set aside the concept of feeling, though in many systems feelings are taken to be specific elements just as simple as sensations.

What the stimulus is to the sensation, the residuum is to the image. Since each separate sensation-element leaves behind it a separate residuum, we have a vast number of these residua in our memory, each of which may be separately aroused, thus providing a certain independence of the original arrangement in which the sensations were experienced. This leads to the theory of the "association mixtures" (*associative Mischwirkungen*) propounded by G. E. Müller (44) and carried to the extreme in a paper by Henning (14).

2. Association: Even under our first heading we have met with the concept of memory. According to current teaching, the chief working principle of memory is association, although the purest of associationists recognize that it is not the only principle. It may suffice to point out in this connection that Rosa Heine (12) concludes from experiments performed in G. E. Müller's laboratory, that recognition is not based upon association; for she failed to detect in recognition any trace of that retroactive inhibition which is so powerful a factor in all associative learning. Likewise, Müller himself, relying upon experiments by L. Schlüter (54) acknowledges the possibility of reproduction by similarity. Yet, despite all this, association holds its position as the primary factor governing the coming and the going of our ideas, and the law of association is based upon the sensation-image concept. Our train of thought having been broken up into separate elements, the question is asked by what law does one element cause the appearance of another, and the answer is, association, the tie that forms between each element and all those other elements with which it has ever been in contiguity. As Wertheimer (65) again has pointed out, the core of this theory is this, that the necessary and sufficient cause for the formation and operation of an association is an original existential connection—the mere coexistence of *a* and *b* gives to each a tendency to reproduce the other. Meaning, far from being regarded as one of the conditions of association, is explained by the working of associations, which in themselves are meaningless.

Another feature of this theory is its statistical nature. At every moment, endless associations are working, reinforcing and inhibiting each other.[3] Since we can never have a complete survey of all the effective forces, it is impossible in any single case to make accurate prediction. As the special laws of association can be discovered by statistical methods only, so our predictions can be only statistical.

3. Attention: It is a recognized fact, that, clear and simple as association and sensation appear to be, there is a good deal of obscurity about the concept of attention.[4] And yet, wherever there is an effect that cannot be explained by sensation or association, there attention appears upon the stage.

---

[3]That the facts of reinforcement and inhibition are far from fitting into the theory can be mentioned only incidentally. The reader is referred to the work of Shepard and Fogelsonger (58), and to that of Fringa (8).

[4]Compare Titchener's recent discussion (62).

In more complex systems attention is the makeshift, or the scapegoat, if you will, which always interferes with the working out of these other principles. If the expected sensation does not follow when its appropriate stimulus is applied, attention to other contents must have caused it to pass unnoticed, or if a sensation does not properly correspond to the stimulus applied, the attention must have been inadequate, thus leading us to make a false judgment. We meet with like instances over and over again which justify the following general statement, that attention must be added as a separate factor which not only influences the texture and the course of our conscious processes, but is also likely to be influenced by them.

Modern psychology has endeavored to give a physiological foundation to its psychological conceptions. Let us therefore glance at the physiological side of these three principles. The substratum of sensation (and image) is supposed to be the arousal of a separate and circumscribed area of the cortex, while the substratum for association is the neural connection established between such areas. Again attention holds an ambiguous position, for some see its essence as a facilitation and some as an inhibition of the nervous processes. Without going more into detail, let us examine the nature of this psycho-physical correspondence. Methodologically the physiological and the psychological aspects of these three principles are in perfect harmony; the cortex has been divided into areas, the immediate experience has been analyzed into elements, and connections are assumed to exist between brain areas as between the elements of consciousness. Furthermore, the nervous processes may be altered functionally and their corresponding psychological elements are subject to the functional factor of attention. Evidently the psychological and the physiological are interdependent, and are not sensation, association, and attention, factual? Do not cortical areas exist, and likewise nervous tracts, and the facilitation and inhibition of excitations? Certainly facts exist which have been interpreted in these ways, but we believe it can be proved that this interpretation is insufficient in the face of other and more comprehensive facts. Furthermore, we maintain that the insufficiency of the older theory cannot be remedied by supplementing the three principles, but that these must be sacrificed and replaced by other principles. It is not a discovery of the *Gestalt-psychologie* that these three concepts are inadequate to cover the abundance of mental phenomena, for many others have held the same opinion, and some have even begun experimental work with this in mind. I need but mention v. Ehrenfels and the Meinong school as one instance, Külpe and the Würzburg school as another. But they all left the traditional concepts intact, and while trying to overcome the difficulties by the expedient of adding new concepts, they could not check the tendency involved in these new concepts to modify the old ones. I must, however, warn the reader not to confound the old term of *Gestalt-Qualität* with the term *Gestalt* as it is employed in the new theory. It was to avoid this very confusion that Wertheimer in his first paper avoided the term (64) and introduced a totally neutral expression for the perception of movement—the *phi-phenomenon.*

Just a line at this point upon certain recent tendencies in American psychology. Behaviorism, excluding as it does all forms of consciousness from its realm, strictly speaking denies the use of these three principles altogether. Therefore we do not find the terms attention and sensation in the behaviorist's writings, and even association has disappeared from the explanation in the sense of a tie that can be formed as an original act. And yet, as I have shown in a paper which discusses the fundamental differences between Wertheimer's theory and that of Meinong and Benussi (26), despite the restriction in his use of terms, the outfit of the Behaviorist is essentially the same as that of the traditional psychologist. He says "reaction" where the latter said "sensation," and in so doing includes the effector side of the process, but apart from this he builds his system in exactly the same manner, joining reflex arcs to reflex arcs entirely in accordance with the method of the "bundle-hypothesis."

However, I find a radical abandonment of this hypothesis in Rahn's monograph (52) and also in a recent paper by Ogden (48). With both of these I can in large measure agree, and both of these writers, it seems to me, could readily assimilate the fundamental working principle of the *Gestalt-Psychologie.*

⁓ 21 ⁓

Wolfgang Köhler, Excerpt from
The mentality of apes (1938).*

1. The animals are supposed to have accidentally got accustomed to such solutions in previous life; an *extremely familiar* action, the result of very much practice, was, it is presumed, observed, which, on account of its extreme familiarity, looks exactly like an intelligent solution. But the best and most obvious solutions which I observed, often occurred suddenly, after the animal had been quite helpless at the beginning of the experiment, and sometimes for hours after. Whoever considers Tachego's first experiment (when the box was in the way at the bars) or Koko's (use of box as a stool) to be the repetition of long-practised, mechanical and meaningless products of habit, does so certainly in opposition to the impression which observation of the procedure must make.

2. The animals are supposed to have so developed, strengthened, and perfected their performance, through the selection by success of "impulses", that they can now "easily" reproduce it *in this form.* No single experiment fulfils this requirement, as practically none is performed twice over in the same way; indeed, the movements by which one single one is performed vary greatly. The door is opened from the ground, but also the animal sitting on top of it; when the box is standing in the way, it is pushed away by a corner from the bars, or thrown back over the bottom edge. If the box is to be brought underneath the objective, the same animal will drag, carry, or roll it along, just as the mood takes him. *The only limit is the sense of the proceeding.* For this reason no observer, even with the best of efforts, can say: "the animal contracts such or such a muscle, carries out this or that impulse". *This would be to accentuate an inessential side-issue, which may change from one case to another.* To give the essentials, it is necessary to use expressions in describing all this, which themselves involve meaningful actions; for instance, "*the animal removed from the bars the box which stood in the way*". Which muscles carry out which actions is entirely immaterial.

3. There are other variations not so unimportant, which likewise run counter to the theory, *but arise directly through unforeseen circumstances,* and represent the answer to

*Köhler, W. (1938). Excepts from *The mentality of apes.* London: Routledge & Kegan Paul, Ch. VII, 215–222. Reprinted by permission of Routledge & Kegan Paul.

these circumstances; these *cannot possibly all have been rehearsed.* The animal then does not continue carrying out a rehearsed programme meaninglessly, but answers to a disturbance by a corresponding variation. This is often the case when using the stick. It is easy to say, that the animal fetches an object with the stick, but in reality it does so each time in a different way, because on uneven ground each movement brings the object into a different position which requires special handling. When Sultan for the first time pulled one stick towards himself with another, the test went very smoothly on favourable ground. But the next time the stick encountered a pebble while he was drawing it to him, and so he could not get it any farther, as it was turned round and pointed straight towards him (lying lengthwise). The animal stopped *at once,* first pushed the stick, with careful little pokes of the second stick, crosswise again, and then pulled it to him. One may truthfully say that in the majority of cases when the stick is used, the solving of the chief problem brings in its course small, unforeseen additional problems, and that, as a rule, the chimpanzee immediately makes the necessary modifications. Of course there are limits here, too—they will be dealt with in the next chapter—but we are not asserting that the chimpanzee can do as much as an adult man. On the other hand, it would be simply nonsense to assert that the animal has gone through special combinations of accidental impulses for all these different cases and variations.

4. *Success* is supposed to have selected and joined together the objectively suitable combinations of impulses out of all those that occurred. But the animals produce complete methods of solution, quite suddenly, and *as complete wholes which may, in a certain sense, be absolutely appropriate to the situation, and yet cannot be carried out. They can never have had any success with them,* and, therefore, such methods were certainly never practised formerly (as they would have to be, according to the theory). I would remind the reader how two animals suddenly lift a box that stands too low, and hold it high against the wall; how several of them endeavour to stand the box diagonally so as to make it reach higher; how Rana joins two sticks that are too small, to make one that looks twice as long; how Sultan steers one stick with another from quite a distance right up to the objective and thus "reaches" it, so to speak. In the second part of this investigation a particularly curious case will be described, in which several animals, when a block of stone prevented them from opening a heavy door, *suddenly* made the greatest efforts to lift the heavy door over the stone. How can selection by success have trained them to such "good errors"?

After all this, as far as I can see, even an adherent of the chance theory must recognize that the reports of experiments here given do not support his explanation. The more he tries to advance more valuable data than the general scheme of his theory, and really think out and show how he would explain and interpret all the experiments in detail, the more will he realize that he is attempting something impossible. Only he must keep in view the condition that not even in the most innocent form or in the smallest detail is intelligence to be allowed to co-operate as insight into the structure of the situation.

Whoever is not sure from the very beginning (as a disciple of scientific economy) that this theory only and no other may be applied to animals, must be asked once again to look through the reports of some of the experiments.

Even if that will give him but a faint idea of what direct observation of the actual occurrences teaches one—that cannot be adequately reproduced—he may perhaps feel that, besides the theory, such extended discussions about it are not suitable here; *to such an extent do observations, and the manner of explaining them, differ from each other.* Unfortunately one is forced, by the small value assigned to psychological observations compared to general principles, to such remote and amazing discussions, which the subject-matter itself does not at all require. Henceforth, I shall refer no more to the theory, and shall discuss the experiments only from the points of view which arise *directly out of them.*

I did not express my attitude towards the general theory of association when discussing the chance-theory, and, at the very beginning, it was pointed out that the question to be answered in this book might be affirmed or denied without thereby affirming anything regarding the relation of the experiments to the doctrine of association. For the time being, this will be assumed. If we accept the doctrine of chance, we shall also have to accept that animals have no insight whatever; this touches the very core of the investigation. Association theorists know and recognize what one calls insight[1] in man, and contend that they can explain this by their principles just as well as the simplest association (or reproduction) by contiguity. The only thing that follows for animal behaviour is that, where it has an intelligent character, they will treat it in the same way; but not at all that the animal lacks that which is usually called insight in man. I can, therefore, dispense with any closer elaboration in this direction and will merely observe here that the first and essential condition of a satisfactory associative explanation of intelligent behaviour would be the following achievement of the theory of association, to wit: what the grasp of a *material, inner* relation of two things to each other means (more universally: the grasp of the structure of a situation) must *strictly* be derived from the principle of association; "relation" here meaning an *interconnexion based on the properties of these things themselves,* not a "frequent following each other" or "occurring together." This problem is the first that should be solved, because such "relations" represent the most elementary function participating in specifically intelligent behaviour, and there is no doubt at all that these relations, among other factors, continually determine the chimpanzee's behaviour[2]. They are not facts merely of the type "sensations" and the like, merely further associable elements, but it can quite definitely be proved (and quantitatively proved)[3] that they determine in a very marked degree the chimpanzee's behaviour, i.e. his inner processes, by their functional proper-

[1]The German word *Einsicht* is rendered by both "intelligence" and "insight," throughout this book. The lack of an adjective derived from the noun "insight," apart from other considerations, makes this procedure necessary. [Tr. Note.]

[2]As they determine memory in man too. (Cf. Selz, *l. c.*).

[3]Cf. *Abhandl. d. Preuss. Akad. d. Wiss,* 1918. Phys.-Math. Section, No. 2.

ties. Either the association theory is capable of clearly explaining the "smaller than," "farther away than," "pointing straight towards," etc., according to their true meaning as mere associations from experience, and then all is well; or else the theory cannot be used as a complete explanation, because it cannot account for those factors primarily effective for the chimpanzees (as for man). In the latter case only a *participation* of the association-principle could be allowed, and at least that other class of processes, relations and *not* exterior connexions, should be recognized as an independent working principle as well.

The following explanation, which is often suggested by non-professionals, but which none who has had much experience with animals will take too seriously, can be dealt with much more shortly. Could the chimpanzees, perhaps, prior to the experiments, have seen similar methods of procedure carried out by human beings, and do they not simply imitate such proceedings?

This idea must first of all be brought into clear relation with the question dealt with in this book. It should only be brought forward in the form of an objection if "mere imitation" means imitation *without a trace of insight* into things that have been seen; for otherwise, instead of an objection, we should be dealing with a very special suggestion as to the interpretation of the intelligent action we have actually before us. I presume that even this slight explanation of the so-called objection will somewhat lessen the tendency to bring it forward. For any sudden introduction of relatively complex proceedings, seen *without a trace of insight,* but now performed just as if they were intelligent, would constitute a phenomenon which, as far as I am aware, has never yet been witnessed either in human or in animal psychology; it would have to be introduced here as a new hypothesis. It appears to me, therefore, that we are faced with the following mistake. For the adult human being nothing is easier, in general, than to "imitate" what he sees, or has seen others do; and particularly such actions as the chimpanzees here carry out would be copied immediately by one human being from another, if occasion arose; in such cases we may certainly speak of "mere imitation." Now this fact, carelessly considered, might lead to the said objection; but when applying it to the chimpanzee, one leaves out of account that the human imitator has long been acquainted with the action, and, as long as the model does not become too complicated, will immediately *understand and intelligently grasp what the action of the other means,* and to what extent it is a "solution" of the situation in question. However, that it may be possible, even after a lapse of time (for the experimenter excludes all opportunity for imitation immediately before the experiment),[1] to achieve complex methods of behaviour in no wise and in no detail understood, as clear and complete actions, simply because they were witnessed once or several times before: I repeat: none of our experience has shown us this, and there is little prospect that it will in the future show us any-

[1]Excepting in those cases in which "imitation" is to be investigated.

thing so remarkable. What is really important is that we consider carefully, and allow not the smallest trace of the insight type to be included in what we are here assuming under "imitation."

Even animal psychologists have not always paid sufficient attention to this fundamental difference between "simple" human imitation and the imitation we so lightly expect from animals, and so people were to a certain extent astonished when it was first shown experimentally that animals do not so easily imitate as expected. Less astonishment would perhaps have been felt if it had been realized that, after all, man has first to *understand*, in some degree, before it even occurs to him to imitate. Now we have to test whether animals also require a certain minimum of understanding of what they have seen, before they can imitate it. Recent experiments by American investigators[1] have proved quite definitely, contrary to Thorndike's results, that some imitation, clumsy and laborious enough, occurs among the higher vertebrates. Their reports bear out the assumption that, in general, the animal must work *hard* to gain some understanding of the model, before it can imitate it. "Simple imitation" I can only say to any who have not yet experimented with animals: when any animal suddenly does manage to imitate a performance enacted before him of which he knew nothing before, he inspires the greatest respect immediately. Unfortunately this is a very rare occurrence even among chimpanzees,[2] and when it does occur, the situation, as well as its solution, must lie just about within the bounds set for spontaneous solutions. It will now be seen how far removed from experience an objection of the "simple imitation" type is.

[Chimpanzees (and also other higher vertebrates) will "imitate" with ease as soon as the same conditions as those required in man are present, i.e. if they are already familiar with, and understand the action to be imitated. If, *in such circumstances*, there is any reason to watch the model (animal or man), and if his actions are of interest, then either the animal "takes part" or "tries the same solution," etc. Thus, in imitation, similar circumstances and qualitative conditions seem to exist in the higher animals as in man. It can easily be shown, that humans do not "simply imitate" either, if they do not sufficiently understand an action, or a line of thought. I shall return to this subject when describing the imitation of chimpanzees.]

Anticipating later accounts, I will, for the present, mention only briefly that four kinds of imitation occur in chimpanzees, but that none of the observations give the slightest ground for thinking that the animals could "simply" and *quite without insight* have "imitated" important parts of their performances. The chimpanzee cannot do this.

[1]Barry, *Journal of Comp. Neurol and Psychol.*, 18, 1908; Haggerty, *ibid.*, 19, 1909.

[2]Compare Pfungst, *Bericht uber den 5 Kongress. f. exper. Psychologie*, 1912, p. 201. Pfungst, however, goes too far; even human beings are imitated by chimpanzees when necessity arises, *if they are understood.*

❦ 22 ❦

Sigmund Freud, Excerpt from *New introductory lectures on psychoanalysis* (1933).*

LADIES AND GENTLEMEN,—If, after an interval of more than fifteen years, I have brought you together again to discuss with you what novelties, and what improvements it may be, the intervening time has introduced into psycho-analysis, it is right and fitting from more than one point of view that we should turn our attention first to the position of the theory of dreams. It occupies a special place in the history of psycho-analysis and marks a turning-point; it was with it that analysis took the step from being a psychotherapeutic procedure to being a depth-psychology. Since then, too, the theory of dreams has remained what is most characteristic and peculiar about the young science, something to which there is no counterpart in the rest of our knowledge, a stretch of new country, which has been reclaimed from popular beliefs and mysticism. The strangeness of the assertions it was obliged to put forward has made it play the part of a shibboleth, the use of which decided who could become a follower of psycho-analysis and to whom it remained for ever incomprehensible. I myself found it a sheet-anchor during those difficult times when the unrecognized facts of the neuroses used to confuse my inexperienced judgement. Whenever I began to have doubts of the correctness of my wavering conclusions, the successful transformation of a senseless and muddled dream into a logical and intelligible mental process in the dreamer would renew my confidence of being on the right track.

It is therefore of special interest to us, in the particular instance of the theory of dreams, on the one hand to follow the vicissitudes through which

*Reprinted from *New introductory lectures on psychoanalysis* by Sigmund Freud, Translated and Edited by James Strachey, by permission of W.W. Norton & Company, Inc. Copyright (c) 1965, 1964 by James Strachey. Copyright 1933 by Sigmund Freud. Copyright renewed 1961 by W. J. H. Sprott.

psycho-analysis has passed during this interval, and on the other hand to learn what advances it has made in being understood and appreciated by the contemporary world. I may tell you at once that you will be disappointed in both these directions.

Let us look through the volumes of the *Internationale Zeitschrift für* (*ärztliche*) *Psychoanalyse* [*International Journal of* (*Medical*) *Psycho-Analysis*], in which, since 1913, the authoritative writings in our field of work have been brought together. In the earlier volumes you will find a recurrent sectional heading 'On Dream-Interpretation', containing numerous contributions on various points in the theory of dreams. But the further you go the rarer do these contributions become, and finally the sectional heading disappears completely. The analysts behave as though they had no more to say about dreams, as though there was nothing more to be added to the theory of dreams. But if you ask how much of dream-interpretation has been accepted by outsiders—by the many psychiatrists and psychotherapists who warm their pot of soup at our fire (incidentally without being very grateful for our hospitality), by what are described as educated people, who are in the habit of assimilating the more striking findings of science, by the literary men and by the public at large—the reply gives little cause for satisfaction. A few formulas have become generally familiar, among them some that we have never put forward—such as the thesis that all dreams are of a sexual nature—but really important things like the fundamental distinction between the manifest content of dreams and the latent dream-thoughts, the realization that the wish-fulfilling function of dreams is not contradicted by anxiety-dreams, the impossibility of interpreting a dream unless one has the dreamer's associations to it at one's disposal, and, above all, the discovery that what is essential in dreams is the process of the dream-work—all this still seems about as foreign to general awareness as it was thirty years ago. I am in a position to say this, since in the course of that period I have received innumerable letters whose writers present their dreams for interpretation or ask for information about the nature of dreams and who declare that they have read my *Interpretation of Dreams,* though in every sentence they betray their lack of understanding of our theory of dreams. But all this shall not deter us from once more giving a connected account of what we know about dreams. You will recall that last time we devoted a whole number of lectures to showing how we came to understand this hitherto unexplained mental phenomenon.[1]

Let us suppose, then, that someone—a patient in analysis, for instance—tells us one of his dreams. We shall assume that in this way he is making us one of the communications to which he has pledged himself by the fact of having started an analytic treatment. It is, to be sure, a communication made by inappropriate means, for dreams are not in themselves social utterances, not a means of giving information. Nor, indeed, do we understand what the dreamer was trying to say to us, and he himself is equally in the dark. And now we

---

[1] [Cf. the whole of Part II of *Introductory Lectures on Psycho-Analysis* (1916–17).]

have to make a quick decision. On the one hand, the dream may be, as non-analytic doctors assure us, a sign that the dreamer has slept badly, that not every part of his brain has come to rest equally, that some areas of it, under the influence of unknown stimuli, endeavoured to go on working but were only able to do so in a very incomplete fashion. If that is the case, we shall be right to concern ourselves no further with the product of a nocturnal disturbance which has no psychical value: for what could we expect to derive from investigating it that would be of use for our purposes? Or on the other hand—but it is plain that we have from the first decided otherwise. We have—quite arbitrarily, it must be admitted—made the assumption, adopted as a postulate, that even this unintelligible dream must be a fully valid psychical act, with sense and worth, which we can use in analysis like any other communication. Only the outcome of our experiment can show whether we are right. If we succeed in turning the dream into an utterance of value of that kind, we shall evidently have a prospect of learning something new and of receiving communications of a sort which would otherwise be inaccessible to us.

Now, however, the difficulties of our task and the enigmas of our subject rise before our eyes. How do we propose to transform the dream into a normal communication and how do we explain the fact that some of the patient's utterances have assumed a form that is unintelligible both to him and to us?

As you see, Ladies and Gentlemen, this time I am taking the path not of a genetic but of a dogmatic exposition. Our first step is to establish our new attitude to the problem of dreams by introducing two new concepts and names. What has been called the dream we shall describe as the text of the dream or the *manifest* dream, and what we are looking for, what we suspect, so to say, of lying behind the dream, we shall describe as the *latent* dream-thoughts. Having done this, we can express our two tasks as follows. We have to transform the manifest dream into the latent one, and to explain how, in the dreamer's mind, the latter has become the former. The first portion is a *practical* task, for which dream-interpretation is responsible; it calls for a technique. The second portion is a *theoretical* task, whose business it is to explain the hypothetical dream-work; and it can only be a theory. Both of them, the technique of dream-interpretation and the theory of the dream-work, have to be newly created.

With which of the two, then, shall we start? With the technique of dream-interpretation, I think; it will present a more concrete appearance and make a more vivid impression on you.

Well then, the patient has told us a dream, which we are to interpret. We have listened passively, without putting our powers of reflection into action.[1] What do we do next? We decide to concern ourselves as little as possible with what we have heard, with the *manifest* dream. Of course this manifest dream

---

[1] [Some illuminating remarks on reflection will be found, in a similar connection, in Chapter II of *The Interpretation of Dreams* (1900a).]

exhibits all sorts of characteristics which are not entirely a matter of indifference to us. It may be coherent, smoothly constructed like a literary composition, or it may be confused to the point of unintelligibility, almost like a delirium; it may contain absurd elements or jokes and apparently witty conclusions; it may seem to the dreamer clear and sharp or obscure and hazy; its pictures may exhibit the complete sensory strength of perceptions or may be shadowy like an indistinct mist; the most diverse characteristics may be present in the same dream, distributed over various portions of it; the dream, finally, may show an indifferent emotional tone or be accompanied by feelings of the strongest joy or distress. You must not suppose that we think nothing of this endless diversity in manifest dreams. We shall come back to it later and we shall find a great deal in it that we can make use of in our interpretations. But for the moment we will disregard it and follow the main road that leads to the interpretation of dreams. That is to say, we ask the dreamer, too, to free himself from the impression of the manifest dream, to divert his attention from the dream as a whole on to the separate portions of its content and to report to us in succession everything that occurs to him in relation to each of these portions—what associations present themselves to him if he focuses on each of them separately.

That is a curious technique, is it not?—not the usual way of dealing with a communication or utterance. And no doubt you guess that behind this procedure there are assumptions which have not yet been expressly stated. But let us proceed. In what order are we to get the patient to take up the portions of his dream? There are various possibilities open to us. We can simply follow the chronological order in which they appeared in the account of the dream. That is what may be called the strictest, classical method. Or we can direct the dreamer to begin by looking out for the 'day's residues' in the dream; for experience has taught us that almost every dream includes the remains of a memory or an allusion to some event (or often to several events) of the day before the dream, and, if we follow these connections, we often arrive with one blow at the transition from the apparently far remote dream-world to the real life of the patient. Or, again, we may tell him to start with those elements of the dream's content which strike him by their special clarity and sensory strength; for we know that he will find it particularly easy to get associations to these. It makes no difference by which of these methods we approach the associations we are in search of.[1]

And next, we obtain these associations. What they bring us is of the most various kinds: memories from the day before, the 'dream-day', and from times long past, reflections, discussions, with arguments for and against, confessions and enquiries. Some of them the patient pours out; when he comes to others he is held up for a time. Most of them show a clear connection to some element of the dream; no wonder, since those elements were their starting-point.

---

[1] [A slightly different list of these alternative methods is given in 'Remarks on the Theory and Practice of Dream-Interpretation' (1923c).]

But it also sometimes happens that the patient introduces them with these words: 'This seems to me to have nothing at all to do with the dream, but I tell it you because it occurs to me.'

If one listens to these copious associations, one soon notices that they have more in common with the content of the dream than their starting-points alone. They throw a surprising light on all the different parts of the dream, fill in gaps between them, and make their strange juxtapositions intelligible. In the end one is bound to become clear about the relation between them and the dream's content. The dream is seen to be an abbreviated selection from the associations, a selection made, it is true, according to rules that we have not yet understood: the elements of the dream are like representatives chosen by election from a mass of people. There can be no doubt that by our technique we have got hold of something for which the dream is a substitute and in which lies the dream's psychical value, but which no longer exhibits its puzzling peculiarities, its strangeness and its confusion.

Let there be no misunderstanding, however. The associations to the dream are not yet the latent dream-thoughts. The latter are contained in the associations like an alkali in the mother-liquor, but yet not quite completely contained in them. On the one hand, the associations give us far more than we need for formulating the latent dream-thoughts—namely all the explanations, transitions, and connections which the patient's intellect is bound to produce in the course of his approach to the dream-thoughts. On the other hand, an association often comes to a stop precisely before the genuine dream-thought: it has only come near to it and has only had contact with it through allusions. At that point we intervene on our own; we fill in the hints, draw undeniable conclusions, and give explicit utterance to what the patient has only touched on in his associations. This sounds as though we allowed our ingenuity and caprice to play with the material put at our disposal by the dreamer and as though we misused it in order to interpret *into* his utterances what cannot be interpreted *from* them. Nor is it easy to show the legitimacy of our procedure in an abstract description of it. But you have only to carry out a dream-analysis yourselves or study a good account of one in our literature and you will be convinced of the cogent manner in which interpretative work like this proceeds.

If in general and primarily we are dependent, in interpreting dreams, on the dreamer's associations, yet in relation to certain elements of the dream's content we adopt a quite independent attitude, chiefly because we have to, because as a rule associations fail to materialize in their case. We noticed at an early stage that it is always in connection with the same elements that this happens; they are not very numerous, and repeated experience has taught us that they are to be regarded and interpreted as *symbols* of something else. As contrasted with the other dream-elements, a fixed meaning may be attributed to them, which, however, need not be unambiguous and whose range is determined by special rules with which we are unfamiliar. Since *we*

know how to translate these symbols and the dreamer does not, in spite of having used them himself, it may happen that the sense of a dream may at once
become clear to us as soon as we have heard the text of the dream, even
before we have made any efforts at interpreting it, while it still remains an
enigma to the dreamer himself. But I have said so much to you in my earlier
lectures about symbolism, our knowledge of it and the problems it poses us,
that I need not repeat it to-day.[1]

   That, then, is our method of interpreting dreams. The first and justifi-
able question is: 'Can we interpret *all* dreams by its help?'[2] And the answer is:
'No, not all; but so many that we feel confident in the serviceability and correctness of the procedure.' 'But why not all?' The answer to this has something important to teach us, which at once introduces us into the psychical
determinants of the formation of dreams: 'Because the work of interpreting
dreams is carried out against a resistance, which varies between trivial dimensions and invincibility (at least so far as the strength of our present methods
reaches).' It is impossible during our work to overlook the manifestations of
this resistance. At some points the associations are given without hesitation
and the first or second idea that occurs to the patient brings an explanation.
At other points there is a stoppage and the patient hesitates before bringing
out an association, and, if so, we often have to listen to a long chain of ideas
before receiving anything that helps us to understand the dream. We are certainly right in thinking that the longer and more roundabout the chain of
associations the stronger the resistance. We can detect the same influence at
work in the forgetting of dreams. It happens often enough that a patient,
despite all his efforts, cannot remember one of his dreams. But after we have
been able in the course of a piece of analytic work to get rid of a difficulty
which had been disturbing his relation to the analysis, the forgotten dream
suddenly re-emerges. Two other observations are also in place here. It very
frequently comes about that, to begin with, a portion of a dream is omitted
and added afterwards as an addendum. This is to be regarded as an attempt
to forget that portion. Experience shows that it is that particular piece which
is the most important; there was a greater resistance, we suppose, in the path
of communicating it than the other parts of the dream.[3] Furthermore, we
often find that a dreamer endeavours to prevent himself from forgetting his
dreams by fixing them in writing immediately after waking up. We can tell him
that that is no use. For the resistance from which he has extorted the preservation of the text of the dream will then be displaced on to its associations and
will make the manifest dream inaccessible to interpretation.[4] In view of these

---

[1] [*See Introductory Lectures* (1916–17). Lecture X.]

[2] [Freud had recently written a special note on 'The Limits to the Possibility of
Interpretation' (1925*t*).]

[3] [Cf. *The Interpretation of Dreams* (1900*a*). Chapter VII (A).]

[4] [Cf. 'The Handling of Dream-Interpretation in Psycho-Analysis' (1911*e*).]

facts we need not feel surprised if a further increase in the resistance suppresses the associations altogether and thus brings the interpretation of the dream to nothing.

From all this we infer that the resistance which we come across in the work of interpreting dreams must also have had a share in their origin. We can actually distinguish between dreams that arose under a slight and under a high pressure of resistance.[1] But this pressure varies as well from place to place within one and the same dream; it is responsible for the gaps, obscurities and confusions which may interrupt the continuity of even the finest of dreams.

But what is creating the resistance and against what is it aimed? Well, the resistance is the surest sign to us of a conflict. There must be a force here which is seeking to express something and another which is striving to prevent its expression. What comes about in consequence as a manifest dream may combine all the decisions into which this struggle between two trends has been condensed. At one point one of these forces may have succeeded in putting through what it wanted to say, while at another point it is the opposing agency which has managed to blot out the intended communication completely or to replace it by something that reveals not a trace of it. The commonest and most characteristic cases of dream-construction are those in which the conflict has ended in a compromise, so that the communicating agency has, it is true, been able to say what it wanted but not in the way it wanted—only in a softened down, distorted and unrecognized form. If, then, dreams do not give a faithful picture of the dream-thoughts and if the work of interpretation is required in order to bridge the gap between them, that is the outcome of the opposing, inhibiting and restricting agency which we have inferred from our perception of the resistance while we interpret dreams. So long as we studied dreams as isolated phenomena independent of the psychical structures akin to them, we named this agency the *censor*[2] *of dreams.*

You have long been aware that this censorship is not an institution peculiar to dream-life. You know that the conflict between the two psychical agencies, which we—inaccurately—describe as the 'unconscious repressed' and the 'conscious', dominates our whole mental life and that the resistance against the interpretation of dreams, the sign of the dream-censorship, is nothing other than the resistance due to repression by which the two agencies are separated. You know too that the conflict between these two agencies may under certain conditions produce other psychical structures which, like dreams, are the outcome of compromises; and you will not expect me to repeat to you here everything that was contained in my introduction to the theory of the neuroses in order to demonstrate to you what we know of the

---

[1][Cf. Section II of 'Remarks on the Theory and Practice of Dream-Interpretation' (1923*c*).]

[2][This is one of the very rare occasions on which Freud uses the personified form '*Zensor*' instead of the impersonal '*Zensur*' (censorship).]

determinants of the formation of such compromises. You have realized that the dream is a pathological product, the first member of the class which includes hysterical symptoms, obsessions and delusions,[1] but that it is distinguished from the others by its transitoriness and by its occurrence under conditions which are part of normal life. For let us bear firmly in mind that, as was already pointed out by Aristotle, dream-life is the way in which our mind works during the state of sleep.[2] The state of sleep involves a turning-away from the real external world, and there we have the necessary condition for the development of a psychosis. The most careful study of the severe psychoses will not reveal to us a single feature that is more characteristic of those pathological conditions. In psychoses, however, the turning-away from reality is brought about in two kinds of way: either by the unconscious repressed becoming excessively strong so that it overwhelms the conscious, which is attached to reality,[3] or because reality has become so intolerably distressing that the threatened ego throws itself into the arms of the unconscious instinctual forces in a desperate revolt. The harmless dream-psychosis is the result of a withdrawal from the external world which is consciously willed and only temporary, and it disappears when relations to the external world are resumed. During the isolation of the sleeping individual an alteration in the distribution of his psychical energy also sets in; a part of the expenditure on repression, which is normally required in order to hold the unconscious down, can be saved, for if the unconscious makes use of its relative liberation for active purposes, it finds its path to motility closed and the only path open to it is the harmless one leading to hallucinatory satisfaction. Now, therefore, a dream can be formed; but the fact of the dream-censorship shows that even during sleep enough of the resistance due to repression is retained.

Here we are presented with a means of answering the question of whether dreams have a function too, whether they are entrusted with any useful achievement. The condition of rest free from stimulus, which the state of sleep wishes to establish, is threatened from three directions: in a relatively accidental manner by external stimuli during sleep, and by interests of the previous day which cannot be broken off, and in an unavoidable manner by unsated repressed instinctual impulses which are on the watch for an opportunity of finding expression. In consequence of the diminishing of repressions at night there would be a risk that the rest afforded by sleep would be interrupted whenever an instigation from outside or from inside succeeded in linking up with an unconscious instinctual source. The process of dreaming allows the product of a collaboration of this kind to find an outlet in a

---

[1][This part of the sentence is repeated almost word for word from the second sentence in Freud's preface to the first edition of *The Interpretation of Dreams* (1900a).]

[2][*The Interpretation of Dreams*, Chapter I.]

[3][The notion occurs already in one of Freud's very earliest psychological papers, his first one on 'The Neuro-Psychoses of Defence' (1894a).]

harmless hallucinatory experience and in that way assures a continuation of sleep. The fact that a dream occasionally awakens the sleeper, to the accompaniment of a generation of anxiety, is no contradiction of this function but rather, perhaps, a signal that the watchman regards the situation as too dangerous and no longer feels able to control it. And very often then, while we are still asleep, a consolation occurs to us which seeks to prevent our waking up: 'But after all it's only a dream!'

This was what I wanted to say to you, Ladies and Gentlemen, about dream-interpretation, whose task it is to lead the way from the manifest dream to the latent dream-thoughts. When this has been achieved, interest in a dream, so far as practical analysis is concerned, is for the most part at an end. We add the communication we have received in the form of a dream to the rest of the patient's communications and proceed with the analysis. We, however, have an interest in dwelling a little longer on the dream. We are tempted to study the process by which the latent dream-thoughts were transformed into the manifest dream. We call this the 'dream-work'. As you will recall, I described it in such detail in my earlier lectures[1] that I can restrict my present survey to the most concise summary.

The process of the dream-work, then, is something entirely new and strange, nothing resembling which was known before. It has given us our first glimpse of the processes which take place in the unconscious system and has shown us that they are quite other than what we know from our conscious thinking and are bound to appear to the latter preposterous and incorrect. The importance of this finding was then increased by the discovery that in the construction of neurotic symptoms the same mechanisms (we do not venture to say 'processes of thought') are operative as those which have transformed the latent dream-thoughts into the manifest dream.

In what follows I shall not be able to avoid a schematic method of exposition. Let us assume that in a particular case we have before us all the latent thoughts, charged with a greater or less amount of affect, by which the manifest dream has been replaced after its interpretation has been completed. We shall then be struck by one difference among these latent thoughts, and that difference will take us a long way. Almost all these dream-thoughts are recognized by the dreamer or acknowledged by him; he admits that he has thought this, now or at some other time, or that he might have thought it. There is only one single thought that he refuses to accept; it is strange to him or even perhaps repellent; he may possibly reject it with passionate feeling. It now becomes evident to us that the other thoughts are portions of a conscious, or, more accurately, a preconscious train of thinking. They might have been thought in waking life too, and indeed they were probably formed during the previous day. This one repudiated thought, however, or, properly speaking, this one impulse, is a child of night; it belongs to the dreamer's unconscious

[1][Introductory Lectures, XI.]

and on that account it is repudiated and rejected by him. It had to wait for the nightly relaxation of repression in order to arrive at any kind of expression. And in any case this expression is a weakened, distorted and disguised one; without our work of dream-interpretation we should not have found it. This unconscious impulse has to thank its link with the other, unobjectionable, dream-thoughts for the opportunity of slipping past the barrier of the censorship in an inconspicuous disguise. On the other hand, the preconscious dream-thoughts have to thank this same link for the power to occupy mental life during sleep as well. For there is no doubt about it: this unconscious impulse is the true creator of the dream; it is what produces the psychical energy for the dream's construction. Like any other instinctual impulse, it cannot strive for anything other than its own satisfaction; and our experience in interpreting dreams shows us too that that is the sense of all dreaming. In every dream an instinctual wish has to be represented as fulfilled. The shutting-off of mental life from reality at night and the regression to primitive mechanisms which this makes possible enable this wished-for instinctual satisfaction to be experienced in a hallucinatory manner as occurring in the present. As a result of this same regression, ideas are transformed in the dream into visual pictures: the latent dream-thoughts, that is to say, are dramatized and illustrated.

This piece of the dream-work gives us information about some of the most striking and peculiar features of dreams. I will repeat the course of events in dream-formation. As an introduction: the wish to sleep and intentional turning away from the external world. Next, two consequences of this for the mental apparatus: first, the possibility for older and more primitive methods of working to emerge in it—regression; secondly, the lowering of the resistance due to repression which weighs down upon the unconscious. As a result of this last factor the possibility arises for the formation of a dream and this is taken advantage of by the precipitating causes, the internal and external stimuli which have become active. The dream which originates in this way is already a compromise-structure. It has a double function; on the one hand it is ego-syntonic,[1] since, by getting rid of the stimuli which are interfering with sleep, it serves the wish to sleep; on the other hand it allows a repressed instinctual impulse to obtain the satisfaction that is possible in these circumstances, in the form of the hallucinated fulfilment of a wish. The whole process of forming a dream which is permitted by the sleeping ego is, however, subject to the condition of the censorship, which is exercised by the residue of the repression still in operation. I cannot present the process more simply: it is not more simple. But I can proceed now with my description of the dream-work.

Let us go back once more to the latent dream-thoughts. Their most powerful element is the repressed instinctual impulse which has created in them

[1][In conformity with the ego.]

an expression for itself on the basis of the presence of chance stimuli and by transference on to the day's residues—though an expression that is toned down and disguised. Like every instinctual impulse, it too presses for satisfaction by action; but its path to motility is blocked by the physiological regulations implied in the state of sleep; it is compelled to take the backwards course in the direction of perception and to be content with a hallucinated satisfaction. The latent dream-thoughts are thus transformed into a collection of sensory images and visual scenes. It is as they travel on this course that what seems to us so novel and so strange occurs to them. All the linguistic instruments by which we express the subtler relations of thought—the conjunctions and prepositions, the changes in declension and conjugation—are dropped, because there are no means of representing them; just as in a primitive language without any grammar, only the raw material of thought is expressed and abstract terms are taken back to the concrete ones that are at their basis. What is left over after this may well appear disconnected. The copious employment of symbols, which have become alien to conscious thinking, for representing certain objects and processes is in harmony alike with the archaic regression in the mental apparatus and with the demands of the censorship.

But other changes made in the elements of the dream-thoughts go far beyond this. Such of those elements as allow any point of contact to be found between them are *condensed* into new unities. In the process of transforming the thoughts into pictures, preference is unmistakably given to such as permit of this putting-together, this condensation; it is as though a force were at work which was subjecting the material to compression and concentration. As a result of condensation, one element in the manifest dream may correspond to numerous elements in the latent dream-thoughts; but, conversely too, one element in the dream-thoughts may be represented by several images in the dream.

Still more remarkable is the other process—*displacement* or shifting of accent—which in conscious thinking we come across only as faulty reasoning or as means for a joke. The different ideas in the dream-thoughts are, indeed, not all of equal value; they are cathected with quotas of affect of varying magnitude and are correspondingly judged to be important and deserving of interest to a greater or less degree. In the dream-work these ideas are separated from the affects attaching to them. The affects are dealt with independently; they may be displaced on to something else, they may be retained, they may undergo alterations, or they may not appear in the dream at all. The importance of the ideas that have been stripped of their affect returns in the dream as sensory strength in the dream-pictures; but we observe that this accent has passed over from important elements to indifferent ones. Thus something that played only a minor part in the dream-thoughts seems to be pushed into the foreground in the dream as the main thing, while, on the contrary, what was the essence of the dream-thoughts finds only passing and indistinct representation in the dream. No other part of the dream-work is so much responsible for making the dream strange and incomprehensible to the dreamer. Displacement is the principal means used in the *dream-distortion* to which the dream-thoughts must submit under the influence of the censorship.

After these influences have been brought to bear upon the dream-thoughts the dream is almost complete. A further, somewhat variable, factor also comes into play—known as 'secondary revision'—after the dream has been presented before consciousness as an object of perception. At that point we treat it as we are in general accustomed to treat the contents of our perception: we fill in gaps and introduce connections, and in doing so are often guilty of gross misunderstandings. But this activity, which might be described as a rationalizing one and which at best provides the dream with a smooth façade that cannot fit its true content, may also be omitted or only be expressed to a very modest degree—in which case the dream will display all its rents and cracks openly. It must not be forgotten, on the other hand, that the dream-work does not always operate with equal energy either; it often restricts itself to certain portions of the dream-thoughts only and others of them are allowed to appear in the dream unaltered. In such cases an impression is given of the dream having carried out the most delicate and complex intellectual operations, of its having speculated, made jokes, arrived at decisions and solved problems, whereas all this is a product of our normal mental activity, may have been performed equally well during the day before the dream as during the night, has nothing to do with the dream-work and brings nothing to light that is characteristic of dreams. Nor is it superfluous to insist once more on the contrast within the dream-thoughts themselves between the unconscious instinctual impulse and the day's residues. While the latter exhibit all the multiplicity of our mental acts, the former, which becomes the motive force proper of the forming of the dream, finds its outlet invariably in the fulfilment of a wish.

I could have told you all this fifteen years ago, and indeed I believe I did in fact tell it to you then. And now let me bring together such changes and new discoveries as may have been made during the interval. I have said already that I am afraid you will find that it amounts to very little, and you will fail to understand why I obliged you to listen to the same thing twice over, and obliged myself to say it. But fifteen years have passed meanwhile and I hope that this will be my easiest way of re-establishing contact with you. Moreover, these are such fundamental things, of such decisive importance for understanding psycho-analysis, that one may be glad to hear them a second time, and it is in itself worth knowing that they have remained so much the same for fifteen years.

In the literature of this period you will of course find a large quantity of confirmatory material and of presentation of details, of which I intend only to give you samples. I shall also, incidentally, be able to tell you a few things that were in fact already known earlier. What is in question is principally the symbolism in dreams and the other methods of representation in them. Now listen to this. Only quite a short while ago the medical faculty in an American University refused to allow psycho-analysis the status of a science, on the ground that it did not admit of any experimental proof. They might have raised the same objection to astronomy; indeed, experimentation with the heavenly bodies is particularly difficult. There one has to fall back on observation. Nevertheless, some Viennese investigators have actually made a beginning with experimental confirmation of our dream symbolism. As long ago as in 1912 a Dr. Schrötter found that if instructions to dream of sexual matters are given to deeply hypnotized subjects, then in the dream that is thus provoked the sexual material emerges with its place taken by the symbols that are familiar to us. For instance, a woman was told to dream of sexual intercourse with a female friend. In her dream this friend appeared with a travelling-bag on which was pasted the label 'Ladies Only'. Still more impressive experiments were carried out by Betlheim and Hartmann in 1924. They worked with patients suffering from what is known as the Korsakoff confusional psychosis. They told these patients stories of a grossly sexual kind and observed the distortions which appeared when the patients were instructed to reproduce what they had been told. Once more there emerged the symbols for sexual organs and sexual intercourse that are familiar to us—among them the symbol of the staircase which, as the writers justly remark, could never have been reached by a conscious wish to distort.[1]

In a very interesting series of experiments, Herbert Silberer [1909 and 1912] has shown that one can catch the dream-work red-handed, as it were, in the act of turning abstract thoughts into visual pictures. If he tried to force himself to do intellectual work while he was in a state of fatigue and drowsiness, the thought would often vanish and be replaced by a vision, which was obviously a substitute for it.

Here is a simple example. 'I thought', says Silberer, 'of having to revise an uneven passage in an essay.' The vision: 'I saw myself planing a piece of wood.' It often happened during these experiments that the content of the vision was not the thought that was being dealt with but his own subjective state while he was making the effort—the state instead of the object. This is described by Silberer as a 'functional phenomenon'. An example will show you at once what is meant. The author was endeavouring to compare the opinions of two philosophers on a particular question. But in his sleepy condition one of these opinions kept on escaping him and finally he had a vision that he was asking for information from a disobliging secretary who was bent over his writing-table and who began by disregarding him and then gave him a disagreeable and uncomplying look. The conditions under which the exper-

---

[1][Longer descriptions of these experiments will be found in Chapter VI (E) of *The Interpretation of Dreams* (1900a).]

iments were made probably themselves explain why the vision that was induced represented so often an event of self-observation.[1]

We have not yet finished with symbols. There are some which we believed we recognized but which nevertheless worried us because we could not explain how *this* particular symbol had come to have *that* particular meaning. In such cases confirmations from elsewhere—from philology, folklore, mythology or ritual—were bound to be especially welcome. An instance of this sort is the symbol of an overcoat or cloak [German '*Mantel*']. We have said that in a woman's dreams this stands for a man.[2] I hope it will impress you when you hear that Theodor Reik (1920) gives us this information: 'During the extremely ancient bridal ceremonial of the Bedouins, the bridegroom covers the bride with a special cloak known as "Aba" and speaks the following ritual words: "Henceforth none save I shall cover thee!"' (Quoted from Robert Eisler [1910, 2, 599 *f.*]). We have also found several fresh symbols, at least two of which I will tell you of. According to Abraham (1922) a spider in dreams is a symbol of the mother, but of the *phallic* mother, of whom we are afraid; so that the fear of spiders expresses dread of mother-incest and horror of the female genitals. You know, perhaps, that the mythological creation, Medusa's head, can be traced back to the same *motif* of fright at castration.[3] The other symbol I want to talk to you about is that of the *bridge*, which has been explained by Ferenczi (1921 and 1922). First it means the male organ, which unites the two parents in sexual intercourse; but afterwards it develops further meanings which are derived from this first one. In so far as it is thanks to the male organ that we are able to come into the world at all, out of the amniotic fluid, a bridge becomes the crossing from the other world (the unborn state, the womb) to this world (life); and, since men also picture death as a return to the womb (to the water), a bridge also acquires the meaning of something that leads to death, and finally, at a further remove from its original sense, it stands for transitions or changes in condition generally. It tallies with this, accordingly, if a woman who has not overcome her wish to be a man has frequent dreams of bridges that are too short to reach the further shore.

In the manifest content of dreams we very often find pictures and situations recalling familiar themes in fairy tales, legends and myths. The interpretation of such dreams thus throws a light on the original interests which

[1] [Freud gave a very much fuller account of Silberer's experiments, with a great many quotations, in some passages added in 1914 to *The Interpretation of Dreams* (1900*a*), Chapter VI (D) and (I).]

[2] [The symbol is referred to in the *Introductory Lectures*, Lecture X, but the fact that this applies to women's dreams is only mentioned among some 'Observations and Examples' published earlier (Freud, 1913*h*).]

[3] [Cf. a posthumously published note by Freud on the subject (1940*c* [1922]).]

created these themes, though we must at the same time not forget, of course, the change in meaning by which this material has been affected in the course of time. Our work of interpretation uncovers, so to say, the raw material, which must often enough be described as sexual in the widest sense, but has found the most varied application in later adaptations. Derivations of this kind are apt to bring down on us the wrath of all non-analytically schooled workers, as though we were seeking to deny or undervalue everything that was later erected on the original basis. Nevertheless, such discoveries are instructive and interesting. The same is true of tracing back the origin of particular themes in plastic art, as, for instance, when M. J. Eisler (1919), following indications in his patients' dreams, gave an analytic interpretation of the youth playing with a little boy represented in the Hermes of Praxiteles. And lastly I cannot resist pointing out how often light is thrown by the interpretation of dreams on mythological themes in particular. Thus, for instance, the legend of the Labyrinth can be recognized as a representation of anal birth: the twisting paths are the bowels and Ariadne's thread is the umbilical cord.

The methods of representation employed by the dream-work—fascinating material, scarcely capable of exhaustion—have been made more and more familiar to us by closer study. I will give you a few examples of them. Thus, for instance, dreams represent the relation of frequency by a multiplication of similar things. Here is a young girl's remarkable dream. She dreamt she came into a great hall and found some one in it sitting on a chair; this was repeated six or eight times or more, but each time it was her father. This is easy to understand when we discover, from accessory details in the interpretation, that this room stood for the womb. The dream then becomes equivalent to the phantasy, familiarly found in girls, of having met their father already during their intra-uterine life when he visited the womb while their mother was pregnant. You should not be confused by the fact that something is reversed in the dream—that her father's 'coming-in' is displaced on to herself; incidentally, this has a special meaning of its own as well. The multiplication of the figure of the father can only express the fact that the event in question occurred repeatedly. After all, it must be allowed that the dream is not taking very much on itself in expressing frequency by multiplicity.[1] It has only needed to go back to the original significance of the former word; to-day it means to us a repetition in time, but it is derived from an accumulation in space. In general, indeed, where it is possible, the dream-work changes temporal relations into spatial ones and represents them as such. In a dream, for instance, one may see a scene between two people who look very small and a long way off, as though one were seeing them through the wrong end of a pair of opera-glasses. Here, both the smallness and the remoteness in space have the same significance: what is meant is remoteness in *time* and we are to understand that the scene is from the remote past.

---

[1] ['*Häufigkeit*' and '*Häufung*' in German. Both words are derived from '*Haufen*'—a 'heap'.]

Again, you may remember that in my earlier lectures I already told you (and illustrated the fact by examples) that we had learnt to make use for our interpretations even of the purely *formal* features of the manifest dream—that is, to transform them into material coming from the latent dream-thoughts.[1] As you already know, all dreams that are dreamt in a single night belong in a single context. But it is not a matter of indifference whether these dreams appear to the dreamer as a continuum or whether he divides them into several parts and into how many. The number of such parts often corresponds to an equal number of separate focal points in the structural formation of the latent dream-thoughts or to contending trends in the dreamer's mental life, each of which finds a dominant, even though never an exclusive, expression in one particular part of the dream. A short introductory dream and a longer main dream following it often stand in the relation of protasis and apodosis [conditional and consequential clauses], of which a very clear instance will be found in the old lectures.[2] A dream which is described by the dreamer as 'somehow interpolated' will actually correspond to a dependent clause in the dream-thoughts. Franz Alexander (1925) has shown in a study on pairs of dreams that it not infrequently happens that two dreams in one night share the carrying-out of the dream's task by producing a wish-fulfilment in two stages if they are taken together, though each dream separately would not effect that result. Suppose, for instance, that the dream-wish had as its content some illicit action in regard to a particular person. Then in the first dream the person will appear undisguised, but the action will be only timidly hinted at. The second dream will behave differently. The action will be named without disguise, but the person will either be made unrecognizable or replaced by someone indifferent. This, you will admit, gives one an impression of actual cunning. Another and similar relation between the two members of a pair of dreams is found where one represents a punishment and the other the sinful wish-fulfilment. It amounts to this: 'if one accepts the punishment for it, one can go on to allow oneself the forbidden thing.'

I cannot detain you any longer over such minor discoveries or over the discussions relating to the employment of dream-interpretation in the work of analysis. I feel sure you are impatient to hear what changes have been made in our fundamental views on the nature and significance of dreams. I have already warned you that precisely on this there is little to report to you. The most disputed point in the whole theory was no doubt the assertion that all dreams are the fulfilments of wishes. The inevitable and ever recurring objection raised by the layman that there are nevertheless so many anxiety-dreams was, I think I may say, completely disposed of in my earlier lectures.[3] With the division into wishful dreams, anxiety-dreams and punishment dreams, we have kept our theory intact.

[1] [Cf. *Introductory Lectures*, XI..]

[2] [*Introductory Lectures*, XII.]

[3] [See *Introductory Lectures*, XIV.]

Punishment-dreams, too, are fulfilments of wishes, though not of wishes of the instinctual impulses but of those of the critical, censoring and punishing agency in the mind. If we have a pure punishment-dream before us, an easy mental operation will enable us to restore the wishful dream to which the punishment-dream was the correct rejoinder and which, owing to this repudiation, was replaced as the manifest dream. As you know, Ladies and Gentlemen, the study of dreams was what first helped us to understand the neuroses, and you will find it natural that our knowledge of the neuroses was later able to influence our view of dreams. As you will hear,[1] we have been obliged to postulate the existence in the mind of a special critical and prohibiting agency which we have named the 'super-ego'. Since recognizing that the censorship of dreams is also a function of this agency, we have been led to examine the part played by the super-ego in the construction of dreams more carefully.

Only two serious difficulties have arisen against the wish-fulfilment theory of dreams. A discussion of them leads far afield and has not yet, indeed, brought us to any wholly satisfying conclusion.

The first of these difficulties is presented in the fact that people who have experienced a shock, a severe psychical trauma—such as happened so often during the war and such as affords the basis for traumatic hysteria—are regularly taken back in their dreams into the traumatic situation. According to our hypotheses about the function of dreams this should not occur. What wishful impulse could be satisfied by harking back in this way to this exceedingly distressing traumatic experience? It is hard to guess.

We meet with the second of these facts almost every day in the course of our analytic work; and it does not imply such an important objection as the other does. One of the tasks of psycho-analysis, as you know, is to lift the veil of amnesia which hides the earliest years of childhood and to bring to conscious memory the manifestations of early infantile sexual life which are contained in them. Now these first sexual experiences of a child are linked to painful impressions of anxiety, prohibition, disappointment and punishment. We can understand their having been repressed; but, that being so, we cannot understand how it is that they have such free access to dream-life, that they provide the pattern for so many dream-phantasies and that dreams are filled with reproductions of these scenes from childhood and with allusions to them. It must be admitted that their unpleasurable character and the dream-work's wish-fulfilling purpose seem far from mutually compatible. But it may be that in this case we are magnifying the difficulty. After all, these same infantile experiences have attached to them all the imperishable, unfulfilled instinctual wishes which throughout life provide the energy for the construction of dreams, and to which we may no doubt credit the possibility, in their mighty uprush, of forcing to the surface, along with the rest, the material of

[1] [In Lecture XXXI below.]

distressing events. And on the other hand the manner and form in which this material is reproduced shows unmistakably the efforts of the dream-work directed to denying the unpleasure by means of distortion and to transforming disappointment into attainment.

With the traumatic neuroses things are different. In their case the dreams regularly end in the generation of anxiety. We should not, I think, be afraid to admit that here the function of the dream has failed. I will not invoke the saying that the exception proves the rule: its wisdom seems to me most questionable. But no doubt the exception does not overturn the rule. If, for the sake of studying it, we isolate one particular psychical function, such as dreaming, from the psychical machinery as a whole, we make it possible to discover the laws that are peculiar to it; but when we insert it once more into the general context we must be prepared to discover that these findings are obscured or impaired by collision with other forces. We say that a dream is the fulfilment of a wish; but if you want to take these latter objections into account, you can say nevertheless that a dream is an *attempt* at the fulfilment of a wish. No one who can properly appreciate the dynamics of the mind will suppose that you have said anything different by this. In certain circumstances a dream is only able to put its intention into effect very incompletely, or must abandon it entirely. Unconscious fixation to a trauma seems to be foremost among these obstacles to the function of dreaming. While the sleeper is obliged to dream, because the relaxation of repression at night allows the upward pressure of the traumatic fixation to become active, there is a failure in the functioning of his dream-work, which would like to transform the memory-traces of the traumatic event into the fulfilment of a wish. In these circumstances it will happen that one cannot sleep, that one gives up sleep from dread of the failure of the function of dreaming. Traumatic neuroses are here offering us an extreme case; but we must admit that childhood experiences, too, are of a traumatic nature, and we need not be surprised if comparatively trivial interferences with the function of dreams may arise under other conditions as well.[1]

[1][The topic of the last three paragraphs was first raised by Freud in Chapters II and III of *Beyond the Pleasure Principle* (1920g). Further allusions to it will be found in Lecture XXXII, p. 106 below.]

VII. Behaviorism

T he story of behaviorism as a system within 20th Century psychology starts with two movements, one in Russian physiology through the pioneering efforts of Ivan Pavlov (1849–1936) and his successors, and the other in the United States beginning with the publication of John B. Watson's (1878–1958) call for a "Psychology as the behaviorist views it" (1913). Interestingly, both movements were compatible only up to a certain point. They agreed about the relevance of observable behavior *per se*, and they rejected mentalistic explanations of human activity. However, while Watson argued that behavior comprised the proper definition of psychology, Pavlov dismissed psychology and interpreted behavior as elaborated reflexes of biological significance.

Beginning with his research on the digestive system, Pavlov established a detailed theory of conditioned reflexes mediated by the cerebral cortex. Somewhat concurrently, the British neurologist, Charles Sherrington (1857–1952), extended the vertebrate neurology advanced by Ramón y Cajal to a systematic neurophysiology, specifically at the spinal level. When refined electrophysiological methods were introduced, the general principles proposed by Sherrington were fully supported. The fate of Pavlov's theory of cortical processes did not meet with the same success (see Konorski, 1967). However, the wealth of observational data collected by Pavlov and his followers were recognized for the exactness of careful experimentation, even if the physiological theory had to be abandoned. In this selection from the 1927 edition of Pavlov's lectures, his views on psychology and its place in science were introduced to an English speaking audience. Pavlov outlines the major features and measures of the fundamental unit of his theory—the reflex.

On the American side, Watson's goal was not to reduce psychology to biologically explained reflexes, but rather to show that an objective psychology could be created by defining the subject matter of the discipline as observable behavior. That is, by limiting the study of the mind to its input and output, the role of the mind itself could be conveniently ignored. His 1913 formulation is repeated here, and it still retains a clarity of purpose that is attractive.

Two additional papers from the American behavioristic movement are included, both of which react to Watson's original formulation. Edward Chase Tolman (1886–1959) attempted to revise Watson's scheme by reintroducing some of the psychological events that he felt were abruptly and unnecessarily discarded. Impressed by contemporary Gestalt psychology, Tolman tried to incorporate cognitive mediation of behavior. Thus, while retaining the importance of behavior, Tolman's contribution attempted to restore to psychology some of the traditional mentalistic concerns. In contrast, B.F. Skinner (1904–1990) was a radical behaviorist in that he advocated a version of environmental determinism in which specific behaviors are controlled by reinforcement contingencies. In this selection, given as an address to the Midwestern Psychological Association in 1950, Skinner asserted his conviction that psychology should be a positive science, guided by data not by theory. Indeed, only by following this positive attitude can psychology succeed unfettered by theory and fulfill the call by Watson as the science of behavior, studied by the objective methods of the natural sciences.

REFERENCES

KONORSKI, J. (1967). *Integrative activity of the brain.* Chicago: University of Chicago Press, 1–3.

PAVLOV, I. (1927, 1960). Lecture I. In G.V. Anrep (transl. & ed.) *Conditioned reflexes: An investigation of the physiological activity of the cerebral cortex.* New York: Dover, 1–15.

SKINNER, B.F. (1950). Are theories of learning necessary? *Psychological Review, 57,* 193–216.

TOLMAN, E.C. (1948). Cognitive maps in rats and men. *Psychological Review, 55,* 189–208.

WATSON, J.B. (1913). Psychology as the behaviorist views it. *Psychological Review, 20,* 158–177.

☙ 23 ☙

Ivan Pavlov, Excerpt from Lecture I of *Conditioned reflexes: An investigation of the physiological activity of the cerebral cortex* (1927).*

LECTURE I

The development of the objective method in investigating the physiological activities of the cerebral hemispheres.—Concept of Reflex.—Variety of Reflexes.—Signal-reflexes, the most fundamental physiological characteristic of the hemispheres.

THE cerebral hemispheres stand out as the crowning achievement in the nervous development of the animal kingdom. These structures in the higher animals are of considerable dimensions and exceedingly complex, being made up in man of millions upon millions of cells—centres or foci of nervous activity—varying in size, shape and arrangement, and connected with each other by countless branchings from their individual processes. Such complexity of structure naturally suggests a like complexity of function, which in fact is obvious in the higher animal and in man. Consider the dog, which has been for so many countless ages the servant of man. Think how he may be trained to perform various duties, watching, hunting, etc. We know that this complex behaviour of the animal, undoubtedly involving the highest nervous activity, is mainly associated with the cerebral hemispheres. If we remove the hemispheres in the dog [Goltz[1] and others[2]], the animal becomes not only incapable of performing these duties but also incapable even of looking after itself. It becomes in fact a helpless invalid, and cannot long survive unless it be carefully tended.

*Pavlov, I. (1927, 1960). Lecture I. In G. V. Anrep (translator & editor) *Conditioned reflexes: An investigation of the physiological activity of the cerebral cortex.* New York: Dover, 1–15. Reprinted by permission of Dover Publications, Inc.

[1]F. Goltz, "Der Hund ohne Grosshirn," Pflüger's *Archiv*, V. li. p. 570, 1892.

[2]M. Rothmann, "Der Hund ohne Grosshirn," *Neurologisches Centralblatt*, V. xxviii, p. 1045, 1909.

In man also the highest nervous activity is dependent upon the structural and functional integrity of the cerebral hemispheres. As soon as these structures become damaged and their functions impaired in any way, so man also becomes an invalid. He can no longer proceed with his normal duties, but has to be kept out of the working world of his fellow men.

In astounding contrast with the unbounded activity of the cerebral hemispheres stands the meagre content of present-day physiological knowledge concerning them. Up to the year 1870, in fact, there was no physiology of the hemispheres; they seemed to be out of reach of the physiologist. In that year the common physiological methods of stimulation and extirpation were first applied to them [Fritsch and Hitzig[1]]. It was found by these workers that stimulation of certain parts of the cortex of the hemispheres (motor cortex) regularly evoked contractions in definite groups of skeletal muscles: extirpation of these parts of the cortex led to disturbances in the normal functioning of the same groups of muscles. Shortly afterwards it was demonstrated [Ferrier,[2] H. Munk[3]] that other areas of the cortex which do not evoke any motor activity in response to stimulation are also functionally differentiated. Extirpation of these areas leads to definite defects in the nervous activity associated with certain receptor organs, such as the retina of the eye, the organ of Corti, and the sensory nerve-endings in the skin. Searching investigations have been made, and still are being made, by numerous workers on this question of localization of function in the cortex. Our knowledge has been increased in precision and filled out in detail, especially as regards the motor area, and has even found useful application in medicine. These investigations, however, did not proceed fundamentally beyond the position established by Fritsch and Hitzig. The important question of the physiological mechanism of the whole higher and complex behaviour of the animal which is—as Goltz showed—dependent upon the cerebral hemispheres, was not touched in any of these investigations and formed no part of the current physiological knowledge.

When therefore we ask the questions: What do those facts which have up to the present been at the disposal of the physiologist explain with regard to the behaviour of the higher animals? What general scheme of the highest nervous activity can they give? or what general rules governing this activity can they help us to formulate?—the modern physiologist finds himself at a loss and can give no satisfactory reply. The problem of the mechanism of this complex structure which is so rich in function has got hidden away in a corner, and this unlimited field, so fertile in possibilities for research, has never been adequately explored.

[1]Fritsch und E. Hitzig, "Ueber die elektrische Erregbarkeit des Grosshirns." *Archiv für (Anatomie und) Physiologie*, p. 300, 1870.

[2]D. Ferrier, *Functions of the Brain*, London, 1876.

[3]H. Munk, *Ueber die Functionen der Grosshirnrinde*, Berlin, 1890 and 1909.

The reason for this is quite simple and clear. These nervous activities have never been regarded from the same point of view as those of other organs, or even other parts of the central nervous system. The activities of the hemispheres have been talked about as some kind of special psychical activity, whose working we feel and apprehend in ourselves, and by analogy suppose to exist in animals. This is an anomaly which has placed the physiologist in an extremely difficult position. On the one hand it would seem that the study of the activities of the cerebral hemispheres, as of the activities of any other part of the organism, should be within the compass of physiology, but on the other hand it happens to have been annexed to the special field of another science—psychology.

What attitude then should the physiologist adopt? Perhaps he should first of all study the methods of this science of psychology, and only afterwards hope to study the physiological mechanism of the hemispheres? This involves a serious difficulty. It is logical that in its analysis of the various activities of living matter physiology should base itself on the more advanced and more exact sciences—physics and chemistry. But if we attempt an approach from this science of psychology to the problem confronting us we shall be building our superstructure on a science which has no claim to exactness as compared even with physiology. In fact it is still open to discussion whether psychology is a natural science, or whether it can be regarded as a science at all.

It is not possible here for me to enter deeply into this question, but I will stay to give one fact which strikes me very forcibly, viz. that even the advocates of psychology do not look upon their science as being in any sense exact. The eminent American psychologist, William James, has in recent years referred to psychology not as a science but as a *hope* of science. Another striking illustration is provided by Wundt, the celebrated philosopher and psychologist, founder of the so-called experimental method in psychology and himself formerly a physiologist. Just before the War (1913), on the occasion of a discussion in Germany as to the advisability of making separate Chairs of Philosophy and Psychology, Wundt opposed the separation, one of his arguments being the impossibility of fixing a common examination schedule in psychology, since every professor had his own special ideas as to what psychology really was. Such testimony seems to show clearly that psychology cannot yet claim the status of an exact science.

If this be the case there is no need for the physiologist to have recourse to psychology. It would be more natural that experimental investigation of the physiological activities of the hemispheres should lay a solid foundation for a future true science of psychology; such a course is more likely to lead to the advancement of this branch of natural science.

The physiologist must thus take his own path, where a trail has already been blazed for him. Three hundred years ago Descartes evolved the idea of the reflex. Starting from the assumption that animals behaved simply as machines, he regarded every activity of the organism as a *necessary* reaction to some external stimulus, the connection between the stimulus and the response being made through a definite nervous path: and this connection, he stated, was the fundamental purpose of the nervous structures in the animal body. This was the basis on which the study of the nervous system was firmly established. In the eighteenth, nineteenth and twentieth centuries the conception of the reflex was used to the full by physiologists. Working at first only on the lower parts of the central nervous system, they came gradually to study more highly developed parts, until quite recently Magnus,[1] continuing the classical investigations of Sherrington[2] upon the spinal reflexes, has succeeded in demonstrating the reflex nature of all the elementary motor activities of the animal organism. Descartes' conception of the reflex was constantly and fruitfully applied in these studies, but its application has stopped short of the cerebral cortex.

It may be hoped that some of the more complex activities of the body, which are made up by a grouping together of the elementary locomotor activities, and which enter into the states referred to in psychological phraseology as "playfulness," "fear," "anger," and so forth, will soon be demonstrated as reflex activities of the subcortical parts of the brain. A bold attempt to apply the idea of the reflex to the activities of the hemispheres was made by the Russian physiologist, I. M. Sechenov, on the basis of the knowledge available in his day of the physiology of the central nervous system. In a pamphlet entitled "Reflexes of the Brain," published in Russian in 1863, he attempted to represent the activities of the cerebral hemispheres as reflex—that is to say, as *determined*. Thoughts he regarded as reflexes in which the effector path was inhibited, while great outbursts of passion he regarded as exaggerated reflexes with a wide irradiation of excitation. A similar attempt was made more recently by Ch. Richet,[3] who introduced the conception of the psychic reflex, in which the response following on a given stimulus is supposed to be determined by the association of this stimulus with the traces left in the hemispheres by past stimuli. And generally speaking, recent physiology shows a tendency to regard the highest activities of the hemispheres as an association of the new excitations at any given time with traces left by old ones (associative memory, training, education by experience).

All this, however, was mere conjecture. The time was ripe for a transition to the experimental analysis of the subject—an analysis which must be as objective as the analysis in any other branch of natural science. An impetus was given to this transition by the rapidly developing science of comparative physiology, which itself sprang up as a direct result of the Theory of Evolution. In dealing with the lower members of the animal kingdom physiologists were,

[1] R. Magnus, *Körperstellung*, Berlin, 1924.

[2] C. S. Sherrington, *The Integrative Action of the Nervous System*, London, 1906.

[3] Ch. Richet, *Réflexes Psychiques. Réflexes Conditionels. Automatisme Mental.* Pavlov's *Jubilee Volume*, Petrograd, 1925.

of necessity, compelled to reject anthropomorphic preconceptions, and to direct all their effort towards the elucidation of the connections between the external stimulus and the resulting response, whether locomotor or other reaction. This led to the development of Loeb's doctrine of Animal Tropisms;[1] to the introduction of a new objective terminology to describe animal reactions [Beer, Bethe and Uexküll[2]]; and finally, it led to the investigation by zoologists, using purely objective methods, of the behaviour of the lower members of the animal kingdom in response to external stimuli—as for example in the classical researches of Jennings.[3]

Under the influence of these new tendencies in biology, which appealed to the practical bent of the American mind, the American School of Psychologists—already interested in the comparative study of psychology—evinced a disposition to subject the highest nervous activities of animals to experimental analysis under various specially devised conditions. We may fairly regard the treatise by Thorndyke, *The Animal Intelligence* (1898),[4] as the starting point for systematic investigations of this kind. In these investigations the animal was kept in a box, and food was placed outside the box so that it was visible to the animal. In order to get the food the animal had to open a door, which was fastened by various suitable contrivances in the different experiments. Tables and charts were made showing how quickly and in what manner the animal solved the problems set it. The whole process was understood as being the formation of an association between the visual and tactile stimuli on the one hand and the locomotor apparatus on the other. This method, with its modifications, was subsequently applied by numerous authors to the study of questions relating to the associative ability of various animals.

At about the same time as Thorndyke was engaged on this work, I myself (being then quite ignorant of his researches) was also led to the objective study of the hemispheres, by the following circumstance: In the course of a detailed investigation into the activities of the digestive glands I had to inquire into the so-called psychic secretion of some of the glands, a task which I attempted in conjunction with a collaborator. As a result of this investigation an unqualified conviction of the futility of subjective methods of inquiry was firmly stamped upon my mind. It became clear that the only satisfactory solution of the problem lay in an experimental investigation by strictly objective methods. For this purpose I started to record all the external stimuli falling on the animal at the time its reflex reaction was manifested (in this particular case the secretion of saliva), at the same time recording all changes in the reaction of the animal.

[1]J. Loeb, *Studies in General Physiology*, Chicago, 1905.

[2]Beer, Bethe und Uexküll, "Vorschläge zu einer objectivirenden Nomenklatur in der Physiologie des Nervensystems," *Biologisches Centralblatt*, V. xix, p. 517, 1899.

[3]H. S. Jennings, *The Behavior of Lower Organisms*, New York, 1906.

[4]E. L. Thorndyke, *The Animal Intelligence, An Experimental Study of the Associative Processes in Animals.* New York, 1898.

This was the beginning of these investigations, which have gone on now for twenty-five years—years in which numerous fellow-workers on whom I now look back with tender affection have united with mine in this work their hearts and hands. We have of course passed through many stages, and only gradually has the subject been opened up and the difficulties overcome. At first only a few scattered facts were available, but to-day sufficient material has been gathered together to warrant an attempt to present it in a more or less systematized form. At the present time I am in a position to present you with a physiological interpretation of the activities of the cerebral hemispheres which is, at any rate, more in keeping with the structural and functional complexity of this organ than is the collection of fragmentary, though very important, facts which up to the present have represented all the knowledge of this subject. Work on the lines of purely objective investigation into the highest nervous activities has been conducted in the main in the laboratories under my control, and over a hundred collaborators have taken part. Work on somewhat similar lines to ours has been done by the American psychologists. Up to the present, however, there has been one essential point of difference between the American School and ourselves. Being psychologists, their mode of experimentation, in spite of the fact that they are studying these activities on their external aspect, is mostly psychological—at any rate so far as the arrangement of problems and their analysis and the formulation of results are concerned. Therefore—with the exception of a small group of "behaviourists"—their work cannot be regarded as purely physiological in character. We, having started from physiology, continue to adhere strictly to the physiological point of view, investigating and systematizing the whole subject by physiological methods alone. As regards other physiological laboratories a few only have directed their attention to this subject, and that recently; nor have their investigations extended beyond the limits of a preliminary inquiry.

I shall now turn to the description of our material, first giving as a preliminary an account of the general conception of the reflex, of specific physiological reflexes, and of the so-called "instincts." Our starting point has been Descartes' idea of the nervous reflex. This is a genuine scientific conception, since it implies necessity. It may be summed up as follows: An external or internal stimulus falls on some one or other nervous receptor and gives rise to a nervous impulse; this nervous impulse is transmitted along nerve fibres to the central nervous system, and here, on account of existing nervous connections, it gives rise to a fresh impulse which passes along outgoing nerve fibres to the active organ, where it excites a special activity of the cellular structures. Thus a stimulus appears to be connected of necessity with a definite response, as cause with effect. It seems obvious that the whole activity of the organism should conform to definite laws. If the animal were not in exact correspondence with its environment it would, sooner or later, assume that one reflex initiates the next following—or, in other words, we must regard it as a chain-reflex. But this linking up of activities is not peculiar to instincts alone. We are familiar with numerous reflexes which most certainly fuse into chains. Thus, for example, if we stimulate an afferent nerve, *e.g.* the sciatic nerve, a reflex rise of blood pressure occurs; the high pressure in the left ventricle of the heart, and first part of the aorta, serves as the effective stimulus to a second reflex, this time a depressor reflex which has a moderating influence on the first. Again, we may take one of the chain reflexes recently established by Magnus. A cat, even when deprived of its cerebral hemispheres, will in most cases land on its feet when thrown from a height. How is this managed? When the position of the otolithic organ in space is altered a definite reflex is evoked which brings about a contraction of the muscles in the neck, restoring the animal's head to the normal position. This is the first reflex. With the righting of the head a fresh reflex is evoked, and certain muscles of the trunk and limbs are brought into play, restoring the animal to the standing posture. This is the second reflex.

Some, again, object to the identification of instincts with reflexes on this ground: instincts, they say, frequently depend upon the internal state of an organism. For instance, a bird only builds its nest in the mating season. Or, to take a simpler case, when an animal is satiated with eating, then food has no longer any attraction and the animal leaves off eating. Again, the same is true of the sexual impulse. This depends on the age of the organism, and on the state of the reproductive glands; and a considerable influence is exerted by hormones (the products of the glands of internal secretion). But this dependence cannot be claimed as a peculiar property of "instincts." The intensity of any reflex, indeed its very presence, is dependent on the irritability of the centres, which in turn depends constantly on the physical and chemical properties of the blood (automatic stimulation of centres) and on the interaction of reflexes.

Last of all, it is sometimes held that whereas reflexes determine only the activities of single organs and tissues, instincts involve the activity of the organism as a whole. We now know, however, from the recent investigations of Magnus and de Kleijn, that standing, walking and the maintenance of postural balance in general, are all nothing but reflexes.

It follows from all this that instincts and reflexes are alike the inevitable responses of the organism to internal and external stimuli, and therefore we have no need to call them by two different terms. Reflex has the better claim of the two, in that it has been used from the very beginning with a strictly scientific connotation.

The aggregate of reflexes constitutes the foundation of the nervous activities both of men and animals. It is therefore of great importance to study in detail all the fundamental reflexes of the organism. Up to the present, unfortunately, this is far from being accomplished, especially, as I have mentioned before, in the case of those reflexes which have been known vaguely as "instincts." Our knowledge of these latter is very limited and fragmentary. Their classification under such headings as "alimentary," "defensive," "sexual," "parental" and "social" instincts, is thoroughly inadequate. Under each of these heads is assembled often a large number of individual reflexes. Some of these are quite unidentified; some are confused with others; and many are still only partially appreciated. I can demonstrate from my own experience to what extent the subject remains inchoate and full of gaps. In the course of the researches which I shall presently explain, we were completely at a loss on one occasion to find any cause for the peculiar behaviour of an animal. It was evidently a very tractable dog, which soon became very friendly with us. We started off with a very simple experiment. The dog was placed in a stand with loose loops round its legs, but so as to be quite comfortable and free to move a pace or two. Nothing more was done except to present the animal repeatedly with food at intervals of some minutes. It stood quietly enough at first, and ate quite readily, but as time went on it became excited and struggled to get out of the stand, scratching at the floor, gnawing the supports, and so on. This ceaseless muscular exertion was accompanied by breathlessness and continuous salivation, which persisted at every experiment during several weeks, the animal getting worse and worse until it was no longer fitted for our researches. For a long time we remained puzzled over the unusual behaviour of this animal. We tried out experimentally numerous possible interpretations, but though we had had long experience with a great number of dogs in our laboratories we could not work out a satisfactory solution of this strange behaviour, until it occurred to us at last that it might be the expression of a special *freedom reflex*, and that the dog simply could not remain quiet when it was constrained in the stand. This reflex was overcome by setting off another against it, the reflex for food. We began to give the dog the whole of its food in the stand. At first the animal ate but little, and lost considerably in weight, but gradually it got to eat more, until at last the whole ration was consumed. At the same time the animal grew quieter during the course of the experiments: the freedom reflex was being inhibited. It is clear that the freedom reflex is one of the most important reflexes, or, if we use a more general term, reactions, of living beings. This reflex has even yet to find its final recognition. In James's writings it is not even enumerated among the special human "instincts." But it is clear that if the animal were not provided with a reflex of protest against boundaries set to its freedom, the smallest obstacle in its path would interfere with the proper fulfilment of its natural functions. Some animals as we all know have this freedom reflex to such a degree that when placed in captivity they refuse all food, sicken and die.

As another example of a reflex which is very much neglected we may refer to what may be called the *investigatory reflex*. I call it the "What-is-it?" reflex. It is this reflex which brings about the immediate response in man and animals to the slightest changes in the world around them, so that they immediately orientate their appropriate receptor organ in accordance with the perceptible quality in the agent bringing about the change, making full investigation of it. The biological significance of this reflex is obvious. If the animal were not provided with such a reflex its life would hang at every moment by a thread. In man this reflex has been greatly developed with far-reaching results, being represented in its highest form by inquisitiveness—the parent of that scientific method through which we may hope one day to come to a true orientation in knowledge of the world around us.

Still less has been done towards the elucidation of the class of negative or inhibitory reflexes (instincts) which are often evoked by any strong stimulus or even by weak stimuli, if unusual. Animal hypnotism, so-called, belongs to this category.

As the fundamental nervous reactions both of men and of animals are inborn in the form of definite reflexes, I must again emphasize how important it is to compile a complete list comprising all these reflexes with their adequate classification. For, as will be shown later on, all the remaining nervous functions of the animal organism are based upon these reflexes. Now, although the possession of such reflexes as those just described constitutes the fundamental condition for the natural survival of the animal, they are not in themselves sufficient to ensure a prolonged, stable and normal existence. This can be shown in dogs in which the cerebral hemispheres have been removed. Leaving out of account the internal reflexes, such a dog still retains the fundamental external reflexes. It is attracted by food; it is repelled by nocuous stimuli; it exhibits the investigatory reflex, raising its head and pricking up its ears to sound. In addition it exhibits the freedom reflex, offering a powerful resistance to any restraint. Nevertheless it is wholly incapable of looking after itself, and if left to itself will very soon die. Evidently something important is missing in its present nervous make-up. What nervous activities can it have lost? It is easily seen that, in this dog, the number of stimuli evoking reflex reaction is considerably diminished; those remaining are of an elemental, generalized nature, and act at a very short range. Consequently the dynamic equilibrium between the inner forces of the animal system and the external forces in its environment has become elemental as compared with the exquisite adaptability of the normal animal, and the simpler balance is obviously inadequate to life.

Let us return now to the simplest reflex from which our investigations started. If food or some rejectable substance finds its way into the mouth, a secretion of saliva is produced. The purpose of this secretion is in the case of food to alter it chemically, in the case of a rejectable substance to dilute and wash it out of the mouth. This is an example of a reflex due to the physical and chemical properties of a substance when it comes into contact with the mucous membrane of the mouth and tongue. But, in addition to this, a similar reflex secretion is evoked when these substances are placed at a distance from the dog and the receptor organs affected are only those of smell and sight. Even the vessel from which the food has been given is sufficient to evoke an alimentary reflex complete in all its details; and, further, the secretion may be provoked even by the sight of the person who brought the vessel, or by the sound of his footsteps. All these innumerable stimuli falling upon the several finely discriminating distance receptors lose their power for ever as soon as the hemispheres are taken from the animal, and those only which have a direct effect on mouth and tongue still retain their power. The great advantage to the organism of a capacity to react to the former stimuli is evident, for it is in virtue of their action that food finding its way into the mouth immediately encounters plenty of moistening saliva, and rejectable substances, often nocuous to the mucous membrane, find a layer of protective saliva already in the mouth which rapidly dilutes and washes them out. Even greater is their importance when they evoke the motor component of the complex reflex of nutrition, *i.e.* when they act as stimuli to the reflex of seeking food.

Here is another example—the reflex of self-defence. The strong carnivorous animal preys on weaker animals, and these if they waited to defend themselves until the teeth of the foe were in their flesh would speedily be exterminated. The case takes on a different aspect when the defense reflex is called into play by the sights and sounds of the enemy's approach. Then the prey has a chance to save itself by hiding or by flight.

How can we describe, in general, this difference in the dynamic balance of life between the normal and the decorticated animal? What is the general mechanism and law of this distinction? It is pretty evident that under natural conditions the normal animal must respond not only to stimuli which themselves bring immediate benefit or harm, but also to other physical or chemical agencies—waves of sound, light, and the like—which in themselves only *signal* the approach of these stimuli; though it is not the sight and sound of the beast of prey which is in itself harmful to the smaller animal, but its teeth and claws.

Now although the *signalling stimuli* do play a part in those comparatively simple reflexes we have given as examples, yet this is not the most important point. The essential feature of the highest activity of the central nervous system, with which we are concerned and which in the higher animals most probably belongs entirely to the hemispheres, consists not in the fact that innumerable signalling stimuli do initiate reflex reactions in the animal, but in the fact that under different conditions these same stimuli may initiate quite different reflex reactions; and conversely the same reaction may be initiated by different stimuli.

In the above-mentioned example of the salivary reflex, the signal at one time is one particular vessel, at another time another; under certain conditions one man, under different conditions another—strictly depending upon which vessel had been used in feeding and which man had brought the vessel and given food to the dog. This evidently makes the machine-like responsive activities of the organism still more precise, and adds to it qualities of yet higher perfection. So infinitely complex, so continuously in flux, are the conditions in the world around, that that complex animal system which is itself in living flux, and that system only, has a chance to establish dynamic equilibrium with the environment. Thus we see that the fundamental and the most general function of the hemispheres is that of reacting to signals presented by innumerable stimuli of interchangeable signification.

≈ 24 ≈

John Broadus Watson, "Psychology as the behaviorist views it" (1913).*

Psychology as the behaviorist views it is a purely objective experimental branch of natural science. Its theoretical goal is the prediction and control of behavior. Introspection forms no essential part of its methods, nor is the scientific value of its data dependent upon the readiness with which they lend themselves to interpretation in terms of consciousness. The behaviorist, in his efforts to get a unitary scheme of animal response, recognizes no dividing line between man and brute. The behavior of man, with all of its refinement and complexity, forms only a part of the behaviorist's total scheme of investigation.

It has been maintained by its followers generally that psychology is a study of the science of the phenomena of consciousness. It has taken as its problem, on the one hand, the analysis of complex mental states (or processes) into simple elementary constituents, and on the other the construction of complex states when the elementary constituents are given. The world of physical objects (stimuli, including here anything which may excite activity in a receptor), which forms the total phenomena of the natural scientist, is looked upon merely as means to an end. That end is the production of mental states that may be 'inspected' or 'observed.' The psychological object of observation in the case of an emotion, for example, is the mental state itself. The problem in emotion is the determination of the number and kind of elementary constituents present, their loci, intensity, order of appearance, etc. It is agreed that introspection is the method *par excellence* by means of which mental states may be manipulated for purposes of psychology. On this assumption, behavior data (including under this term everything which goes

*Watson, J. B. (1913). Psychology as the behaviorist views it. *Psychological Review*, 20, 158–177. Reprinted by permission of the American Psychological Association.

under the name of comparative psychology) have no value *per se*. They possess significance only in so far as they may throw light upon conscious states.[1] Such data must have at least an analogical or indirect reference to belong to the realm of psychology.

Indeed, at times, one finds psychologists who are sceptical of even this analogical reference. Such scepticism is often shown by the question which is put to the student of behavior, "what is the bearing of animal work upon human psychology?" I used to have to study over this question. Indeed it always embarrassed me somewhat. I was interested in my own work and felt that it was important, and yet I could not trace any close connection between it and psychology as my questioner understood psychology. I hope that such a confession will clear the atmosphere to such an extent that we will no longer have to work under false pretences. We must frankly admit that the facts so important to us which we have been able to glean from extended work upon the senses of animals by the behavior method have contributed only in a fragmentary way to the general theory of human sense organ processes, nor have they suggested new points of experimental attack. The enormous number of experiments which we have carried out upon learning have likewise contributed little to human psychology. It seems reasonably clear that some kind of compromise must be effected: either psychology must change its viewpoint so as to take in facts of behavior, whether or not they have bearings upon the problems of 'consciousness'; or else behavior must stand alone as a wholly separate and independent science. Should human psychologists fail to look with favor upon our overtures and refuse to modify their position, the behaviorists will be driven to using human beings as subjects and to employ methods of investigation which are exactly comparable to those now employed in the animal work.

Any other hypothesis than that which admits the independent value of behavior material, regardless of any bearing such material may have upon consciousness, will inevitably force us to the absurd position of attempting to *construct* the conscious content of the animal whose behavior we have been studying. On this view, after having determined our animal's ability to learn, the simplicity or complexity of its methods of learning, the effect of past habit upon present response, the range of stimuli to which it ordinarily responds, the widened range to which it can respond under experimental conditions,— in more general terms, its various problems and its various ways of solving them,—we should still feel that the task is unfinished and that the results are worthless, until we can interpret them by analogy in the light of consciousness. Although we have solved our problem we feel uneasy and unrestful because of our definition of psychology: we feel forced to say something about the possible mental processes of our animal. We say that, having no eyes, its stream of consciousness cannot contain brightness and color sensations as we

---

[1]That is, either directly upon the conscious state of the observer or indirectly upon the conscious state of the experimenter.

know them,—having no taste buds this stream can contain no sensations of sweet, sour, salt and bitter. But on the other hand, since it does respond to thermal, tactual and organic stimuli, its conscious content must be made up largely of these sensations; and we usually add, to protect ourselves against the reproach of being anthropomorphic, "if it has any consciousness." Surely this doctrine which calls for an analogical interpretation of all behavior data may be shown to be false: the position that the standing of an observation upon behavior is determined by its fruitfulness in yielding results which are interpretable only in the narrow realm of (really human) consciousness.

This emphasis upon analogy in psychology has led the behaviorist somewhat afield. Not being willing to throw off the yoke of consciousness he feels impelled to make a place in the scheme of behavior where the rise of consciousness can be determined. This point has been a shifting one. A few years ago certain animals were supposed to possess 'associative memory,' while certain others were supposed to lack it. One meets this search for the origin of consciousness under a good many disguises. Some of our texts state that consciousness arises at the moment when reflex and instinctive activities fail properly to conserve the organism. A perfectly adjusted organism would be lacking in consciousness. On the other hand whenever we find the presence of diffuse activity which results in habit formation, we are justified in assuming consciousness. I must confess that these arguments had weight with me when I began the study of behavior. I fear that a good many of us are still viewing behavior problems with something like this in mind. More than one student in behavior has attempted to frame criteria of the psychic—to devise a set of objective, structural and functional criteria which, when applied in the particular instance, will enable us to decide whether such and such responses are positively conscious, merely indicative of consciousness, or whether they are purely 'physiological.' Such problems as these can no longer satisfy behavior men. It would be better to give up the province altogether and admit frankly that the study of the behavior of animals has no justification, than to admit that our search is of such a 'will o' the wisp' character. One can assume either the presence or the absence of consciousness anywhere in the phylogenetic scale without affecting the problems of behavior by one jot or one tittle; and without influencing in any way the mode of experimental attack upon them. On the other hand, I cannot for one moment assume that the paramecium responds to light; that the rat learns a problem more quickly by working at the task five times a day than once a day, or that the human child exhibits plateaux in his learning curves. These are questions which vitally concern behavior and which must be decided by direct observation under experimental conditions.

This attempt to reason by analogy from human conscious processes to the conscious processes in animals, and *vice versa*: to make consciousness, as the human being knows it, the center of reference of all behavior, forces us into a situation similar to that which existed in biology in Darwin's time. The whole Darwinian movement was judged by the bearing it had upon the origin and development of the human race. Expeditions were undertaken to collect material which would establish the position that the rise of the human race was a perfectly natural phenomenon and not an act of special creation. Variations were carefully sought along with the evidence for the heaping up effect and the weeding out effect of selection; for in these and the other Darwinian mechanisms were to be found factors sufficiently complex to account for the origin and race differentiation of man. The wealth of material collected at this time was considered valuable largely in so far as it tended to develop the concept of evolution in man. It is strange that this situation should have remained the dominant one in biology for so many years. The moment zoölogy undertook the experimental study of evolution and descent, the situation immediately changed. Man ceased to be the center of reference. I doubt if any experimental biologist today, unless actually engaged in the problem of race differentiation in man, tries to interpret his findings in terms of human evolution, or ever refers to it in his thinking. He gathers his data from the study of many species of plants and animals and tries to work out the laws of inheritance in the particular type upon which he is conducting experiments. Naturally, he follows the progress of the work upon race differentiation in man and in the descent of man, but he looks upon these as special topics, equal in importance with his own yet ones in which his interests will never be vitally engaged. It is not fair to say that all of his work is directed toward human evolution or that it must be interpreted in terms of human evolution. He does not have to dismiss certain of his facts on the inheritance of coat color in mice because, forsooth, they have little bearing upon the differentiation of the *genus homo* into separate races, or upon the descent of the *genus homo* from some more primitive stock.

In psychology we are still in that stage of development where we feel that we must select our material. We have a general place of discard for processes, which we anathematize so far as their value for psychology is concerned by saying, "this is a reflex"; "that is a purely physiological fact which has nothing to do with psychology." We are not interested (as psychologists) in getting all of the processes of adjustment which the animal as a whole employs, and in finding how these various responses are associated, and how they fall apart, thus working out a systematic scheme for the prediction and control of response in general. Unless our observed facts are indicative of consciousness, we have no use for them, and unless our apparatus and method are designed to throw such facts into relief, they are thought of in just as disparaging a way. I shall always remember the remark one distinguished psychologist made as he looked over the color apparatus designed for testing the responses of animals to monochromatic light in the attic at Johns Hopkins. It was this: "And they call this psychology!"

I do not wish unduly to criticize psychology. It has failed signally, I believe, during the fifty-odd years of its existence as an experimental discipline to make its place in the world as an undisputed natural science. Psychology, as it is generally thought of, has something *esoteric* in its methods. If you fail to reproduce my findings, it is not due to some fault in your apparatus or in the control of your stimulus, but it is due to the fact that your introspection is untrained.[1] The attack is made upon the observer and not upon the experimental setting. In physics and in chemistry the attack is made upon the experimental conditions. The apparatus was not sensitive enough, impure chemicals were used, etc. In these sciences a better technique will give reproducible results. Psychology is otherwise. If you can't observe 3–9 states of clearness in attention, your introspection is poor. If, on the other hand, a feeling seems reasonably clear to you, your introspection is again faulty. You are seeing too much. Feelings are never clear.

The time seems to have come when psychology must discard all reference to consciousness; when it need no longer delude itself into thinking that it is making mental states the object of observation. We have become so enmeshed in speculative questions concerning the elements of mind, the nature of conscious content (for example, imageless thought, attitudes, and Bewusseinslage, etc.) that I, as an experimental student, feel that something is wrong with our premises and the types of problems which develop from them. There is no longer any guarantee that we all mean the same thing when we use the terms now current in psychology. Take the case of sensation. A sensation is defined in terms of its attributes. One psychologist will state with readiness that the attributes of a visual sensation are *quality, extension, duration,* and *intensity*. Another will add *clearness*. Still another that of *order*. I doubt if any one psychologist can draw up a set of statements describing what he means by sensation which will be agreed to by three other psychologists of different training. Turn for a moment to the question of the number of isolable sensations. Is there an extremely large number of color sensations—or only four, red, green, yellow and blue? Again, yellow, while psychologically simple, can be obtained by superimposing red and green spectral rays upon the same diffusing surface! If, on the other hand, we say that every *just noticeable difference* in the spectrum is a simple sensation, and that every just noticeable increase in the white value of a given color gives simple sensations, we are forced to admit that the number is so large and the conditions for obtaining them so complex that the concept of sensation is unusable, either for the purpose of analysis or that of synthesis. Titchener, who has fought the most valiant fight in this country for a psychology based upon introspection, feels that these differences of opinion as to the number of sensations and their attributes; as to whether there are relations (in the sense of elements) and on

---

[1]In this connection I call attention to the controversy now on between the adherents and the opposers of imageless thought. The 'types of reactors' (sensory and motor) were also matters of bitter dispute. The complication experiment was the source of another war of words concerning the accuracy of the opponents' introspection.

the many others which seem to be fundamental in every attempt at analysis, are perfectly natural in the present undeveloped state of psychology. While it is admitted that every growing science is full of unanswered questions, surely only those who are wedded to the system as we now have it, who have fought and suffered for it, can confidently believe that there will ever be any greater uniformity than there is now in the answers we have to such questions. I firmly believe that two hundred years from now, unless the introspective method is discarded, psychology will still be divided on the question as to whether auditory sensations have the quality of 'extension,' whether intensity is an attribute which can be applied to color, whether there is a difference in 'texture' between image and sensation and upon many hundreds of others of like character.

The condition in regard to other mental processes is just as chaotic. Can image type be experimentally tested and verified? Are recondite thought processes dependent mechanically upon imagery at all? Are psychologists agreed upon what feeling is? One states that feelings are attitudes. Another finds them to be groups of organic sensations possessing a certain solidarity. Still another and larger group finds them to be new elements correlative with and ranking equally with sensations.

My psychological quarrel is not with the systematic and structural psychologist alone. The last fifteen years have seen the growth of what is called *functional psychology*. This type of psychology decries the use of elements in the static sense of the structuralists. It throws emphasis upon the biological significance of conscious processes instead of upon the analysis of conscious states into introspectively isolable elements. I have done my best to understand the difference between functional psychology and structural psychology. Instead of clarity, confusion grows upon me. The terms sensation, perception, affection, emotion, volition are used as much by the functionalist as by the structuralist. The addition of the word 'process' ('mental act as a whole,' and like terms are frequently met) after each serves in some way to remove the corpse of 'content' and to leave 'function' in its stead. Surely if these concepts are elusive when looked at from a content standpoint, they are still more deceptive when viewed from the angle of function, and especially so when function is obtained by the introspection method. It is rather interesting that no functional psychologist has carefully distinguished between 'perception' (and this is true of the other psychological terms as well) as employed by the systematist, and 'perceptual process' as used in functional psychology. It seems illogical and hardly fair to criticize the psychology which the systematist gives us, and then to utilize his terms without carefully showing the changes in meaning which are to be attached to them. I was greatly surprised some time ago when I opened Pillsbury's book and saw psychology defined as the 'science of behavior.' A still more recent text states that psychology is the 'science of mental behavior.' When I saw these promising statements I thought, now surely we will have texts based upon different lines. After a few pages the science of behavior is dropped and one finds the conventional treatment of sensation, perception, imagery, etc., along with certain shifts in emphasis and additional facts which serve to give the author's personal imprint.

One of the difficulties in the way of a consistent functional psychology is the parallelistic hypothesis. If the functionalist attempts to express his formulations in terms which make mental states really appear to function, to play some active rôle in the world of adjustment, he almost inevitably lapses into terms which are connotative of interaction. When taxed with this he replies that it is more convenient to do so and that he does it to avoid the circumlocution and clumsiness which are inherent in any thoroughgoing parallelism.[1] As a matter of fact I believe the functionalist actually thinks in terms of interaction and resorts to parallelism only when forced to give expression to his views. I feel that *behaviorism* is the only consistent and logical functionalism. In it one avoids both the Scylla of parallelism and the Charybdis of interaction. Those time-honored relics of philosophical speculation need trouble the student of behavior as little as they trouble the student of physics. The consideration of the mind-body problem affects neither the type of problem selected nor the formulation of the solution of that problem. I can state my position here no better than by saying that I should like to bring my students up in the same ignorance of such hypotheses as one finds among the students of other branches of science.

This leads me to the point where I should like to make the argument constructive. I believe we can write a psychology, define it as Pillsbury, and never go back upon our definition: never use the terms consciousness, mental states, mind, content, introspectively verifiable, imagery, and the like. I believe that we can do it in a few years without running into the absurd terminology of Beer, Bethe, Von Uexküll, Nuel, and that of the so-called objective schools generally. It can be done in terms of stimulus and response, in terms of habit formation, habit integrations and the like. Furthermore, I believe that it is really worth while to make this attempt now.

The psychology which I should attempt to build up would take as a starting point, first, the observable fact that organisms, man and animal alike, do adjust themselves to their environment by means of hereditary and habit equipments. These adjustments may be very adequate or they may be so inadequate that the organism barely maintains its existence; secondly, that certain stimuli lead the organisms to make the responses. In a system of psychology completely worked out, given the response the stimuli can be predicted; given the stimuli the response can be predicted. Such a set of statements is crass and raw in the extreme, as all such generalizations must be. Yet they are hardly more raw and less realizable than the ones which appear in the psychology texts of the day. I possibly might illustrate my point better by choosing an

---

[1]My colleague, Professor H. C. Warren, by whose advice this article was offered to the REVIEW, believes that the parallelist can avoid the interaction terminology completely by exercising a little care.

everyday problem which anyone is likely to meet in the course of his work. Some time ago I was called upon to make a study of certain species of birds. Until I went to Tortugas I had never seen these birds alive. When I reached there I found the animals doing certain things: some of the acts seemed to work peculiarly well in such an environment, while others seemed to be unsuited to their type of life. I first studied the responses of the group as a whole and later those of individuals. In order to understand more thoroughly the relation between what was habit and what was hereditary in these responses, I took the young birds and reared them. In this way I was able to study the order of appearance of hereditary adjustments and their complexity, and later the beginnings of habit formation. My efforts in determining the stimuli which called forth such adjustments were crude indeed. Consequently my attempts to control behavior and to produce responses at will did not meet with much success. Their food and water, sex and other social relations, light and temperature conditions were all beyond control in a field study. I did find it possible to control their reactions in a measure by using the nest and egg (or young) as stimuli. It is not necessary in this paper to develop further how such a study should be carried out and how work of this kind must be supplemented by carefully controlled laboratory experiments. Had I been called upon to examine the natives of some of the Australian tribes, I should have gone about my task in the same way. I should have found the problem more difficult: the types of responses called forth by physical stimuli would have been more varied, and the number of effective stimuli larger. I should have had to determine the social setting of their lives in a far more careful way. These savages would be more influenced by the responses of each other than was the case with the birds. Furthermore, habits would have been more complex and the influences of past habits upon the present responses would have appeared more clearly. Finally, if I had been called upon to work out the psychology of the educated European, my problem would have required several lifetimes. But in the one I have at my disposal I should have followed the same general line of attack. In the main, my desire in all such work is to gain an accurate knowledge of adjustments and the stimuli calling them forth. My final reason for this is to learn general and particular methods by which I may control behavior. My goal is not "the description and explanation of states of consciousness as such," nor that of obtaining such proficiency in mental gymnastics that I can immediately lay hold of a state of consciousness and say, "this, as a whole, consists of gray sensation number 350, of such and such extent, occurring in conjunction with the sensation of cold of a certain intensity; one of pressure of a certain intensity and extent," and so on *ad infinitum.* If psychology would follow the plan I suggest, the educator, the physician, the jurist and the business man could utilize our data in a practical way, as soon as we are able, experimentally, to obtain them. Those who have occasion to apply psychological principles practically would find no need to complain as they do at the present time. Ask any physician or jurist today whether scientific psychology plays a practical part in his daily routine and you will hear him deny that the psychology of the laboratories finds a place in his scheme of work. I think the criticism is extremely just. One of the earliest conditions which made me dissatisfied with psychology was the feeling that there was no realm of application for the principles which were being worked out in content terms.

What gives me hope that the behaviorist's position is a defensible one is the fact that those branches of psychology which have already partially withdrawn from the parent, experimental psychology, and which are consequently less dependent upon introspection are today in a most flourishing condition. Experimental pedagogy, the psychology of drugs, the psychology of advertising, legal psychology, the psychology of tests, and psychopathology are all vigorous growths. These are sometimes wrongly called "practical" or "applied" psychology. Surely there was never a worse misnomer. In the future there may grow up vocational bureaus which really apply psychology. At present these fields are truly scientific and are in search of broad generalizations which will lead to the control of human behavior. For example, we find out by experimentation whether a series of stanzas may be acquired more readily if the whole is learned at once, or whether it is more advantageous to learn each stanza separately and then pass to the succeeding. We do not attempt to apply our findings. The application of this principle is purely voluntary on the part of the teacher. In the psychology of drugs we may show the effect upon behavior of certain doses of caffeine. We may reach the conclusion that caffeine has a good effect upon the speed and accuracy of work. But these are general principles. We leave it to the individual as to whether the results of our tests shall be applied or not. Again, in legal testimony, we test the effects of recency upon the reliability of a witness's report. We test the accuracy of the report with respect to moving objects, stationary objects, color, etc. It depends upon the judicial machinery of the country to decide whether these facts are ever to be applied. For a 'pure' psychologist to say that he is not interested in the questions raised in these divisions of the science because they relate indirectly to the application of psychology shows, in the first place, that he fails to understand the scientific aim in such problems, and secondly, that he is not interested in a psychology which concerns itself with human life. The only fault I have to find with these disciplines is that much of their material is stated in terms of introspection, whereas a statement in terms of objective results would be far more valuable. There is no reason why appeal should ever be made to consciousness in any of them. Or why introspective data should ever be sought during the experimentation, or published in the results. In experimental pedagogy especially one can see the desirability of keeping all of the results on a purely objective plane. If this is done, work there on the human being will be comparable directly with the work upon animals. For example, at Hopkins, Mr. Ulrich has obtained certain results upon the distribution of effort in learning—using rats as subjects. He is prepared to give comparative results upon the effect of having an animal work at the problem once per day, three times per day, and five times per day. Whether it is advisable to have the animal learn only one problem at a time or to learn three abreast. We need to have similar experiments made upon man, but we care as little about his 'conscious processes' during the conduct of the experiment as we care about such processes in the rats:

I am more interested at the present moment in trying to show the necessity for maintaining uniformity in experimental procedure and in the method of stating results in both human and animal work, than in developing any ideas I may have upon the changes which are certain to come in the scope of human psychology. Let us consider for a moment the subject of the range of stimuli to which animals respond. I shall speak first of the work upon vision in animals. We put our animal in a situation where he will respond (or learn to respond) to one of two monochromatic lights. We feed him at the one (positive) and punish him at the other (negative). In a short time the animal learns to go to the light at which he is fed. At this point questions arise which I may phrase in two ways: I may choose the psychological way and say "does the animal see these two lights as I do, *i. e.*, as two distinct colors, or does he see them as two grays differing in brightness, as does the totally color blind?" Phrased by the behaviorist, it would read as follows: "Is my animal responding upon the basis of the difference in intensity between the two stimuli, or upon the difference in wave-lengths?" He nowhere thinks of the animal's response in terms of his own experiences of colors and grays. He wishes to establish the fact whether wave-length is a factor in that animal's adjustment.[1] If so, what wave-lengths are effective and what differences in wave-length must be maintained in the different regions to afford bases for differential responses? If wave-length is not a factor in adjustment he wishes to know what difference in intensity will serve as a basis for response, and whether that same difference will suffice throughout the spectrum. Furthermore, he wishes to test whether the animal can respond to wave-lengths which do not affect the human eye. He is as much interested in comparing the rat's spectrum with that of the chick as in comparing it with man's. The point of view when the various sets of comparisons are made does not change in the slightest.

However we phrase the question to ourselves, we take our animal after the association has been formed and then introduce certain control experiments which enable us to return answers to the questions just raised. But there is just as keen a desire on our part to test man under the same conditions, and to state the results in both cases in common terms.

The man and the animal should be placed as nearly as possible under the same experimental conditions. Instead of feeding or punishing the human subject, we should ask him to respond by setting a second apparatus

---

[1]He would have exactly the same attitude as if he were conducting an experiment to show whether an ant would crawl over a pencil laid across the trail or go round it.

until standard and control offered no basis for a differential response. Do I lay myself open to the charge here that I am using introspection? My reply is not at all; that while I might very well feed my human subject for a right choice and punish him for a wrong one and thus produce the response if the subject could give it, there is no need of going to extremes even on the platform I suggest. But be it understood that I am merely using this second method as an abridged behavior method.[1] We can go just as far and reach just as dependable results by the longer method as by the abridged. In many cases the direct and typically human method cannot be safely used. Suppose, for example, that I doubt the accuracy of the setting of the control instrument, in the above experiment, as I am very likely to do if I suspect a defect in vision? It is hopeless for me to get his introspective report. He will say: "There is no difference in sensation, both are reds, identical in quality." But suppose I confront him with the standard and the control and so arrange conditions that he is punished if he responds to the 'control' but not with the standard. I interchange the positions of the standard and the control at will and force him to attempt to differentiate the one from the other. If he can learn to make the adjustment even after a large number of trials it is evident that the two stimuli do afford the basis for a differential response. Such a method may sound nonsensical, but I firmly believe we will have to resort increasingly to just such method where we have reason to distrust the language method.

There is hardly a problem in human vision which is not also a problem in animal vision: I mention the limits of the spectrum, threshold values, absolute and relative, flicker, Talbot's law, Weber's law, field of vision, the Purkinje phenomenon, etc. Every one is capable of being worked out by behavior methods. Many of them are being worked out at the present time.

I feel that all the work upon the senses can be consistently carried forward along the lines I have suggested here for vision. Our results will, in the end, give an excellent picture of what each organ stands for in the way of function. The anatomist and the physiologist may take our data and show, on the one hand, the structures which are responsible for these responses, and, on the other, the physico-chemical relations which are necessarily involved (physiological chemistry of nerve and muscle) in these and other reactions.

The situation in regard to the study of memory is hardly different. Nearly all of the memory methods in actual use in the laboratory today yield

---

[1]I should prefer to look upon this abbreviated method, where the human subject is told in words, for example, to equate two stimuli; or to state in words whether a given stimulus is present or absent, etc., as the *language method* in behavior. It in no way changes the status of experimentation. The method becomes possible merely by virtue of the fact that in the particular case the experimenter and his animal have systems of abbreviations or shorthand behavior signs (language), any one of which may stand for a habit belonging to the repertoire both of the experimenter and his subject. To make the data obtained by the language method virtually the whole of behavior—or to attempt to mould all of the data obtained by other methods in terms of the one which has by all odds the most limited range—is putting the cart before the horse with a vengeance.

the type of results I am arguing for. A certain series of nonsense syllables or other material is presented to the human subject. What should receive the emphasis are the rapidity of the habit formation, the errors, peculiarities in the form of the curve, the persistence of the habit so formed, the relation of such habits to those formed when more complex material is used, etc. Now such results are taken down with the subject's introspection. The experiments are made for the purpose of discussing the mental machinery[1] involved in learning, in recall, recollection and forgetting, and not for the purpose of seeking the human being's way of shaping his responses to meet the problems in the terribly complex environment into which he is thrown, nor for that of showing the similarities and differences between man's methods and those of other animals.

The situation is somewhat different when we come to a study of the more complex forms of behavior, such as imagination, judgment, reasoning, and conception. At present the only statements we have of them are in content terms.[2] Our minds have been so warped by the fifty-odd years which have been devoted to the study of states of consciousness that we can envisage these problems only in one way. We should meet the situation squarely and say that we are not able to carry forward investigations along all of these lines by the behavior methods which are in use at the present time. In extenuation I

---

[1]They are often undertaken apparently for the purpose of making crude pictures of what must or must not go on in the nervous system.

[2]There is need of questioning more and more the existence of what psychology calls imagery. Until a few years ago I thought that centrally aroused visual sensations were as clear as those peripherally aroused. I had never accredited myself with any other kind. However, closer examination leads me to deny in my own case the presence of imagery in the Galtonian sense. The whole doctrine of the centrally aroused image is, I believe, at present, on a very insecure foundation. Angell as well as Fernald reach the conclusion that an objective determination of image type is impossible. It would be an interesting confirmation of their experimental work if we should find by degrees that we have been mistaken in building up this enormous structure of the centrally aroused sensation (or image).

The hypothesis that all of the so-called 'higher thought' processes go on in terms of faint reinstatements of the original muscular act (including speech here) and that these are integrated into systems which respond in serial order (associative mechanisms) is, I believe, a tenable one. It makes reflective processes as mechanical as habit. The scheme of habit which James long ago described—where each return or afferent current releases the next appropriate motor discharge—is as true for 'thought processes' as for overt muscular acts. Paucity of 'imagery' would be the rule. In other words, wherever there are thought processes there are faint contractions of the systems of musculature involved in the overt exercise of the customary act, and especially in the still finer systems of musculature involved in speech. If this is true, and I do not see how it can be gainsaid, imagery becomes a mental luxury (even if it really exists) without any functional significance whatever. If experimental procedure justifies this hypothesis, we shall have at hand tangible phenomena which may be studied as behavior material. I should say that the day when we can study reflective processes by such methods is about as far off as the day when we can tell by physico-chemical methods the difference in the structure and arrangement of molecules between living protoplasm and inorganic substances. The solutions of both problems await the advent of methods and apparatus.

should like to call attention to the paragraph above where I made the point that the introspective method itself has reached a *cul-de-sac* with respect to them. The topics have become so threadbare from much handling that they may well be put away for a time. As our methods become better developed it will be possible to undertake investigations of more and more complex forms of behavior. Problems which are now laid aside will again become imperative, but they can be viewed as they arise from a new angle and in more concrete settings.

Will there be left over in psychology a world of pure psychics, to use Yerkes' term? I confess I do not know. The plans which I most favor for psychology lead practically to the ignoring of consciousness in the sense that that term is used by psychologists today. I have virtually denied that this realm of psychics is open to experimental investigation. I don't wish to go further into the problem at present because it leads inevitably over into metaphysics. If you will grant the behaviorist the right to use consciousness in the same way that other natural scientists employ it—that is, without making consciousness a special object of observation—you have granted all that my thesis requires.

In concluding, I suppose I must confess to a deep bias on these questions. I have devoted nearly twelve years to experimentation on animals. It is

[After writing this paper I heard the addresses of Professors Thorndike and Angell, at the Cleveland meeting of the American Psychological Association. I hope to have the opportunity to discuss them at another time. I must even here attempt to answer one question raised by Thorndike.

Thorndike (see this issue) casts suspicions upon ideo-motor action. If by ideo-motor action he means just that and would not include sensori-motor action in his general denunciation, I heartily agree with him. I should throw out imagery altogether and attempt to show that practically all natural thought goes on in terms of sensori-motor processes in the larynx (but not in terms of 'imageless thought') which rarely come to consciousness in any person who has not groped for imagery in the psychological laboratory. This easily explains why so many of the well-educated laity know nothing of imagery. I doubt if Thorndike conceives of the matter in this way. He and Woodworth seem to have neglected the speech mechanisms.

It has been shown that improvement in habit comes unconsciously. The first we know of it is when it is achieved—when it becomes an object. I believe that 'consciousness' has just as little to do with *improvement* in thought processes. Since, according to my view, thought processes are really motor habits in the larynx, improvements, short cuts, changes, etc., in these habits are brought about in the same way that such changes are produced in other motor habits. This view carries with it the implication that there are no reflective processes (centrally initiated processes): The individual is always *examining objects*, in the one case objects in the now accepted sense, in the other their substitutes, viz., the movements in the speech musculature. From this it follows that there is no theoretical limitation of the behavior method. There remains, to be sure, the practical difficulty, which may never be overcome, of examining speech movements in the way that general bodily behavior may be examined.]

natural that such a one should drift into a theoretical position which is in harmony with his experimental work. Possibly I have put up a straw man and have been fighting that. There may be no absolute lack of harmony between the position outlined here and that of functional psychology. I am inclined to think, however, that the two positions cannot be easily harmonized. Certainly the position I advocate is weak enough at present and can be attacked from many standpoints. Yet when all this is admitted I still feel that the considerations which I have urged should have a wide influence upon the type of psychology which is to be developed in the future. What we need to do is to start work upon psychology, making *behavior*, not *consciousness*, the objective point of our attack. Certainly there are enough problems in the control of behavior to keep us all working many lifetimes without ever allowing us time to think of consciousness *an sich*. Once launched in the undertaking, we will find ourselves in a short time as far divorced from an introspective psychology as the psychology of the present time is divorced from faculty psychology.

SUMMARY

1. Human psychology has failed to make good its claim as a natural science. Due to a mistaken notion that its fields of facts are conscious phenomena and that introspection is the only direct method of ascertaining these facts, it has enmeshed itself in a series of speculative questions which, while fundamental to its present tenets, are not open to experimental treatment. In the pursuit of answers to these questions, it has become further and further divorced from contact with problems which vitally concern human interest.

2. Psychology, as the behaviorist views it, is a purely objective, experimental branch of natural science which needs introspection as little as do the sciences of chemistry and physics. It is granted that the behavior of animals can be investigated without appeal to consciousness. Heretofore the viewpoint has been that such data have value only in so far as they can be interpreted by analogy in terms of consciousness. The position is taken here that the behavior of man and the behavior of animals must be considered on the same plane; as being equally essential to a general understanding of behavior. It can dispense with consciousness in a psychological sense. The separate observation of 'states of consciousness' is, on this assumption, no more a part of the task of the psychologist than of the physicist. We might call this the return to a non-reflective and naïve use of consciousness. In this sense consciousness may be said to be the instrument or tool with which all scientists work. Whether or not the tool is properly used at present by scientists is a problem for philosophy and not for psychology.

3. From the viewpoint here suggested the facts on the behavior of amoebae have value in and for themselves without reference to the behavior of man. In biology studies on race differentiation and inheritance in amoebae form a separate division of study which must be evaluated in terms of the laws found there. The conclusions so reached may not hold in any other form. Regardless of the possible lack of generality, such studies must be made if evolution as a whole is ever to be regulated and controlled. Similarly the laws of behavior in amoebae, the range of

responses, and the determination of effective stimuli, of habit formation, persistency of habits, interference and reinforcement of habits, must be determined and evaluated in and for themselves, regardless of their generality, or of their bearing upon such laws in other forms, if the phenomena of behavior are ever to be brought within the sphere of scientific control.

4. This suggested elimination of states of consciousness as proper objects of investigation in themselves will remove the barrier from psychology which exists between it and the other sciences. The findings of psychology become the functional correlates of structure and lend themselves to explanation in physico-chemical terms.

5. Psychology as behavior will, after all, have to neglect but few of the really essential problems with which psychology as an introspective science now concerns itself. In all probability even this residue of problems may be phrased in such a way that refined methods in behavior (which certainly must come) will lead to their solution.

∽25∽

Edward C. Tolman, "Cognitive maps in rats and men" (1948).*1

I shall devote the body of this paper to a description of experiments with rats. But I shall also attempt in a few words at the close to indicate the significance of these findings on rats for the clinical behavior of men. Most of the rat investigations, which I shall report, were carried out in the Berkeley laboratory. But I shall also include, occasionally, accounts of the behavior of non-Berkeley rats who obviously have misspent their lives in out-of-State laboratories. Furthermore, in reporting our Berkeley experiments I shall have to omit a very great many. The ones I *shall* talk about were carried out by graduate students (or underpaid research assistants) who, supposedly, got some of their ideas from me. And a few, though a very few, were even carried out by me myself.

Let me begin by presenting diagrams for a couple of typical mazes, an alley maze and an elevated maze. In the typical experiment a hungry rat is put at the entrance of the maze (alley or elevated), and wanders about through the various true path segments and blind alleys until he finally comes to the food box and eats. This is repeated (again in the typical experiment) one trial every 24 hours and the animal tends to make fewer and fewer errors (that is, blind-alley entrances) and to take less and less time between start and goal-box until finally he is entering no blinds at all and running in a very few seconds from start to goal. The results are usually presented in the form of

*Tolman, E. C. (1948). Cognitive maps in rats and men. *Psychological Review, 55*, 189–208. Reprinted by permission of the American Psychological Association.

[1]34th Annual Faculty Research Lecture, delivered at the University of California, Berkeley, March 17, 1947. Presented also on March 26, 1947 as one in a series of lectures in Dynamic Psychology sponsored by the division of psychology of Western Reserve University, Cleveland, Ohio.

average curves of blind-entrances, or of seconds from start to finish, for groups of rats.

All students agree as to the facts. They disagree, however, on theory and explanation.

(1) First, there is a school of animal psychologists which believes that the maze behavior of rats is a matter of mere simple stimulus-response connections. Learning, according to them, consists in the strengthening of some of these connections and in the weakening of others. According to this 'stimulus-response' school the rat in progressing down the maze is helplessly responding to a succession of external stimuli—sights, sounds, smells, pressures, etc. impinging upon his external sense organs—plus internal stimuli coming from the viscera and from the skeletal muscles. These external and internal stimuli call out the walkings, runnings, turnings, retracings, smellings, rearings, and the like which appear. The rat's central nervous system, according to this view, may be likened to a complicated telephone

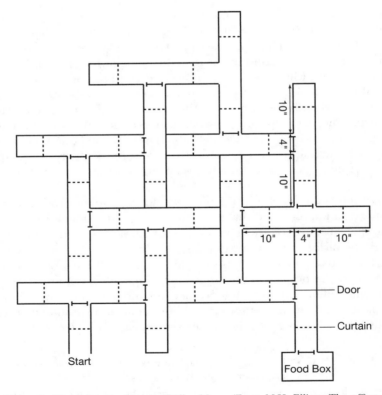

Figure 1   Plan of maze: 14-unit, T-Alley Maze. (From M.H. Elliott, The effect of change of reward on the maze performance of rats. *Univ. Calif. Publ. Psychol.*, 1928, 4, p.20.)

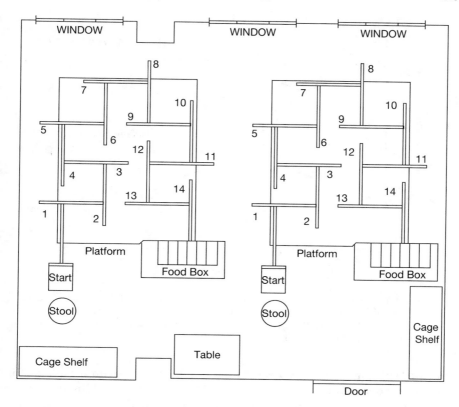

Figure 2 14-Unit, T-Elevated Mazes. (From C. H. Honzik, The sensory basis of maze learning in rats. *Compar. Psychol. Monogr.*, 1936, 13, No. 4, p. 4. These were two identical mazes placed side by side in the same room.)

switchboard. There are the incoming calls from sense-organs and there are the outgoing messages to muscles. Before the learning of a specific maze, the connecting switches (synapses according to the physiologist) are closed in one set of ways and produce the primarily exploratory responses which appear in the early trials. *Learning*, according to this view, consists in the respective strengthening and weakening of various of these connections; those connections which result in the animal's going down the true path become relatively more open to the passage of nervous impulses, whereas those which lead him into the blinds become relatively less open.

It must be noted in addition, however, that this stimulus-response school divides further into two subgroups.

(a) There is a subgroup which holds that the mere mechanics involved in the running of a maze is such that the crucial stimuli from the maze get presented simultaneously with the correct responses more frequently than

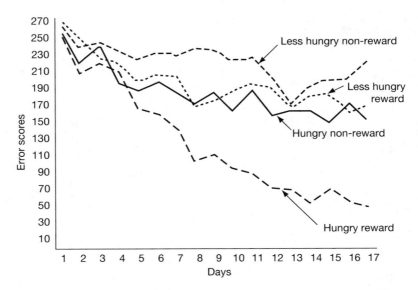

Figure 3   Error curves for four groups, 36 rats.(From E. C. Tolman and C. H. Honzik, Degrees of hunger, reward, and non-reward, and maze learning in rats. *Univ. Calif. Publ. Psychol.*, 1930, 4, No. 16, p. 246. A maze identical with the alley maze shown in Figure 25.1 was used.)

they do with any of the incorrect responses. Hence, just on a basis of this greater frequency, the neural connections between the crucial stimuli and the correct responses will tend, it is said, to get strengthened at the expense of the incorrect connections.

(b) There is a second subgroup in this stimulus-response school which holds that the reason the appropriate connections get strengthened relatively to the inappropriate ones is, rather, the fact that the responses resulting from the correct connections are followed more closely in time by need-reductions. Thus a hungry rat in a maze tends to get to food and have his hunger reduced *sooner* as a result of the true path responses than as a result of the blind alley responses. And such immediately following need-reductions or, to use another term, such 'positive reinforcements' tend somehow, it is said, to strengthen the connections which have most closely preceded them. Thus it is as if—although this is certainly not the way this subgroup would themselves state it—the satisfaction-receiving part of the rat telephoned back to Central and said to the girl: "Hold that connection; it was good; and see to it that you blankety-blank well use it again the next time these same stimuli come in." These theorists also assume (at least some of them do some of the time) that, if bad results—'annoyances,' 'negative reinforcements'—follow, then this same satisfaction-and-annoyance-receiving part of the rat will telephone back and say, "Break that connection and don't you dare use it next time either."

So much for a brief summary of the two subvarieties of the 'stimulus-response,' or telephone switchboard school.

(2) Let us turn now to the second main school. This group (and I belong to them) may be called the field theorists. We believe that in the course of learning something like a field map of the environment gets established in the rat's brain. We agree with the other school that the rat in running a maze is exposed to stimuli and is finally led as a result of these stimuli to the responses which actually occur. We feel, however, that the intervening brain processes are more complicated, more patterned and often, pragmatically speaking, more autonomous than do the stimulus-response psychologists. Although we admit that the rat is bombarded by stimuli, we hold that his nervous system is surprisingly selective as to which of these stimuli it will let in at any given time.

Secondly, we assert that the central office itself is far more like a map control room than it is like an old-fashioned telephone exchange. The stimuli, which are allowed in, are not connected by just simple one-to-one switches to the outgoing responses. Rather, the incoming impulses are usually worked over and elaborated in the central control room into a tentative, cognitive-like map of the environment. And it is this tentative map, indicating routes and paths and environmental relationships, which finally determines what responses, if any, the animal will finally release.

Finally, I, personally, would hold further that it is also important to discover in how far these maps are relatively narrow and strip-like or relatively broad and comprehensive. Both strip-maps and comprehensive-maps may be either correct or incorrect in the sense that they may (or may not), when acted upon, lead successfully to the animal's goal. The differences between such strip maps and such comprehensive maps will appear only when the rat is later presented with some change within the given environment. Then, the narrower and more strip-like the original map, the less will it carry over successfully to the new problem; whereas, the wider and the more comprehensive it was, the more adequately it will serve in the new set-up. In a strip-map the given position of the animal is connected by only a relatively simple and single path to the position of the goal. In a comprehensive-map a wider arc of the environment is represented, so that, if the starting position of the animal be changed or variations in the specific routes be introduced, this wider map will allow the animal still to behave relatively correctly and to choose the appropriate new route.

But let us turn, now, to the actual experiments. The ones, out of many, which I have selected to report are simply ones which seem especially important in reinforcing the theoretical position I have been presenting. This position, I repeat, contains two assumptions: First, that learning consists not in stimulus-response connections but in the building up in the nervous system of sets which function like cognitive maps, and second, that such cognitive maps may be usefully characterized as varying from a narrow strip variety to a broader comprehensive variety.

The experiments fall under five heads: (1) "latent learning," (2) "vicarious trial and error" or "VTE," (3) "searching for the stimulus," (4) "hypotheses" and (5) "spatial orientation."

(1) *"Latent Learning" Experiments.* The first of the latent learning experiments was performed at Berkeley by Blodgett. It was published in 1929. Blodgett not only performed the experiments, he also originated the concept. He ran three groups of rats through a six-unit alley maze, shown in Fig. 4. He had a control group and two experimental groups. The error curves for these groups appear in Fig. 5. The solid line shows the error curve for Group I, the control group. These animals were run in orthodox fashion. That is, they were run one trial a day and found food in the goal-box at the end of each trial. Groups II and III were the experimental groups. The animals of Group II, the dash line, were not fed in the maze for the first six days but only in their home cages some two hours later. On the seventh day (indicated by the small cross) the rats found food at the end of the maze for the first time and continued to find it on subsequent days. The animals of Group III were treated similarly except that they first found food at the end of the maze on the third day and continued to find it there on subsequent days. It will be observed that the experimental groups as long as they were not finding food did not appear to learn much. (Their error curves did not drop.) But on the days immediately succeeding their first finding of the food their error curves did drop astoundingly. It appeared, in short, that during the non-rewarded trials these animals had been learning much more than they had exhibited. This learn-

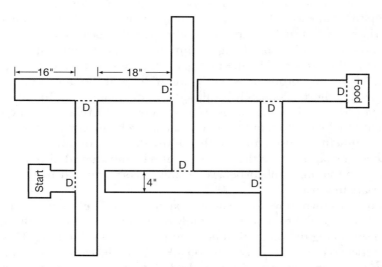

Figure 4   6-Unit Alley T-Maze. (From H. C. Blodgett, The effect of the introduction of reward upon the maze performance of rats. *Univ. Calif. Publ. Psychol.*, 1929, 4, No. 8, p. 117.)

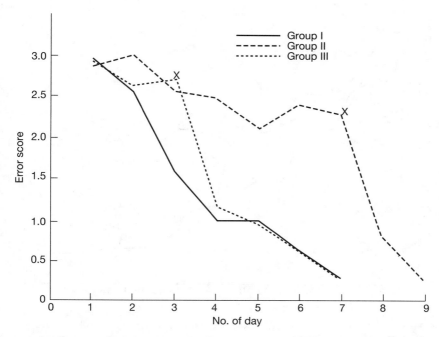

Figure 5   (From H. C. Blodgett, The effect of the introduction of reward upon the maze performance of rats. *Univ. Calif. Publ. Psychol.*, 1929, 4, No. 8, p. 120.)

ing, which did not manifest itself until after the food had been introduced, Blodgett called "latent learning." Interpreting these results anthropomorphically, we would say that as long as the animals were not getting any food at the end of the maze they continued to take their time in going through it—they continued to enter many blinds. Once, however, they knew they were to get food, they demonstrated that during these preceding non-rewarded trials they had learned where many of the blinds were. They had been building up a 'map,' and could utilize the latter as soon as they were motivated to do so.

Honzik and myself repeated the experiments (or rather he did and I got some of the credit) with the 14-unit T-mazes shown in Fig. 1, and with larger groups of animals, and got similar results. The resulting curves are shown in Fig. 6. We used two control groups—one that never found food in the maze (HNR) and one that found it throughout (HR). The experimental group (HNR-R) found food at the end of the maze from the 11th day on and showed the same sort of a sudden drop.

But probably the best experiment demonstrating latent learning was, unfortunately, done not in Berkeley but at the University of Iowa, by Spence and Lippitt. Only an abstract of this experiment has as yet been published. However, Spence has sent a preliminary manuscript from which the following account is summarized. A simple Y-maze (see Fig. 7) with two goal-boxes was

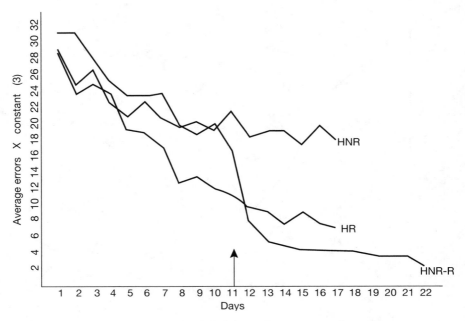

Figure 6 Error curves for HR, HNR, and HNR-R. (From E. C. Tolman and
C. H. Honzik, Introduction and removal of reward, and maze performance in rats.
Univ. Calif. Publ. Psychol., 1930, 4, No. 19, p. 267.)

used. Water was at the end of the right arm of the Y and food at the end of
the left arm. During the training period the rats were run neither hungry nor
thirsty. They were satiated for both food and water before each day's trials.
However, they were willing to run because after each run they were taken out
of whichever end box they had got to and put into a living cage, with other
animals in it. They were given four trials a day in this fashion for seven days,
two trials to the right and two to the left.

In the crucial test the animals were divided into two subgroups one
made solely hungry and one solely thirsty. It was then found that on the first
trial the hungry group went at once to the left, where the food had been, statistically more frequently than to the right; and the thirsty group went to the
right, where the water had been, statistically more frequently than to the left.
These results indicated that under the previous non-differential and very mild
rewarding conditions of merely being returned to the home cages the animals
had nevertheless been learning where the water was and where the food was.
In short, they had acquired a cognitive map to the effect that food was to the
left and water to the right, although during the acquisition of this map they
had not exhibited any stimulus-response propensities to go more to the side
which became later the side of the appropriate goal.

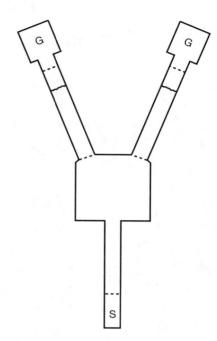

Figure 7   Ground plan of the apparatus. (Taken from K. W. Spence and R. Lippitt, An experimental test of the sign-gestalt theory of trial and error learning. *J. Exper. Psychol.*, 1946, 36, p. 494. In this article they were describing another experiment but used the same maze.)

There have been numerous other latent learning experiments done in the Berkeley laboratory and elsewhere. In general, they have for the most part all confirmed the above sort of findings.

Let us turn now to the second group of experiments.

(2) *"Vicarious Trial and Error" or "VTE."* The term Vicarious Trial and Error (abbreviated as VTE) was invented by Prof. Muenzinger at Colorado[1] to designate the hesitating, looking-back-and-forth, sort of behavior which rats can often be observed to indulge in at a choice-point before actually going one way or the other.

Quite a number of experiments upon VTEing have been carried out in our laboratory. I shall report only a few. In most of them what is called a discrimination set-up has been used. In one characteristic type of visual discrimination apparatus designed by Lashley (shown in Fig. 8) the animal is put on a jumping stand and faced with two doors which differ in some visual property say, as here shown, vertical stripes vs. horizontal stripes.

One of each such pair of visual stimuli is made always correct and the other wrong; and the two are interchanged from side to side in random fashion. The animal is required to learn, say, that the vertically striped door is always the correct one. If he jumps to it, the door falls open and he gets to

---

[1] *Vide:* K. F. Muenzinger, Vicarious trial and error at a point of choice: I. A general survey of its relation to learning efficiency. *J. genet. Psychol.*, 1938, 53, 75–86.

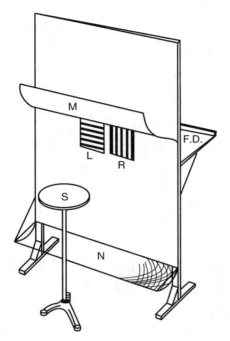

Figure 8 Apparatus used for testing discrimination of visual patterns. (From K. S. Lashley, The mechanism of vision. I. A method for rapid analyses of pattern-vision in the rat. *J. Genet. Psychol.*, 1930, 37, p. 454.)

food on a platform behind. If, on the other hand, he jumps incorrectly, he finds the door locked and falls into a net some two feet below from which he is picked up and started over again.

Using a similar set-up (see Fig. 9), but with landing platforms in front of the doors so that if the rat chose incorrectly he could jump back again and start over, I found that when the choice was an easy one, say between a white door and a black door, the animals not only learned sooner but also did more VTEing than when the choice was difficult, say between a white door and a gray door (see Fig. 10). It appeared further (see Fig. 11) that the VTEing began to appear just as (or just before) the rats began to learn. After the learning had become established, however, the VTE's began to go down. Further, in a study of individual differences by myself, Geier and Levin[1] (actually done by Geier and Levin) using this same visual discrimination apparatus, it was found that with one and the same difficulty of problem the smarter animal did the more VTEing.

To sum up, in *visual discrimination* experiments the better the learning, the more the VTE's. But this seems contrary to what we would perhaps have expected. We ourselves would expect to do more VTEing, more sampling of the two stimuli, when it is difficult to choose between them than when it is easy.

[1]F. M. Geier, M. Levin & E. C. Tolman, Individual differences in emotionality, hypothesis formation, vicarious trial and error and visual discrimination learning in rats. *Compar. Psychol. Monogr.*, 1941, 17, No. 3.

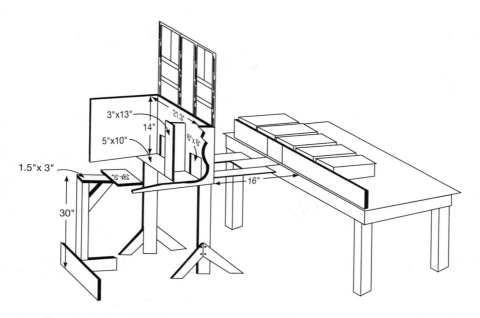

Figure 9 (From E. C. Tolman, Prediction of vicarious trial and error by means of the schematic sowbug. *Psychol. Rev.*, 1939, 46, p. 319.)

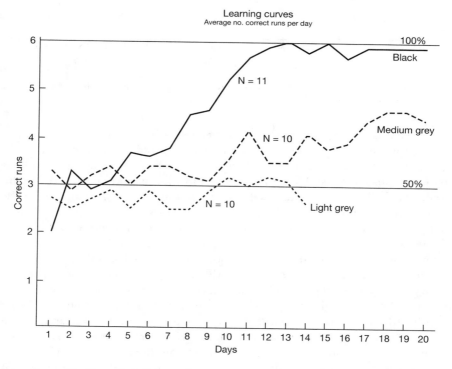

Figure 10 (From E. C. Tolman, Prediction of vicarious trial and error by means of the schematic sowbug. *Psychol. Rev.*, 1939, 46, p. 319.)

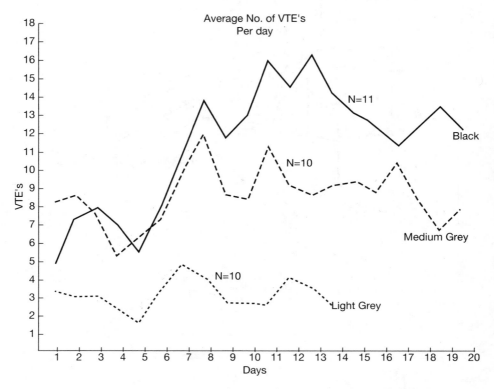

Figure 11   (From E. C. Tolman, Prediction of vicarious trial and error by means of the schematic sowbug. *Psychol. Rev.*, 1939, 46, p. 320.)

What is the explanation? The answer lies, I believe, in the fact that the manner in which we set the visual discrimination problems for the rats and the manner in which we set similar problems for ourselves are different. *We* already have our 'instructions.' We know beforehand what it is we are to do. We are told, or we tell ourselves, that it is the lighter of the two grays, the heavier of the two weights, or the like, which is to be chosen. In such a setting we do more sampling, more VTEing, when the stimulus-difference is small. But for the rats the usual problem in a discrimination apparatus is quite different. They do not know what is wanted of them. The major part of their learning in most such experiments seems to consist in their discovering the instructions. The rats have to discover that it is the differences in visual brightness, not the differences between left and right, which they are to pay attention to. Their VTEing appears when they begin to 'catch on.' The greater the difference between the two stimuli the more the animals are attracted by this difference. Hence the sooner they catch on, and during this catching on, the more they VTE.

That this is a reasonable interpretation appeared further, from an experiment by myself and Minium (the actual work done, of course, by

Minium) in which a group of six rats was first taught a white vs. black discrimination, then two successively more difficult gray vs. black discriminations. For each difficulty the rats were given a long series of further trials beyond the points at which they had learned. Comparing the beginning of each of these three difficulties the results were that the rats did more VTEing for the easy discriminations than for the more difficult ones. When, however, it came to a comparison of amounts of VTEing during the final performance after each learning had reached a plateau, the opposite results were obtained. In other words, after the rats had finally divined their instructions, then they, like human beings, did more VTEing, more sampling, the more difficult the discrimination.

Finally, now let us note that it was also found at Berkeley by Jackson[1] that in a maze the difficult maze units produce more VTEing and also that the more stupid rats do the more VTEing. The explanation, as I see it, is that, in the case of mazes, rats know their instructions. For them it is natural to expect that the same spatial path will always lead to the same outcome. Rats in mazes don't have to be told.

But what, now, is the final significance of all this VTEing? How do these facts about VTEing affect our theoretical argument? My answer is that these facts lend further support to the doctrine of a building up of maps. VTEing,

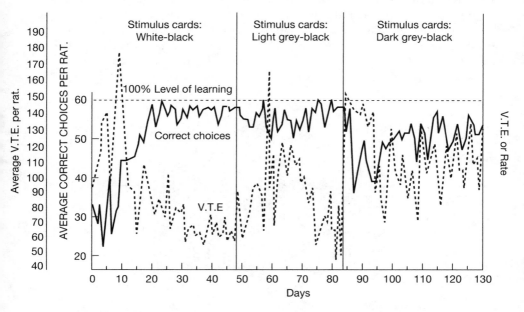

Figure 12   (From E. C. Tolman and E. Minium, VTE in rats: overlearning and difficulty of discrimination. *J. comp. Psychol.*, 1942, 34, p. 303.)

[1]L. L. Jackson, V. T. E. on an elevated maze. *J. comp. Psychol.*, 1943, 36, 99–107.

as I see it, is evidence that in the critical stages—whether in the first picking up of the instructions or in the later making sure of which stimulus is which— the animal's activity is not just one of responding passively to discrete stimuli, but rather one of the active selecting and comparing of stimuli. This brings me then to the third type of experiment.

(3) *"Searching for the Stimulus."* I refer to a recent, and it seems to me extremely important experiment, done for a Ph.D. dissertation by Hudson. Hudson was first interested in the question of whether or not rats could learn an avoidance reaction in one trial. His animals were tested one at a time in a living cage (see Fig. 13) with a small striped visual pattern at the end, on which was mounted a food cup. The hungry rat approached this food cup and ate. An electrical arrangement was provided so that when the rat touched the cup he could be given an electric shock. And one such shock did appear to be enough. For when the rat was replaced in this same cage days or even weeks afterwards, he usually demonstrated immediately strong avoidance reactions to the visual pattern. The animal withdrew from that end of the cage, or piled up sawdust and covered the pattern, or showed various other amusing responses all of which were in the nature of withdrawing from the pattern or making it disappear.

But the particular finding which I am interested in now appeared as a result of a modification of this standard procedure. Hudson noticed that the animals, anthropomorphically speaking, often seemed to look around *after* the shock to see what it was that had hit them. Hence it occurred to him that, if the pattern were made to disappear the instant the shock occurred, the rats might not establish the association. And this indeed is what happened in the case of many individuals. Hudson added further electrical connections so that

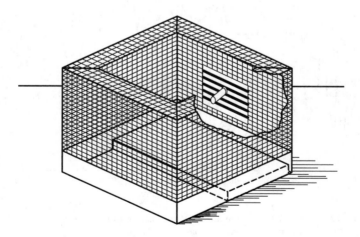

Figure 13   (From Bradford Hudson. Ph.D. Thesis: 'One trial learning: A study of the avoidance behavior of the rat.' On deposit in the Library of the University of California, Berkeley, California.)

when the shock was received during the eating, the lights went out, the pattern and the food cup dropped out of sight, and the lights came on again all within the matter of a second. When such animals were again put in the cage 24 hours later, a large percentage showed no avoidance of the pattern. Or to quote Hudson's own words:

> "Learning what object to avoid . . . may occur exclusively during the period *after* the shock. For if the object from which the shock was actually received is removed at the moment of the shock, a significant number of animals fail to learn to avoid it, some selecting other features in the environment for avoidance, and others avoiding nothing."

In other words, I feel that this experiment reinforces the notion of the largely active selective character in the rat's building up of his cognitive map. He often has to look actively for the significant stimuli in order to form his map and does not merely passively receive and react to all the stimuli which are physically present.

Turn now to the fourth type of experiment.

(4) *The "Hypothesis" Experiments.* Both the notion of hypotheses in rats and the design of the experiments to demonstrate such hypotheses are to be credited to Krech. Krech used a four-compartment discrimination-box. In such a four-choice box the correct door at each choice-point may be determined by the experimenter in terms of its being lighted or dark, left or right, or various combinations of these. If all possibilities are randomized for the 40 choices made in 10 runs of each day's test, the problem could be made insoluble.

When this was done, Krech found that the individual rat went through a succession of systematic choices. That is, the individual animal might perhaps begin by choosing practically all right-hand doors, then he might give this up for choosing practically all left-hand doors, and then, for choosing all dark doors, and so on. These relatively persistent, and well-above-chance systematic types of choice Krech called "hypotheses." In using this term he obviously did not mean to imply verbal processes in the rat but merely referred to what I have been calling cognitive maps which, it appears from his experiments, get set up in a tentative fashion to be tried out first one and then another until, if possible, one is found which works.

Finally, it is to be noted that these hypothesis experiments, like the latent learning, VTE, and "looking for the stimulus" experiments, do not, as

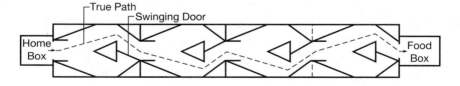

Figure 14   (From I. Krechevsky (Now D. Krech), The genesis of "hypotheses" in rats. *Univ. Calif. Publ. Psychol.*, 1932, 6, No. 4, p. 46.)

such, throw light upon the widths of the maps which are picked up but do indicate the generally map-like and self-initiated character of learning.

For the beginning of an attack upon the problem of the width of the maps let me turn to the last group of experiments.

(5) *"Spatial Orientation" Experiments.* As early as 1929, Lashley reported incidentally the case of a couple of his rats who, after having learned an alley maze, pushed back the cover near the starting box, climbed out and ran directly across the top to the goal-box where they climbed down in again and ate. Other investigators have reported related findings. All such observations suggest that rats really develop wider spatial maps which include more than the mere trained-on specific paths. In the experiments now to be reported this possibility has been subjected to further examination.

In the first experiment, Tolman, Ritchie and Kalish (actually Ritchie and Kalish) used the set-up shown in Fig. 15.

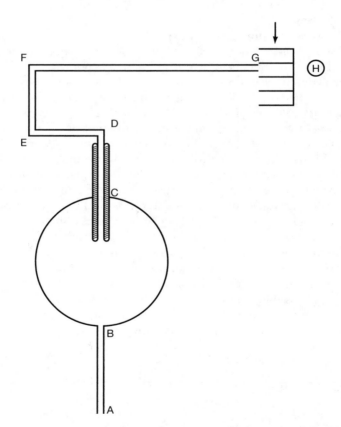

Figure 15   Apparatus used in preliminary training. (From E. C. Tolman, B. F. Ritchie and D. Kalish, Studies in spatial learning. I. Orientation and the short-cut. J. exp. Psychol., 1946, 36, p. 16.)

This was an elevated maze. The animals ran from A across the open circular table through CD (which had alley walls) and finally to G, the food box. H was a light which shone directly down the path from G to F. After four nights, three trials per night, in which the rats learned to run directly and without hesitation from A to G, the apparatus was changed to the sun-burst shown in Fig. 16. The starting path and the table remained the same but a series of radiating paths was added.

The animals were again started at A and ran across the circular table into the alley and found themselves blocked. They then returned onto the table and began exploring practically all the radiating paths. After going out a few inches only on any one path, each rat finally chose to run all the way out on one. The percentages of rats finally choosing each of the long paths from 1 to 12 are shown in Fig. 17. It appears that there was a preponderant tendency to choose path No. 6 which ran to a point some four inches in front of where the entrance to the food-box had been. The only other path chosen with any appreciable frequency was No. 1—that is, the path which pointed perpendicularly to the food-side of the room.

These results seem to indicate that the rats in this experiment had learned not only to run rapidly down the original roundabout route but also,

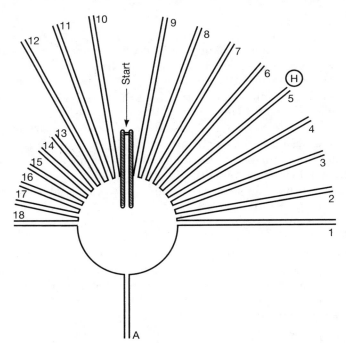

Figure 16 Apparatus used in the test trial. (From E. C. Tolman, B. R. Ritchie and D. Kalish, Studies in spatial learning. I. Orientation and short-cut. *J. exp. Psychol.*, 1946, 36, p. 17.)

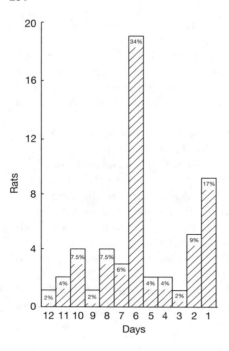

Figure 17   Numbers of rats which chose each of the paths. (From E. C. Tolman, B. F. Ritchie and D. Kalish, Studies in spatial learning. I. Orientation and the short-cut. *J. exp. Psychol.*, 1946, 36, p. 19.)

when this was blocked and radiating paths presented, to select one pointing rather directly towards the point where the food had been or else at least to select a path running perpendicularly to the food-side of the room.

As a result of their original training, the rats had, it would seem, acquired not merely a strip-map to the effect that the original specifically trained-on path led to food but, rather, a wider comprehensive map to the effect that food was located in such and such a direction in the room.

Consider now a further experiment done by Ritchie alone. This experiment tested still further the breadth of the spatial map which is acquired. In this further experiment the rats were again run across the table—this time to the arms of a simple T. (See Fig. 18.)

Twenty-five animals were trained for seven days, 20 trials in all, to find food at F_1; and twenty-five animals were trained to find it at F_2. The L's in the diagram indicate lights. On the eighth day the starting path and table top were rotated through 180 degrees so that they were now in the position shown in Fig. 19. The dotted lines represent the old position. And a series of radiating paths was added. What happened? Again the rats ran across the table into the central alley. When, however, they found themselves blocked, they turned back onto the table and this time also spent many seconds touching and trying out for only a few steps practically all the paths. Finally, however, within seven minutes, 42 of the 50 rats chose one path and ran all the way out on it. The paths finally chosen by the 19 of these animals that had been fed at F_1 and by the 23 that had been fed at F_2 are shown in Fig. 20.

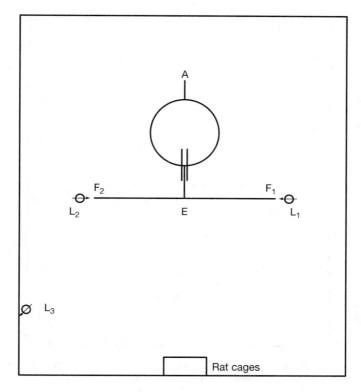

Figure 18   (From B. F. Ritchie. Ph.D. Thesis: 'Spatial learning in rats.' On deposit in the Library of the University of California, Berkeley, California.)

This time the rats tended to choose, not the paths which pointed directly to the spots where the food had been, but rather paths which ran perpendicularly to the corresponding sides of the room. The spatial maps of these rats, when the animals were started from the opposite side of the room, were thus not completely adequate to the precise goal positions but were adequate as to the correct sides of the room. The maps of these animals were, in short, not altogether strip-like and narrow.

This completes my report of experiments. There were the *latent learning experiments,* the *VTE experiments,* the *searching for the stimulus experiment,* the *hypothesis experiments,* and these last *spatial orientation experiments.*

And now, at last, I come to the humanly significant and exciting problem: namely, what are the conditions which favor narrow strip-maps and what are those which tend to favor broad comprehensive maps not only in rats but also in men?

There is considerable evidence scattered throughout the literature bearing on this question both for rats and for men. Some of this evidence was obtained in Berkeley and some of it elsewhere. I have not time to present it in

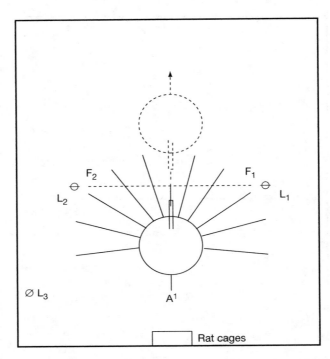

Figure 19   (From B. F. Ritchie. Ph.D. Thesis: 'Spatial learning in rats.' On deposit in the Library of the University of California, Berkeley, California.)

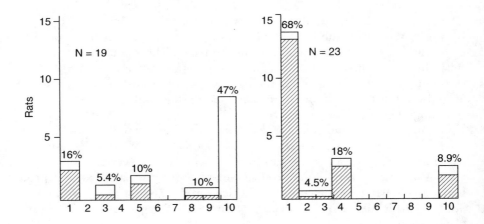

Figure 20   (a) Paths chosen by rats in the F_1 group; (b) Paths chosen by rats in the F_2 group. (From B. F. Ritchie. Ph.D. Thesis: "Spatial learning in rats.' On deposit in the Library of the University of California, Berkeley, California.)

any detail. I can merely summarize it by saying that narrow strip maps rather than broad comprehensive maps seem to be induced: (1) by a damaged brain, (2) by an inadequate array of environmentally presented cues, (3) by an overdose of repetitions on the original trained-on path and (4) by the presence of too strongly motivational or of too strongly frustrating conditions.

It is this fourth factor which I wish to elaborate upon briefly in my concluding remarks. For it is going to be my contention that some, at least, of the so-called 'psychological mechanisms' which the clinical psychologists and the other students of personality have uncovered as the devils underlying many of our individual and social maladjustments can be interpreted as narrowings of our cognitive maps due to too strong motivations or to too intense frustration.

My argument will be brief, cavalier, and dogmatic. For I am not myself a clinician or a social psychologist. What I am going to say must be considered, therefore, simply as in the nature of a *rat* psychologist's *rat*iocinations offered free.

By way of illustration, let me suggest that at least the three dynamisms called, respectively, "regression," "fixation," and "displacement of aggression onto outgroups" are expressions of cognitive maps which are too narrow and which get built up in us as a result of too violent motivation or of too intense frustration.

(a) Consider *regression*. This is the term used for those cases in which an individual, in the face of too difficult a problem, returns to earlier more childish ways of behaving. Thus, to take an example, the overprotected middle-aged woman (reported a couple of years ago in *Time Magazine*) who, after losing her husband, regressed (much to the distress of her growing daughters) into dressing in too youthful a fashion and into competing for their beaux and then finally into behaving like a child requiring continuous care, would be an illustration of regression. I would not wish you to put too much confidence in the reportorial accuracy of *Time*, but such an extreme case is not too different from many actually to be found in our mental hospitals or even sometimes in ourselves. In all such instances my argument would be (1) that such regression results from too strong a present emotional situation and (2) that it consists in going back to too narrow an earlier map, itself due to too much frustration or motivation in early childhood. *Time*'s middle-aged woman was presented by too frustrating an emotional situation at her husband's death and she regressed, I would wager, to too narrow adolescent and childhood maps since these latter had been originally excessively impressed because of over-stressful experiences at the time she was growing up.

(b) Consider *fixation*. Regression and fixation tend to go hand in hand. For another way of stating the fact of the undue persistence of early maps is to say that they were fixated. This has even been demonstrated in rats. If rats are too strongly motivated in their original learning, they find it very difficult to relearn when the original path is no longer correct. Also after they have relearned, if they are given an electric shock they, like *Time*'s woman, tend to regress back again to choosing the earlier path.

(c) Finally, consider the *"displacement of aggressions onto outgroups."* Adherence to one's own group is an ever-present tendency among primates. It is found in chimpanzees and monkeys as strongly as in men. We primates operate in groups. And each individual in such a group tends to identify with his whole group in the sense that the group's goals become his goals, the group's life and immortality, his life and immortality. Furthermore, each individual soon learns that, when as an individual he is frustrated, he must not take out his aggressions on the other members of his own group. He learns instead to displace his aggressions onto outgroups. Such a displacement of aggression I would claim is also a narrowing of the cognitive map. The individual comes no longer to distinguish the true locus of the cause of his frustration. The poor Southern whites, who take it out on the Negroes, are displacing their aggressions from the landlords, the southern economic system, the northern capitalists, or wherever the true cause of their frustration may lie, onto a mere convenient outgroup. The physicists on the Faculty who criticize the humanities, or we psychologists who criticize all the other departments, or the University as a whole which criticizes the Secondary School system or, vice versa, the Secondary School system which criticizes the University—or, on a still larger and far more dangerous scene—we Americans who criticize the Russians and the Russians who criticize us, are also engaging, at least in part, in nothing more than such irrational displacements of our aggressions onto outgroups.

I do not mean to imply that there may not be some true interferences by the one group with the goals of the other and hence that the aggressions of the members of the one group against the members of the other are necessarily *wholly* and *merely* displaced aggressions. But I do assert that often and in large part they are such mere displacements.

Over and over again men are blinded by too violent motivations and too intense frustrations into blind and unintelligent and in the end desperately dangerous hates of outsiders. And the expression of these their displaced hates ranges all the way from discrimination against minorities to world conflagrations.

What in the name of Heaven and Psychology can we do about it? My only answer is to preach again the virtues of reason—of, that is, broad cognitive maps. And to suggest that the child-trainers and the world-planners of the future can only, if at all, bring about the presence of the required rationality (*i.e.*, comprehensive maps) if they see to it that nobody's children are too over-motivated or too frustrated. Only then can these children learn to look before and after, learn to see that there are often round-about and safer paths to their quite proper goals—learn, that is, to realize that the well-beings of White and of Negro, of Catholic and of Protestant, of Christian and of Jew, of

American and of Russian (and even of males and females) are mutually inter-dependent.

We dare not let ourselves or others become so over-emotional, so hungry, so ill-clad, so over-motivated that only narrow strip-maps will be developed. All of us in Europe as well as in America, in the Orient as well as in the Occident, must be made calm enough and well-fed enough to be able to develop truly comprehensive maps, or, as Freud would have put it, to be able to learn to live according to the Reality Principle rather than according to the too narrow and too immediate Pleasure Principle.

We must, in short, subject our children and ourselves (as the kindly experimenter would his rats) to the optimal conditions of moderate motivation and of an absence of unnecessary frustrations, whenever we put them and ourselves before that great God-given maze which is our human world. I cannot predict whether or not we will be able, or be allowed, to do this; but I *can* say that, only insofar as we *are* able and *are* allowed, have we cause for hope.

26

B. F. Skinner, Excerpt from "Are theories of learning necessary?" (1950).*[1]

    Certain basic assumptions, essential to any scientific activity, are sometimes called theories. That nature is orderly rather than capricious is an example. Certain statements are also theories simply to the extent that they are not yet facts. A scientist may guess at the result of an experiment before the experiment is carried out. The prediction and the later statement of result may be composed of the same terms in the same syntactic arrangement, the difference being in the degree of confidence. No empirical statement is wholly nontheoretical in this sense, because evidence is never complete, nor is any prediction probably ever made wholly without evidence. The term "theory" will not refer here to statements of these sorts but rather to any explanation of an observed fact which appeals to events taking place somewhere else, at some other level of observation, described in different terms, and measured, if at all, in different dimensions.

    Three types of theory in the field of learning satisfy this definition. The most characteristic is to be found in the field of physiological psychology. We are all familiar with the changes that are supposed to take place in the nervous system when an organism learns. Synaptic connections are made or broken, electrical fields are disrupted or reorganized, concentrations of ions are built up or allowed to diffuse away, and so on. In the science of neurophysiology statements of this sort are not necessarily theories in the present sense. But in a science of behavior, where we are concerned with whether or not an

    *Skinner, B. F. (1950). Excerpt from Are theories of learning necessary? *Psychological Review*, 57, 193–199. Reprinted by permission of the American Psychological Association. Numbers in parentheses refer to citations not included in this excerpt.

    [1]Address of the president, Midwestern Psychological Association, Chicago, Illinois, May, 1949.

organism secretes saliva when a bell rings, or jumps toward a gray triangle, or says *bik* when a card reads *tuz*, or loves someone who resembles his mother, all statements about the nervous system are theories in the sense that they are not expressed in the same terms and could not be confirmed with the same methods of observation as the facts for which they are said to account.

A second type of learning theory is in practice not far from the physiological, although there is less agreement about the method of direct observation. Theories of this type have always dominated the field of human behavior. They consist of references to "mental" events, as in saying that an organism learns to behave in a certain way because it "finds something pleasant" or because it "expects something to happen." To the mentalistic psychologist these explanatory events are no more theoretical than synaptic connections to the neurophysiologist, but in a science of behavior they are theories because the methods and terms appropriate to the events to be explained differ from the methods and terms appropriate to the explaining events.

In a third type of learning theory the explanatory events are not directly observed. The writer's suggestion that the letters CNS be regarded as representing, not the Central Nervous System, but the Conceptual Nervous System (2, p. 421), seems to have been taken seriously. Many theorists point out that they are not talking about the nervous system as an actual structure undergoing physiological or bio-chemical changes but only as a system with a certain dynamic output. Theories of this sort are multiplying fast, and so are parallel operational versions of mental events. A purely behavioral definition of expectancy has the advantage that the problem of mental observation is avoided and with it the problem of how a mental event can cause a physical one. But such theories do not go so far as to assert that the explanatory events are identical with the behavioral facts which they purport to explain. A statement about behavior may support such a theory but will never resemble it in terms of syntax. Postulates are good examples. True postulates cannot become facts. Theorems may be deduced from them which, as tentative statements about behavior, may or may not be confirmed, but theorems are not theories in the present sense. Postulates remain theories until the end.

It is not the purpose of this paper to show that any of these theories cannot be put in good scientific order, or that the events to which they refer may not actually occur or be studied by appropriate sciences. It would be foolhardy to deny the achievements of theories of this sort in the history of science. The question of whether they are necessary, however, has other implications and is worth asking. If the answer is no, then it may be possible to argue effectively against theory in the field of learning. A science of behavior must eventually deal with behavior in its relation to certain manipulable variables. Theories—whether neural, mental, or conceptual—talk about intervening steps in these relationships. But instead of prompting us to search for and explore relevant variables, they frequently have quite the opposite effect.

When we attribute behavior to a neural or mental event, real or conceptual, we are likely to forget that we still have the task of accounting for the neural or mental event. When we assert that an animal acts in a given way because it expects to receive food, then what began as the task of accounting for learned behavior becomes the task of accounting for expectancy. The problem is at least equally complex and probably more difficult. We are likely to close our eyes to it and to use the theory to give us answers in place of the answers we might find through further study. It might be argued that the principal function of learning theory to date has been, not to suggest appropriate research, but to create a false sense of security, an unwarranted satisfaction with the *status quo*.

Research designed with respect to theory is also likely to be wasteful. That a theory generates research does not prove its value unless the research is valuable. Much useless experimentation results from theories, and much energy and skill are absorbed by them. Most theories are eventually overthrown, and the greater part of the associated research is discarded. This could be justified if it were true that productive research requires a theory, as is, of course, often claimed. It is argued that research would be aimless and disorganized without a theory to guide it. The view is supported by psychological texts that take their cue from the logicians rather than empirical science and describe thinking as necessarily involving stages of hypothesis, deduction, experimental test, and confirmation. But this is not the way most scientists actually work. It is possible to design significant experiments for other reasons and the possibility to be examined is that such research will lead more directly to the kind of information that a science usually accumulates.

The alternatives are at least worth considering. How much can be done without theory? What other sorts of scientific activity are possible? And what light do alternative practices throw upon our present preoccupation with theory?

It would be inconsistent to try to answer these questions at a theoretical level. Let us therefore turn to some experimental material in three areas in which theories of learning now flourish and raise the question of the function of theory in a more concrete fashion.[2]

THE BASIC DATUM IN LEARNING

What actually happens when an organism learns is not an easy question. Those who are interested in a science of behavior will insist that learning is a change in behavior, but they tend to avoid explicit references to responses or acts as such. "Learning is adjustment, or adaptation to a situation." But of

---

[2]Some of the material that follows was obtained in 1941–42 in a cooperative study on the behavior of the pigeon in which Keller Breland, Norman Guttman, and W. K. Estes collaborated. Some of it is selected from subsequent, as yet unpublished, work on the pigeon conducted by the author at Indiana University and Harvard University. Limitations of space make it impossible to report full details here.

what stuff are adjustments and adaptations made? Are they data, or inferences from data? "Learning is improvement." But improvement in what? And from whose point of view? "Learning is restoration of equilibrium." But what is in equilibrium and how is it put there? "Learning is problem solving." But what are the physical dimensions of a problem—or of a solution? Definitions of this sort show an unwillingness to take what appears before the eyes in a learning experiment as a basic datum. Particular observations seem too trivial. An error score falls; but we are not ready to say that this is learning rather than merely the result of learning. An organism meets a criterion of ten successful trials; but an arbitrary criterion is at variance with our conception of the generality of the learning process.

This is where theory steps in. If it is not the time required to get out of a puzzle box that changes in learning, but rather the strength of a bond, or the conductivity of a neural pathway, or the excitatory potential of a habit, then problems seem to vanish. Getting out of a box faster and faster is not learning; it is merely performance. The learning goes on somewhere else, in a different dimensional system. And although the time required depends upon arbitrary conditions, often varies discontinuously, and is subject to reversals of magnitude, we feel sure that the learning process itself is continuous, orderly, and beyond the accidents of measurement. Nothing could better illustrate the use of theory as a refuge from the data.

But we must eventually get back to an observable datum. If learning is the process we suppose it to be, then it must appear so in the situations in which we study it. Even if the basic process belongs to some other dimensional system, our measures must have relevant and comparable properties. But productive experimental situations are hard to find, particularly if we accept certain plausible restrictions. To show an orderly change in the behavior of the *average* rat or ape or child is not enough, since learning is a process in the behavior of the individual. To record the beginning and end of learning or a few discrete steps will not suffice, since a series of cross-sections will not give complete coverage of a continuous process. The dimensions of the change must spring from the behavior itself; they must not be imposed by an external judgment of success or failure or an external criterion of completeness. But when we review the literature with these requirements in mind, we find little justification for the theoretical process in which we take so much comfort.

The energy level or work-output of behavior, for example, does not change in appropriate ways. In the sort of behavior adapted to the Pavlovian experiment (respondent behavior) there may be a progressive increase in the magnitude of response during learning. But we do not shout our responses louder and louder as we learn verbal material, nor does a rat press a lever harder and harder as conditioning proceeds. In operant behavior the energy or magnitude of response changes significantly only when some arbitrary value is differentially reinforced—when such a change is what is learned.

The emergence of a right response in competition with wrong responses is another datum frequently used in the study of learning. The maze and the discrimination box yield results which may be reduced to these terms. But a behavior-ratio of right *vs.* wrong cannot yield a continuously changing measure in a single experiment on a single organism. The point at which one response takes precedence over another cannot give us the whole history of the change in either response. Averaging curves for groups of trials or organisms will not solve this problem.

Increasing attention has recently been given to latency, the relevance of which, like that of energy level, is suggested by the properties of conditioned and unconditioned reflexes. But in operant behavior the relation to a stimulus is different. A measure of latency involves other considerations, as inspection of any case will show. Most operant responses may be emitted in the absence of what is regarded as a relevant stimulus. In such a case the response is likely to appear before the stimulus is presented. It is no solution to escape this embarrassment by locking a lever so that an organism cannot press it until the stimulus is presented, since we can scarcely be content with temporal relations that have been forced into compliance with our expectations. Runway latencies are subject to this objection. In a typical experiment the door of a starting box is opened and the time that elapses before a rat leaves the box is measured. Opening the door is not only a stimulus, it is a change in the situation that makes the response possible for the first time. The time measured is by no means as simple as a latency and requires another formulation. A great deal depends upon what the rat is doing at the moment the stimulus is presented. Some experimenters wait until the rat is facing the door, but to do so is to tamper with the measurement being taken. If, on the other hand, the door is opened without reference to what the rat is doing, the first major effect is the conditioning of favorable waiting behavior. The rat eventually stays near and facing the door. The resulting shorter starting-time is not due to a reduction in the latency of a response, but to the conditioning of favorable preliminary behavior.

Latencies in a single organism do not follow a simple learning process. Relevant data on this point were obtained as part of an extensive study of reaction time. A pigeon, enclosed in a box, is conditioned to peck at a recessed disc in one wall. Food is presented as reinforcement by exposing a hopper through a hole below the disc. If responses are reinforced only after a stimulus has been presented, responses at other times disappear. Very short reaction times are obtained by differentially reinforcing responses which occur very soon after the stimulus (4). But responses also come to be made very quickly without differential reinforcement. Inspection shows that this is due to the development of effective waiting. The bird comes to stand before the disc with its head in good striking position. Under optimal conditions, without differential reinforcement, the mean time between stimulus and response will be of the order of ⅓ sec. This is not a true reflex latency, since the stimulus is discriminative rather than eliciting, but it is a fair example of the latency used in the study of learning. The point is that this measure does not vary continuously or in an orderly fashion. By giving the bird more food, for example, we induce a condition in which it does not always respond. But the responses that occur show approximately the same temporal relation to the stimulus (Fig. 1, middle curve). In extinction, of special interest here, there is a scattering of latencies because lack of reinforcement generates an emotional condition. Some responses occur sooner and others are delayed, but the commonest value remains unchanged (bottom curve in Fig. 1). The longer latencies are easily explained by inspection. Emotional behavior, of which examples will be mentioned later, is likely to be in progress when the ready-signal is presented. It is often not discontinued before the "go" signal is presented, and the result is a long starting-time. Cases also begin to appear in which the bird simply does not respond at all during a specified time. If we average a large number of readings, either from one bird or many, we may create what looks like a progressive lengthening of latency. But the data for an individual organism do not show a continuous process.

Another datum to be examined is the rate at which a response is emitted. Fortunately the story here is different. We study this rate by designing a situation in which a response may be freely repeated, choosing a response (for example, touching or pressing a small lever or key) that may be easily observed and counted. The responses may be recorded on a polygraph, but a more convenient form is a cumulative curve from which rate of responding is immediately read as slope. The rate at which a response is emitted in such a situation comes close to our preconception of the learning process. As the organism learns, the rate rises. As it unlearns (for example, in extinction) the rate falls. Various sorts of discriminative stimuli may be brought into control of the response with corresponding modifications of the rate. Motivational changes alter the rate in a sensitive way. So do those events which we speak of as generating emotion. The range through which the rate varies significantly may be as great as of the order of 1000:1. Changes in rate are satisfactorily

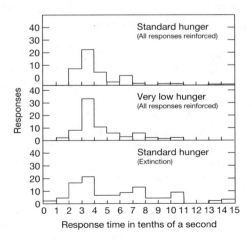

Figure 1   Response time in tenths of a second

smooth in the individual case, so that it is not necessary to average cases. A given value is often quite stable: in the pigeon a rate of four or five thousand responses per hour may be maintained without interruption for as long as fifteen hours.

Rate of responding appears to be the only datum that varies significantly and in the expected direction under conditions which are relevant to the "learning process." We may, therefore, be tempted to accept it as our long-sought-for measure of strength of bond, excitatory potential, etc. Once in possession of an effective datum, however, we may feel little need for any theoretical construct of this sort. Progress in a scientific field usually waits upon the discovery of a satisfactory dependent variable. Until such a variable has been discovered, we resort to theory. The entities which have figured so prominently in learning theory have served mainly as substitutes for a directly observable and productive datum. They have little reason to survive when such a datum has been found.

It is no accident that rate of responding is successful as a datum, because it is particularly appropriate to the fundamental task of a science of behavior. If we are to predict behavior (and possibly to control it), we must deal with *probability of response*. The business of a science of behavior is to evaluate this probability and explore the conditions that determine it. Strength of bond, expectancy, excitatory potential, and so on, carry the notion of probability in an easily imagined form, but the additional properties suggested by these terms have hindered the search for suitable measures. Rate of responding is not a "measure" of probability but it is the only appropriate datum in a formulation in these terms.

As other scientific disciplines can attest, probabilities are not easy to handle. We wish to make statements about the likelihood of occurrence of a single future response, but our data are in the form of frequencies of responses that have already occurred. These responses were presumably similar to each other and to the response to be predicted. But this raises the troublesome problem of response-instance *vs.* response-class. Precisely what responses are we to take into account in predicting a future instance? Certainly not the responses made by a population of different organisms, for such a statistical datum raises more problems than it solves. To consider the frequency of repeated responses in an individual demands something like the experimental situation just described.

This solution of the problem of a basic datum is based upon the view that operant behavior is essentially an emissive phenomenon. Latency and magnitude of response fail as measures because they do not take this into account. They are concepts appropriate to the field of the reflex, where the all but invariable control exercised by the eliciting stimulus makes the notion of probability of response trivial. Consider, for example, the case of latency. Because of our acquaintance with simple reflexes we infer that a response that is more likely to be emitted will be emitted more quickly. But is this true?

What can the word "quickly" mean? Probability of response, as well as prediction of response, is concerned with the moment of emission. This is a point in time, but it does not have the temporal dimension of a latency. The execution may take time after the response has been initiated, but the moment of occurrence has no duration.[3] In recognizing the emissive character of operant behavior and the central position of probability of response as a datum, latency is seen to be irrelevant to our present task.

Various objections have been made to the use of rate of responding as a basic datum. For example, such a program may seem to bar us from dealing with many events which are unique occurrences in the life of the individual. A man does not decide upon a career, get married, make a million dollars, or get killed in an accident often enough to make a rate of response meaningful. But these activities are not responses. They are not simple unitary events lending themselves to prediction as such. If we are to predict marriage, success, accidents, and so on, in anything more than statistical terms, we must deal with the smaller units of behavior which lead to and compose these unitary episodes. If the units appear in repeatable form, the present analysis may be applied. In the field of learning a similar objection takes the form of asking how the present analysis may be extended to experimental situations in which it is impossible to observe frequencies. It does not follow that learning is not taking place in such situations. The notion of probability is usually extrapolated to cases in which a frequency analysis cannot be carried out. In the field of behavior we arrange a situation in which frequencies are available as data, but we use the notion of probability in analyzing and formulating instances or even types of behavior which are not susceptible to this analysis.

Another common objection is that a rate of response is just a set of latencies and hence not a new datum at all. This is easily shown to be wrong. When we measure the time elapsing between two responses, we are in no doubt as to what the organism was doing when we started our clock. We know that it was just executing a response. This is a natural zero—quite unlike the arbitrary point from which latencies are measured. The free repetition of a

---

[3]It cannot, in fact, be shortened or lengthened. Where a latency appears to be forced toward a minimal value by differential reinforcement, another interpretation is called for. Although we may differentially reinforce more energetic behavior or the faster execution of behavior after it begins, it is meaningless to speak of differentially reinforcing responses with short or long latencies. What we actually reinforce differentially are (a) favorable waiting behavior and (b) more vigorous responses. When we ask a subject to respond "as soon as possible" in the human reaction-time experiment, we essentially ask him (a) to carry out as much of the response as possible without actually reaching the criterion of emission, (b) to do as little else as possible, and (c) to respond energetically after the stimulus has been given. This may yield a minimal measurable time between stimulus and response, but this time is not necessarily a basic datum nor have our instructions altered it as such. A parallel interpretation of the differential reinforcement of long "latencies" is required. This is easily established by inspection. In the experiments with pigeons previously cited, preliminary behavior is conditioned that postpones the response to the key until the proper time. Behavior that "marks time" is usually conspicuous.

response yields a rhythmic or periodic datum very different from latency. Many periodic physical processes suggest parallels.

We do not choose rate of responding as a basic datum merely from an analysis of the fundamental task of a science of behavior. The ultimate appeal is to its success in an experimental science. The material which follows is offered as a sample of what can be done. It is not intended as a complete demonstration, but it should confirm the fact that when we are in possession of a datum which varies in a significant fashion, we are less likely to resort to theoretical entities carrying the notion of probability of response.

VIII. The Third Force Movement

It may be easier to specify what the "Third Force" movement is not, rather than what it is. It is not psychoanalysis, nor is it an experimentally based, objective psychology, such as behaviorism. While consistent with preconceptions of mental activity, the Third Force movement draws its intellectual underpinnings from the literature and methodologies of European existentialism and phenomenology and from American writers who called for a humanistic psychology that is not necessarily rigorously scientific like the natural sciences. The Third Force Movement has found success in clinical applications, which is appropriate since the Third Force Movement tries to understand the person as an individual, existing in particular context and times, wrestling with the choices of life and assuming responsibility for those choices.

The excerpt from the 1970 work by Amadeo Giorgi (b. 1931) attempts to resolve the tension between psychology defined as the study of human mental activity and science. In defining psychology as a human science, Giorgi distinguishes between the description of the "actual" in order to reveal the "structural". The former must be exact in order to let the description lead to ideas. Acknowledging the immaturity of psychological science compared to the natural sciences, Giorgi argues for an openness, without preconceptions of psychological events, so that true science can progress and not delimit the actual events.

Maurice Merleau-Ponty (1908–1961) applied the phenomenological method to a new consideration of the individual in a unique context. For Merleau-Ponty, psychology cannot be treated as an objective science in the same way as the natural sciences, because psychological events are not stimuli, nor are they responses in terms of behavior, reflexes or synaptic exchanges of neurotransmitters. Rather, a psychological event is a dynamic interchange between the organism and environment, involving layers of processing, but having characteristic unity and intention. In this excerpt from *The structure of behavior* (1942), Merleau-Ponty attempts to distinguish psychology from other modes of inquiry.

The final reading of this section is a classic article originally published in 1955 by the American humanistic psychologist, Carl Rogers (1902–1987). In this paper, Rogers offers an American perspective on some of the same issues raised by Merleau-Ponty—namely, the basic definition of psychology and how it should be studied. While many of the specific concerns Rogers raised are no longer central, the basic question of psychology's place in the study of human activity is still a source of intriguing debate. As more contemporary studies move among the neurosciences and the cognitive sciences, psychology's place in the intellectual pursuit of knowledge about human activity is expanded, but still has not earned consensus.

REFERENCES

GIORGI, A. (1970). *Psychology as a human science: A phenomenologically based approach.* New York: Harper & Row, 178–206.

MERLEAU-PONTY, M. (1942, 1963). *The structure of behavior* (A. Fisher, transl.). Boston: Beacon Press, 124–128, 221–228.

ROGERS, C. R. (1955). Person or science? A philosophical question. *American Psychologist, 10*, 267–278.

~ 27 ~

Amedeo Giorgi, Excerpt from *Psychology as a human science: A phenomenologically based approach* (1970).*

SOME CHARACTERISTICS OF THE APPROACH OF PSYCHOLOGY CONCEIVED AS A HUMAN SCIENCE

Where the characteristics are repetitious from earlier discussions, they will simply be stated here. Discussions will deal only with new characteristics. The minimum characteristics of the approach are listed below.

The Privileged Position of Human Scientific Psychology

With respect to privileged position, the life-world is the most basic frame of reference from which psychology must take its point of departure and with which it must be in constant dialogue. Psychology does not remain within the attitude of the life-world. It must develop its own specialized attitude, which also must be clarified, but it begins with life-world phenomena and must dialogue with them constantly so that it is not cut off from its source of raw data.

Origins of Psychological Data

As implied earlier, psychology must return to the phenomenal origins of any psychological process and then move toward closure if it is to be understood adequately. One corollary of this assumption is that psychological phenomena are essentially dynamic and they must be understood in their temporal aspects. A second one is that there must be a constant dialogue among

*"Some Characteristics of the Approach of Psychology Conceived as a Human Science" (pages 178–206) from *Psychology as a Human Science: A phenomenologically based approach* by Amedeo Giorgi. Copyright © 1970 by Amedeo Giorgi. Reprinted by permission of Harper Collins, Publishers, Inc.

the approach, the method and the phenomenon (or content) in any specific research or theoretical project as discussed earlier.

A related presupposition is also raised by this assumption, but it is a difficult one and it will require a lengthy discussion. This is the problem of the terms to be employed to express both the phenomenal origins of a psychological process and the mature phase of the same process, or the point at which sufficient closure has resulted for it to be established as a relevant psychological datum or reality. We propose to use the term "structure" to speak of the phenomenal origins, and for the lack of a better term, we shall use the term "psychological meaning" for the matured phase of the process. By the latter term we simply mean the best way of interpreting and expressing psychological reality. As we have indicated, our position implies that we must come to grips with the meaning of behavior as a uniquely psychological phenomenon.

Far more complicated is the understanding of the term "structure." We adopt Merleau-Ponty's usage of this term. Merleau-Ponty (1963, p. 47) defines structure as follows:

> . . . [structures] are defined as total processes which may be indiscernible from each other while their "parts," compared to each other, differ in absolute size: in other words the systems are defined as transposable wholes. We will say that there is form whenever the properties of a system are modified by every change brought about in a single one of its parts and, on the contrary, are conserved when they all change while maintaining the same relationship among themselves.

Thus, "structure" is a comprehensive term that nevertheless implies an invariant meaning based upon the relationship of discriminable parts. One of its values for us is that it is precisely structure that is the reality that one responds to at the phenomenal level. Merleau-Ponty (1962, 1963) has argued this point convincingly by showing the priority of structure as opposed to either elements, things, objects, ideas, etc. Over time, as one moves toward concretion, i.e., toward objects, things, or ideas, the structural context does not disappear, but rather it is transformed. Thus, there is still *some* context, but the total situation is no longer best described as a basically structural one as understood at the phenomenal level. For psychology, then, one must move from an understanding of a phenomenon in its structural sense to its "psychological meaning," which would seem to be the best type of concretion or closure for psychology. It should be noted that this is a very different kind of progress from beginning with a natural scientific idea of a psychological phenomenon and attempting to move toward a more properly psychological understanding of it.

Merleau-Ponty speaks about the distinction between structure and idea in another passage which may help clarify our point. He (Merleau-Ponty, 1962, p.429) states:

... what constitutes the difference between the Gestalt of a circle and the significance "circle," is that the latter is recognized by an understanding which engenders it as the abode of points equidistant from a center, the former by a subject familiar with his world and able to seize it as a modulation of that world, as a circular physiognomy. We have no way of knowing what a picture or a thing is other than by looking at them, and their significance is revealed only if we look at them ... from a certain *direction*, in short only if we place, at the service of the spectacle, our collusion with the world.

Thus, we can see that the context or frame of reference for significance is far more specifiable than that for structure; it is somewhat like the distinction we reported earlier that Merleau-Ponty makes between world and universe. Universes can be specified far more readily than worlds, but they are ultimately dependent upon and intrinsically related to the life-world. For a proper human scientific psychology, a progress akin to the movement from the life-world to a universe is also necessary. We simply wanted to clarify, however, that one must at least begin with structures if one is to return to the phenomenal level.

Merleau-Ponty has elucidated the meaning of structure in another way that is highly revelant for psychology conceived as a human science. Merleau-Ponty (1963, p. 184) distinguishes three orders of structure, which are not powers of being but what he calls "three dialectics"; they are the physical, the vital, and the human orders. The physical structure is an equilibrium that is achieved with respect to the forces of the milieu; the vital structure is a stability that is achieved for itself by an organism based upon needs and instincts; and the human structure is a third dialectic whereby "signification" is the chief means of achieving stability. Another way that Merleau-Ponty expresses these orders is in terms of the following pairs: for the physical order we have "stimulus-reflex"; for the vital order, "situation-instinctive reaction"; and for the human order there is "perceived situation-work." These three orders are irreducible to each other. If these orders are accepted, and they are by us, then one can see more clearly the difficulties of trying to account for man in terms of stimuli and reflexes, or of even trying to account for him in terms of needs or drives. Rather, the challenge facing a human scientific psychology is that of trying to establish concepts, categories, techniques, and methods that will enable us to work with the dialectic "perceived situation-work." In other words, one of the primary responsibilities of psychology conceived as a human science is that it remain strictly within the human order. Except for some implicit breakthroughs, traditional psychology has not generally worked in this realm nor conceived of its problems in these terms.

Finally, another reason we feel that the term "structure," which emerges precisely because of the concern for origins, is valuable is because of its integrational possibilities. We have especially in mind here the possibility of integrating both the external and internal viewpoints that have caused so much difficulty in psychological history. The value of the concept of approach comes to the fore again because it should be understood that we are speaking about internal and external viewpoints and not methods or contents. In first trying to understand the internal viewpoint adequately, psychologists spoke about "inner contents" and the whole idea that what the self was present to were private data soon became prevalent (although this idea certainly ante-dated the existence of psychology). This idea is so strong that it exists to the present (e.g., Brody and Oppenheim, 1966). However, this idea could not persist so strongly if there were not a confusion between the internal view-point and internal contents.

Similarly, there has been confusion between the internal viewpoint and internal methods. Thus, for example, introspection has consistently been characterized as a method of internal observation. In fact, however, it is assuming an external viewpoint towards oneself. It can be called a "method of inner observation" only if one first believes in "inner contents"; but it really means stating the facts about oneself as any other person would do *if* he could be observing what the introspector happens to be observing. This means that the introspector must ignore his personal viewpoint and his unique proximi-ty to his own experiencing. This is why it can be classified as an external atti-tude or viewpoint toward oneself.

Consequently, it must be emphasized that this value of structure is in the integration of internal and external *viewpoints*. That both viewpoints are nec-essary for the proper growth of psychology is clearly attested to by the history of psychology. The tension concerning the proper subject matter of psychol-ogy has always implied the tension between internal and external view-points—those preferring an internal viewpoint defining psychology as the study of consciousness, and those preferring an external viewpoint defining it as the study of behavior (this does not imply that in all cases either con-sciousness or behavior was properly understood). An examination of the act versus content controversy can serve as an illustration of the necessity of both viewpoints (see Boring, 1950). The act school held that regardless of what the content of a conscious act was, an *act* was necessary to have any content what-soever. Therefore, they defined psychology as essentially being an investiga-tion of the acts of consciousness, or consciousness in general. But what turned out to be embarrassing for this viewpoint were acts whose sources were not conscious, plus various types of habitual behavior. Thus, the total range of top-ics of interest to psychologists could not be subsumed under this viewpoint. The content theorists, on the other hand, stress the fact that regardless of what the act is, a *content* is given to someone and what is important is the rela-tionship between the content and the conditions in which it was produced. Thus, their investigations led to systematic variation of conditions which were held to be more valid because they were in the public realm and easily acces-sible to any observer. However, what is a constant source of difficulty with this viewpoint is the factor of "experimental error" or the variance that accompanies any experimental situation. In addition, it has been demonstrated that one can keep stimuli constant and obtain different responses, or one can vary stimuli and obtain the same response; thus, the subject's response to some extent at least also depends on the subject's viewpoint on the situation. Therefore, in either case, one reaches the limit of the viewpoint without exhausting all the possible topics of interest to psychology. Clearly, then, a complementarity is suggested by these facts. But it is not a case of a simple side-by-side complementarity, but a dialectical one because it will be necessary to have internal and external viewpoints with respect to the "same situation" in some meaning of that term. We feel that the concept of structure of behavior will allow us to do this because Merleau-Ponty's idea of it implies that behavioral structures contain an intrinsic intelligibility—or its parts are internally related—and this type of relation is accessible from an internal viewpoint. On the other hand, behavioral structures are not wholly private phenomena, but on the contrary, they are also visible to the external viewpoint because they are also in the perceptual world. In other words, it is just as difficult to completely hide one's behavior—i.e., to be totally inexpressive—as it is to be completely open about oneself. Thus, by adopting a descriptive approach, Merleau-Ponty unveils behavior as the ambiguous phenomenon that it is, and he implicitly challenges the criteria of full clarity that we have been taught to expect about phenomena, as well as challenging the "either-or" notions of public and private.

In addition, Merleau-Ponty also shows that the whole problem of viewpoints is far from settled. The assumption is often made that an internal viewpoint must refer back to the self, and that an external viewpoint must refer to an other. However, this distinction is too simplistic. It is too simplistic because it presupposes that all viewpoints are limited to being mere passive attitudes. However, in assuming an active stance, which a reflective act is, a subject is able to grasp the meanings of experience or behavior, whether they be his own or another's. In other words, a reflective attitude is neutral with respect to the distinction between internal and external experience (Merleau-Ponty, 1964, p. 65). Moreover, another complication comes in when we consider that the distinction between internal and external is often ambiguous. Does internal or external refer to the attitude, or to the object that is being attended to? If we consider that it is the former, then it should be emphasized that one may take either an internal or an external attitude toward oneself; or an internal or external attitude toward the other. While the proper explanation of this ability may be lacking, the fact that it can be done is an experiential given. Otherwise, the method of introspection would not be possible. Even though it is not a complete explanation, the process seems less mysterious if one remembers that an external viewpoint is really a *highly specialized internal viewpoint* in the sense that it is still the viewpoint of *one*, or a position that that *one* must be capable of assuming. For example, I can approximate the viewpoint that my wife might assume with respect to a certain house, and I have some idea of what the earth must look like from the moon. In both cases the viewpoints are not naturally mine, but I have access to them. In other words, we constantly move from internal to external viewpoints in the course of everyday living; but this also means that an internal viewpoint may not be as inaccessible as it is often assumed to be. This does not mean that we know an internal viewpoint wholly or *exactly as* the other knows it, but as we said above about behavior, it would be just as difficult to know nothing about it.

These are the kinds of problems that the concern for origins initiates. Our position is not so much a concrete solution as the offering of a direction in which certain key problems may receive more precise articulation which ultimately will lead to concrete solutions.

Some Key Presuppositions

There are at least three key presuppositions for psychology conceived as a human science. They are presented below.

Fidelity to the Phenomenon of Man as a Person   We mentioned previously that for any science the priority should be with the relationships among the approach, the method and the content. We still agree with this position, but what we want to emphasize here is that within the context of such a trialogue, a human scientific psychology would stress fidelity to the phenomenon of man as a person. This would be stressed, first of all, to counter any reductionistic tendencies that may be prevalent. This is especially important when operating within a scientific perspective because there is a strong bias in our culture that believes that a human person cannot be studied scientifically. However, the problem usually arises when one simply assumes the current cultural meaning of science as indicating primarily the natural sciences, and then one is left wondering how to fit man as a person into that context. Our aim, however, is to broaden the understanding of science by trying to devise ways in which to study man as a person rigorously and systematically. It is for this reason that fidelity to man as a person is a constant concern. In our understanding of the term, "person" includes all the specifically human characteristics attributed to man in the life-world as well as any other type of behavior that has been recorded and observed whether for good or evil.

Special Concern for Uniquely Human Phenomena   We mentioned earlier that one of the insights from phenomenological philosophy was that all positions were perspectival. If so, what is the special intention guiding our own approach that opens up possibilities that are worth pursuing? More than anything else, we would say that the concern for understanding uniquely human phenomena in a psychologically rigorous and valid way is the prime motivating factor. However, while we began with this intention, our understanding of it has expanded in a way we had not anticipated. That is, while initially we thought that problems of freedom, choice, destiny, death, etc., would be paramount, it became increasingly evident that far more areas than we originally were willing to allow were also relevant. This was one consequence of the introduction of the notion of human order by Merleau-Ponty. If the human order is irreducible, and if it consists of the dialectic "perceived situation-work," then many more processes that could have been considered more or less autonomous, or as belonging to a range of organisms rather than just to man, suddenly also become "uniquely human." Thus, Merleau-Ponty's thought opens up considerably the array of researchable human phenomena.

Nevertheless, as with all perspectives, some possibilities are closed off too. The chief domain that remains untouched by our approach is that of animal psychology. This is not to demean that area: it is simply a matter of recognizing legitimate limits of our approach.

The Primacy of Relationships   The third presupposition we adopt is the primacy of relationships as opposed to seemingly independent units and entities. This is, of course, one of the fundamental insights of phenomenology, and it specifically refers to the primary relation of man and world. In practice this means that one is hard pressed to put a priority on the side of the world conceived independently of man, or on the side of man conceived as existing prior to his engagement in the world. Consequently, whatever phenomenon is considered has to be understood as already involving both man and world. The challenge facing human scientific psychology is the one of realizing this "primacy of relationships" in a concrete way and of being able to express its variables as the "related" variables they de facto are. Of course, there is an awareness of this fact within traditional psychology, but we feel that this notion has to be emphasized even more than it is and it must be formalized in a more systematic way.

A good example of the primacy of relationships is provided by Berger (1963). Berger speaks against the myth that in courtships some irresistible force can strike a person from anywhere and attract him toward "anyone." He points out how sociological investigations reveal "patterns" of courtships and uncover a complex web of motives related in many ways to the entire institutional structure within which an individual lives his life, e.g., class, career, geography, economic ambition, aspirations of power and prestige, etc. In such analyses, the "miracle of love" begins to look very synthetic or fictional. In short, these complex relationships preceded and even guided the awakening of "love" which from the point of view of the individual was an "individual phenomenon arising almost spontaneously from nowhere."

However it is not just with social or cultural phenomena that the importance of relations are being recognized. Rock (1966, p.260), for example, speaking of perception, writes:

> . . . assuming the existence of bounded and shaped things, the relationship of their images to one another corresponds very closely to the relationship of the things themselves to one another in the real world. Thus relative orientation, position and size and the intra-figural or object-relative aspect of shape are all directly given by the relationship of the retinal images of objects to one another.

The fact that relations among objects in the real world are reflected in the relations among their corresponding images provides, in my opinion, one major explanation for the veridicality of perception.

While we do not necessarily agree with all of the expressions in the above paragraph, it does show how there is an increasing awareness of the role of relationships as an explanatory factor. In other words, what Rock is saying is important is not the relation between object and image, but the relation between the relationship among objects and the relationship among images. This also shows that there is a more explicit movement on the part of psychology toward the contextual, a matter we shall discuss shortly. In any event, by beginning our analyses with the concept of structure, we simultaneously presuppose the priority of relations in this sense.

Some Characteristics of the Attitude of Human Scientific Psychology

The attitude toward psychological phenomena will be different in a human-scientific psychology. There are two particular characteristics of the attitude we would like to discuss.

Necessity of a Broadening or Open Attitude   We have already indicated the distinction between a universe of discourse and the world, and how science functions by attempting to delimit the world in such a way that a universe is constituted. Operationally, this task has been simplified by setting up, as one of the restrictions, the analysis of only those events that have been completed, or in other words, of *past* events. When an event is past, it is closed, and even if one cannot know all of the factors determining an event or a phenomenon immediately, one can at least be sure that new factors cannot interfere. Consequently, if one can replicate conditions perhaps one can take closer and closer looks at the phenomenon until its enigmatic aspects disappear, or at least until the investigator is satisfied that he has coped with this phenomenon adequately.

The attitude of closure, or a constant narrowing or zeroing in on a phenomenon, is an attitude that is adequate for trying to understand "past" events or "closed phenomena." However, once a human being is introduced into a phenomenon as a constitutive aspect, a "closing" attitude is no longer adequate; rather, if we are to be able to stick to the primary criterion of our approach, viz., fidelity to the phenomenon, then we shall have to utilize an attitude that is more open, more indeterminate and consisting of gaps as well as "filled" sections. Not so much because these factors are desirable in themselves; but simply because they are *there*, and we want to note what actually happens. But then one may object: is this still science?

Our answer would be that it may not be natural science, but it is the attitude that one must use for a human science, and indeed, such an attitude is incompatible only with the articulate views of existing natural science, but not necessarily against the idea of a human science, if for no other reason than that it has not as yet been articulated. It should be evident to the reader that this is a problem of *approach*, and therefore one that is not ordinarily explicitly articulated within the realm of psychological science. What makes the set of criteria for which we are arguing difficult to reconcile with the idea of science is that the latter is supposed to yield certitude, be a basis for prediction, operate deterministically in the sense of assuming a closed system of causal factors, etc. But these are characteristics of the approach to natural science, and not necessarily science per se. It still remains to be seen what list of characteristics a human science would consist of. An analysis of the human science characteristics *and* those of the natural sciences might yield a deeper and more clarifying view of what science as a whole actually is. However—and this is the main point we wish to establish in this section—it is clear that whatever else is necessary, an attitude that requires an opening up rather than closure, one that allows for future possibilities as well as past facticities, and one that does not foreclose the reality of indeterminacy and ambiguity, will be a necessary point of departure—because, to repeat, the main emphasis is fidelity to the phenomenon as it appears, including processes, and *not* to an idea of science that has been developed in a different context. The essential point is that an "open" or "expansive" attitude should not be judged against the criteria of the approach of the natural sciences, e.g., predictability, certitude, etc. Rather, the key factor to consider is whether or not an "open" attitude can lead to the establishment of "actual happenings" or facts in a rigorous way. It is our assertion that it can and we hope to demonstrate this point in the next section.

The Necessity for an "Engaged" Attitude   We have spoken at length above about how an objective attitude was not really a removal of the presence of a scientist, but rather a special kind of presence. Once that point is clarified the question of whether or not the objective attitude still remains the best possible attitude for all situations can then be raised. Our answer to the question is that it is not, and that for psychology conceived as a human science, a fully engaged attitude is required. By this is meant that if attempts to keep man, as a researcher, out of the situation fail, then perhaps the solution is to put him completely in it. Similarly, instead of trying to have human subjects respond unidimensionally, a better procedure might be to let the subject be completely in the situation. The idea here is to catch man more totally "engaged" rather than being present in more limited ways that are not spontaneously constituted by him. We must learn to delineate an attitude that reflects precisely man's involvement with the world. This necessity applies to both the experimenter and the subject, but in different ways, because their thematic presence is different. The experimenter's engagement is in the pursuit of science, and in specifying situations in such a way that subjects who behave more or less "normally" reveal patterns or styles of living that are presumably typical for those situations. Nevertheless, once the data are obtained, they are organized, interpreted, and written up according to the researcher's view of the situation. The major protection against bias is for the viewpoint itself to be made explicit, so that its validity may be circumscribed. It is not the sheer presence of a bias that vitiates data, it is the extension of limited biases to situations where they are not relevant and thus they lose their fruitfulness. Precisely because man is always in a limited situation, in a perspective, we feel that an engaged attitude which acknowledges such a perspective is a more accurate description than an "objective" one, and thus we feel that a more accurate understanding of why research situations have validity may be achieved.

What should be thematic for subjects of research is that they respond to the situation according to the instructions they are given. However, they too are engaged in the situation, and it would be wrong to think that they could be merely "objectively" present. Any experienced researcher knows that instructions can be interpreted in a number of ways, and this means that it is the subjects who actually complete the constitution of a research situation. In other words, they are engaged. If this is actually what takes place, then it must be described and understood as such.

Thus, we have a researcher who is engaged in the project of pursuing scientific psychology, partially constituting a situation that he believes will help clarify his understanding of a certain psychological phenomenon coming together with other persons (subjects) who also partially constitute the situation and who are engaged in the project of responding to certain instructions in what they believe to be typical ways. Any research situation in psychology is always a place where the engaged projects of two different attitudes intersect, even if it is only one subject responding to a stimulus. If we keep in mind what we have said about the primacy of relations and the necessity of contexts, it becomes apparent that the change in terminology is not just a semantic difference, but one that points to a more accurate description of a research situation in psychology. Anything that will throw light on the "projects" of the two attitudes, or on their respective theories, will help in understanding the situation better. That is why the notion of engagement is potentially so valuable. Moreover, the above description once again points out that psychology is essentially an intersubjective science.

The Subject Matter of Psychology Conceived as a Human Science

In this section we shall try to clarify more sharply what we conceive to be the subject matter of human scientific psychology. We shall do this by discussing attitudinal differences and then by trying to clarify the phenomena of experience and behavior.

Human Scientific Psychology: The Discovery of the Actual in Order to Learn the Contextual   Within the perspective of psychology conceived as a human science, the main concern is to discover the actual, by means of description, in order to learn about the structure of the situation as a whole, which is done by revealing the context. The full psychological meaning of the event is also uncovered by this process. This approach emphasizes the youthfulness of psychology, where there are still so many relevant findings to be discovered, as opposed to the emphasis in the natural sciences whereby, because of their maturity, they are able to "create" their data (Mead, 1964) by structuring a situation and then observing if their *ideas* about a phenomenon or theory are correct. The natural sciences are mature enough to have many specific and precise ideas about their experiments; but with human scientific psychology the researcher has only some vague anticipations or expectations about what to observe, and his attitude must remain more open-ended and general, and his precision is directed toward a description of the actual occurrence rather than to any kind of treatment of the actual. Thus, the difference in emphasis we are articulating is that, because of its subject matter, human scientific psychology remains open to the emergence of the *actual* and tries to capture it as faithfully as possible so that *ideas* of it may be formed. In the natural sciences, the research paradigm is mostly (but not exclusively) one where a researcher tries to test his *idea* of the phenomenon. This is another reason why direct imitation of contemporary natural sciences is an erroneous procedure, because for the most part they are at a more developed phase of their history. Psychology might even be better off trying to imitate the *beginnings* of the natural sciences; but curiously enough, that would involve an historical analysis which would once again put us in the realm of the human sciences.

The above discussion concerned a difference in emphasis, but now we want to speak about an essential difference between human scientific psychology and the natural scientific approach. In the natural scientific approach, methodologically speaking, once a unit or a whole is established the analytic process is then usually applied, which means that the whole is broken down into elements or parts and then the whole is understood in terms of this analysis. In a human scientific approach, we are suggesting that once the unit or whole is established it is then conceived to be merely a constituent of a larger-structured context, and through the process of explicitation (Giorgi, 1966) precisely how the constituent under consideration is related to the whole becomes known and its meaning can be ascertained. In other words, in this perspective the discovery of the actual (understood as what is present, but not necessarily limited to its physical aspects) is the point of departure for uncovering relationships, contexts, and meaning. This is necessary because the latter types of information are far more valuable for the human sciences than mere facts, physical dimensions, or quantitative expressions. While the exact procedures used in the process of explicitation can still undergo further clarification, our position is that they can be applied as rigorously, in principle, as any analytic procedures.

An example of the application of this method is provided by Colaizzi (1967) who was interested in discovering how nonsense syllables changed in their appearance during the course of learning. Consequently he interrupted subjects during their learning at various phases of the process in order to obtain descriptions of their experience. One interruption took place after a single exposure of the ten syllables and we shall concentrate on this phase to demonstrate our point. First of all, the fact emerged that not one subject was able to repeat a single syllable correctly, although he was asked to do so. Secondly, if one were to ask about the facts that were discovered, one would find a seemingly uncorrelated array: some subjects spoke about the apparatus, some mentioned the instructions, some talked about the experimenter, some spoke about the shock of being interrupted, some mentioned unfamiliar items or letters, etc. These were the facts that the descriptions produced. With the method of explicitation one tries to understand the actual context within which the facts emerge. Consequently one continually studies the protocols in order to see what is common or typical about the context that would permit precisely these facts to appear. One looks for the meaning that relates these specific facts to the context, as parts to a whole, that would render them all intelligible. Colaizzi concluded that awareness of the learning *situation* is the functional or lived contextual unity that co-relates the seemingly disparate facts that emerge after the experience with a single learning trial. Thus, while subjects reported different facts—the experimenter, the apparatus, unfamiliarity—the reason that these particular facts were able to emerge was that they were related in a functionally significant way (i.e., meaningfully) to the experience of the situation as the initial phase of a learning process. Thus, more accurately, one could say that the subjects experienced "the-apparatus-as-*part*-of-the-learning-situation," or "the-unfamiliarity-as-*part*-of-the-learning-situation," etc., rather than merely the apparatus or unfamiliarity as such. At this phase of the process the *context itself is experientially figural* even though *parts* of it serve as the vehicle of expression. Moreover, it should not be forgotten that the items themselves were what were sought, and eventually do emerge, at the end of the process. Descriptions reported from different phases of the process reveal different facts, contexts and meanings that can be ascertained in the same manner.

The above example of explicitation may clarify the notion somewhat, but it probably will not silence all questions. Colleagues will surely ask about its validity, reliability, objectivity, etc. At this stage of our experience with this method, we can only reply with the following comments: (1) Undoubtedly, we admit that the method can stand further clarification, articulation, and refinement. (2) One must be careful not merely to superimpose the criteria of the natural scientific approach on this method. It is more a matter of discovering its own internal criteria. (3) We can point to the fact that this method *does* work even though we cannot as yet fully state *why* it works. But this is very often the case in science; certain things work and just why they do is something that emerges only after years of experience with the technique. The real difference is that this method does not *look scientific* according to the expectations of the natural scientific approach. That is why we feel that it is important to overcome this prejudice and allow the development of methods that look different, as they should, when different phenomena are being studied and different questions are being asked. All of this implies a different outlook on science and this in turn explains why we insist on the relevance of the approach. In any event, we are not claiming that human scientific procedures are already in existence and ready for use, but only that they are possible.

The Delineation of Experience and Behavior   One of the major tasks still confronting psychology, and this includes human scientific psychology, is the proper understanding of experience, of behavior and of the relationship between the two. Our position is that a structural approach offers a good possibility for such an understanding, although whether or not it will ultimately be the most fruitful approach will of course depend upon how well it fares. At any rate, a structural approach makes possible the study of experiential-behavioral dialectics, which for us is the subject matter of psychology, from a unified point of departure (Giorgi, 1967). Many other psychologists have stated that both experience and behavior are necessary for psychology, but very frequently this is understood in a side-by-side manner. That is, familiar objective techniques are used for studying behavior, and familiar introspective methods are used for the study of experience. The difficulty is that both methods already imply a disruption of experience and behavior; they have developed from viewpoints that considered either behavior or experience as self-enclosed entities. It is our position that behavior and experience are related in an intrinsic way that has not as yet been fully captured.

The way we would propose to attempt this—and we admit that this is still only an attempt—is by trying to understand the experiential-behavioral dialectics in terms of a more comprehensive concept such as structure or situation. As implied above, heretofore one tried to center on either experience *or* behavior, but by making either one figural, the other was implicitly cut off and then one could relate them only externally. Our position is that behavior and experience are best understood in terms of internal relationships.

We will again draw upon a phenomenological perspective to help us formulate the problem. Van Kaam (1966) has spoken of understanding behavior in terms of intentional-functional relations and Gurwitsch (1964) has restressed the presentational function of consciousness or experience. We propose to utilize these ideas to come up with a framework for understanding the experiential-behavioral dialectics. Our proposal is that these dialectics can be understood by considering them in terms of the following pair of relations: (a) intentional functional-fulfilling relations, and (b) intentional-presentational fulfilling relations. First, a general comment about the relations themselves is in order. We interpret these to be internal relations, i.e., intrinsic ones that are discovered over time by a process of unfolding or development. Moreover, both sets of relations occur simultaneously in an even larger context than we are considering, so in that sense, there are limits to the usefulness of these relations in understanding human behavior and experience, but the precise limits cannot be known until much more experience in their application is accumulated. Lastly, we have used a more comprehensive set of relations precisely because of our concern for contexts and the primacy of relations. For example, in the history of psychology, there have always been functional schools and structural schools, but they have always been defined too narrowly. Functionalism usually means stressing the functions or activities of organisms, but then these functions were always related to experience or the world in an external way. Similarly, structural schools usually stressed the invariant features of content, but then tried to relate these contents back to the organism or to the conditions of research in an external way. That is why the approach adopted is so important; it helps to establish the fact that the *way* in which one views phenomena is what is so important. In this context it is precisely the internal viewpoint that has been misunderstood so often.

Hence, van Kaam's idea that behavior should be understood in terms of intentional-functional relations is an important breakthrough, but we feel he stopped short. It is not only the sources (intentions) of behavior that must be understood in terms of internal relations, but also their consequences (fulfillments, implying also their lack). However, a human person is so complex that it is difficult to comprehend him solely in terms of one set of relations. Thus, capitalizing upon Gurwitsch's reemphasis on the presentational function of consciousness, and also recognizing that it, too, has sources and consequences (obviously Gurwitsch does too but he does not express it in this way), then we can also try to understand man in terms of intentional-presentational-fulfilling relationships.

It should not be forgotten that these analyses are always performed within the context of a more comprehensive structure or situation. This point is essential because it is the only way in which the unity of experiential-behavioral dialectics can be understood. In other words, it is not the same situation seen *first* experientially and *then* behaviorally; rather, it is one situation *containing* experiential and behavioral *aspects*. Experience and behavior are not sheer substitutes for each other, one known to the actor and the other to the observer. The problem is more complicated because experience and behavior literally reveal different aspects of a given situation *at the same time that they overlap* each other. They are different kinds of "openings" to a situation that neither exist merely "side-by-side" nor are reducible to each other. The internal viewpoint (actor) is the *privileged position* for unveiling experience, and the external viewpoint (observer) is the *privileged position* for access to behavior, but neither the internal viewpoint nor the external viewpoint is limited *exclu-

sively to either experience or behavior. Both viewpoints have access to both phenomena, but not equally so. Consequently, once one adopts a structural or situational viewpoint, one sees that the experiential-behavioral relation is a unified action on or response to a situation that is complementary precisely because different aspects of the situation are revealed by either side of the relation. This is the real danger of trying to reduce one to the other; it inevitably reduces the situation and the phenomenon under investigation. Thus, it is necessary to adopt attitudes that will comprehend the entire situation (and this process overcomes the problem of the two sciences of psychology because one is still bound by the *unity* of the situation or structure), and then within that attitude intentional-presentational-fulfillment relations will help to clarify the internal viewpoint and the experiential aspects, and intentional-functional-fulfilling relations will help to clarify the external viewpoint and the behavioral aspects of the situation.

Still another point implicit in all these discussions should be made explicit, otherwise some of the value of enlarging the horizons in the way we have suggested may be lost. It is most important to realize that from a human scientific perspective the "actual" or the real cannot be reduced to physical presence. However we ultimately come to understand the presence of contexts or relationships, it is clear that they are experientially given and not in a physical sense. Once again we would follow Merleau-Ponty (1968) here, this time in the direction that his notions of the visible and the invisible suggest. Merleau-Ponty points out how man, as embodied subjectivity, is the perceivable perceiver, the touchable toucher, the sensible sensor; and he generalizes this under the notion of the visible and the invisible. The point is that the real consists precisely of a dialectic between these two and not of just one half. Moreover, that which is visible is not understood in precisely the same way as the one who is doing the seeing, and vice versa. In other words, phenomena are constituted by both halves of this dialectic, and it is only because of empiricistic and positivistic biases that we are surprised to discover that the real consists of more than just the sensory or physical. Applied to the discussion at hand, we would say that from an external viewpoint, experience is the invisible aspect of a situation in which the behavior is visible; and that from an internal viewpoint, behavior is the invisible aspect of a situation in which the experience is the visible. However, these should not be conceived as dichotomous or in an all-or-none sense. As implied before, we affirm that the internal viewpoint is the privileged position for access to experience and that an external viewpoint is the privileged position for access to behavior, but that these are not exclusive. Merleau-Ponty also holds not only that the two perspectives of visible and invisible are not exclusive, but that they do imply each other, and overlap, and "encroach" upon one another. They meet within the lived-body, and it is difficult to tell where one leaves off and the other picks up. We would say the same about experience and behavior. They intersect within the lived-body, and without the latter notion—a valuable contribution of Merleau-Ponty—it would indeed be difficult to locate the point where behavior and experience intersect.

Psychology's Subject Matter Requires a New Concept of Nature   We mentioned earlier that in speaking of consciousness, experience, or behavior, intentional relations are always involved, and thus trying to understand these phenomena within a cause-effect paradigm or in terms of external relations (or, in short, with a strictly naturalistic viewpoint) is not an adequate approach for psychology conceived as a human science. Insofar as the natural scientific approach in its theoretical formulations explicitly, and in its praxis almost exclusively (there are some implicit deviations), considers man as *part of the world*, it studies him without reference to his intentional relations to the world. But man is also one *for whom the world exists* and this side of him hardly ever receives explicit reference within the natural scientific viewpoint. Psychology as a human science especially wishes to do justice to the latter aspect—not to detract from the former, but to integrate it.

Perhaps the difference between our approach and the natural scientific approach can best be understood in these terms. We follow Merleau-Ponty's (1963) line of reasoning here. It is not that the natural scientific approach to psychology yields nothing or deals with phenomena that are nonexistent. Rather, it deals with the behavior of man at levels that are lower than his most integrated functioning. Most of its theories, concepts, hypotheses, definitions, etc., are derived from or refer to the vital level of integration and not yet to a more properly human structural level. Many of these phenomena are found with pathological cases or with traditional laboratory studies, both of which, for different reasons, allow only a reduced level of functioning to appear (Merleau-Ponty, 1963). The difficulties in communication between the two viewpoints is perhaps greatest just at this point. Because the human scientific viewpoint is holistic it asserts that when one is interested in studying man at his highest level of functioning, at the level of the unequivocally human, then facts obtained at lower levels of functioning are not necessarily relevant as such. They may or may not be, depending upon the extent to which a human context was implicitly present. Natural scientific psychologists often interpret this attitude as a mere dismissal of their data; human scientific psychologists, however, intend to communicate caution because they realize that crossing contexts uncritically can be just as misleading as comparing data when methods differ. We feel that the caution is justified because it is not merely a matter of adding up such facts in order to build a human order, nor is it simply a matter of interpreting the "same" facts differently; it is literally a matter of trying to determine what the relevant facts at the human level would be. Thus, to integrate the "naturalistic" aspects of man literally means a transformation of them. On the other hand, when such "naturalistic" behaviors appear, one can also assume that the person to whom they belong is not behaving in the most integrated fashion possible vis-à-vis his particular situation. This is why we must learn to conceive of research situations in such a way that the higher levels of functioning are given at least an equal chance of appearing. Only in this way will facts concerning them be discovered and understood.

The above comments lead to a direct confrontation with the problem of the meaning of nature. We do not intend to resolve this complex issue here, but we feel that some minimal clarification is in order. Because of the aim of the human sciences to study systematically the human level as it is lived, and the fact that man is also a creature for whom the world exists, the natural scientific conception of nature is not adequate. Within the latter perspective Cartesian influences are dominant, and nature came to be defined in opposition to consciousness and vice versa. Thus, as Merleau-Ponty (1963) states, nature came to mean the reference to a multiplicity of events external to each other and bound together by relations of causality. To the extent that psychology has attempted to be a natural science, it has remained faithful to realism and to causal thinking (Merleau-Ponty, 1963), and our own analyses have indicated how often psychology has expressed such an ideal.

However, Merleau-Ponty (1963, p. 3) himself does not accept this definition of nature, but because many practitioners of science are often guided by such a concept, he wishes to bring its meaning to the level of explicit awareness, in order to show how theories of nature must be brought into better harmony with the facts. The long history of success in the natural sciences has made most of us uncritical with respect to all of its aspects, and thus many provisional conceptual formulations of science are often accepted as absolute ones. Thus it is not surprising that the natural scientific understanding of nature was almost universally accepted. Due to the prevalence of this conception of nature, then, one must either state that man is in part nonnatural in order to comprehend him adequately, or the concept of nature itself must be broadened so that *all* aspects of *human* nature can be included. Either choice is fraught with difficulties, but we prefer the latter alternative. In either case, however, the natural scientific conception of nature is not adequate for the phenomenon of man as a person. Primarily this is because it was conceived too narrowly, and because it neglects to take into account the complex relationships that the phenomenon of consciousness introduces. The last statement, of course, presupposes that the study of man can be undertaken without necessarily assuming the historical dichotomy between consciousness and nature understood in its more narrow sense.

It is also important to realize that one does not have to leave the realm of science in order to try to understand the complexities that consciousness introduces, or the fact that the world also exists for man: one must simply go beyond the realm of the sciences of nature as they have been traditionally understood. In other words, the *aim* of the human sciences is similar to the *aim* of the natural sciences, namely, to observe, describe, and try to render intelligible all of the phenomena that man experiences or is capable of experiencing. But the implementation of human scientific psychology must differ because the way human phenomena reveal themselves also differs; the way man relates to the phenomena of the physical world and the way he relates to, *and is related to by,* the phenomenon of man, is radically different in the life-world. It is this difference that we take seriously and try to systematize into a scientific viewpoint. It is possible to achieve this scientific ambition because we must remember that seeing the phenomena of the world in terms of cause-effect relations, in an objective way or in thing-like categories, is ultimately due to a certain *attitude* toward the world (Kockelmans, 1965); and in order to see human phenomena in terms of intentional relations or in terms of a human category system, one must also assume a certain *attitude* toward those phenomena, but not the same attitude in both cases. All that is necessary is that science admit more than a single attitude into its domain, and this it already does. It seems to us that what should characterize a scientific perspective is the relevancy and the fruitfulness of the attitude that science assumes with respect to a group of phenomena, and the rigor with which it is applied, but not the absolutization of a single attitude or of a single technique for being rigorous. One would be more conscious of these distinctions if more attention were paid to the role of approach in science.

One can certainly understand the desire of natural scientific psychology to attempt to place the totality of phenomena within one unified perspective or under one concept. Such a unity is the constant striving of man be he scientist, philosopher, poet, or mystic. Our objection is not to the intention so much as to the specific concept or perspective that purports to be all-encompassing. We feel that the specific conception of nature being offered as the basis for unity is too narrow, too one-sided, and unduly influenced by the perspective of the natural sciences. As we indicated above, we also feel that the very understanding of science itself has been too closely associated with the praxis of the natural sciences. That is why our own approach is more open-ended—why we would argue for a broadened conception of nature, so that inputs from different perspectives could be readily assimilated. Precisely because we do not know the exact meaning of nature, it is for us still a problem to be solved, rather than an answer to be defended. We do know, however, that the answer to the meaning of nature being offered by the natural scientific perspective would exclude many legitimate psychological phenomena, and that is too heavy a price. Because of our insistence that the life-world is the ground for science, and especially the source of its raw data, we turn the problem around. We assert that the proper investigation of many concrete psychological problems, if they are formulated precisely as they reveal themselves, will put increasing pressure on established psychological concepts and theories to cope with them. The result of this confrontation between the concrete problems and the established theories, we believe, will be the broadening of the theories, including their concept of nature.

To say that our approach is open-ended also means that we have no specific commitments as to what the answer to the problem of nature should be. If the study of all of the phenomena that man can experience demonstrates that they are all of one nature, and can be subsumed under one concept yet to be defined, that is agreeable to us. If, on the other hand, the above described phenomena can only be understood by positing multiple natures, then that is also agreeable. The only alternative we would not permit is the achievement of unity at the price of the exclusion of some phenomena for whatever reason. The discovery of phenomena that upset man's categorical systems have more often than not proved to be rewarding for man. Hence, we argue for the broadening of concepts rather than the delimiting of phenomena.

One last point. While we have been mostly arguing against a natural scientific approach in this section, these arguments should not be interpreted as arguments for an opposite mentalistic position. As with Merleau-Ponty (1968), we do not wish to choose sides with respect to the classical antinomies, but we prefer to emphasize the embodied human person in the most comprehensive sense, so that a means of integrating the truths of "naturalism" and "mentalism" may be found in a way that goes beyond the excesses of either.

The Inevitable Presence of the Scientist in the Constitution of Science

This notion has been discussed at length but there are two more implications we would like to emphasize.

The Context for Investigating Man as a Person Cannot be Less Than the Context for Understanding Man the Investigator This is an extremely significant point that is often neglected—partly because it is not as problematic within the context of the natural sciences, partly because it is recognized in theoretical discussions but not necessarily carried through in practice, and partly because it can be justified by claiming that science must limit in order to function. Obviously, we agree with the latter principle; the only question at issue is the type of limits that are set. The point at issue is that man as subject of research can in no way have assumptions attributed to him that one would deny to man as researcher. Stated positively, one would have to assert of man as subject of research all the assumptions and attributes that one holds concerning man the researcher. And even more importantly, one would have to *conduct* research within the context of these assumptions. Probably many psychologists would object that the imposition of such demands would make research in psychology impossible, or they would try to argue that such demands are unnecessary because there is obviously a lot of successful research currently being conducted outside the context we recommend. However, we must remember that such objections come from within the context of the natural scientific approach, and the assumptions that are valid in that context do not hold within our perspective. Unfortunately, one of the major difficulties of conceiving psychology as a human science is that it is simultaneously the problem of conceiving of the proper functioning of the human sciences themselves. In other words, there are few precedents to go by, and because of this, many of the notions that are introduced seem to be "far out" or absurd, but we feel that they can only be competently judged by criteria that have yet to be devised, and certainly not by the present standard criteria.

In any event, we would posit that the investigator and the subject are equals with respect to basic assumptions about their humanity. What does differ, as we explained before, is their *thematic presence* in a situation. This is true whether one is speaking of an experimental situation or a therapeutic one. This way of describing psychological situations once again reveals the radical intersubjectivity of psychology conceived as a human science.

A Non-Manipulative Paradigm is Necessary   This is a direct implication of the above point. Understanding human psychological research in terms of cause-effect analyses or in terms of "a function of x variables," etc., will no longer be desirable. The relationship between experimenter and researcher will have to be based upon appeal and cooperation and understood in that sense as well. Moreover, research designs will always have to be open-ended so that the final closure can be made by the subject himself. When the closure is accomplished, data are obtained, but now they are obtained from a perspective that includes the subject's more spontaneous participation. In short, if one truly believes that humans should not manipulate other humans, then it seems to be absurd to try to build a human science on the basis of a paradigm that violates this essential point. Obviously here we are referring only to the direct or indirect manipulation of other humans and not to the manipulation of the physical environment.

IMPLICATIONS OF THE CHARACTERISTICS OF HUMAN SCIENTIFIC PSYCHOLOGY FOR ITS PARADIGM

In this section we will merely try to articulate a direction rather than come up with definitive answers. Earlier we characterized the approach to natural scientific psychology as being empirical, positivistic, reductionistic, objective, analytic, quantitative, deterministic, concerned with prediction and largely operating within the genetic bias and with the assumption of an independent observer. All of these factors have operated in such a way that the paradigm of natural scientific psychology was structured primarily to ask a measurement question and to reveal the quantitative dimensions of reality. It also favored a paradigm that sought specificity and explanations that were within the context of cause-effect relations. This, in turn, has led to designs that favor isolation of variables with the assumption of a constant relation between specific variables and the conditions of the experiment, but this constancy is understood as being due to external relations between man and the world.

From what we have said thus far, it is readily apparent that the paradigm for conducting research within the context of psychology conceived as a human science will be very different. The approach of the human sciences may be characterized as being concerned with meaning, description, qualitative differences, the process of explicitation, investigating intentional relations, dealing with human phenomena in a human sense and in a human way, articulating the phenomena of consciousness and behavior within the context of a broadened conception of nature, and assuming the privileged position of the life-world, the primacy of relations and the presence of an involved scientist. These characteristics will have to lead to a paradigm that is far more dialectical than the traditional paradigm, one in which the implications of every decision that the researcher makes will have to be pursued and one in which the precise meaning of the researcher's presence will have to be ascertained. It implies a paradigm that must be far more open-ended than the traditional paradigm, and one that will allow the presence of indeterminateness and generalities because such phenomena exist in research situations. It will be more open-ended also because subjects are seen as co-constituting the closure of the paradigm with the meanings *they* bring to the situation. Consequently, because of the last two reasons, precisely what variables were operating in the experiment or research situation can be ascertained only *after* the research is completed—not before. This fact clearly indicates that while a human scientific psychology is not empiricistic or positivistic, it is *empirical* (based on experience) and *positive* (it affirms a reality). This is also why we feel we can include this project within the context of a science, because it is the aim of science to be faithful to experience and to unravel the mysteries of the world. The only problem with empiricism and positivism is that these philosophies defined experience and the real too narrowly, and by means of certain *ideas* of experience and the real which brought closure too rapidly. Consequently, this is why we argue that the approach is absolutely vital, and why an approach must be characterized as including the vague, the general, and the indeterminate. First of all, existentially speaking, they are *there*. Secondly, as Merleau-Ponty (1962) asserts, they are positive phenomena. We must not see them as merely the lack of specificity, but as contexts and horizons that give the specific objects, things, and ideas their meaning. Lastly, the difficulty is not so much with experience and the real, as with our formulated ideas of them. Thus our ideas of these phenomena must change, and this can only be done by turning away momentarily (bracketing from the established ideas, then by trying to be present to experiences and the real in a fresh way, and only then trying to formulate more accurate ideas about them. Only after the newer ideas have emerged can they be compared to the older ones. But all of the above implies an openness for new attitudes and a tolerance for new styles of thinking—especially when they are in their beginning phases.

The last sentence might be interpreted as a plea, and perhaps it is. Undoubtedly, to argue for a new paradigm means that one is essentially dissatisfied with the existing one. It also means that many supporters of the older paradigm will have to disagree with the newer one if only for the simple reason that the existing paradigm is for them fruitful. Our only concern is that the suggested new paradigm be judged according to intrinsic criteria rather than in terms of the criteria of the older paradigm. Thus, it would be wrong to state that the new paradigm we suggest is erroneous because it violates the principle of determinism. It is precisely the principle of determinism applied to human phenomena that helped to create the need for a new paradigm. This is why the concept of approach had to be introduced. In a sense, it deals with the whole problem of the criteria of criteria, which cannot be irrelevant for the conduct of science. Still, there will be problems in trying to establish the idea of a human science in general, and we would like to speak to some of these problems in the next section.

28

Maurice Merleau-Ponty, Excerpts from *The structure of behavior* (1942).*

The preceding chapters teach us only not to explain the higher by the lower, as they say, but also not to explain the lower by the higher. Traditionally, lower or mechanical reactions which, like physical events, are functions of antecedent conditions and thus unfold in objective time and space are distinguished from "higher" reactions which do not depend on stimuli, taken materially, but rather on the meaning of the situation, and which appear therefore to presuppose a "view" of this situation, a prospection, and to belong no longer to the order of the in-itself (*en soi*) but to the order of the for-itself (*pour soi*). Both of these orders are transparent for the mind: the first is transparent for the mode of thinking in physics and is like the external order in which events govern each other from the outside; the second is transparent for reflective consciousness and is like the internal order in which that which takes place always depends upon an intention. *Behavior,* inasmuch as it has a structure, is not situated in either of these two orders. It does not unfold in objective time and space like a series of physical events; each moment does not occupy one and only one point of time; rather, at the decisive moment of learning, a "now" stands out from the series of "nows," acquires a particular value and summarizes the groupings which have preceded it as it engages and anticipates the future of the behavior; this "now" transforms the singular situation of the experience into a typical situation and the effective reaction into an aptitude. From this moment on behavior is detached from the order of the in-itself (*en soi*) and becomes the projection outside the organism of a *possibility* which is internal to it. The world, inasmuch as it harbors living beings,

*Merleau-Ponty, M. (1942, 1963). Excerpts from *The structure of behavior* (A. Fisher, translator). Boston: Beacon Press, 124-128, 221-228. Reprinted by permission of Duquesne University Press.

ceases to be a material plenum consisting of juxtaposed parts; it opens up at the place where behavior appears.

Nothing would be served by saying that it is we, the spectators, who mentally unite the elements of the situation to which behavior is addressed in order to make them meaningful, that it is we who project into the exterior the intentions of our thinking, since we would still have to discover what it is, what kind of phenomenon is involved upon which this *Einfühlung* rests, what is the sign which invites us to anthropomorphism. Nor would anything be served by saying that behavior "is conscious" and that it reveals to us, as its other side, a being for-itself (*pour soi*) hidden behind the visible body. The gestures of behavior, the intentions which it traces in the space around the animal, are not directed to the true world or pure being, but to being-for-the-animal, that is, to a certain milieu characteristic of the species; they do not allow the showing through of a consciousness, that is, a being whose whole essence is to know, but rather a certain manner of treating the world, of "being-in-the-world" or of "existing." A consciousness, according to Hegel's expression, is a "penetration in being," and here we have nothing yet but an opening up. The chimpanzee, which physically can stand upright but in all urgent cases reassumes the animal posture, which can assemble boxes but gives them only a tactile equilibrium, in this way manifests a sort of adherence to the here and now, a short and heavy manner of existing. Gelb and Goldstein's patient, who no longer has the "intuition" of numbers, no longer "understands" analogies and no longer "perceives" simultaneous wholes, betrays a weakness, a lack of density and vital amplitude, of which the cognitive disorders are only the secondary expression. It is only at the level of symbolic conduct, and more exactly at the level of exchanged speech, that foreign existences (at the same time as our own, moreover) appear to us as ordered to the true world; it is only at this level that, instead of seeking to insinuate his stubborn norms, the subject of behavior "de-realizes himself" and becomes a genuine *alter ego*. And yet the constitution of the other person as another I is never completed since his utterance, even having become a pure phenomenon of expression, always and indivisibly remains expressive as much of himself as of the truth.

There is, then, no behavior which certifies a pure consciousness behind it, and the other person is never given to me as the exact equivalent of myself thinking. In this sense it is not only to animals that consciousness must be denied. The supposition of a *foreign consciousness* immediately reduces the world which is given to me to the status of a private spectacle; the world is broken up into a multiplicity of "representations of the world" and can no longer be anything but the meaning which they have in common, or the invariant of a system of monads. But in fact I am aware of perceiving the world as well as behavior which, caught in it, intends numerically one and the same world, which is to say that, in the experience of behavior, I effectively surpass the alternative of the for-itself (*pour soi*) and the in-itself (*en soi*). Behaviorism, solipsism, and "projective" theories all accept that behavior is given to me like something spread out in front of me. But to reject consciousness in animals in the sense of pure consciousness, the *cogitatio*, is not to make them automatons without interiority. The animal, to an extent which varies according to the integration of its behavior, is certainly *another existence*; this existence is perceived by everybody; we have described it; and it is a phenomenon which is independent of any notional theory concerning the soul of brutes. Spinoza would not have spent so much time considering a drowning fly if this behavior had not offered to the eye something other than a fragmant of extension; the theory of animal machines is a "resistance" to the phenomenon of behavior. Therefore this phenomenon must still be conceptualized. The structure of behavior as it presents itself to perceptual experience is neither thing nor consciousness; and it is this which renders it opaque to the mind.

The object of the preceding chapters was not only to establish that behavior is irreducible to its alleged parts. If we had had nothing other in view, instead of this long inductive research—which can never be finished, since behaviorism can always invent other mechanical models with regard to which the discussion will have to be recommenced—a moment of reflection would have provided us with a certitude in principle. Does not the *cogito* teach us once and for all that we would have no knowledge of any *thing* if we did not first have a knowledge of our thinking and that even the escape into the world and the resolution to ignore interiority or to never leave things, which is the essential feature of behaviorism, cannot be formulated without being transformed into consciousness and without presupposing existence for-itself (*pour soi*)? Thus behavior is constituted of relations; that is, it is conceptualized and not in-itself (*en soi*), as is every other object moreover; this is what reflection would have shown us. But by following this short route we would have missed the essential feature of the phenomenon, the paradox which is constitutive of it: behavior is not a thing, but neither is it an idea. It is not the envelope of a pure consciousness and, as the witness of behavior, I am not a pure consciousness. It is precisely this which we wanted to say in stating that behavior is a form.

Thus, with the notion of "form," we have found the means of avoiding the classical antitheses in the analysis of the "central sector" of behavior as well as in that of its visible manifestations. More generally, this notion saves us from the alternative of a philosophy which juxtaposes externally associated terms and of another philosophy which discovers relations which are intrinsic to thought in all phenomena. But precisely for this reason the notion of form is ambiguous. Up until now it has been introduced by physical examples and defined by characteristics which made it appropriate for resolving problems of psychology and physiology. Now this notion must be understood in itself, without which the philosophical significance of what precedes would remain equivocal.

Yet until now we have considered only the perspectivism of true perception. Instances in which lived experience appears clothed with a signification which breaks apart, so to speak, in the course of subsequent experience and is not verified by concordant syntheses would still have to be analyzed. We have not accepted the causal explanation which naturalism provides in order to account for this subjectivity in the second degree. What is called bodily, psychological or social determinism in hallucination and error has appeared to us to be reducible to the emergence of imperfect dialectics, of partial structures. But why, *in existendo,* does such a dialectic at the organic-vegetative level break up a more integrated dialectic, as happens in hallucination? Consciousness is not only and not always consciousness of truth; how are we to understand the inertia and the resistance of the inferior dialectics which stand in the way of the advent of the pure relations of impersonal subject and true object and which affect my knowledge with a coefficient of subjectivity? How are we to understand the adherence of a fallacious signification to the lived, which is constitutive of illusion?

We have rejected Freud's causal categories and replaced his energic metaphors with structural metaphors. But although the complex is not a thing outside of consciousness which would produce its effects in it, although it is only a structure of consciousness, at least this structure tends as it were to conserve itself. It has been said that what is called unconsciousness[58] is only an inapperceived signification: it may happen that we ourselves do not grasp the true meaning of our life, not because an unconscious personality is deep within us and governs our actions, but because we understand our lived states only through an idea which is not adequate for them.

But even unknown to us, the efficacious law of our life is constituted by its true signification. Everything happens as if this signification directed the flux of mental events. Thus it will be necessary to distinguish their ideal signification, which can be true or false, and their immanent signification, or—to employ a clearer language which we will use from now on—their ideal *signification* and their actual *structure.* Correlatively, it will be necessary to distinguish in development an ideal liberation, on the one hand, which does not transform us in our being and changes only the consciousness which we have of ourselves, and on the other, a real liberation which is the *Umgestaltung* of which we spoke, along with Goldstein. We are not reducible to the ideal consciousness which we have of ourselves any more than the existent thing is reducible to the signification by which we express it.

It is easy to argue in the same way, in opposition to the sociologist, that the structures of consciousness which he relates to a certain economic structure are in reality the consciousness of certain structures. This argument hints at a liberty very close to mind, capable by reflection of grasping itself as spontaneous source, and naturizing from below the contingent forms with which it has clothed itself in a certain milieu. Like Freud's complex, the economic structure is only one of the objects of a transcendental consciousness. But "transcendental consciousness," the full consciousness of self, is not ready made; it is to be achieved, that is, realized in existence. In opposition to

Durkheim's "collective consciousness" and his attempts at sociological explanation of knowledge, it is rightly argued that consciousness cannot be treated
as an effect since it is that which constitutes the relation of cause and effect.
But beyond a causal thinking which can be all too easily challenged, there is
a truth of sociologism. Collective consciousness does not produce categories,
but neither can one say that collective representations are only the objects of
a consciousness which is always free in their regard, only the consciousness in
a "we" of an object of consciousness in an "I."

The mental, we have said,[59] is reducible to the structure of behavior.
Since this structure is visible from the outside and for the spectator at the
same time as from within and for the actor, another person is in principle
accessible to me as I am to myself; and we are both objects laid out before an
impersonal consciousness[60]. But just as I can be mistaken concerning myself
and grasp only the apparent or ideal signification of my conduct, so can I be
mistaken concerning another and know only the envelope of his behavior.
The perception which I have of him is never, in the case of suffering or
mourning, for example, the equivalent of the perception which he has of
himself unless I am sufficiently close to him that our feelings constitute
together a single "form" and that our lives cease to flow separately. It is by this
rare and difficult consent that I can be truly united with him, just as I can
grasp my natural movements and know myself sincerely only by the decision
to belong to myself. Thus I do not know myself because of my special position,
but neither do I have the innate power of truly knowing another. I communicate with him by the signification of his conduct; but it is a question of
attaining its structure, that is of attaining, beyond his words or even his
actions, the region where they are prepared.

As we have seen,[61] the behavior of another expresses a certain manner
of existing before signifying a certain manner of thinking. And when this
behavior is addressed to me, as may happen in dialogue, and seizes upon my
thoughts in order to respond to them—or more simply, when the "cultural
objects" which fall under my regard suddenly adapt themselves to my powers,
awaken my intentions and make themselves "understood" by me—I am then
drawn into a *coexistence* of which I am not the unique constituent and which
founds the phenomenon of social nature as perceptual experience founds
that of physical nature. Consciousness can *live* in existing things without
reflection, can abandon itself to their concrete structure, which has not yet
been converted into expressible signification; certain episodes of its life,
before having been reduced to the condition of available memories and inof-
fensive objects, can imprison its liberty by their proper inertia, shrink its perception of the world, and impose stereotypes on behavior; likewise, before
having conceptualized our class or our milieu, we *are* that class or that milieu.

Thus, the "I think" can be as if hallucinated by its objects. It will be
replied (which is true) that it "should be able" to accompany all our representations and that it is presupposed by them, if not as term of an act of actu-

al consciousness at least as a possiblity in principle. But this response of critical philosophy poses a problem. The conversion of seeing which transforms
the life of consciousness into a pure dialectic of subject and object, which
reduces the thing in its sensible density to a bundle of significations, the traumatic reminiscence into an indifferent memory, and submits the class structure of my consciousness to examination—does this conversion make explicit an eternal "condition of possibility" or does it bring about the appearance
of a new structure of consciousness? It is a problem to know what happens, for
example, when consciousness disassociates itself from time, from this uninterrupted gushing forth at the center of itself, in order to apprehend it as an
intellectual and manipulable signification. Does it lay bare only what was
implicit? Or, on the contrary, does it not enter as into a lucid dream in which
indeed it encounters no opaqueness, not because it has clarified the existence
of things and its own existence, but because it lives at the surface of itself and
on the envelope of things? Is the reflexive passage to intellectual consciousness an adequation of our knowing to our being or only a way for consciousness to create for itself a separated existence—a quietism? These questions
express no empiricist demand, no complaisance for "experiences" which
would not have to account for themselves. On the contrary, we want to make
consciousness equal with the whole of experience, to gather into consciousness for-itself (*pour soi*) all the life of consciousness in-itself (*en soi*).

A philosophy in the critical tradition founds moral theory on a reflection which discovers the thinking subject in its liberty behind all objects. If,
however, one acknowledges—be it in the status of phenomenon—an existence of consciousness and of its resistant structures, our knowledge depends
upon what we are; moral theory begins with a pyschological and sociological
critique of oneself; man is not assured ahead of time of possessing a source of
morality; consciousness of self is not given in man by right; it is acquired only
by the elucidation of his concrete being and is verified only by the active integration of isolated dialectics—body and soul—between which it is initially broken up. And finally, death is not *deprived of meaning*, since the contingency of
the lived is a perpetual menace for the eternal significations in which it is
believed to be completely expressed. It will be necessary to assure oneself that
the experience of eternity is not the unconsciousness of death, that it is not
on this side but beyond; similarly, moreover, it will be necessary to distinguish
the love of life from the attachment to biological existence. The sacrifice of
life will be philosophically impossible; it will be a question only of "staking'"
one's life, which is a deeper way of living.

If one understands by perception the act which makes us know existences, all the problems which we have just touched on are reducible to the
problem of perception. It resides in the duality of the notions of structure and
signification. A "form," such as the structure of "figure and ground," for example, is a whole which has a meaning and which provides therefore a base for
intellectual analysis. But at the same time it is not an idea: it constitutes, alters

and reorganizes itself before us like a spectacle. The alleged bodily, social and psychological "causalities" are reducible to this contingency of lived perspectives which limit our access to eternal significations. The "horizontal localizations" of cerebral functioning, the adhesive structures of animal behavior and those of pathological behavior are only particularly striking examples of this. "Structure" is the philosophical truth of naturalism and realism. What are the relations of this naturized consciousness and the pure consciousness of self? Can one conceptualize perceptual consciousness without eliminating it as an original mode; can one maintain its specificity without rendering inconceivable its relation to intellectual consciousness? If the essence of the critical solution consists in driving existence back to the limits of knowledge and of discovering intellectual signification in concrete structure, and if, as has been said, the fate of critical thought is bound up with this intellectualist theory of perception, in the event that this were not acceptable, it would be neccessary to define transcendental philosophy anew in such a way as to integrate with it the very phenomenon of the real. The natural "thing," the organism, the behavior of others and my own behavior exist only by their meaning; but this meaning which springs forth in them is not yet a Kantian object; the intentional life which constitutes them is not yet a representation; and the "comprehension" which gives access to them is not yet an intellection.

≈29≈

Carl Rogers, Person or science?
A philosophical question
(1955).*

This is a highly personal document, written primarily for myself, to clarify an issue which has become increasingly puzzling. It will be of interest to others only to the extent that the issue exists for them. I shall therefore describe first something of the way in which the paper grew.

As I have acquired experience as a therapist, carrying on the exciting, rewarding experience of psychotherapy, and as I have worked as a scientific investigator to ferret out some of the truth about therapy, I have become increasingly conscious of the gap between these two roles. The better therapist I have become (as I believe I have), the more I have been vaguely aware of my complete subjectivity when I am at my best in this function. And as I have become a better investigator, more "hardheaded" and more scientific (as I believe I have) I have felt an increasing discomfort at the distance between the rigorous objectivity of myself as scientist and the almost mystical subjectivity of myself as therapist. This paper is the result.

What I did first was to let myself go as therapist, and describe, as well as I could do in a brief space, what is the essential nature of psychotherapy as I have lived it with many clients. I would stress the fact that this is a very fluid and personal formulation, and that if it were written by another person, or if it were written by me two years ago, or two years hence, it would be different in some respects. Then I let myself go as scientist—as tough-minded fact-finder in this psychological realm—and endeavored to picture the meaning which science can give to therapy. Following this I carried on the debate which exist-

*Rogers, C. R. (1955). Person or science? A philosophical question. *American Psychologist, 10*, 267–278. Reprinted by permission of the American Psychological Association.

[1]Also published in *Cross Currents: A Quarterly Review*, 1953, 3, 289–306.

ed in me, raising the questions which each point of view legitimately asks the other.

When I had carried my efforts this far I found that I had only sharpened the conflict. The two points of view seemed more than ever irreconcilable. I discussed the material with a seminar of faculty and students, and found their comments very helpful. During the following year I continued to mull over the problem until I began to feel an integration of the two views arising in me. More than a year after the first sections were written I tried to express this tentative and perhaps temporary integration in words.

Thus the reader who cares to follow my struggles in this matter will find that it has quite unconsciously assumed a dramatic form—all of the dramatis personæ being contained within myself: First Protagonist, Second Protagonist, The Conflict, and finally, The Resolution. Without more ado let me introduce the first protagonist, myself as therapist, portraying as well as I can, what the *experience* of therapy seems to be.

THE ESSENCE OF THERAPY IN TERMS OF ITS EXPERIENCE

I launch myself into the therapeutic relationship having a hypothesis, or a faith, that my liking, my confidence, and my understanding of the other person's inner world, will lead to a significant process of becoming. I enter the relationship not as a scientist, not as a physician who can accurately diagnose and cure, but as a person, entering into a personal relationship. Insofar as I see him only as an object, the client will tend to become only an object.

I risk myself, because if, as the relationship deepens, what develops is a failure, a regression, a repudiation of me and the relationship by the client, then I sense that I will lose myself, or a part of myself. At times this risk is very real, and is very keenly experienced.

I let myself go into the immediacy of the relationship where it is my total organism which takes over and is sensitive to the relationship, not simply my consciousness. I am not consciously responding in a planful or analytic way, but simply in an unreflective way to the other individual, my reaction being based (but not consciously) on my total organismic sensitivity to this other person. I live the relationship on this basis.

The essence of some of the deepest parts of therapy seems to be a unity of experiencing. The client is freely able to experience his feeling in its complete intensity, as a "pure culture," without intellectual inhibitions or cautions, without having it bounded by knowledge of contradictory feelings: and I am able with equal freedom to experience my understanding of this feeling, without any conscious thought about it, without any apprehension or concern as to where this will lead, without any type of diagnostic or analytic thinking, without any cognitive or emotional barriers to a complete "letting go" in understanding. When there is this complete unity, singleness, fullness of experiencing in the relationship, then it acquires the "out-of-this-world" quality which many therapists have remarked upon, a sort of trance-like feeling in the relationship from which both the client and I emerge at the end of the hour, as if from a deep well or tunnel. In these moments there is, to borrow Buber's phrase, a real "I-Thou" relationship, a timeless living in the experience which is *between* the client and me. It is at the opposite pole from seeing the client, or myself, as an object. It is the height of personal subjectivity.

I am often aware of the fact that I do not *know*, cognitively, where this immediate relationship is leading. It is as though both I and the client, often fearfully, let ourselves slip into the stream of becoming, a stream or process which carries us along. It is the fact that the therapist has let himself float in this stream of experience or life previously, and found it rewarding, that makes him each time less fearful of taking the plunge. It is my confidence that makes it easier for the client to embark also, a little bit at a time. It often seems as though this stream of experience leads to some goal. Probably the truer statement, however, is that its rewarding character lies within the process itself, and that its major reward is that it enables both the client and me, later, independently, to let ourselves go in the process of becoming.

As to the client, as therapy proceeds, he finds that he is daring to become himself, in spite of all the dread consequences which he is sure will befall him if he permits himself to become himself. What does this becoming one's self mean? It appears to mean less fear of the organismic, nonreflective reactions which one has, a gradual growth of trust in and even affection for the complex, varied, rich assortment of feelings and tendencies which exist in one at the organic or organismic level. Consciousness, instead of being the watchman over a dangerous and unpredictable lot of impulses, of which few can be permitted to see the light of day, becomes the comfortable inhabitant of a richly varied society of impulses and feelings and thoughts, which prove to be very satisfactorily self-governing when not fearfully or authoritatively guarded.

Involved in this process of becoming himself is a profound experience of personal choice. He realizes that he can choose to continue to hide behind a facade, or that he can take the risks involved in being himself; that he is a free agent who has it within his power to destroy another or himself, and also the power to enhance himself and others. Faced with this naked reality of decision, he chooses to move in the direction of being himself.

But being himself doesn't "solve problems." It simply opens up a new way of living in which there is more depth and more height in the experience of his feelings, more breadth and more range. He feels more unique and hence more alone, but he is so much more real that his relationships with others lose their artificial quality, become deeper, more satisfying, and draw more of the realness of the other person into the relationship.

Another way of looking at this process, this relationship, is that it is a learning by the client (and by the therapist, to a lesser extent). But it is a strange type of learning. Almost never is the learning notable by its complexity, and at its deepest the learnings never seem to fit well into verbal symbols.

Often the learnings take such simple forms as "I *am* different from others"; "I do feel hatred for him"; "I *am* fearful of feeling dependent"; "I do feel sorry for myself"; "I am self-centered"; "I do have tender and loving feelings"; "I could be what I want to be"; etc. But in spite of their seeming simplicity these learnings are vastly significant in some new way which is very difficult to define. We can think of it in various ways. They are self-appropriated learnings, for one thing, based somehow in experience, not in symbols. They are analogous to the learning of the child who knows that "two and two make four" and who one day playing with two objects and two objects, suddenly realizes in *experience* a totally new learning, that "two and two *do* make four."

Another manner of understanding these learnings is that they are a belated attempt to match symbols with meanings in the world of feelings, an undertaking long since achieved in the cognitive realm. Intellectually, we match carefully the symbol we select with the meaning which an experience has for us. Thus I say something happened "gradually," having quickly (and largely unconsciously) reviewed such terms as "slowly," "imperceptibly," "step-by-step," etc., and rejected them as not carrying the precise shade of meaning of the experience. But in the realm of feelings, we have never learned to attach symbols to experience with any accuracy of meaning. This something which I feel welling up in myself, in the safety of an acceptant relationship— what is it? Is it sadness, is it anger, is it regret, is it sorrow for myself, is it anger at lost opportunities—I stumble around trying out a wide range of symbols, until one "fits," "feels right," seems really to match the organismic experience. In doing this type of thing the client discovers that he has to learn the language of feeling and emotion as if he were an infant learning to speak; often, even worse, he finds he must unlearn a false language before learning the true one.

Let us try still one more way of defining this type of learning, this time by describing what it is not. It is a type of learning which cannot be taught. The essence of it is the aspect of self-discovery. With "knowledge" as we are accustomed to think of it, one person can teach it to another, providing each has adequate motivation and ability. But in the significant learning which takes place in therapy, one person *cannot* teach another. The teaching would destroy the learning. Thus I might teach a client that it is safe for him to be himself, that freely to realize his feelings is not dangerous, etc. The more he learned this, the less he would have learned it in the significant, experiential, self-appropriating way. Kierkegaard regards this latter type of learning as true subjectivity, and makes the valid point that there can be no direct communication of it, or even about it. The most that one person can do to further it in another is to create certain conditions which make this type of learning *possible*. It cannot be compelled.

A final way of trying to describe this learning is that the client gradually learns to symbolize a total and unified state, in which the state of the organism, in experience, feeling, and cognition may all be described in one unified way. To make the matter even more vague and unsatisfactory, it seems quite unnecessary that this symbolization should be expressed. It usually does occur, because the client wishes to communicate at least a portion of himself to the therapist, but it is probably not essential. The only necessary aspect is the inward realization of the total, unified, immediate, "at-this-instant," state of the organism which is me. For example, to realize fully that at this moment the oneness in me is simply that "I am deeply frightened at the possibility of becoming something different" is of the essence of therapy. The client who realizes this will be quite certain to recognize and realize this state of his being when it recurs in somewhat similar form. He will also, in all probability, recognize and realize more fully some of the other existential feelings which occur in him. Thus he will be moving toward a state in which he is more truly himself. He will *be*, in more unified fashion, what he organismically *is*, and this seems to be the essence of therapy.

THE ESSENCE OF THERAPY IN TERMS OF SCIENCE

I shall now let the second protagonist, myself as scientist, take over and give his view of this same field.

In approaching the complex phenomena of therapy with the logic and methods of science, the aim is to work toward an *understanding* of the phenomena. In science this means an objective knowledge of events and of functional relationships between events. Science may also give the possibility of increased prediction of and control over these events, but this is not a necessary outcome of scientific endeavor. If the scientific aim were fully achieved in this realm, we would presumably know that, in therapy, certain elements were associated with certain types of outcomes. Knowing this it is likely that we would be able to predict that a particular instance of a therapeutic relationship would have a certain outcome (within certain probability limits) because it involved certain elements. We could then very likely control outcomes of therapy by our manipulation of the elements contained in the therapeutic relationship.

It should be clear that no matter how profound our scientific investigation, we could never by means of it discover any absolute truth, but could only describe relationships which had an increasingly high probability of occurrence. Nor could we discover any underlying reality in regard to persons, interpersonal relationships, or the universe. We could only describe relationships between observable events. If science in this field followed the course of science in other fields, the working models of reality which would emerge (in the course of theory building) would be increasingly removed from the reality perceived by the senses. The scientific description of therapy and therapeutic relationships would become increasingly *unlike* these phenomena as they are experienced.

It is evident at the outset that since therapy is a complex phenomenon, measurement will be difficult. Nevertheless "anything that exists can be mea-

sured," and since therapy is judged to be a significant relationship, with implications extending far beyond itself, the difficulties may prove to be worth sur-
mounting in order to discover laws of personality and interpersonal relationships.

Since, in client-centered therapy, there already exists a crude theory
(though not a theory in the strictly scientific sense), we have a starting point
for the selection of hypotheses. For purposes of this discussion, let us take
some of the crude hypotheses which can be drawn from this theory, and see
what a scientific approach will do with them. We will, for the time being, omit
the translation of the total theory into a formal logic which would be acceptable, and consider only a few of the hypotheses.

Let us first state three of these in their crude form.

1. Acceptance of the client by the therapist leads to an increased acceptance of self
   by the client.
2. The more the therapist perceives the client as a person rather than as an object,
   the more the client will come to perceive himself as a person rather than an
   object.
3. In the course of therapy an experiential and effective type of learning about self
   takes place in the client.

How would we go about translating each of these[2] into operational
terms and how would we test the hypotheses? What would be the general outcomes of such testing?

This paper is not the place for a detailed answer to these questions, but
research already carried on supplies the answers in a general way. In the case
of the first hypothesis, certain devices for measuring acceptance would be
selected or devised. These might be attitude tests, objective or projective, Q
technique or the like. Presumably the same instruments, with slightly different instructions or mind set, could be used to measure the therapist's acceptance of the client, and the client's acceptance of self. Operationally then, the
degree of therapist acceptance would be equated to a certain score on this
instrument. Whether client self-acceptance changed during therapy would be
indicated by pre- and post-measurements. The relationship of any change to
therapy would be determined by comparison of changes in therapy to
changes during a control period or in a control group. We would finally be
able to say whether a relationship existed between therapist acceptance and
client self-acceptance, as operationally defined, and the correlation between
the two.

---

[2]I believe it is now commonly accepted that the most subjective feelings, apprehensions,
tensions, satisfactions, or reactions, may be dealt with scientifically, providing only that they may
be given clear-cut operational definition. William Stephenson, among others, presents this point
of view forcefully (in his *Postulates of Behaviorism*) and through his Q technique, has contributed
importantly to the objectification of such subjective materials for scientific study.

The second and third hypotheses involve real difficulty in measurement, but there is no reason to suppose that they could not be objectively studied, as our sophistication in psychological measurement increases. Some type of attitude test or Q sort might be the instrument for the second hypothesis, measuring the attitude of therapist toward client, and of client toward self. In this case the continuum would be from objective regard of an external object to a personal and subjective experiencing. The instrumentation for hypothesis three might be physiological, since it seems likely that experiential learning has physiologically measurable concomitants. Another possibility would be to infer experiential learning from its effectiveness, and thus measure the effectiveness of learning in different areas. At the present stage of our methodology hypothesis three might be beyond us, but certainly within the foreseeable future, it too could be given operational definition and tested.

The findings from these studies would be of this order. Let us become suppositious, in order to illustrate more concretely. Suppose we find that therapist acceptance leads to client self-acceptance, and that the correlation is in the neighborhood of .70 between the two variables. In hypothesis two we might find the hypothesis unsupported, but find that the more the therapist regarded the client as a person, the more the client's self-acceptance increased. Thus we would have learned that person-centeredness is an element of acceptance, but that it has little to do with the client becoming more of a person to himself. Let us also suppose hypothesis three upheld with experiential learning of certain describable sorts taking place much more in therapy than in the control subjects.

Glossing over all the qualifications and ramifications which would be present in the findings, and omitting reference to the unexpected leads into personality dynamics which would crop up (since these are hard to imagine in advance), the preceding paragraph gives us some notion of what science can offer in this field. It can give us a more exact description of the events of therapy and the changes which take place. It can begin to formulate some tentative laws of the dynamics of human relationships. It can offer public and replicable statements, that if certain operationally definable conditions exist in the therapist or in the relationship, then certain client behaviors may be expected with a known degree of probability. It can presumably do this for the field of therapy and personality change as it is in the process of doing for such fields as perception and learning. Eventually theoretical formulations should draw together these different areas, enunciating the laws which appear to govern alteration in human behavior, whether in the situations we classify as perception, those we classify as learning, or the more global and molar changes which occur in therapy, involving both perception and learning.

SOME ISSUES

Here are two different methods of perceiving the essential aspects of psychotherapy, two different approaches to forging ahead into new territory in this field. As presented here, and as they frequently exist, there seems almost no common meeting ground between the two descriptions. Each represents a vigorous way of seeing therapy. Each seems to be an avenue to the significant truths of therapy. When each of these is held by a different individual or group, it constitutes a basis of sharp disagreement. When each of these approaches seems true to one individual, like myself, then he feels himself conflicted by these two views. Though they may superficially be reconciled, or regarded as complementary to each other, they seem to me to be basically antagonistic in many ways. I should like to raise certain issues which these two viewpoints pose for me.

The Scientist's Questions

First let me pose some of the questions which the scientific viewpoint asks of the experiential (using scientific and experiential simply as loose labels to indicate the two views). The hardheaded scientist listens to the experiential account, and raises several searching questions.

1. First of all he wants to know, "How can you know that this account, or any account given at a previous or later time, is true? How do you know that it has any relationship to reality? If we are to rely on this inner and subjective experience as being the truth about human relationships or about ways of altering personality, then Yogi, Christian Science, dianetics, and the delusions of a psychotic individual who believes himself to be Jesus Christ, are all true, just as true as this account. Each of them represents the truth as perceived inwardly by some individual or group of individuals. If we are to avoid this morass of multiple and contradictory truths, we must fall back on the only method we know for achieving an ever-closer approximation to reality, the scientific method."

2. "In the second place, this experiential approach shuts one off from improving his therapeutic skill, or discovering the less than satisfactory elements in the relationship. Unless one regards the present description as a perfect one, which is unlikely, or the present level of experience in the therapeutic relationship as being the most effective possible, which is equally unlikely, then there are unknown flaws, imperfections, blind spots, in the account as given. How are these to be discovered and corrected? The experiential approach can offer nothing but a trial-and-error process for achieving this, a process which is slow and which offers no real guarantee of achieving this goal. Even the criticisms or suggestions of others are of little help, since they do not arise from within the experience and hence do not have the vital authority of the relationship itself. But the scientific method, and the procedures of a modern logical positivism, have much to offer here. Any experience which can be described at all can be described in operational terms. Hypotheses can be formulated and put to test, and the sheep of truth can thus be separated from the goats of error. This seems the only sure road to improvement, self-correction, growth in knowledge."

3. The scientist has another comment to make. "Implicit in your description of the therapeutic experience seems to be the notion that there are elements in it which *cannot* be predicted—that there is some type of spontaneity or (excuse the term) free will operative here. You speak as though some of the client's behavior—and

perhaps some of the therapist's—is not caused, is not a link in a sequence of cause and effect. Without desiring to become metaphysical, may I raise the question as to whether this is defeatism? Since surely we can discover what causes *much* of behavior—you yourself speak of creating the conditions where certain behavioral results follow—then why give up at any point? Why not at least *aim* toward uncovering the causes of *all* behavior? This does not mean that the individual must regard himself as an automaton, but in our search for the facts we shall not be hampered by a belief that some doors are closed to us."

4. Finally, the scientist cannot understand why the therapist, the experientialist, should challenge the one tool and method which is responsible for almost all the advances which we value. "In the curing of disease, in the prevention of infant mortality, in the growing of larger crops, in the preservation of food, in the manufacture of all the things that make life comfortable, from books to nylon, in the understanding of the universe, what is the foundation stone? It is the method of science, applied to each of these, and to many other problems. It is true that it has improved methods of warfare, too, serving man's destructive as well as his constructive purposes, but even here the potentiality for social usefulness is very great. So why should we doubt this same approach in the social science field? To be sure advances here have been slow, and no law as fundamental as the law of gravity has as yet been demonstrated, but are we to give up this approach out of impatience? What possible alternative offers equal hope? If we are agreed that the social problems of the world are very pressing indeed, if psychotherapy offers a window into the most crucial and significant dynamics of change in human behavior, then surely the course of action is to apply to psychotherapy the most rigorous canons of scientific method, on as broad a scale as possible, in order that we may most rapidly approach a tentative knowledge of the laws of individual behavior and of attitudinal change."

The Questions of the Experientialist

While the scientist's questions may seem to some to settle the matter, his comments are far from being entirely satisfying to the therapist who has lived the experience of therapy. Such an individual has several points to make in regard to the scientific view.

1. "In the first place," this "experientalist" points out, "science always has to do with the other, the object. Various logicians of science, including Stevens, show that it is a basic element of science that it always has to do with the observable object, the observable other. This is true, even if the scientist is experimenting on himself, for to that degree he treats himself as the observable other. It never has anything to do with the experiencing me. Now does not this quality of science mean that it must forever be irrelevant to an experience such as therapy, which is intensely personal, highly subjective in its inwardness, and dependent entirely on the relationship of two individuals each of whom is an experiencing me? Science can of course study the events which occur, but always in a way which is irrelevant to what is occurring. An analogy would be to say that science can conduct an autopsy of the dead events of therapy, but by its very nature it can never enter into the living physiology of therapy. It is for this reason that therapists recognize—usually intu-

itively—that any advance in therapy, any fresh knowledge of it, any significant new hypotheses in regard to it must come from the experience of the therapists and clients, and can never come from science. Again, to use an analogy, certain heavenly bodies were discovered solely from examination of the scientific measurements of the courses of the stars. Then the astronomers searched for these hypothesized bodies and found them. It seems decidedly unlikely that there will ever be a similar outcome in therapy, since science has nothing to say about the internal personal experience which 'I' have in therapy. It can only speak of the events which occur in 'him.' "

2. "Because science has as its field the 'other,' the 'object,' it means that everything it touches is transformed into an object. This has never presented a problem in the physical sciences. In the biological sciences it has caused certain difficulties. A number of medical men feel some concern as to whether the increasing tendency to view the human organism as an object, in spite of its scientific efficacy, may not be unfortunate for the patient. They would prefer to see him again regarded as a person. It is in the social sciences, however, that this becomes a genuinely serious issue. It means that the people studied by the social scientist are always objects. In therapy, both client and therapist become objects for dissection, but not persons with whom one enters a living relationship. At first glance, this may not seem important. We may say that only in his role as scientist does the individual regard others as objects. He can also step out of this role and become a person. But if we look a little further we will see that this is a superficial answer. If we project ourselves into the future, and suppose that we had the answers to most of the questions which psychology investigates today, what then? Then we would find ourselves increasingly impelled to treat all others, and even ourselves, as objects. The knowledge of all human relationships would be so great that we would know it rather than live the relationships unreflectively. We see some foretaste of this in the attitude of sophisticated parents who know that affection 'is good for the child.' This knowledge frequently stands in the way of their being themselves, freely, unreflectively, affectionate or not. Thus the development of science in a field like therapy is either irrelevant to the experience, or may actually make it more difficult to live the relationship as a personal, experiential event."

3. The experientialist has a further concern. "When science transforms people into objects, as mentioned above, it has another effect. The end result of science is to lead toward manipulation. This is less true in fields like astronomy, but in the physical and social sciences, the knowledge of the events and their relationships leads to manipulation of some of the elements of the equation. This is unquestionably true in psychology, and would be true in therapy. If we know all about how learning takes place, we use that knowledge to manipulate persons as objects. This statement places no value judgment on manipulation. It may be done in highly ethical fashion. We may even manipulate ourselves as objects, using such knowledge. Thus, knowing that learning takes place more rapidly with repeated review rather than long periods of concentration of one lesson, I may use this knowledge to manipulate my learning of Spanish. But knowledge is power. As I learn the laws of learning I use them to manipulate others through advertisements, through propaganda, through prediction of their responses, and the control of those responses. It is not too strong a statement to say that the growth of knowledge in the social sciences contains within itself a powerful tendency toward social control, toward

control of the many by the few. An equally strong tendency is toward the weakening or destruction of the existential person. When all are regarded as objects, the subjective individual, the inner self, the person in the process of becoming, the unreflective consciousness of being, the whole inward side of living life, is weakened, devalued, or destroyed. Perhaps this is best exemplified by two books. Skinner's *Walden Two* is a psychologist's picture of paradise. To Skinner it must have seemed desirable, unless he wrote it as a tremendous satire. At any rate it is a paradise of manipulation, in which the extent to which one can be a person is greatly reduced, unless one can be a member of the ruling council. Huxley's *Brave New World* is frankly satire, but portrays vividly the loss of personhood which he sees as associated with increasing psychological and biological knowledge. Thus, to put it bluntly, it seems that a developing social science (as now conceived and pursued) leads to social dictatorship and individual loss of personhood. The dangers perceived by Kierkegaard a century ago in this respect seem much more real now, with the increase of knowledge, than they could have then."

4. "Finally," says the experientialist, "doesn't all this point to the fact that ethics is a more basic consideration than science? I am not blind to the value of science as a tool, and am aware that it can be a very valuable tool. But unless it is the tool of ethical *persons*, with all that the term persons implies, may it not become a Juggernaut? We have been a long time recognizing this issue, because in physical science it took centuries for the ethical issue to become crucial, but it has at last become so. In the social sciences the ethical issues arise much more quickly, because persons are involved. But in psychotherapy the issue arises most quickly and most deeply. Here is the maximizing of all that is subjective, inward, personal; here a relationship is lived, not examined, and a person, not an object, emerges; a person who feels, chooses, believes, acts, not as an automaton, but as a person. And here too is the ultimate in science—the objective exploration of the most subjective aspects of life; the reduction to hypotheses, and eventually to theorems, of all that has been regarded as most personal, most completely inward, most thoroughly a private world. And because these two views come so sharply into focus here, we must make a choice—an ethical personal choice of values. We may do it by default, by not raising the question. We may be able to make a choice which will somehow conserve both values—but choose we must. And I am asking that we think long and hard before we give up the values that pertain to being a person, to experiencing, to living a relationship, to becoming, that pertain to one's self as a process, to one's self in the existential moment, to the inward subjective self that lives."

The Dilemma

There you have the contrary views as they occur sometimes explicitly, more often implicitly, in current psychological thinking. There you have the debate as it exists in me. Where do we go? What direction do we take? Has the problem been correctly described or is it fallacious? What are the errors of perception? Or if it is essentially as described, must we choose one or the other? And if so, which one? Or is there some broader, more inclusive formulation which can happily encompass both of these views without damage to either?

A CHANGED VIEW OF SCIENCE

In the year which has elapsed since the foregoing material was written, I have from time to time discussed the issues with students, colleagues, and friends. To some of them I am particularly indebted for ideas which have taken root in me.[3] Gradually I have come to believe that the most basic error in the original formulation was in the description of science. I should like, in this section, to attempt to correct that error, and in the following section to reconcile the revised points of view.

The major shortcoming was, I believe, in viewing science as something "out there," something spelled with a capital S, a "body of knowledge," existing somewhere in space and time. In common with many psychologists I thought of science as a systematized and organized collection of tentatively verified fact, and saw the methodology of science as the socially approved means of accumulating this body of knowledge, and continuing its verification. It has seemed somewhat like a reservoir into which all and sundry may dip their buckets to obtain water—with a guarantee of 99% purity. When viewed in this external and impersonal fashion, it seems not unreasonable to see Science not only as discovering knowledge in lofty fashion, but as involving depersonalization, a tendency to manipulate, a denial of the basic freedom of choice which I have met experientially in therapy. I should like now to view the scientific approach from a different, and I hope, a more accurate perspective.

Science in Persons

Science exists only in people. Each scientific project has its creative inception, its process, and its tentative conclusion, in a person or persons. Knowledge—even scientific knowledge—is that which is subjectively acceptable. Scientific knowledge can be communicated only to those who are subjectively ready to receive its communication. The utilization of science also occurs only through people who are in pursuit of values which have meaning for them. These statements summarize very briefly something of the change in emphasis which I would like to make in my description of science. Let me follow through the various phases of science from this point of view.

The Creative Phases

Science has its inception in a particular person who is pursuing aims, values, purposes, which have personal and subjective meaning for him. As a part

[3]I would like to mention my special debt to discussions with, and published and unpublished papers by Robert M. Lipgar, Ross L. Mooney, David A. Rodgers, and Eugene Streich. My own thinking has fed so deeply on theirs, and become so intertwined with theirs, that I would be at a loss to acknowledge specific obligations. I only know that in what follows there is much which springs from them through me. I have also profited from correspondence regarding the paper with Anne Roe and Walter Smet.

of this pursuit, he, in some area, "wants to find out." Consequently, if he is to be a good scientist, he immerses himself in the relevant experience, whether that be the physics laboratory, the world of plant or animal life, the hospital, the psychological laboratory or clinic, or whatever. This immersion is complete and subjective, similar to the immersion of the therapist in therapy, described previously. He senses the field in which he is interested. He lives it. He does more than "think" about it—he lets his organism take over and react to it, both on a knowing and on an unknowing level. He comes to sense more than he could possibly verbalize about his field, and reacts organismically in terms of relationships which are not present in his awareness.

Out of this complete subjective immersion comes a creative forming, a sense of direction, a vague formulation of relationships hitherto unrecognized. Whittled down, sharpened, formulated in clearer terms, this creative forming becomes a hypothesis—a statement of a tentative, personal, subjective faith. The scientist is saying, drawing upon all his known and unknown experience, that "I have a hunch that such and such a relationship exists, and the existence of this phenomenon has relevance to my personal values."

What I am describing is the initial phase of science, probably its most important phase, but one which American scientists, particularly psychologists, have been prone to minimize or ignore. It is not so much that it has been denied as that it has been quickly brushed off. Kenneth Spence has said that this aspect of science is "simply taken for granted."[4] Like many experiences taken for granted, it also tends to be forgotten. It is indeed in the matrix of immediate personal, subjective experience that all science, and each individual scientific research, has its origin.

Checking with Reality

The scientist has then creatively achieved his hypothesis, his tentative faith. But does it check with reality? Experience has shown each one of us that it is very easy to deceive himself, to believe something which later experience shows is not so. How can I tell whether this tentative belief has some real relationship to observed facts? I can use, not one line of evidence only, but several. I can surround my observation of the facts with various precautions to make sure I am not deceiving myself. I can consult with others who have also been concerned with avoiding self-deception, and learn useful ways of catching myself in unwarranted beliefs, based on misinterpretation of observations.

---

[4]It may be pertinent to quote the sentences from which this phrase is taken. ". . . the data of all sciences have the same origin—namely, the immediate experience of an observing person, the scientist himself. That is to say, immediate experience, the initial matrix out of which all sciences develop, is no longer considered a matter of concern for the scientist. He simply takes it for granted and then proceeds to the task of describing the events occurring in it and discovering and formulating the nature of the relationships holding among them." Kenneth W. Spence, in *Psychological Theory*, M. H. Marx (Ed.), Macmillan, 1951, p. 173.

I can, in short, begin to use all the elaborate methodology which science has accumulated. I discover that stating my hypothesis in operational terms will avoid many blind alleys and false conclusions. I learn that control groups can help me to avoid drawing false inferences. I learn that correlations, and *t* tests and critical ratios and a whole array of statistical procedures can likewise aid me in drawing only reasonable inferences.

Thus scientific methodology is seen for what it truly is—a way of preventing me from deceiving myself in regard to my creatively formed subjective hunches which have developed out of the relationship between me and my material. It is in this context, and perhaps only in this context, that the vast structure of operationism, logical positivism, research design, tests of significance, etc., have their place. They exist, not for themselves, but as servants in the attempt to check the subjective feeling or hunch or hypothesis of a person with the objective fact.

And even throughout the use of such rigorous and impersonal methods, the important choices are all made subjectively by the scientist. To which of a number of hypotheses shall I devote time? What kind of control group is most suitable for avoiding self-deception in this particular research? How far shall I carry the statistical analysis? How much credence may I place in the findings? Each of these is necessarily a subjective personal judgment, emphasizing that the splendid structure of science rests basically upon its subjective use by persons. It is the best instrument we have yet been able to devise to check upon our organismic sensing of the universe.

The Findings

If, as scientist, I like the way I have gone about my investigation, if I have been open to all the evidence, if I have selected and used intelligently all the precautions against self-deception which I have been able to assimilate from others or to devise myself, then I will give my tentative belief to the findings which have emerged. I will regard them as a springboard for further investigation and further seeking.

It seems to me that in the best of science, the primary purpose is to provide a more satisfactory and dependable hypothesis, belief, faith, for the investigator himself. To the extent that the scientist is endeavoring to prove something to someone else—an error into which I have fallen more than once—then I believe he is using science to bolster a personal insecurity, and is keeping it from its truly creative role in the service of the person.

In regard to the findings of science, the subjective foundation is well shown in the fact that at times the scientist may refuse to believe his own findings. "The experiment showed thus and so but I believe it is wrong," is a theme which every scientist has experienced at some time or other. Some very fruitful scientific discoveries have grown out of the persistent *disbelief,* by a scientist, in his own findings and those of others. In the last analysis he may place more trust in his total organismic reactions than in the methods of science.

There is no doubt that this can result in serious error as well as in scientific discoveries, but it indicates again the leading place of the subjective in the use of science.

Communication of Scientific Findings

Wading along a coral reef in the Caribbean this morning, I saw a blue fish—I think. If you, quite independently, saw it too, then I feel more confidence in my own observation. This is what is known as intersubjective verification, and it plays an important part in our understanding of science. If I take you (whether in conversation or in print or behaviorally) through the steps I have taken in an investigation, and it seems to you too that I have not deceived myself, and that I have indeed come across a new relationship which is relevant to my values, and that I am justified in having a tentative faith in this relationship, then we have the beginnings of Science with a capital S. It is at this point that we are likely to think we have created a body of scientific knowledge. Actually there is no such body of knowledge. There are only tentative beliefs, existing subjectively, in a number of different persons. If these beliefs are not tentative, then what exists is dogma, not science. If on the other hand, no one but the investigator believes the finding, then this finding is either a personal and deviant matter, an instance of psychopathology, or else it is an unusual truth discovered by a genius, which as yet no one is subjectively ready to believe. This leads me to comment on the group which can put tentative faith in any given scientific finding.

Communication to Whom?

It is clear that scientific findings can be communicated only to those who have agreed to the same ground rules of investigation. The Australian bushman will be quite unimpressed with the findings of science regarding bacterial infection. He knows that illness truly is caused by evil spirits. It is only when he too agrees to scientific method as a good means of preventing self-deception, that he will be likely to accept its findings.

But even among those who have adopted the ground rules of science, tentative belief in the findings of a scientific research can only occur where there is a subjective readiness to believe. One could find many examples. Most psychologists are quite ready to believe evidence showing that the lecture system produces significant increments of learning, and quite unready to believe that the turn of an unseen card may be called through an ability labeled extrasensory perception. Yet the scientific evidence for the latter is considerably more impeccable than for the former. Likewise when the so-called "Iowa studies" first came out, indicating that intelligence might be considerably altered by environmental conditions, there was great disbelief among psychologists, and many attacks on the imperfect scientific methods used. The scientific evidence for this finding is not much better today than it was when the Iowa studies first appeared, but the subjective readiness of psychologists to believe such a finding has altered greatly. A historian of science has noted that empiricists, had they existed at the time, would have been the first to disbelieve the findings of Copernicus.

It appears then that whether I believe the scientific findings of others, or those of my own studies, depends in part on my readiness to put a tentative belief in such findings.[5] One reason we are not particularly aware of this subjective fact is that in the physical sciences particularly, we have gradually agreed that in a very large area of experience we are ready to believe any finding which can be shown to rest upon the rules of the scientific game, properly played.

The Use of Science

But not only is the origin, process, and conclusion of science something which exists only in the subjective experience of persons—so also is its utilization. "Science" will never depersonalize, or manipulate, or control individuals. It is only persons who can and will do that. This is surely a most obvious and trite observation, yet a deep realization of it has had much meaning for me. It means that the use which will be made of scientific findings in the field of personality is and will be a matter of subjective personal choice—the same type of choice as a person makes in therapy. To the extent that he has defensively closed off areas of his experience from awareness, the person is more likely to make choices which are socially destructive. To the extent that he is open to all phases of his experience we may be sure that this person will be more likely to use the findings and methods of science (or any other tool or capacity) in a manner which is personally and socially constructive.[6] There is, in actuality then, no threatening entity of "Science" which can in any way affect our destiny. There are only people. While many of them are indeed threatening and dangerous in their defensiveness, and modern scientific

[5]One example from my own experience may suffice. In 1941 a research study done under my supervision showed that the future adjustment of delinquent adolescents was best predicted by a measure of their realistic self-understanding and self-acceptance. The instrument was a crude one, but it was a better predictor than measures of family environment, hereditary capacities, social milieu, and the like. At that time I was simply not ready to believe such a finding, because my own belief, like that of most psychologists, was that such factors as the emotional climate in the family and the influence of the peer group were the real determinants of future delinquency and nondelinquency. Only gradually, as my experience with psychotherapy continued and deepened, was it possible for me to give my tentative belief to the findings of this study and of a later one (1944) which confirmed it. (For a report of these two studies see "The role of self understanding in the prediction of behavior" by C. R. Rogers, B. L. Kell, and H. McNeil, *J. consult. Psychol.*, 1948, 12, 174–186.)

[6]I have spelled out much more fully the rationale for this view in two recent papers: "The concept of the fully functioning person" (unpublished manuscript), and "Toward a theory of creativity," *ETC*, 1954, 11, 249–260.

knowledge multiplies the social threat and danger, this is not the whole picture. There are two other significant facets. (*a*) There are many other persons who are relatively open to their experience and hence likely to be socially constructive. (*b*) Both the subjective experience of psychotherapy and the scientific findings regarding it indicate that individuals are motivated to change, and may be helped to change, in the direction of greater openness to experience, and hence in the direction of behavior which is enhancing of self and society, rather than destructive.

To put it briefly, Science can never threaten us. Only persons can do that. And while individuals can be vastly destructive with the tools placed in their hands by scientific knowledge, this is only one side of the picture. We already have subjective and objective knowledge of the basic principles by which individuals may achieve the more constructive social behavior which is natural to their organismic process of becoming.

A NEW INTEGRATION

What this line of thought has achieved for me is a fresh integration in which the conflict between the "experientialist" and the "scientific" tends to disappear. This particular integration may not be acceptable to others, but it does have meaning to me. Its major tenets have been largely implicit in the preceding section, but I will try to state them here in a way which takes cognizance of the arguments between the opposing points of view.

Science, as well as therapy, as well as all other aspects of living, is rooted in and based upon the immediate, subjective experience of a person. It springs from the inner, total, organismic experiencing which is only partially and imperfectly communicable. It is one phase of subjective living.

It is because I find value and reward in human relationships that I enter into a relationship known as therapeutic, where feelings and cognition merge into one unitary experience which is lived rather than examined, in which awareness is nonreflective, and where I am participant rather than observer. But because I am curious about the exquisite orderliness which appears to exist in the universe and in this relationship I can abstract myself from the experience and look upon it as an observer, making myself and/or others the objects of that observation. As observer I use all the hunches which grow out of the living experience. To avoid deceiving myself as observer, to gain a more accurate picture of the order which exists, I make use of all the canons of science. Science is not an impersonal something, but simply a person living subjectively another phase of himself. A deeper understanding of therapy (or of any other problem) may come from living it, or from observing it in accordance with the rules of science, or from the communication within the self between the two types of experience. As to the subjective experience of choice, it is not only primary in therapy, but it is also primary in the use of scientific method by a person. I have even come to see that freedom of choice is not necessarily antithetical to the determinism which is a part of our framework for thinking scientifically. Since I have recently tried to spell out this relationship elsewhere[7], I will not take the space to do so here.

What I will do with the knowledge gained through scientific method—whether I will use it to understand, enhance, enrich, or use it to control, manipulate, and destroy—is a matter of subjective choice dependent upon the values which have personal meaning for me. If, out of fright and defensiveness, I block out from my awareness large areas of experience—if I can see only those facts which support my present beliefs, and am blind to all others—if I can see only the objective aspects of life, and cannot perceive the subjective—if in any way I cut off my perception from the full range of its actual sensitivity—then I am likely to be socially destructive, whether I use as tool the knowledge and instruments of science, or the power and emotional strength of a subjective relationship. And on the other hand if I am open to my experience, and can permit all of the sensings of my intricate organism to be available to my awareness, then I am likely to use myself, my subjective experience, *and* my scientific knowledge, in ways which are realistically constructive.

This, then, is the degree of integration I have currently been able to achieve between two approaches first experienced as conflicting. It does not completely resolve all the issues posed in the earlier section, but it seems to point toward a resolution. It rewrites the problem or reperceives the issue, by putting the subjective, existential person, with the values which he holds, at the foundation and the root of the therapeutic relationship and of the scientific relationship. For science too at its inception, is an "I-Thou" relationship with the world of perceived objects, just as therapy at its deepest is an "I-Thou" relationship with a person or persons. And only as a subjective person can I enter either of these relationships.

[7]In my paper on "The concept of the fully functioning person."

⤚ Index ⤙